SOCIOLOGY
IN
AMERICA

AMERICAN SOCIOLOGICAL ASSOCIATION PRESIDENTIAL SERIES

Volumes in this series are edited by successive presidents of the American Sociological Association and are based upon sessions at the Annual Meeting of the organization. Volumes in this series are listed below.

Editor
Herbert J. Gans

SOCIOLOGY IN AMERICA

American Sociological Association Presidential Series

SAGE PUBLICATIONS
The International Professional Publishers
Newbury Park   London   New Delhi

For information address:

SAGE Publications, Inc.
2111 West Hillcrest Drive
Newbury Park, California 91320

SAGE Publications Ltd.
28 Banner Street
London EC1Y 8QE
England

SAGE Publications India Pvt. Ltd.
M-32 Market
Greater Kailash I
New Delhi 110 048 India

Printed in the United States of America

Library of Congress Cataloging-in-Publication Data

Sociology in America / edited by Herbert J. Gans.
        p.   cm. -- (American Sociological Association presidential series)
        Papers presented at the 82nd annual meeting of the American Sociological Association in Atlanta, August 1988.
        Includes bibliographical references.
        ISBN 0-8039-3826-8. -- ISBN 0-8039-3827-6 (pbk.)
        1. Sociology--United States--Congresses.   I. Gans, Herbert J. II. American Sociological Association.   Meeting (82nd : 1988 : Atlanta, Ga.)   III. Series.
        HM22.U5S58   1990
        301'.0973--dc20   90-8218
                                                                              CIP

FIRST PRINTING, 1990
Sage Production Editor: Amy Kleiman

Contents

Part V: Sociology and Its Constituencies

Part VI: Sociology and Social Criticism

Part VII: Foreign Sociologists Look at U.S. Sociology

Part VIII: Sociology and the Other Social Sciences

About the Authors

ROBERT APONTE is a doctoral candidate in sociology at the University of Chicago, where he has worked under the general direction of William Julius Wilson. His dissertation focuses on poverty among the major Hispanic groups in Chicago, and he has authored or coauthored a number of papers on poverty. He has taught sociology at Indiana University and Michigan State University, where he is at present a research associate at the Julian Samora Research Institute.

PAUL J. BAKER is Professor of Educational Administration at Illinois State University. He is coauthor (with Louis Anderson) of *Social Problems: A Critical Thinking Approach*. Currently he is studying leadership and organizational change in public schools.

R. W. CONNELL is Professor of Sociology at Macquarie University in Sydney, Australia. A recent president of the Sociological Association of Australia and New Zealand, he is active in the labor movement as well as academic social science. He has published 10 books on politics, class, education, and gender, one of which, *Gender and Power*, was recently published in the United States. He is now researching masculinity, antipoverty education, and AIDS prevention.

LEWIS A. COSER is Distinguished Professor Emeritus at State University of New York, Stony Brook, and Adjunct Professor of Sociology at Boston College. Among his books are *The Functions of Social Conflict, Masters of Sociological Thought, Men of Ideas, The American Communist Party: A Critical History* (with Irving Howe), and, most recently, *A Handful of Thistles*, a volume of critical essays. He is a Fellow of the American Academy of Arts and Sciences and a former president of the American Sociological Society as well as the Eastern Sociological Society.

WILLIAM A. GAMSON is Professor of Sociology at Boston College. He is writing a book on how people think and talk about political issues and the ways in which they make use of media discourse and the larger political culture that it reflects. He also directs the Media Research and Action Project at Boston College, a group focused on the media and public education strategies of social change organizations.

HERBERT J. GANS is the Robert S. Lynd Professor of Sociology at Columbia University. Trained as both a sociologist and a planner, he has done research in urban and community studies, poverty, antipoverty policy and equality, ethnicity, mass communications, and political sociology. He is the author of seven books, among them *The Urban Villagers, More Equality, Popular Culture and High Culture*, and, most recently, *Middle American Individualism*. Now he is writing one on the underclass concept and antipoverty policy. A former president of the Eastern Sociological Society, he is a Fellow of the American Academy of Arts and Sciences.

TODD GITLIN, Professor of Sociology and Director of the Mass Communications Program at the University of California, Berkeley, is the author of *The Whole World Is Watching, Inside Prime Time*, and *The Sixties: Years of Hope, Days of Rage* and editor of *Watching Television*.

JACK A. GOLDSTONE is Professor of Sociology and Director, Center for Comparative Research in History, Society, and Culture, at the University of California, Davis. He is the author of *Revolution and Rebellion in the Early Modern World* and coeditor of *Revolutions of the Late Twentieth Century*.

JOSEPH R. GUSFIELD is Professor of Sociology at the University of California, San Diego. He has conducted research and written extensively on the topics of social movements, sociology of law, higher education, new nations, and the social construction of social problems. Among his books are *Symbolic Crusade: Status Politics and the American Temperance Movement* and *The Culture of Public Problems: Drinking-Driving and the Symbolic Order*.

LEWIS M. KILLIAN is Professor Emeritus of Sociology, University of Massachusetts, Amherst, and Faculty Associate in Sociology, University of West Florida, Pensacola. From 1952 until 1968, he taught at Florida State University in Tallahassee. In 1989, he was president of the Southern Sociological Association.

JOYCE LADNER is Professor in the School of Social Work at Howard University, where she teaches courses on public policy, child welfare, and the family. She is the author and editor of several books, including *Tomorrow's Tomorrow: The Black Woman*, and numerous articles on the impact of poverty and race on blacks.

NIKLAS LUHMANN has been Professor of Sociology at the University of Bielefeld, West Germany, since 1968. His work is devoted mainly to social systems theory and the theory of society. Among his major books are *Soziologische Aufklaerung, Gesellschaftsstruktur und Semantik, Soziale Sys-*

tems, and *Die Wirtschaft der Gesellschaft* as well as two published in English: *Love as Passion* and *The Differentiation of Society.*

PETER MARRIS is Professor in the Urban Planning Program at the University of California, Los Angeles, and is the author of *Meaning and Action, Loss and Change, Dilemmas of Social Reform* (with Martin Rein), *Widows and Their Families* as well as several other books, including a novel, *The Dreams of General Jerusalem.* He was for many years with the Institute of Community Studies in London and has been conducting research on antipoverty programs in the United States and Britain since 1964.

MARSHALL W. MEYER is Professor of Management and Anheuser-Busch Term Professor in the Wharton School and Professor of Sociology at the University of Pennsylvania. His books include *Environments and Organizations* (with several coauthors), *Change in Public Bureaucracies, Limits to Bureaucratic Growth, Bureaucracy in Modern Society* (with Peter M. Blau), and *Permanently Failing Organizations* (with Lynne Zucker).

HARVEY MOLOTCH is Professor of Sociology at the University of California, Santa Barbara, where he is affiliated with the Economy and Society group. His past research has been in the areas of mass media, conversation analysis, and city growth. His latest book, with John Logan, *Urban Fortunes,* which received the Distinguished Contributor to Sociology Award and the Robert Park Award, investigates the sociology of land markets and the property development process.

JOAN MOORE is Professor of Sociology at the University of Wisconsin — Milwaukee. Her research concentrates on urban minority communities. She is currently coediting a volume on drug use in Hispanic communities and is completing a book based on research on long-standing Chicano gangs.

WILLIAM C. RAU is Associate Professor of Sociology at Illinois State University. He is presently engaged in research on the research productivity and quality of graduate education among doctoral-referring programs in the social and natural sciences.

PETER H. ROSSI is the S. A. Rice Professor of Sociology, and Acting Director, Social and Demographic Research Institute, University of Massachusetts at Amherst. His recent books include *Down and Out in America, Of Human Bonding* (with Alice Rossi), *Evaluation: A Systematic Approach* (with Howard E. Freeman), *Thinking About Program Evaluation* (with Richard A. Berk) and *Armed and Considered Dangerous* (with J. D. Wright). He is past president of the American Sociological Association and a recipient of the Common Wealth award for contributions to sociology.

ALLAN SILVER is Professor of Sociology at Columbia University, where he mostly teaches political sociology. His essay in this book derives from research on the historical vicissitudes of friendship and trustful relations in the Western cultural tradition and their implications for sociological theory.

NEIL J. SMELSER is University Professor of Sociology at the University of California, Berkeley, where he has been a faculty member since 1958. Among his publications are *Theory of Collective Behavior* (1962), *Comparative Methods in the Social Sciences* (1976), and *Handbook of Sociology* (editor, 1988). He is a member of the Executive Committee of the International Sociological Association, a Fellow of the American Academy of Arts and Sciences, and a Member of the American Philosophical Society.

CHARLES U. SMITH is Distinguished Professor of Sociology and Dean of the School of Graduate Studies, Florida Agricultural and Mechanical University, and Courtesy Professor of Sociology, Florida State University. He is also a past president of the Southern Sociological Society and the Council of Historically Black Graduate Schools. The author or coauthor of 13 books and monographs, his latest is *The Civil Rights Movement in Florida and the United States*, for which he also served as editor.

WALTER W. STAFFORD is Associate Professor at New York University, Wagner School of Public Affairs. His articles, on race relations, planning, and employment, have appeared in the *Journal of the American Institute of Planners, Phylon*, and *Urban Education*, and most recently in the volume *The Myth of Black Progress*. His latest publication is *Closed Labor Markets*, and he is now completing a study on racial, ethnic, and gender segmentation in New York City.

ALAIN TOURAINE is Director of Studies at the Ecole des Hautes Etudes en Sciences Sociales in Paris, and his own major research fields include industrial sociology, social movements, and sociological theory. A former president of the French Sociological Society and vice president of the International Sociological Association, he is the author of many books, seven of which have been translated into English, the most recent being *Solidarity* and *The Labour Movement*.

DENNIS H. WRONG is Professor of Sociology at New York University. He is the author of *Population and Society, Skeptical Sociology*, and *Power: Its Forms, Bases and Uses* and was the editor of "Social Research" (1962-64) and "Contemporary Sociology" (1972-74). He held a Guggenheim Fellowship in 1984-85.

Preface

This book is a collection of papers on the theme *Sociology in America*, which were presented at the 82nd Annual Meeting of the American Sociological Association in Atlanta in August 1988. Therefore, the book's title is the same as that of the meeting.

Choosing the theme of the annual meeting is one of the few intellectual prerogatives of the association's president, and I chose mine because I wanted a theme that would be or should be of interest to all sociologists, not just those working in one or another sociological specialty. However, I also chose my theme because I had been thinking about the subject for a number of years, having taken part in discussions earlier in the decade about whether or not sociology was in the doldrums. (I actually thought then and think now that in some respects the field is in the doldrums, along with several other social sciences.) Like every other president-elect preparing for his or her annual program, I drafted a thematic statement and it read as follows:

> About 150 years ago, Alexis de Tocqueville wrote the classic *Democracy in America* which examined the promise and problems of the U.S. For the Annual Meeting we have borrowed part of de Tocqueville's title to examine the promise and problems of sociology in the U.S. Specifically, the 1988 Thematic Sessions will use sociological and other analytic tools to ask what sociology's roles are and have been, as well as what they should be. We want to explore the results of our work as researchers, writers, teachers and practitioners — but also as critics, commentators and policy analysts — in order to discover what sociology and sociologists have done with, for, and to, society as a whole and some of its major sectors, from underdogs to top dogs.

> In this process we will look once more at a number of the traditional fields and topics of the discipline, as well as some new ones, but always with the prescript "sociology of," to learn whether and how we have affected the institutions, organizations and people relevant to these fields and topics. In addition, we shall ask what we have done, are doing, and should be doing for and to ourselves. (Some of the Special Sessions will examine our relations with several other social science disciplines.) The ultimate purpose of the 1988 Thematic Sessions is to foster a disciplinary self analysis that will help us to enhance the intellectual and social usefulness of sociology in the years to come.

The actual thematic sessions were chosen by a hardworking Practical Committee consisting of the late and greatly missed Richard J. Hill, Vice President of the ASA in 1988, David Heise, Paul M. Hirsch, Hylan G. Lewis, Elizabeth Long, S. M. Miller, Victor Nee, Ruth A. Wallace, and Eviatar Zerubavel as well as Michael I. Aiken, Janet Astner, and William V. D'Antonio, ex officio. They went over my initial proposals for specific sessions, offering advice, consent, and occasional opposition, the latter especially to a session I proposed on the doldrums matter. The papers themselves were chosen by the session organizers, many of them members of the Program Committee, this being one of *their* few prerogatives. (I organized a few sessions myself when others could not be recruited.) The final list of papers presented in Atlanta can be found in Appendix A of the book. The list is in the order in which the Program Committee originally formulated it, an order that was impossible to follow in Atlanta for various scheduling reasons but that is approximated in this book.

The papers published here are, however, a specific selection from those presented in Atlanta. The list differs from the Atlanta list for a variety of not very unusual reasons: A number of the presentations were never turned into written papers, some were unavailable for publication for other reasons, others did not hew closely enough to the theme, and a few simply did not work as written papers. (As I was editing the book, I was sometimes reminded of what a wise old predecessor in the ASA presidency said to me shortly after I began planning for Atlanta: that the only way to get the book I wanted was to write all the papers myself. I assume, however, that he was only joking.)

The book is thus a skewed sample of the Atlanta meeting. Further, a book has its own logic and this one, therefore, could not follow the organization of the Atlanta sessions completely. Instead, the volume is divided into eight parts, some of the titles of which follow more or less the sessions from which they originated, but other titles were invented for this book. In any case, the book stands on its own.

Its major purpose is to explore a topic to which not much attention has recently been paid in the discipline. In the immediate past, we have been more concerned with sociology's survival and growth, a natural consequence of the financial problems of the 1970s and the intense governmental antipathy to sociology of the Reagan years — which has unfortunately still not ended. Of course, there is a long tradition of concern in the discipline with sociology's usefulness, and the best known ancestor of this book, at least as far as annual sessions themes go, was on "the uses of sociology," which Paul Lazarsfeld took as his theme for the 1962 annual meeting when he was president. (It later became a volume with the same title, edited by him, William Sewell, and Harold Wilensky, and published in 1967.) This book, like others before and after, focused mainly on demonstrating sociology's practicality, but my purpose was different. I proposed that we would look at sociology from the point of view of the country and sectors of it, that we would define the word uses more broadly, and that we would think also about the misuses of sociology: what we have been doing wrong.

By and large, we sociologists have been too distant from the society in which we operate and in which we are embedded, which funds us even if too poorly and which influences us surely more than we influence it. We are so busy trying to understand how that society functions, which is a large part of our job, that we rarely think about our own functions — and dysfunctions. To some extent, our failure to do so stems from our concern with adding to knowledge (or "the literature"), developing theory, and satisfying our various sponsors and constituents. Even so, we also suffer from a typical professional blindness, which results in our inability to distance ourselves sufficiently from ourselves and our routines to look systematically at what we are doing for and to whom. But then we rarely apply sociological knowledge and insight to the solution of the discipline's problems either.

The papers collected here make one start in what I think needs to be done. I do not agree with everything the authors say or how they say it, but I have reprinted my presidential address, as originally published in the *American Sociological Review*, in Appendix B. There my own views on "sociology in America" are on display once more. Which approaches to the theme turn out to be most productive and appropriate remains to be seen, but first things first: I hope that the social and political conditions of the future and the professional and personal interests of future sociologists will make it possible to go further with this topic in the years to come, and that this book will be helpful in that endeavor.

THE ORGANIZATION OF THIS VOLUME

This book is, as already noted, divided into eight parts and two appendixes. I have given each of the parts broad titles, with the papers included in each to be read as samplers of what could be done.

Part I is intended, as it was in Atlanta, to assess some of sociology's general effects on the country, and both Wrong and Gusfield have stayed away from the more obvious effects to discuss some that might not come immediately to mind. Part II purposely reverses the aim of Part I, to insist at once that we cannot look at sociology's effects on America until we understand America's effects on sociology. This topic is already being explored by intellectual historians, but sociology must participate more energetically in this task, if only to make sure that the structural and cultural contexts in which American sociology has developed are fully brought out. In this volume, Smelser concerns himself with some contemporary contexts while Silver traces several of the discipline's principle preoccupations to earlier centuries and to England. In so doing, he reminds us that any good sociological study should begin with a historical analysis.

The next several parts of the book deal with more specific aspects of sociology in America. In Part III, devoted to public policy, Marris analyzes some not usually mentioned roles sociologists play in doing policy-oriented research, while Gamson's paper reviews sociology's activities in always the most urgent policy issue of our time, the prevention of nuclear war. Part IV, the longest in the book, is concerned with sociology's roles in the most basic domestic issues of the last half of the century (at least), race, class, and gender — and because they are so basic, they are intertwined. Smith and Killian sketch the roles sociology and sociologists have played in the civil rights movement, while Aponte, and Stafford and Ladner, look at what sociologists (and others) have done with one of the most widely discussed concepts of the late 1980s, the *underclass*.[1] Aponte's comprehensive review of the history of the term's definitions shows the interplay between its usage by sociologists, economists, and journalists; Stafford and Ladner place more emphasis on what they call the "politics of definition," especially racial politics. Connell continues the critical analytic pattern of this part of the book, addressing what American sociology has done, not yet done, and should be doing in gender analysis.

Part V is concerned with identifying sociology's constituencies and how it serves or fails to serve them. Although we may not have noticed it, sociology has constituencies — and diverse ones, especially now that academic constituencies are no longer as dominant as in the past. In this book, Baker and Rau focus on what remains our most numerous set of constituents, undergraduate students; Meyer, taking a very different approach, examines organizational sociology, noting its expansion and change as it moves toward and develops constituencies in business schools. (Because of my long-standing interest in journalists as one of our constituencies, the Atlanta program included a session about sociology and journalism, but unfortunately the presentations were not turned into published papers.)

Constituents are, of course, only part of the picture and only one way of conceptualizing other groups whom we serve, well or badly. We must also look at what we do for sociology's sponsors, customers, clients, victims, and, perhaps most important, the various interest groups, organized and other, that interact with and impinge on the discipline. (I had hoped that someone could present a survey of what sociology department faculties fight about with each other — and with students — as one way of calling attention to the interest groups inside sociology — but that study, which is conceptually and methodologically not very difficult, remains to be done.) Until we look at our various relations with others, from constituencies to interest groups, we cannot begin to understand, as we must, the political economy of our discipline.

One of our constituencies should be the targets and users of social criticism, and Part VI deals with them and with sociological social criticism. Sociology has always supplied some social criticism and critics, although not enough to my mind, but how we carry out social criticism and for whom remains a matter of debate. In Atlanta, that topic occasioned a lively debate and I am, therefore, publishing both the presentations and the commentaries on them. Coser and Gitlin, who gave the papers, argue among other things that the sociological

1. Although this volume will be published during the presidency of William Julius Wilson, the underclass session and the selection of papers for it took place long before Wilson was even nominated for the ASA presidency.

social critic should be modeled on the national public intellectual who, in the United States, tends to come out of a literary, historical, or philosophical background. Moore and Rossi, the discussants, disagreed. Moore, taking the perspective of minority sociologists, questions the elitism of national public intellectuals, while Rossi emphasizes the importance of empirical sociological research as a primary but easily forgotten prerequisite for good social criticism. I have yet a different view of the sociologist as social critic, which I discuss in my presidential address, but diversity in the conception of the critic is desirable, especially at this stage. What is most important is that we start thinking explicitly again about sociological social criticism and perhaps even make a field or specialty out of it.

The author from whom I borrowed my thematic title was a foreign student of the United States, and Part VII of the book is appropriately devoted to foreign analyses of American sociology. Overseas colleagues who have long paid attention to the U.S. branch of the discipline are an invaluable resource for us, because in many respects they see us more clearly than we can see ourselves and can thus tell us more wisely, with fewer cultural blinders and political inhibitions, what we are doing and doing wrong. The papers by Touraine, Luhmann, and Connell are good examples of what is needed, for each looks at the United States and at us from perspectives difficult to establish here.

Just as we can learn from foreigners, we can learn from other disciplines. The final part of the book represents one of a series of "special" sessions we organized to report on what we can learn from a variety of such disciplines — in the social sciences and in the humanities — and what they can learn from us. (We even planned a session on sociologists and novelists, but none of the novelists we contacted was available in late August.) The session that produced publishable papers covers two of our most important sibling disciplines, with Goldstone looking at history and sociology to lay out the need for and content of comparative history, and Molotch outlining both a more economic sociology and a more sociological economics.

ACKNOWLEDGMENTS

I am grateful to many people without whom this book could not have been put together: my program committee; the session organizers who commissioned the presentation versions of the papers that appear in this volume; ASA's Washington staff, for making the Atlanta meeting run smoothly; and the contributors to this book, who rewrote their Atlanta presentations and, for the most, held to the several deadlines I set. The ASA budget being what it is, the papers from overseas colleagues could not have come into being without travel grants to bring these colleagues to Atlanta in the first place. These came from the German Marshall Fund of the United States and the French-American foundation, who provided aid for professors Luhmann and Touraine; and the International Research and Exchanges Board, which funded the trip of Dr. Igor Kon—although he did not turn his Atlanta presentation into a paper for this book. Mitch Allen and, also on the Sage Publications staff, Amy Kleiman, supplied editorial advice and services; the vital but rarely mentioned copy editor, Janet Brown, provided textual and other corrections.

— Herbert J. Gans

Part I
Sociology's Effects on America

1

The Influence of Sociological
Ideas on American Culture

Dennis H. Wrong

My aim in this chapter is to identify broadly concepts and notions originating in academic sociology that have entered the awareness, or at least the vocabulary, of Americans during the past half century. Surprisingly few discussions, let alone empirical investigations, exist of the influence of sociological thought on the beliefs and attitudes of Americans. On the other hand, the reverse relationship, that is, the influence of American culture and society on American sociology, has been examined to a fare-thee-well, the sociology of knowledge having become a recognized perspective and even an established subfield.

The relevance of sociological researches to public policy has, of course, been widely acknowledged. Sociologists have collected data bearing on social policies and have sometimes played a role in formulating and even executing policy in various areas. Criminology and demography are two major subfields, antedating the birth of sociology itself as an academic discipline, that were always tied to the activities of governments. The impact of sociology as a "policy science" on American society is not, however, my concern in the present chapter. I am interested in the less direct, often highly nuanced, influence of themes and ideas, including mere catchwords and popular labels, that have diffused from academic sociologists to some segments of the American public.

SOCIOLOGY WITHIN THE UNIVERSITY

The first and most direct influence of sociology and sociological ideas has inevitably been on its own students and on colleagues and students in neighboring disciplines within the university. When I encountered sociology for the first time as an undergraduate in the 1940s, the field was still infused with a missionary spirit. My teachers continually emphasized its newness, conveying the definite impression that it had come into being only yesterday, challenging the older disciplines in the university, especially the other social sciences. These were often pictured as ancient bodies of lore hopelessly addicted to antiquated conceptual formulas utterly incapable of grasping the dynamic realities of the twentieth century. Not surprisingly, the hostility to sociology of representatives of the older social sciences and the humanities gave added plausibility to this view of sociology as gadfly, maverick, and intrepid intellectual pioneer, assaulting the complacencies and gentilities of the established academic order. Several professors of history tried to dissuade me from majoring as an undergraduate in so newfangled and disreputable a pseudodiscipline, deigning to bestow such attention on a lowly sophomore only because it so happened that my grandfather had founded the university's history department and my father had also briefly taught history there. Both of *them*, needless to say, also regarded sociology as a presumptuous upstart of little or no value.

It was quite some time before I realized that all of the social sciences and most of the humanities were not much more than half a century old as clearly demarcated subjects of instruction and fields of research. Sociology was at most only a decade or two younger than the others. If it pretended to a youthfulness to which it was not truly entitled, most of the other academic disciplines fell back on traditionalist legitimations that also lacked solid foundation in reality.

Sociology's sense of mission and insistence on its youthfulness had roots in the global intellectual reach of the early nineteenth-century philosophers of history. Auguste Comte, the name-giver of the field, was but one of the thinkers whom Frank Manuel has called "the prophets of Paris," and Paris was but one of the locales where social and historical prophecy flourished in the high noon of the modern era. The institutionalization of sociology as an academic discipline diluted and restricted the prophetic role assigned to it by Comte. The fledgling sociologist of forty or fifty years ago was usually admonished that he or she should aspire to no more than the status of humble laborer in the great unfinished temple of science, content to lay the small brick of a modest piece of completed empirical research on the slowly rising walls of an edifice whose ultimate completion lay far in the future.

Such diffidence failed to mollify practitioners of the other human disciplines who continued to take a skeptical view of the totalistic ambitions of the collective enterprise no matter how self-effacing a posture was assumed by its individual servants. Even the more modest quest of latter-day sociologists for limited "middle-range" generalizations as opposed to sweeping sociohistorical laws seemed to downgrade the patient accumulation of knowledge about highly particularized persons and events that characterized the humanities. The inclination of sociology to present itself as what C. Wright Mills called "the methodological specialty" also appeared to devalue the scholarly labors of those who were more interested in their subject matter than in the methods they used to examine it. Nor did the subordination of topic to method quite eliminate the apparent boundlessness of the area — human social life in all of its manifestations — that sociology aspired to conquer as the Comtean "queen of the sciences," the *scientia scientorum*. The critics of sociology from the other disciplines with their more clearly defined and delimited fields of inquiry were not, therefore, altogether wrong in detecting remnants of the grandiose programmatic project of the nineteenth-century fathers in the more modest "value-free" union of theory and research that became the goal of their mid-twentieth century successors.

DEBUNKER OF POPULAR BELIEFS

The identification of sociology with science building on the model of the natural sciences was primarily relevant to interdisciplinary relations within the university. In confronting nonacademic publics, sociology has often presented itself as the relentless critic of popular belief, the debunker of hoary folklore and social myth, the exposer of alleged common sense as common prejudice or even nonsense. This particular rationale for the existence of sociology has proved more durable than the goal of creating a science, which has come under widespread attack within sociology itself since the 1960s with the result that "positivism" has acquired inescapably pejorative overtones. Some years ago no less a figure than Robert K. Merton (1961) advanced this "scourge of popular fallacies" justification for sociology in the *New York Times Magazine* in attempting to rebut the conventionally "humanistic" antisociological strictures of Russell Kirk.[1] Introductory textbooks frequently if not habitually present as the main task of sociology the scrutiny of popular opinions and attitudes, which are invariably declared to be unsupported by sociological data and deformed by ideological biases endemic to the American or the bourgeois or liberal or capitalist way of life.

One sometimes receives the impression that the authors of introductory textbooks see themselves as addressing an allegedly typical American male frozen in the attitudinal and ideological postures of the late 1930s or the early 1940s, the era when major publishing houses began to produce their own comprehensive lines of textbooks covering all subjects taught at the college level. The typical American of the texts naively believes in windy "July 4th oratory" denying any class differences in the United States; he is full of nostalgia for the small-town life depicted in Norman Rockwell's legendary *Saturday Evening Post* covers though himself a resident of a big city; he is convinced that woman's place is in the home, and that homosexuality and premarital and extramarital sexual intercourse are morally wrong; despite formal denials, he remains incurably "racist" and antiforeign in his attitude toward those who are not middle-class white Anglo-Saxon Protestants like himself. Textbook writers quite often to this day cite the Lynds' famous chapter "The Middletown Spirit" from *Middletown in Transition*, published in 1937, as an accurate description of *prevailing* American "values" or "culture," although elsewhere they are apt to emphasize the tremendous changes they see America as having undergone in the past half century, particularly when contemplating a president like Ronald Reagan, who unapologetically embodies the older attitudes. Reagan, come to think of it, actually took courses in sociology in the 1930s at a small-town college in the Midwest.

The assumption that Americans are forever committed to a set of beliefs that run counter to sociological knowledge certainly suggests that the teaching and diffusion of sociology must be a peculiarly futile enterprise. Millions and millions of students have taken introductory courses and have been assigned textbooks and books of readings. Many of the people who report the news and current affairs in both the print and the nonprint media are, though they usually were not fifty years ago, college graduates who have been exposed to and quite often even majored in sociology. A fair number of professional politicians and officials in the executive branch of the federal government have studied sociology more fully, and more recently, than Ronald Reagan.

THE INTERACTION OF TOPIC AND RESOURCE

Textbook authors are perhaps a special case. Yet in the past most sociologists were inclined, at least implicitly, to regard sociology as providing a completely autonomous and independent point of view quite distinct from that of the human subjects it studied. The latter were seen as contaminated and, therefore, atypical if they had encountered and been influenced by sociology in college courses. Back in the 1950s, a researcher on class structure in the new suburbs wondered cautiously whether "the awareness of class differences might in some part be due to the social science courses these suburbanites took during their undergraduate days." "May it not be," he went on to ask, "the voice of sociology feeding back on itself through the voice of a corrupted respondent?" (Dobriner 1963, p. 37). Today, after the antipositivist revolts inside sociology in the 1960s, we are less disposed to insist on, or even to regard as desirable, a total insulation of "topic" from "resource," to use the language of ethnomethodology. Few sociologists would nowadays deny or deplore the inescapable and ubiquitous interaction between sociology and a wider public whose views on many matters have been increasingly shaped by the transmission of sociological ideas through media ranging from formal education to television.

The impact of sociological perspectives on the very opinions and behavior of the human beings that constitute the subject matter of sociology as a discipline has been recognized as a crucial epistemological difference between the human

sciences and the natural sciences. Far from being no more than intriguing
oddities, Merton's "self-fulfilling" and "suicidal" prophecies reflect possibilities inherent in the relationship between social science and its object domain.
Only a hermetic insulation of social scientists from their lay subjects — at least
after the former have gathered their "data" from the latter — might eliminate the
infection of the subjects by the findings and conclusions about themselves
presented in diverse public forums by social scientists.[2] Such insulation savors
of authoritarian rule by an elite of protected experts. The repudiation of this
possibility, which seemed implicit in such phrases as "social engineering" that
were popular a few decades ago, has contributed to the prevalent skepticism
about science building or "positivist" models for sociology.

THE SOCIOLOGY OF SOCIOLOGY

The opposite extreme from the conception of a totally independent sociology
is to treat sociology as nothing but a particular reflection of the social realities
it pretends to study from a delusive vantage point of Olympian detachment. A
decade and a half ago, at the peak of the revolts against the "establishment" then
allegedly dominating sociology, there sometimes seemed to be more sociologists of sociology than students of the social world outside the academy that was
the field's ostensible subject matter. Facile, crudely reductive readings of
sociology as a mere reflection of the times, often of the ideological coloration
of whatever political party happens to be in office, are legion. Only slightly more
subtle interpretations have imputed ineradicable national or class or ethnic or
secularized religious biases to various sociological standpoints. In regarding
sociology as possessing its own partly autonomous intellectual tradition, one
need not reject altogether such influences. One can accept what has been called
the "weak program" in the sociology of knowledge while disavowing the
"strong program" as reductionist. I am, in any case, prepared to make the
assumption that familiarity with the leading ideas of sociology amounts to more
than merely the adoption of a new language in which to couch a preexisting
awareness of contemporary life.

Neither the view that sociology partly shapes, nor the opposed view that it
merely reflects, the beliefs and attitudes of the society in which it is practiced
sustains the spirit of missionary enthusiasm that pervaded the field in my youth.
If sociologists merely rationalize the ideological tenets and cultural presuppositions of their own society or some subgroup within it, they were never the
prophets they evidently took themselves to be. If, on the other hand, they have
succeeded to some degree in converting their audience, then their message no
longer comes across as a new dispensation, although it may have done so in the
part. Charles Page recently observed: "Among outsiders in recent decades much
of sociology's rhetoric and bits and pieces of its substance have become

'common knowledge,' thereby diminishing its status as a popular field that nevertheless requires special study" (Page 1985, p. 6). The sociological researcher who assumes that he or she is exploring a pristine social world untainted by previous exposure to the thoughtways of academic sociology may find him- or herself in the undignified posture of a dog chasing its own tail.

How can one identify the source of an idea common to both academic sociologists and a larger public? Given that both groups are reacting to the same external reality, they may have independently come to perceive it in much the same way: Great minds and small — or at least sociologically untutored — minds may think alike. Whatever the original source of the idea, the fact that it is shared by experts and their subjects or clients may reinforce its authority in the eyes of both. Such convergences of outlook may be more frequent than unilateral influence in either direction. A "sociological idea," in short, need not be the exclusive property or creation of academic sociologists, although my interest here is in ideas that are at least widely held and disseminated by them.

CATCHWORDS AND CLICHÉS

At the most obvious and direct level, a few terms of unmistakable academic sociological provenance have passed into popular parlance, or at least into the common argot of journalists. "Charisma" and "charismatic" are the most visible — painfully so, one is constrained to add in election years — and have been so promiscuously used that they are now freely applied to just about any politician able to hold an audience's attention for longer than several minutes. There is a woman's dress shop in Brooklyn named "Charisma," which advertises on local television. A few years ago a boutique named "Gemeinschaft" existed on the Upper West Side of Manhattan. The term "life-style" is even more ubiquitous than "charisma" and also derives from Max Weber. In his Sunday *New York Times* column "On Language," William Safire traced "life-style" to the psychoanalyst Alfred Adler in whose theory of personality it played a prominent part. I am fairly sure he is mistaken that this was its source.[3] Adlerian psychotherapy was never very popular in America. "Life-style" is of more recent origin: The term spread like wildfire at the height of the student protest movements of the late 1960s. As is well known, sociology students played a leading role in these movements. They were familiar with Max Weber on the "style of life" of status groups and often extolled their own "alternative life-styles" as a revolutionary break with the past while damning the materialistic, "consumerist," suburban, or bourgeois "life-styles" of their hopelessly unredeemed parents and teachers. However, in treating "life-style" as a psychological notion, Safire correctly gauges a movement away from its original sociological, that is, collective, connotation when people speak of "my" life-style as a personal possession like "my" toothbrush, pet goldfish, or soft brown eyes. True, it is also still used as a synonym for a shared set of beliefs and habits, a "culture," or, closer to the original Weberian usage, a "subculture." But the blurring of the line between the individual and the collective is itself a very American tendency.

SOCIOLOGY AS SOCIAL CRITICISM AND WORLDVIEW

I shall now make a leap from these simple examples of sociological terms that have become banalities through overuse to a much more uncertain realm of vague and inchoate sociological "ideas" affecting the outlook of Americans, bypassing altogether Page's more restricted "bits and pieces of [sociology's] substance" that have shaped public definitions of social problems. I want to discuss three such ideas or themes: (1) the loss of community and the wish to recover it; (2) society made us, so we should not be blamed; (3) the social construction of reality, or we made society and can remake it into something different.

(1) The claim that the greater size, territorial scope, and internal differentiation of modern society have robbed individuals of close, lifelong, protective group memberships is almost coterminous with the birth of sociology itself. It was, of course, asserted earlier, in broad terms, most saliently by Rousseau. The classical sociological version of the emergence of modernity is the transition from *Gemeinschaft* to *Gesellschaft* with emphasis on the dissolution of community and the alienation of the individual as the painful outcome of the process. "Alienation" and "anomie," counterconcepts to "community," specifying just what has been lost as a result of its decline, have become only slightly less popular outside the ranks of sociologists than "charisma" and "life-style." Here if anywhere is the central or root idea with which sociological thought confronts the modern world. Consider the following roster of familiar phrases: "the quest for community," "the eclipse of community," "the need for roots," "the alienation of modern man," "the lonely crowd," "the pursuit of loneliness," "escape from freedom," "the homeless mind," "the world we have lost." All of these were titles of books by social scientists published in the past forty or fifty years, some of which reached a large, nonacademic reading public.

The "search for community" has become virtually the standard sociological explanation for just about any new social phenomenon. It plays the same all-purpose explanatory role for American sociologists that the ever-impending final crisis of capitalism has long played for Marxists. It was invoked to account for the populism and class solidarity of the 1930s, the appeal of totalitarian ideologies to the atomized "mass man" of the 1940s, the baby boom and the great migration to the suburbs of the 1950s, the discontents of "alienated" student protesters in the 1960s, the proliferation of new religious cults in the 1970s, and the rise of a New Right committed to Christian fundamentalism and traditional family values in the 1980s. It is hard not to greet with a certain skepticism the recent insistence by a number of prominent social scientists that today, in the wake of the so-called Me Decade, Americans are yet again experiencing a yearning for community, a sense that their present social bonds are "superficial, transitory and ultimately unsatisfying," a "hunger for deeper social relationships," for greater "spontaneity," more "expressive" rather than "instrumental" ties to others, and "tremendous nostalgia . . . for the idealized 'small town.' "[4]

We have heard all this many times before and there may be less to it than meets the ear. The current president of our Association, Herbert Gans, suggests in his new book *Middle American Individualism* that recent authors of what he calls the "communal critique" of American life have placed "a heavy load of cultural and political expectations on community and on actual communities which neither can bear" (Gans 1988, p. 113). Nor does Gans miss the note of moral censoriousness underlying the critique. The people interviewed by social researchers are unlikely to have had no inkling of it. They can, in any case, hardly be expected to declare that all their ambitions have been realized and that their lives are without moral blemishes or spiritual deficiencies. Casting about for an appropriate, fairly toothless critical gambit, they may very well come up with what might be called, in the mode of George Bush, "the community thing." The wish for more community may, accordingly, have no greater significance than the ritualistic expression of a hope for more love, peace, and altruism in the world; indeed, complaints about the lack of community may, not to put too fine a point upon it, amount to just such a pious hope expressed less sentimentally in what is taken to be the more acceptable "objective" language of academic social science.

(2) Social determinism and its limits have always been a major theme in sociological thought from the belief of the nineteenth-century fathers in "iron," naturelike laws governing society and history to contemporary theoretical debates over the relative importance of "agency" and "structure." The contention that "social conditions," or "social forces," or the imperatives of the "social system" or capitalism or whatever, powerfully shape the lives we lead comes as close as anything does to having been the essence of the sociological outlook from its beginnings. Clearly, it lends itself to a wide range of morally exculpatory uses by individuals. The mocking song of the delinquent youths in *West Side Story* claiming to be victims of poverty and "broken homes" is only the most obvious of such uses.

Yet one of the standard beliefs attributed to Americans by introductory sociology textbooks is their readiness to assume individual moral responsibility for the circumstances of their lives, praising or blaming themselves alone as the case may be. This attitude is often interpreted as a secularized echo of the Protestant ethic, or as congruent with the economic individualism allegedly buttressing a capitalistic market economy. It is also sometimes treated as the antisociological illusion par excellence that sociology aspires to correct. "Individualism" is identified with a belief that human beings are fully formed by biological or psychological influences that operate independently of, or at most underlie, variations in culture and social structure. Treating such a view as the dominant popular one allows sociologists to swing into their ancient rain dance intended to exorcise biological and genetic factors as well as undue stress on differences in individual personality, whatever their origin.

"Individualism" is often regarded as a characteristically American ideology. If so, it surely illustrates the apparent futility of the sociological enterprise to which I previously referred, for a larger public has been exposed to sociology for a longer time in the United States than in any other Western country. Since the 1930s, the stock example of the imputed tendency of Americans to blame themselves as individuals for social conditions clearly beyond their control has been unemployment of a cyclical or structural nature (in the economist's language). I remember C. Wright Mills expatiating on this example in class when elaborating his well-known distinction between personal troubles and public issues, or milieu and structure. But there is obviously a great deal of evidence that Americans, as their voting behavior since at least the New Deal demonstrates, regard the economy as a supraindividual system that can be managed more or less effectively by the government. Americans are certainly "individualists" in Herbert Gans's sense of wishing to "obtain personal control over the general environment so as to minimize threat and unwanted surprise, and in order to lay the groundwork for self-development" (Gans 1988, p. 2). But this need not entail any insistence on the primacy of biological or individual psychological determinants, nor even ignorance of the distinction between micro and macro levels of social reality, or the collapsing of the latter into the former. It does imply, however, a preference by "middle Americans" for what Gans calls their "micro society" of informal personal and family relations as opposed to the "macro society" of large-scale formal organizations and impersonal market forces and, it should be added, social and political mass movements.

(3) This sociological theme appears to be the direct opposite of the preceding one. Although there is no reason why the public mind, nor, for that matter, sociologists themselves, might not entertain contrary ideas at the same time, the "we" implicitly refers to different groups in each case. The "society made us" dictum is applied primarily to lower-class victims of poverty, racial discrimination, or negative labeling for deviant behavior. Exemplifying what Paul Hollander (1973) has called "selective determinism," it lends itself to easy conversion into the left-wing taboo against "blaming the victim." On the other hand, the voluntarism as opposed to determinism implicit in the "social construction of reality" formulation refers to humanity at large as a collective actor. It insists on the fact that society and history are the products of human actions rather than effects of divine ordinance, invariant social laws, or a historical

fatality working silently "behind men's backs." When beliefs and practices are described as "socially constructed," the meaning is much the same as that intended in calling them "culturally patterned," as was more commonly done not so long ago.

There is a difference: "Social construction" suggests that institutions are the products not, certainly, of any unitary collective will or plan guiding action like the blueprint for a building, but at least of intersecting, frequently clashing wills or plans. The clear implication is that the existing order, any existing order, despite its seeming solidity, or — as the phenomenologists like to say — massive "facticity," is nothing but a human artifact, a thrown-together contraption, an exercise in *bricolage* quite unworthy of sanctification and lacking the impersonal inevitability of natural law. Applied to the future, however, the phrase communicates the promise that what has been constructed can be altered and improved, a wing added here, a barrier broken down there, the foundations strengthened and broadened. Or the whole building can be demolished and replaced with something more satisfactory. There is an echo here of Marx's contrast between prehistory and history. The popularity of the "social construction" image is largely accounted for by the possibility it projects of far-reaching planned social change, which gives it special appeal to sociologists of a left-liberal persuasion, that is, to the vast majority of sociologists. Ironically, the two authors most responsible for the popularity of the concept, Peter Berger and Thomas Luckmann (1966), are fairly conservative fellows not at all disposed to regard what has been socially constructed as ephemeral and insubstantial, ready to be instantly razed for rebuilding.

The phrase, with its particular resonances, is largely limited to sociologists. The "social construction of reality" has certainly not become a household cliché like "charisma" or "life-style" or even formulations of the other two sociological ideas I have discussed. Yet awareness of the purely manmade and largely provisional nature of the social order has, I think, entered popular consciousness, and the diffusion of sociology deserves some credit or blame for this. It perhaps represents sociology's major contribution to the "relativist" outlook complained of by conservative thinkers such as Allan Bloom.

"To our customs and beliefs, the very ones we hold sacred," Raymond Aron (1984, p. 76) has written, "sociology ruthlessly attaches the adjective 'arbitrary.' " This goes to the heart of the matter. The arbitrariness, the humanly invented and makeshift character of our routines and institutional practices, is the most general and also the most pervasive impression transmitted by sociology to a wider public. Modern men and women are conscious of having been thrust into a world they never made, but unlike most of the men and women of the past they know it was made by other people not so very different from themselves rather than by God, natural law, or deep-seated covert historical forces. Sociology is, therefore, an agent of disenchantment.

But if the notion of "social construction" seems to delegitimate the present order by regarding it as the contingent outcome of a series of historical accidents that might easily have produced something different, it also throws into question confidence in progressive social change. If it accentuates the vulnerability and precariousness of the status quo, it also casts doubt on the grounding in social reality of efforts to reform or transform that status quo. If social constructionism lends support to the convictions that "things don't have to be the way they are" and that it is possible purposefully to "make the world over" in the image of our most cherished ideals, it also robs the left of any assurance that its project is rooted in immanent currents of change reflecting powerful underlying social forces.

Social constructionism amounts to final and total abandonment of the nineteenth-century belief in laws governing society and history comparable to the laws of nature discovered by the physical sciences. Marxism, only occasionally convergent with "bourgeois" sociology in the past, represented the most elaborate version of the claim that history was subject at least to "tendential laws" that could be looked to for political guidance. But since at least the 1960s, the most fashionable readings of Marxism, especially by American sociologists in sympathy with it, have been voluntaristic rather than deterministic and entirely congruent with social constructionism. The political lesson of social constructionism would seem to be that "where there's a will, there's a way," understood, of course, in collective rather than individual terms. But this constitutes a reversion to utopianism. Moreover, optimism of the will, in Gramsci's phrase, is likely to flag in periods of stability such as the present.

Sociology, therefore, provides no comfort for radicalism anymore than for necessitarian arguments of a conservative character. In this sense, it may have contributed both to what has been called the "end of ideology" and to "legitimation crisis." Indeed, it perhaps suggests that ultimately these are twins, different aspects of the same thing, rather than the opposites they are usually represented as being.

NOTES

1. Merton (1961, p. 21) wrote: "One of its [sociology's] principal functions is to subject popular beliefs about man and his works to responsible investigations."

2. One of the best discussions of the epistemological issue and its larger implications that I have seen is in Apel (1977).

3. Ned Polsky contends that, although he borrowed the term from Alfred Adler, he himself is responsible for its spread through his book originally published in 1967 and later widely excerpted in anthologies for college courses. I remain unpersuaded that Weber was not the original source. Polsky (1985, p. ix), incidentally, properly notes that " 'lifestyle' has been horrendously overworked and indeed become a cliche of the adman [and] should now be avoided by any serious writer."

4. The phrases in quotation marks are drawn from Yankelovich (1981) and from Bellah et al. (1985).

REFERENCES

Apel, Karl Otto. 1977. "Types of Social Science in the Light of Human Interests of Knowledge." *Social Research* 44(Autumn):425-70.

Aron, Raymond. 1984. *Politics and History*. New Brunswick, NJ: Transaction.

Bellah, Robert N., Richard Madsen, William M. Sullivan, Ann Swidler, and Steven M. Tipton. 1985. *Habits of the Heart*. New York: Harper & Row.

Berger, Peter and Thomas Luckmann. 1966. *The Social Construction of Reality*. Garden City, NY: Doubleday Anchor.

Dobriner, William L. 1963. *Class in Suburbia*. Englewood Cliffs, NJ: Prentice-Hall.

Gans, Herbert. 1988. *Middle American Individualism*. New York: Free Press.

Hollander, Paul. 1973. "Sociology, Selective Determinism and the Rise of Expectations." *American Sociologist* 8(November):147-53.

Merton, Robert K. 1961. "Now the Case for Sociology." *New York Times Magazine*, July 16, pp. 14, 19-21.

Page, Charles. 1985. "The Decline of Sociology's Constituency." *History of Sociology* 6(Fall):1-10.

Polsky, Nelson. 1985. "Preface." In *Hustlers, Beats, and Others*. Chicago: University of Chicago Press.

Yankelovich, Daniel. 1981. *New Rules*. New York: Random House.

2

Sociology's Critical Irony:
Countering American Individualism

Joseph R. Gusfield

Teaching undergraduates exposes vulnerable professors to the innocent and naive insights of the uninformed and the uninitiated. The remark of a student in a course in social stratification many years ago is a good place at which to begin.

We had been reading one of the then-major works in stratification literature — a volume in W. Lloyd Warner's Yankee City series of studies. In it he presented a method for discovering the social class structure of a community. In my attempts to enliven the discussion, I asked a young woman to categorize her family into one of Warner's six social classes. When she replied that she couldn't do this, I followed by asking her how she would go about doing it, hoping that her answer would show an understanding of Professor Warner's techniques for class analysis. Her answer pointed in another and perhaps more pertinent direction. Unashamedly, she responded, "I'd ask a sociologist." This chapter is a commentary on that answer.

In my mind that response has two possible meanings, each of which bears on the history and functions of sociology in America. One meaning is suggestive of the sociologist as the arbiter of public issues through his or her knowledge and scientific expertise. The sociologist can give us the definitive categorization of people into classes based on his or her research. The second meaning is less respectful of sociological accomplishment as science. It suggests that the categorizations of class are as much the invention of the sociologist as they are descriptions of a factual America. Here the sociologist is the interpreter of events and conditions.

There is a third perspective that takes a little from each of the other two. It visualizes a sociology that sees itself as a set of concepts, a way of understanding and explaining but also a way that is not random or arbitrary. In this discussion of the influence of sociology on American society, I want to focus on this amalgam of art, in the form of a particular perspective, and science, in the form of a systematized attempt to learn what is factually correct about a segment of human behavior. What I shall argue is that sociology has a salient impact on American society through its language, its concepts, and the particular implication of these on American political and social issues.

In the structured society of today, various groups become the accepted sources of the meanings of events and processes beyond the immediate and the local experience of people. Often particular institutions become the authoritative sites for fact and meaning. The phenomenon called "mental illness" is today in the custody of the medical institutions, especially psychiatry. Indeed, the very term *mental illness* puts it in an institutional "place." I have referred to this mode of custodianship as a form of the "ownership of social problems" (Gusfield 1975, 1981). Religious institutions no longer are credible authorities on such questions. Medical personnel constitute an authoritative elite in this area. Sociologists are among the elites and would-be elites creating knowledge and destroying beliefs about Americans and American society. It is largely with their functions as purveyors of the meanings of events and processes that I am concerned in this chapter.

There are two sections to this chapter. In the first I will consider the form of sociology, with particular attention to sociology's cultural products — its writings and teachings. Here I want to assert the significance of sociological concepts on public discussion. In the second section I will consider its particular political and ethical meanings in American society.

In their consequences, the general premises of the sociological perspective have political significance through the concepts and perspectives inherent in them. I want to assert that, as a particular perspective toward human behavior, sociology has served as ideological support for challenges to the domination of individualist thought on American explanations of behavior.

THE SOCIAL CONSTRUCTION OF THE INDIVIDUAL

Sociology and Public Discourse

Among the many aphorisms attributed to Robert Park was one that allegedly was uttered in a moment of pessimistic despair. Park said, "Sociology is at best a pedagogical device." If by that remark he meant that what sociologists do in American society — talk to students and write papers and books — was a form of instruction and interpretation, then Park's aphorism has set the tone for my remarks. One of the ways in which sociologists have affected the understanding of human behavior and society is largely through their impact on the ways in which human actions are interpreted and discussed.

This should be distinguished from a more technical, scientific impact. I once knew an educational psychologist who could not understand the energy and emotion of American electoral campaigns. He thought that we should devise tests to give to candidates. These tests would then determine who was the best person to be president. That is an extreme view and I know no other social scientist with such a limited sense of the sources of conflict and contention in the contemporary society. It is, however, an image of a thoroughly rationalized world operating under scientific expertise. It is a world in which social technologies solve human problems without the disorder of political or intellectual conflict.

In this manner, the social sciences might become the intelligent arbiter of much of the conflict and inexactness that marks societies where sharp cultural, social, and economic differences cannot be mitigated by a common faith in a religious or philosophical standard. The utopian vision of the social sciences qua positive technical science was a vision of an arena of technical discourse, accessible to those qualified through experience and/or training who possessed the requisite credentials. Saint-Simon put it this way:

> Hitherto, the method of the sciences of observation has not been introduced into political questions; every man has imported his point of view, method of reasoning and judging, and hence there is not yet any precision in the answers or universality in the results. The time has come when this infancy of the science should cease, and certainly it is desirable that it should cease, for *the troubles of the social order arise from obscurities in political theory.* (Saint-Simon 1964, p. 40, italics added)

In this chapter I am not concerned with the technical contribution of sociology. My subject is rather the ways in which sociological concepts and the sociological perspective contribute to a consciousness of the individual (sociologists are fonder of the word *person*). In particular I am directing my attention to the conceptions of the individual and the political, economic, and cultural significance of the sociological perspective for the power and dominance of American individualism.

Individualism and Sociological Concepts

At least since Tocqueville, many critics, analysts, and observers of America have pointed to the dominance of individualist principles of political and economic action in the arenas of public and private life (Tocqueville [1831-35] 1969, Pt. II, chaps. 2-4; Lukes 1973; Gans 1988). Their uses of the term are by no means identical. Tocqueville defined *individualism* in terms of its implications for public life.

> I have shown how, in ages of equality, every man finds his beliefs within himself and I shall now go on to show how all his feelings are turned in on himself. . . .

> Individualism is a calm and considered feeling which disposes each citizen to isolate himself from the mass of his fellows and withdraw into the circle of family and friends; . . . he gladly leaves the greater society to look after itself. (Tocqueville [1831-35] 1969, p. 507)

Tocqueville's definition is by no means the definitive one nor is there any such. It is certainly beyond the scope of this chapter to offer one. Like many terms it is best seen in the light of its contrasts. Tocqueville uses it as a contrast to a feeling of commonality with others. Elie Halevy presents a more cognitive view of the term, emphasizing beliefs about society:

> In the whole of modern Europe it is a fact that individuals have assumed consciousness of their autonomy . . . society appears, and perhaps appears more and more, as issuing from the considered will of the individuals which make it up. (Quoted in Lukes 1973, p. ix)

It is this sharp distinction between society and the individual, between self-interests and public interests, between the self as controller of one's destiny and the social contexts of institutions, cultures, and groups as constraining and channeling behavior, that provides my focus. My concern in this section is less with the nature of ideologies than with the ways in which the concepts and perspectives of a discipline lead to the construction of the object — the individual — in varying ways.

Both clinical psychology and economics can be contrasted with sociology in the presentation of the person as an object isolated from institutional, group, and historical settings. Understanding action as the impact of "personality" or "rational self-interest" divorces the individual from social contexts. For the sociologist, behavior, whatever its individual elements, is always examined in reference to social organization and shared culture, to institutions, groups, and, as in this chapter, to the common categories used to interpret events and direct awareness.

Social Constructions

In one of many ways the term *culture* has been used, it points to the stock of meanings that are available, and even exclusive, in a society. In this chapter I am concerned with culture as a set of meanings about things. I leave the subject — things — in so vague a form to emphasize that culture includes the very terms in use to describe and direct our attentions. Language includes the concepts with which we form the experience. In the field of alcohol problems, where I have been working for many years, the term *substance abuse* has come into wide use as the generic concept under which alcohol and illegal drug use are studied or acted upon. The concept places attention on how a substance is used, or misused. An alternative concept, not widely used today, is "abusive substance." In the latter form, the attention is drawn to the existence and availability of drugs and alcohol as an explanation of alcohol and drug problems. Each concept organizes the understanding and meaning of its subject in a different manner. "Substance abuse" is more psychological. It places the focus of study on the person who uses alcohol or drugs. "Abusive substance" has a more sociological thrust. It leads to inquiries about where and when the substances are available. It emphasizes contexts of use rather than the personal characteristics of consumers.

It is in this sense that I refer to such concepts and paradigms as "social constructions." This concept points to the active, creative element by which the world of fact is enmeshed with an interpretive character; a world constructed rather than discovered. The concepts, theories, and problems with which we confront reality color and direct our perceptions and our understandings of what we perceive (Berger and Luckmann 1966; Gusfield 1984).

In a perhaps overquoted passage, Kenneth Burke has expressed this thought in his characteristic witty and vivid manner:

> Any performance is discussible, either from the standpoint of what it *attains* or what it *misses*. Comprehensiveness can be discussed as superficiality, intensiveness as stricture, tolerance as uncertainty — and the poor *pedestrian* abilities of a fish are clearly explainable in terms of his excellence as a *swimmer*. A way of seeing is also a way of not seeing — a focus upon object A involves a neglect of object B. (Burke 1965, p. 49)

Concepts as Meaning

It is difficult to perceive the world without the help of concepts. At the same time, concepts define and limit perceptions. It is no accident, as Herbert Blumer wrote, that conceiving has two meanings. One is as a way of looking at things. Another is as a way of bringing things into existence (Blumer 1969, p. 163). The process of naming is also a process of conferring meaning onto objects and events.

I have given several instances of how the concept of medicine is the framework within which medical practices operate. To perceive an object as medical is to put it within a specific institution and to act toward it accordingly. This is what the medicalization of "alcoholism" has done.

Much recent criticism of medicalization as a process in several fields has taken a critical approach. Witness the attack on the meaning of "mental illness" by such writers as Szaz (1961), Goffman (1961), Foucault (1966), and Scheff (1966). Much of that shift in meaning has involved seeing what has been seen as medical therapy and is now seen as one form of social control. The meaning of "mental illness" was changed when it became institutionalized in medicine (Foucault 1966).

There is an ironic quality to the meaning of "mental illness" as social control. It converts what was seen as beneficent and disinterested healing into something more self-oriented and repressive. In the sociologist's attack on "medicalization" as social control, the idea of medicine as a form of social control removes the behavior from the realm of the image of doctor and patient, of a personal affliction or disease, and places it in a wider context of social structure, of deviance, of control (Conrad and Schneider 1980). All these concepts provide a "way of seeing" that reconstructs (and deconstructs) the nature of the interaction. It looks at it anew. I shall want later to explore more fully the ironic quality of much of contemporary sociology in its intellectual and political impact on American culture.

Meaning and Text

There is no necessity to assume that objects and events have one and only one definitive meaning. That view leaves us locked in the prison house in which any specific theory, concept, or framework of relevance can lock us. There is, I assert, much merit in Paul Ricoeur's view of meaningful action considered as a text (Ricoeur 1979). From his viewpoint the range of the meanings of things are not fixed but are constantly being revealed as we interpret them. Ricoeur puts it this way:

> The meaning of human action is also something which is *addressed* to an indefinite range of possible "readers." . . . That means that, like a text, human action is an open work, the meaning of which is "in suspense." It is because it "opens up" new references and receives fresh relevance from them, that human deeds are also waiting for fresh interpretations which decide their meaning . . . the meaning of an event is the sense of its forthcoming interpretations. (Ricoeur 1979, p. 86)

The Art of Sociological Language

In one of his many essays, Kenneth Burke makes a distinction between semantic and poetic meaning (Burke 1957). Semantic meanings are the language of technical research and analysis in which an act or object has one and only one clear and unambiguous meaning. As Burke (1957, p. 123) puts it, its aim is "to give the name and address of every event in the universe." Poetic meaning utilizes the multiplicity of meanings that a given act can have. The two kinds of meanings are not irreconcilable. To choose one is not necessarily to eschew the other. But they are different. Poetic meaning opens up new, even unexpected, meanings. To say, as Lenore Weitzman has in her recent study of no-fault divorce, that poverty is being "feminized" is poetic (Weitzman 1985, chap. 10). It forces us to see poverty through a wider process. It is a form of metaphorical speech. Poverty is given a gender image to highlight the ways in which divorce is creating a large segment of the poor who are divorced women with children.

I am returned to Park's aphorism. There is much merit in that view, seeing as it does an educational, cultural consequence to the creation and destruction of meanings. Much of that impact is conveyed through the written and spoken language of sociologists. The images, metaphors, and concepts of sociological talk and writing, I assert here, form a large measure of its influence.

Metaphor, Analogy, and Rhetoric

I have been making a distinction between sociology as technical knowledge invested with the authority of science and sociological knowledge that is unique being neither science nor art but something of both. It is the nontechnical, less "research-designed" work that has provided much of the conceptual and discourse material out of which sociologists and their publics have "made sense" of our world. The names of many come to mind. For these meetings it is symbolic that Herbert Gans has selected Tocqueville as the model of sociologists who studied American society. The Holy Trinity of Durkheim, Marx, and Weber have been followed by a long line of creators of meaning: Tocqueville and the "tyranny of the masses"; Veblen and "conspicuous consumption"; Galbraith and the "techno-structure"; Olsen and the "free rider"; Riesman and "inner- and other-directed"; Rieff and "the triumph of the therapeutic"; Bourdieu and "cultural capital"; Bellah et al. and "life-style enclaves." Doubtless you can supply many others. Such concepts and metaphors provide an imagery and a focus that puts a particular clothing on the bare bones of raw reality.

The influence of sociology, as well as other social sciences, has affected the discourse with which public discussion is conducted. They develop the tools with which modern societies are given understandability. There is a great stock of such sociological concepts, including anomie, alienation, social mobility, and many more. There are also the paired terms that express both historical change and institutional differences. Among these are tradition-modernity, community-society, caste and class, formal and informal, bureaucratic and the charismatic. The metaphors of "role" are drawn from the stage; of "stratification" from geology. They add an element of visual imagery to verbal formulations. They are transmitted through classrooms, readings, and the content of American intellectual and cultural life. They have become part of the common categories and language of more American publics. Such concepts bring into play vivid and directing metaphors and analogies that make the new or the strange familiar.

Two aspects of sociological concepts stand out in this focus on individualism. The first is the consciousness of the individual as part of a group. An anecdote of one of my mentors, Louis Wirth, expresses the idea succinctly. Four professors come upon a human body at the base of a bridge. The physicist examines it as matter that has been in motion from the bridge. The biologist examines it to determine if it is still alive. The psychologist speculates on the possibility of suicidal motives. The sociologist examines the pockets to find to what groups the person belonged. Sociological explanations have been, and still are, explanations that look to institutions, to cultural continuities, to group commitments, norms, roles, and interactions. The "scene" and not the "agent," to use Burke's pentad, is the dominating image. Culture, social structure, group, and institutions are the scenic essentials of sociological thought. They form a perception of the individual as other than an isolated, self-contained, and self-directed being.

The existence and persistence of imagery, analogy, and metaphor are more than an admission of rhetorical skill. Metaphor expresses one thing in terms of another but it also enables us to expand the potential meaning by seeing the object in another setting. It is part of another reading of the text. Blau and Duncan's use of a path as a way of expressing individual social mobility is one such art form (Blau and Duncan 1963). Goffman's terms, "frontstage" and "backstage," are another (Goffman 1959). New metaphors surprise and, in surprising, expand the meanings of its primary object, the ones for which metaphors are found. The process of creating new metaphors is also the process of thinking in a new vein, of disturbing what is conventional and literal (Ricoeur 1977, 1978). To refer to *education* as "cultural capital" is to see the uses of education in a different fashion than in conventional usage, emphasizing both the utility of education on the market and the particular nature of culture in defining place and group membership in modern societies (Bourdieu and Passeron 1977).

An instance of the transmission of a sociological term into common usage is found in Veblen's terms "status symbol" and "conspicuous consumption" (Veblen [1899] 1934). Though first published at the end of the nineteenth century, Veblen's terms have been adopted into language to serve to sharpen the consciousness of Americans in the character of much consumership in the United States. In doing so Veblen paid attention to how a commonly perceived act of individual rationality is to be interpreted in an audience context. In the concept, the economic uses of consumership are redrawn.

Sociological Irony

In presenting alternative meanings to familiar events and processes, the sociologist is supremely the ironist. In showing how people and organizations pursue courses of action opposite to declared intentions, he or she becomes the ironist as debunker. (Consider here the many studies of organizational constraints.) Language and thought become ironic when that which is familiar and commonplace is depicted as strange and problematic. The object is interpreted in opposite fashion from its conventional meaning.

Kristen Luker's study of the abortion and antiabortion movements is a good illustration of sociological irony at work (Luker 1984). As she reads her interviews, prochoice partisans are modern feminists. Having children is a good in life among a number of other goods. Marriage need not entail the loss of individuality or career for a woman. Their social position supports their ideology. They are well educated and fairly high in the income structure. Antiabortion activist women are the opposite both in the meanings of abortion and in their social position. They see legalized abortion as a demeaning of the female role as wife and mother. But indeed their capacity to utilize the feminist gains through the labor force, through individualized sexual pleasure, or through easier divorce are limited. They have comparatively little education or other skills. Their life chances are dependent on husbands. Recreational sex is more a threat than an opportunity.

Luker summarizes her study in writing:

> Thus, the sides are fundamentally opposed to each other not only on the issue of abortion but also on what abortion *means*. . . . In order for pro-choice women to achieve their goals, therefore, they *must* argue that motherhood is not a primary, inevitable, or "natural" role for all women; for pro-life women to achieve their goals, they *must* argue that it is. In short, the debate restores the question of whether women's fertility is to be socially recognized as a resource or a handicap." (Luker 1984, p. 202)

Luker has ended in reversing the meaning of the abortion issue. What appears as a moral issue, over right and wrong (right to privacy versus right of the fetus to survive), now is described in terms of an issue over resources and opportunities. She has found newer and different meanings to the abortion issue than those of which partisans or observers were aware. The phrase "in terms of" is a way of saying that what may be relevant from one standpoint may not be from another. The individual is not presented as someone devoid of occupation, group affiliation, or historical moment. Even though Luker's is an interpretation of self-interest, she does not portray her subjects as isolated people characterized by beliefs apart from a context.

The Transfiguration of the Commonplace

In these forms the cultural frameworks of understanding, within which beliefs are couched, are made reflective, are rendered an object of awareness. There is much analogy here to Arthur Danto's (1981) view of artistic creation as the "transfiguration of the commonplace" and to Marcus and Fischer's (1986) idea of anthropology as cultural critique. Such critical functions involve the perception of the familiar in new and strange ways that render alternative ways of seeing possible. It is in this sense that the sociologist is in the business of manufacturing or creating meaning through "destroying" conventional perspectives.

THE POLITICAL PERSPECTIVE OF SOCIOLOGY

If sociology has an artistic component in "transfiguring the commonplace," what is the character of the commonplace and what is the nature of sociological transfiguration? Paradigms in the study of human behavior are seldom, whatever the intent of their founders and users, neutral to the world of social and political conflict. How we see constrains and conducts what we are likely to espouse. The sociological conception of the individual has implications for how social problems are conceived and how they appear to be resolved. That, in turn, has implications for the reception of sociology as a discipline in the world of public affairs as well as intellectual life.

Critical Irony

Whether or not the sociologist consistently engages in what Burke has called a "perspective by incongruity" (Burke 1954, Pt. II.), there is an ironic component to much that is done in the art of social science. It consists in rendering problematic what has been taken as nonproblematic. It involves what Richard Brown (1987, p. 190) calls "the capacity to derealize the present." Luker has done that in rendering problematic what were accepted meanings at the outset that viewed abortion as wholly a moralistic conflict.

All of us in contemporary societies live in a world of presumed facts. Yet fact, as we have tried to show, is elusive, ambiguous, and often a product of diverse interpretations. The sociologist acts as a critical ironist in turning a cool eye to the presumptions of facticity and the theoretical frameworks conventionally in use. It is not so much a matter of seeing this or that as correct or incorrect but in uncovering the cultural categories at work. I have tried to do this for the phenomena of drinking-driving, showing that the "facts" of drinking and driving and the perspective toward them involve a fixed presupposition that the central figure in traffic safety is the motorist. Others, with other perspectives, emphasize the auto, the roads, the leisure time patterns, and the contexts of driving and alcohol sale (Gusfield 1981, 1985). For the traffic safety "expert," alcohol is only one element, and not necessarily the central one in the effort to lessen auto fatalities and injuries. For others, such as MADD (Mothers Against Drunk Driving) the issue is as much a matter of doing justice and redressing victimage with punishment as it is one of deterring future casualties. The political and ethical differences are uncovered as Luker has uncovered the possible rational interests that can underlie what is conventionally understood as a moral conflict.

This view of sociology departs from the form of authoritative certainty implicit in the Simonean vision of a technical science. It presents an arena within which the quest for order is paralleled by a quest for disorder; the creation of meaning and the destruction of meaning ride in tandem. The result is the presentation of alternatives that would not have entered the arenas of public possibilities without the work and perspective of sociologists. Though its attainment is more complex and difficult than he may have thought, there is much merit in Karl Mannheim's alternative vision of the social scientist as the "free-floating" intellectual (Mannheim 1949).

Knowledge, both as fact and as theory, is seldom neutral to the world of political and social action. In the social sciences it is especially the case. What is asserted as fact has consequences for action, for policy. A genetic explanation of behavior withdraws support for policies to change or maintain institutional and cultural conditions. A sociological theory of crime moves us in different policy directions than does a biological one or a psychological one. It focuses attention on the institutional and cultural elements that operate to develop the individual and to create a particular environment in which some actions are more likely than others.

The paradigms of sociological thought and study are, whether or not the sociologist intends it, a critique of orientations and political positions that are premised on contrasting theoretical or factual conclusions. Sociology becomes a critique of some political programs and a supporter of others. Such critiques are inherent in its existence as a discipline. Despite the endless methodological and theoretical debates and discussions, there is a sociological perspective that unites us. However broad the umbrella under which we huddle, it is not the same umbrella under which the psychologist or the economist finds shelter. In American life it gives sociology a position as a particular kind of critic.

In some respects, American sociology is a creature of the growth in public and governmental obligations toward the poor, the suffering, and the disadvantaged. Undergraduate teaching and governmentally sponsored research remain the major sources of the sociologist's livelihood. These rest, to a major degree, on the relation of sociology to the occupations that deal with troubled and troublesome people; with social problems as distinct from the clinical psychologist and psychiatrist's concern for the individual self.

American Individualism and the
Sociological Perspective

Irony depends for its effect on the discrepancy between an existing understanding and new meanings with which the object is seen that contradict the original. What makes "abusive substance" an ironic concept is its opposite character to the dominating image of "substance abuse." What makes the view of "mental illness" as social control ironic is its contrast with "mental illness" as the caring behavior of physicians.

In considering the sources of sociological irony, it is important to recognize the audiences, the publics to which sociological writing and teaching is directed. American culture and politics have been dominated by a perspective of individualism throughout much of nineteenth- and twentieth-century history and, especially, since the end of the Civil War. The tensions and conflicts generated by political and philosophical commitment to a market-oriented individualism have been at the center of American public issues. Sociology has served a political and moral role as a critic of that individualism. The individual as an isolated concept has different implications for political and social programs than does the perception of the individual as a being-in-context. It is within the discourse of the American tension between a market-oriented, libertarian, and individualist conception of human action and an institutional and group-directed social science that sociology has had its impact on the American political and cultural scene.

And *scene* is the characteristic term and image of the sociologist. Whatever the identifying marks on our T-shirts (T for Theory), what constitutes the unifying and persistent emphasis of sociology is its focus on contexts in the explanation of human action.

In academic arenas, the tension between sociology and anthropology, on the one hand, and economics, on the other, has provided a great deal of the intellectual history of the social sciences. From Durkheim's critique of Herbert Spencer's attempt to use exchange as the source of social life to Mancur Olsen's critique of group sentiment or ideology as the source of collective action, the dialogue between individualist and societal accounts of human action has been a central part of intellectual history. Sociology has been a critic of classical economics and a critic of individualist interpretations of American life. Whatever the political intentions of individual sociologists, the ideological constraints on their research or the particular theoretical dedications of sociologists, a particular perspective toward human behavior has political and ethical implications. In the challenge to biological and individualist interpretations, sociologists cannot help developing doctrines that are inconsistent with market-oriented nineteenth-century laissez-faire liberalism and its contemporary embodiments.

The particular and exceptional way in which American individualism has dominated life and thought in the United States has been commented on above. Elsewhere, especially in Europe, the term was not used as a support for a liberal democracy and a market-dominated economics. Often it possessed a pejorative connotation (Lukes 1973, Pt. 1). Tocqueville saw the American form of individualism as isolating Americans from involvement with the community and with public life (Tocqueville [1831-35] 1969, pp. 506-507). The perception of the person as unrelated to others beyond the family is deep in the paradigms of clinical psychology and economics. It is that consciousness of the person as the isolated unit of analysis that is inconsistent with sociological paradigms.

A recent comparison of American and Japanese legal systems states the distinction well. The central differences are traced to the assumed individual autonomy and choice in American law, which leads to a view of individual interests in isolation and competition with others. Law is used to cope with the tensions between such individuals. In contrast, Japanese law perceives persons as parts of the social organism and uses law as a means of bringing those who have become outside the group into harmonious relations (Wagatsuma and Rosett 1986).

The Ethical and Political Thrust of Sociology

In recent years a renaissance of market-oriented policies by political administrations, as in the Thatcher and Reagan administrations, has been marked by an evident hostility to sociological studies, both in allocation of grants and in attitudes toward universities, especially in England. From the perspective of this chapter such hostility is by no means irrational. A highly individualistic ethic places responsibility for both causal and policy measures on the individual. It finds institutionalist explanations and policy measures that stress the structure of institutions or the interactional features of group life anathema to a perception of society as made up of individuals apart from their contexts. The consciousness of what the sociologist calls "the person" in the disciplines of clinical psychology and economics has political ramifications.

Historically, both in Europe and in the United States, sociology has represented a political critique of modern life in its individualist, capitalist, and bureaucratic forms. One wing of this critique has had affinity with a more European form of conservatism, which has seen the sources of modern malaise in the demise of the small community and the *Gemeinschaftliche* organization. Here the roots of alienation and "social pathology" have been traced to anomie, to "social disorganization," to the disruptive consequences of geographical and social mobility, to the individualizing effects of urbanization and capitalism, and the depersonalizing effects of formal organization. The underlying theme has been a contrast with a past in which authority, hierarchy, and community provided the person and family with continuity and cultural consistency. The individualizing consequences of modern life and modern social structure are the bête noire of such critiques.

While this form of social criticism, with its emphasis on the importance of authority and hierarchy, has not been a clear element in American political criticism, it has been a source of the glorification of the rural community and the derogation of the urbanism that has been an important element in American sociology. It has affinity with a classic European conservatism and to those critiques of social and cultural change that have deplored the loss of traditional continuities and the decline of cultural hierarchy represented by familial and religious authority. It has also been an important source of the communal movement of the 1960s. It is not that sociology "causes" an ideology but that it provides a language and a cultural authority that gives it expression and public standing. Bellah et al. have shown how this process operates in reverse through the individualistic language of psychotherapy and clinical psychology (Bellah et al. 1985).

A second political impact of sociology has been its support of reformist and radical critiques of American society. An emphasis on context, on structure, has been the support of a welfare-oriented ethics of communal responsibility and a reformist liberalism that directed attention to institutional change rather than the psychology of individual motivation. A sociology of drug abuse says No to saying No to Drugs and looks instead at the structure of law, of markets, of criminality and youth cultures. The rise of labeling theory as an explanation of crime and deviance is a sociological supplanting of the person with the institution and the social structure as the source of explanation.

In a similar vein the utopianism of a radical critique has emphasized the institutional bases of American life and has sought change through a radical transformation of the economic structure and/or the nature of formal organization. Both the radical and the reformist strains in American sociology have produced a critique of individualist egalitarianism based on the analysis of social stratification. Here again the contextualism of the sociological perspective provides a contrast to an unalloyed individualism.

No single perspective is able to provide a complete, accepted, uncriticized vision of the world. Sociologists differ in the degree to which they subscribe without qualification to their disciplinary perspective. As Dennis Wrong pointed out so well, sociologists oversociologize (Wrong 1961). So too biologists overbiologize, economists overeconomize, and psychologists over-psychologize. Disciplines and departments are as much a product of university organization and politics as of intellectual perspectives. There are always alliances across and between disciplines; institutional economists, rational choice political scientists, historical sociologists, sociological historians. But in its persistent and central mode of explaining human behavior and society, sociology has proven a corrective to the overly economistic and psychologistic perspectives that have dominated American public discourse. The growing adoption of sociological concepts into ordinary language, whatever its aesthetic results, is a politically meaningful process.

As a part of American intellectual, scholarly, and educational life, sociology has been an accepted field for study for approximately fifty years. In that period it has affected American life through millions of students, through its impact on intellectual circles, on policy developments, on popular culture and elite

Joseph R. Gusfield

46

thought. It lacks the clinical activities of psychology or the polic
orientations of economics. As is true of many areas of scholars
unintegrated into American life, still a suspect discipline, mor
welfare state than to a free market. For a discipline that is inhei
one, that is not an unmixed blessing. In a society still dominate
implicit in the paradigms of psychology and economics, it is also an inescapable
one.

REFERENCES

Bellah, Robert, Richard Madsen, William M. Sullivan, Ann Swidler, and Steven M. Tipton. 1985. *Habits of the Heart*. Berkeley: University of California Press.

Berger, Peter and Thomas Luckmann. 1966. *The Social Construction of Reality*. Garden City, NY: Doubleday Anchor.

Blau, Peter and Otis Dudley Duncan. 1963. *The American Occupational Structure*. New York: John Wiley.

Blumer, Herbert. 1969. *Symbolic Interactionism*. Englewood Cliffs, NJ: Prentice-Hall.

Bourdieu, Pierre and Jean-Claude Passeron. 1977. *Reproduction in Education, Society, and Culture*. Beverly Hills, CA: Sage.

Brown, Richard H. 1987. *Sociology as Text*. Chicago: University of Chicago Press.

Burke, Kenneth. 1954. *The Philosophy of Literary Form*. New York: Vintage.

————. 1965. *Permanence and Change*. Indianapolis: Bobbs-Merrill.

Conrad, Peter and Joseph W. Scheider. 1980. *Deviance and Medicalization: From Badness to Sickness*. St. Louis: C. V. Mosby.

Danto, Arthur. 1981. *The Transfiguration of the Commonplace*. Cambridge, MA: Harvard University Press.

Foucault, Michel. 1966. *Madness and Civilization*. New York: New American Library.

Gans, Herbert. 1988. *Middle American Individualism*. New York: Free Press.

Goffman, Erving. 1959. *Asylums*. Garden City, NY: Doubleday.

Gusfield, Joseph. 1975. "Categories of Ownership and Responsibility in Social Issues: Alcohol Abuse and Automobile Use." *Journal of Drug Issues* 5:285-303.

————. 1981. *The Culture of Public Problems: Drinking-Driving and the Symbolic Order*. Chicago: University of Chicago Press.

————. 1984. "On the Side: Practical Action and Social Constructivism." In *Studies in the Sociology of Social Problems*, edited by J. Schneider and J. Kitsuse. Norwood, NJ: Ablex.

————. 1985. "Social and Cultural Contexts of the Drinking-Driving Event." *Journal of Studies on Alcohol* (Supp. no. 10), pp. 70-77.

Luker, Kristen. 1984. *Abortion and the Politics of Motherhood*. Berkeley: University of California Press.

Lukes, Steven. 1973. *Individualism*. Oxford: Basil Blackwell.

Mannheim, Karl. 1949. *Ideology and Utopia*. New York: Harcourt, Brace.

Marcus, George and Michael Fischer. 1986. *Anthropology as Cultural Critique*. Chicago: University of Chicago Press.

Ricoeur, Paul. 1977. *The Rule of Metaphor*. Toronto: University of Toronto Press.

————. 1978. "Metaphor and the Problem of Meaning in Hermeneutics." In *The Philosophy of Paul Ricoeur*, edited by C. Reagan and D. Stewart. Boston: Beacon.

————. 1979. "The Model of the Text: Meaningful Action Considered as a Text." In *Interpretive Social Science,* edited by P. Rabinow and W. M. Sullivan. Berkeley: University of California Press.

Saint-Simon, Henri. 1964. *Social Organization, the Science of Man and Other Writings,* edited by Felix Markham. New York: Harper & Row.

Scheff, Thomas. 1966. *Being Mentally Ill.* Chicago: Aldine.

Szaz, Thomas. 1961. *The Myth of Mental Illness.* New York: Harper/Modern Library.

Tocqueville, Alexis de. [1831-35] 1969. *Democracy in America.* Garden City, NY: Doubleday.

Veblen, Thorstein. [1899] 1934. *The Theory of the Leisure Class.* New York: Random House/The Modern Library.

Wagatsuma, Hiroshi and Arthur Rosett. 1986. "The Implication of Apology: Law and Culture in Japan and the United States." *Law and Society Review* 20:461-498.

Weitzman, Lenore. 1985. *The Divorce Revolution.* New York: Free Press.

Wrong, Dennis. 1961. "The Over-Socialized Conception of Man in Modern Sociology." *American Sociological Review* 26(April):183-93.

Part II
America's Effects on Sociology

3

External Influences on Sociology

Neil J. Smelser

It is common — and helpful — to distinguish between internal or autonomous forces that shape the development of scientific inquiry on the one hand and those that arise externally in the cultural and social milieus of that scientific enterprise on the other. By the former we refer to the power of unsolved paradigmatic puzzles and implications to drive scientific thought. The readiest examples come from the "pure" sciences of mathematics, logic, and philosophy: Efforts to solve Xeno's paradox, efforts to fathom the nature of infinity and the logic of negative numbers, and (perhaps) efforts to divine the existential characteristics of an omnipresent God come to mind. By the latter we refer to those factors that are subsumed under the heading of the sociology of knowledge; these include the influences found in the larger cultural and linguistic contexts within which scientists work, the influences imparted by the social origins and positions of scientists, the hostility or receptivity of the political environment, and the organizational setting (e.g., university, research academy, industry, government) in which scientific work is executed.

It is not always easy to observe this distinction in practice. For example, it is apparent that the main "forces" that have shaped neo-Marxist sociological thought have been scholars' efforts to come to terms with the fact that many of the predictions that Marx derived from his theoretical diagnosis of capitalism have apparently not come to pass historically — the failure of the major capitalist classes to polarize because of the internal differentiation of each, the failure of the proletariat to develop into a world revolutionary force, and so on. That is to say, new theoretical work has arisen as the original Marxian paradigm has been adapted or elaborated to account for these evident predictive failures. But are those "forces" internal or external to Marxian thought? They are internal in that they are logical parts of the organized corpus of that theory, and any change in their validity status ramifies out and presses for change in its theoretical foundations. They are external, however, in the sense that they are the products of independently generated historical processes that are observable in the development of capitalist societies.

This apparent ambiguity complicates any neat effort to identify the precise status of the factors that have influenced the historical development of a field like sociology. In this chapter I will allude to the ambiguity from time to time but will make an effort to identify factors that appear to be primarily external to sociology.

There is a certain tradition of inquiry in the sociology of sociology with respect to these external factors. We have interpretations of early industrial sociology (that of Mayo 1949); Roethisberger and Dickson (1944) as "managerial sociology" (e.g., Burawoy 1979), suggesting either a direct or indirect domination of the subfield by the ideology and interests of the business classes; we have Gouldner's critique (1970) of Parsons's sociological theory as directed toward fending off, if not denying, the crisis revolutionary forces in America associated with the Great Depression and subsequent developments; we have a general book on Western sociology (Reynolds 1977), which is also critical in tone, suggesting the domination of the field by establishmentarian forces; we have the critique of Habermas (1973) and other critical theorists, who regard mainline (i.e., positivist) sociology as a kind of handmaiden of the instrumental/rational/technological interests of the postindustrial state apparatus; and we have at least one example of an analysis that regards sociological developments mainly as a result of sociometric and generational dynamics (Mullins 1973). Most of these treatments — and my illustrations are not exhaustive — are critical in character and focus on the business and/or political establishment as the main determining forces in question. As such they tend to be somewhat one-dimensional in character, and can be criticized as such. Reflection alone should tell us that there is a multiplicity of cultural, economic, political, and organizational influences involved in the evolution of a field of knowledge as large and complex as sociology.

In keeping with this critical remark, I will develop not one line of analysis but several, and these will fall under the headings of cultural, social, scientific, and political influences on the development and status of sociology. Some general observations will be included, but consistent with the theme of the symposium — "America's Impact on Sociology" — in which this essay was originally presented, most points made will apply to the American scene.

CULTURAL INFLUENCES

To speak of cultural influences is to suggest that major motifs and emphases in any national sociological tradition will reflect the implications of the major value and ideological components of the larger culture that harbors it. Several examples come readily to mind:

- In Latin American sociology, there is a special emphasis on the political and class dimensions. It has been declared that even though the starting point of inquiry may be work, health, or social protest, all sociological analysis in Latin America ends up as political analysis. This is clearly an exaggeration, but any review of theoretical writings and empirical research in these countries reveals the salience of that theme.
- In Great Britain is found a special scholarly fascination with social stratification and social classes, and the manifestation of these in all other areas of social life, such as education, culture, and family.
- Sociological theory in the Soviet Union and the socialist countries of eastern Europe was for a long time under the ideological shadow of often orthodox Marxist-Leninist doctrines that proscribed official interpretations of capitalist and socialist societies that left little room for the development of alternative lines of thought; as that shadow has lifted and as other "cultures" are infusing those societies, sociological theory is becoming increasingly variegated.
- American research on social stratification has stressed individual mobility more than collective mobility, and upward mobility more than downward mobility. These emphases can be seen as manifesting a special preoccupation with the American cultural value of individual achievement. That research also has focused on rates of individual mobility over time and above all with blockages to mobility (e.g., racial discrimination), which no doubt reveals a sensitivity to the degree to which the American cultural value of equality of opportunity is or is not being realized (Blau and Duncan 1967).

Turning to the American value system more generally, it is possible to cull from the insights of various observers and analysts (Tocqueville 1841; Parsons 1951; Williams 1963) a number of recurrent themes:

- individualism, with an assumption of responsibility for one's conduct
- mastery of nature and of one's fate
- voluntary cooperation as the basis of interaction
- social order based on moral consensus as contrasted with hierarchical ordering, class, or authority (consistent with the early Republican rejection of European patterns of monarchy and aristocracy)
- pragmatism, incrementalism, and reform as principles of social changes
- a resultant optimism

It would be a serious oversimplification to argue that these themes have dominated American sociology and, more broadly, the behavioral and social sciences in general, but it would also be a mistake to ignore them. Perhaps the case could be best made for two of our sister disciplines of economics and psychology, with the former's emphasis on voluntary exchange, freedom from constraint, entrepreneurship, and survival through success, and the latter's emphasis on individual adjustment, competence, and coping. It might also be remembered that one of the distinctively American adaptations of Freudian psychoanalytic theory (largely pessimistic in character) was ego psychology, which stressed individual adaptation and flexibility above all.

Similar continuities might be observed in many schools of thought that have had indigenous American origins. It can be argued, for example, that role theory is based on the assumption of socialization into and more or less voluntary compliance with the "expectations" of others, and the mechanisms of social control associated with role theory stress conformity rather than obedience to authority or submission to coercion. The school of symbolic interaction, rooted in the pragmatic philosophies of Dewey, Mead, and Blumer, conceives of the actor as an agent, an active user and manipulator of his or her symbolic environment and not in any way enslaved by the structural forces of society, by instinct, or by mechanical principles such as behavioral conditioning; in this sense the tenets of symbolic interactionism can be regarded as a kind of celebration of individual mastery and freedom, in contrast to the more deterministic theories against which it is counterpoised. Much of exchange theory, too, while it has origins in economic theories of competition, shared with these the underlying assumption that exchange is a matter of freely supplying and demanding resources and rewards to and from others. And, finally, the central features of Parsonian sociology and functionalism in general are voluntarism and consensus around a moral order.

To point out these continuities, of course, is to simplify matters greatly. American sociology has also been characterized by theoretical formulations that stand in critical dialogue with these strands and stress themes of inequality, domination, and coercion. Many of these theories are of European origin and have found their way into American sociology through the works of those who came from Europe (for example, Sorokin 1928) or studied in Europe (e.g., Parsons 1937) or who were otherwise inspired by the European masters (e.g., Mills 1956).

These system/collectivist/critical/radical perspectives have themselves come to constitute a major part of sociology in this country and continue to be nourished by the more contemporary contributions of European scholars such as Habermas, Touraine, Bourdieu, Giddens, and others. The field can be regarded as a kind of continuous dialogue and ferment among these strands of thought, some consonant with and some in critical opposition to the dominant themes of the American cultural tradition.

This notion of a continuous cultural dialogue within the discipline is closely connected with an observable but not very well understood phenomenon of the periodic rise and fall of the great historic figures of the field in sociological research and explanation. Durkheim and Freud held great sway in the two postwar decades in American sociology and social science generally, but the fortunes of both, especially the latter, have now faded somewhat and the neo-Marxian and neo-Weberian themes have risen in salience. European sociology has witnessed an ebbing of Marxian sociology as such but continues to generate and nurture theories that cannot be described as Marxian but that retain some distinctive thread of Marxian thought, such as the ideas of domination and protest (new critical theory and the new social movements school, for example). As indicated, we do not understand the vicissitudes of the masters very well. Some of these might be a generational matter; one cohort of sociologists may embrace and make productive use of the insights of a Tocqueville or a Freud, while the next, facing new intellectual problems and perhaps eager to distance itself from the work of its teachers, will forsake those figures and resurrect others; still another cohort will call up the heroes of their teachers' teachers. In any event, this invocation of the notion of myriad cultural dialogues within sociology that mirror larger cultural themes brings into question once again the strict distinction between internal and external influences on the evolution of a field of inquiry.

KEEPING UP WITH SOCIETY

One of the key influences in the development of sociology — if not the social and behavioral sciences generally — is the fact that much of its subject matter is dictated by real and perceived social trends in the larger society. If one examines the rise of new areas of interest in the past several decades, one will find the family and unemployment emerging in the years of the Great Depression, propaganda and public opinion and rumor in World War II, a burst of new interests in the sociology of poverty, sociology of education, sociology of youth, and feminist sociology in the 1960s and immediately thereafter, and environmental sociology, the sociology of energy, and the sociology of risk more recently. All these are evident reactions to social problematics, and a quantitative study might reveal a quite real correspondence between the appearance of these problematics and a flurry in the literature, if the appropriate time lags for funding, research, execution, and publication delays are taken into account.

The rise and fall of major figures, mentioned before, might also be explained in part by the changing historical circumstances of any given society. The evident rise of interest in Marx and Weber in this society in the 1960s and 1970s can be regarded as a kind of intellectual mirror of the group conflict and political turmoil of those decades. It also makes sense that, as colonial countries are struggling under the yoke of the colonial powers and subsequently are fighting to consolidate their own independence, they may turn to the Marxian notions of exploitation and dominance to enlighten their understanding; when they move actively into the phase of building institutions and promoting economic growth, the theories of a Joseph Schumpeter might appear more attractive.

A closely related tendency to these is for our subject matter to run ahead of the conceptual frameworks under which we study it. The most important illustration of this concerns the study of international relations and international interdependencies. If we examine our major sociological heritage, it is apparent that most of our theories are based on the postulate that most of what transpires in social life does so *within* single societies and, indeed, intrasocietal forces are the main operative determinants. Put another way, sociologists have tended to regard the single society, nation, or culture as the principal unit of analysis for their studies. When we look around the contemporary world, however, it is apparent that the relevance of this kind of approach grows less and less. Nations grow more dependent on one another; the major forces affecting the decisions of national governments are not within the hands of national decision makers but lie outside their control; in short, it is systems of societies, not single societies, that constitute the most important level of analysis. Accordingly, analyses built on the idea of single societies, states, nation-based ideologies, and the like are less powerful. But with few exceptions the corpus of our inherited traditions does not provide very many theories and frameworks for moving to the higher systemic levels.

INFLUENCES FROM SCIENCE

One of the remarkable features of human history during the past several hundred years is the extent to which science as a culture has come to be such a dominant feature of Western culture in general. Its conquest has been selective, with the early strides being in astronomy and physics, with subsequent developments being made in chemistry and the life sciences, and, finally, beginning in the late eighteenth and nineteenth centuries, in economics and psychology, then in political science, anthropology, and sociology. In all instances the scientific impulse displaced a preexisting religious or philosophical one, and in no case was that transition an easy one, involving as it did a threat to established claims to legitimacy and to individuals and groups who represented those claims.

It is important to recognize, moreover, that as the scientific impulse emerged in one intellectual area after another, it arose in a unique historical context, and its character was influenced by that context. Here the contrast between the histories of European and American sociology are instructive. The emergence of the field in continental Europe — associated above all with the efforts of Émile Durkheim and Max Weber — occurred in two principal contexts: first the distinctive emphases in European social thought and second the simultaneous emergence of the scientific impulse in economics and psychology. With respect to the first, European sociology oriented itself above all to the intellectual traditions of European thought as represented in the study of history, philosophy, law, and the classics in the academy and in the critical intellectual traditions focusing on the state, social classes, and the economy, to be found both in the academy and in the more general intellectual life of those countries. It also oriented itself to the emerging social scientific emphases of the day, as Durkheim's negative polemic toward psychology and Weber's suspicion of the assumptions of formal economics reveal this second stress. The current preoccupation of European sociology with macroscopic and critical issues — phenomenology excepted — of the state, classes, and the economy, and the critical treatment of each, bears witness to the power of these traditions.

(England is something of an exception here — while not totally exempt from continental traditions, English sociology arose in the context of the rise of first liberal and later labor reformist politics and in the peculiar context of English empiricism, manifested in the early "survey" techniques of Booth (1892, 1902) and Rowntree (1922). This put a permanent, somewhat left-wing but simultaneously fact-oriented stamp to British sociology.)

America is also something of an exception. Just as its nation arose without the necessity to fight off the burdens of European feudalism, so its sociology arose in a context that did not include (with exceptions to be noted presently) the peculiar intellectual history of European nations. Our sociology grew up in two major intellectual and social contexts. First, it made its appearance in the public institutions of higher education in this country several decades after the passage of the Morell Act of 1862, which solidly established the scientific and applied impulses (mechanical and agricultural) in American higher education; a related part of this development was that economics and psychology preceded sociology and had fully adopted the scientific "definition" of their own fields. Second, in the 1890s the reform theme was in the air and sociology picked up that theme from both the social gospel and the progressivist movements. It is not surprising that sociology, struggling to establish its legitimacy in those days, picked up the twin themes of scientific respectability and social reform as its motifs to broadcast to the academy and to the larger society. Those themes persist to the present day. They also fit comfortably into the American cultural emphases on pragmatism, reform, and optimism identified in the previous section. American sociology appears to have had an odd preoccupation with how scientific it is or is not, and upon what model of the scientific method it is built.

POLITICAL INFLUENCES

We know enough about the systemic character of societies to be able to assert with confidence that sociology — or any other field of inquiry, for that matter — never exists in isolation from the polity but is embedded in its complex ways. In particular, sociology's general relations with national governments and its many publics are always fraught with uncertainty and ambivalence. These relations may be likened to a troubled marriage. The two partners may constantly irritate one another as governments and publics raise ideological concerns and pressures that threaten to compromise the freedom of thinkers and researchers in the discipline, and sociologists forever generate information and ways of describing social events and situations that have an unsettling, needling, and even debunking effect. At the same time the two may find that they cannot live without one another, governments and publics being dependent on data, information, and perspectives for their policies and their interpretations of the social world, and sociology requiring autonomy as well as financial and institutional support. This inevitable ambivalence can be resolved in a variety of ways. Sociology may be afforded a free and happy welcome as part of the academy; it may be given only low status and a bad press in the public eye; or it may be constantly hounded to be something that it is not or driven underground altogether by oppressive measures.

One of the remarkable features of American sociology is that it has been housed in academic departments in universities, which have as a matter of historical fact been institutionally removed from the political winds, despite periodic forays of interested legislators and usually right-wing political groups that have imperiled academic freedom in the universities. This is a relative statement, of course, but if one compares the American case with others — including those of eastern European societies — the field has emerged as one that is, by and large, nonpoliticized from the standpoint of its environment. (The field is in another sense a very political one, because it sometimes manifests skeptical if not critical views of its subject matter — the institutions of the country — views that perforce trigger political reactions; in still another sense it is a political field, in that it shares with others political striving within its ranks.)

As the functions of the state have grown, and the welfare state in particular, sociology and the other social sciences have taken on a different kind of political significance. Government agencies, pursuing their various missions, are inevitably called upon to justify both their concerns with societal problems and their policies relating to these problems in terms of some kind of factual base. For example, in order to define teenage pregnancy as a "problem," it is necessary to establish some kind of empirical scope of its incidence, and presumably to hold this scope up to some kind of standard that would make it a "nonproblem." In establishing this kind of empirical scope, various political agencies have borrowed both methods (mainly survey) and findings from sociology and the other social sciences, giving them applied or political significance, if you will. In many respects the research carried out by agents is very similar to social science research in general.

Where sociology has come under greater political influences is not in its significance as an academic discipline in the university setting but in its significance as a science based on research, with the support for that research coming from the science establishment (and ultimately from the Congress and the executive branch); it is the case, furthermore, that the phenomenon of research has a political dimension, and I would like to spend the remainder of my remarks on this topic.

Organizationally, the behavioral and social sciences are a part of the National Science Foundation and are supported by the same general budget that is appropriated for the foundation annually by Congress. Yet it is apparent that these disciplines occupy a minor place in that agency; the Science Board (its policymaking board of trustees) has virtually no behavioral or social sciences as a subpart of a division known as the Biological, Behavioral, and Social Sciences, the director of which is invariably a biological scientist. Furthermore, the sums available to the behavioral and social sciences within the foundation are minuscule in comparison with the total budget. Perhaps more decisive, however, and perhaps the ultimate reason for all of the above, is the fact that much of the "hard-science" leadership of the National Science Foundation and the science establishment in Washington, while they grant a place for the behavioral and social sciences, still regard these enterprises as basically "soft" and not really "scientific."

The other important point to mention about the National Science Foundation — and all other government granting agencies — is that they are publicly visible and come under annual review at budget time by the Office of Budget and Management in the executive branch and both houses of Congress. The view of the behavioral and social sciences in the halls of government, moreover, is fraught with ambivalence. On the one hand government officials are forever faced with and must deal with pressing social problems of poverty, unemployment, crime, mental health, economic instability, and so on, all of which are most directly related to and informed by behavioral and social science research. This concern tends to generate a positive attitude toward the behavioral and social sciences, and to incline governmental officials to support research in those areas out of the conviction that increased knowledge about those problems will be enlightening and will lead to more effective attacks on them.

On the other hand there are pockets of hostility toward the behavioral and social sciences on the part of government officials, and while these vary in importance and salience over time, they are identifiable and take the following forms:

- Research in the behavioral and social sciences produces trivial, obvious, and unimportant results, and expenditures on that kind of research are wasteful of public funds. This attitude is symbolized in the annual "Golden Fleece" awards named by Senator William Proxmire, the intent of which is to show that the federal government has been fleeced of its gold by studies funded to study the sex life of goats, the sociology of love, and other such subjects.
- Research in the behavioral and social science system is of no use to the government and, therefore, should not be funded; this opinion is associated with public statements by David Stockman, President Reagan's former budget adviser, made during congressional budgetary hearings in the early 1980s.
- Research in the behavioral and social sciences is basically unscientific — according to the canons of "hard" science, and is, therefore, undeserving of study. This is a kind of spillover of the above-mentioned attitude on the part of many physical and life scientists.
- Research in some branches of the behavioral and social sciences (such as the study of race relations, fundamentalist religious beliefs, family life, and other areas) is basically dangerous ideologically, because it is likely that suggesting changes in such areas will generate criticism of institutions and practices that are either considered sacred or uneasily taken for granted.

This kind of hostility is difficult to document, because it is often shrouded in one of the less frank forms just listed; nevertheless, it exists and reflects both right-wing political sentiments and the fact that social scientists themselves are more politically liberal and critical than other groups in the political spectrum. From time to time this ideological hostility breaks into the open and results in direct assaults on certain kinds of social science research; in the early Reagan years, for example, budget cuts in the National Science Foundation, National Institute of Mental Health, and elsewhere were directed toward discouraging research that focused on systemic (class, race, for example) accounts and explanations of social problems, but budgets in other areas were left alone or encouraged research that involved genetic and psychogenic understandings of them.

It is difficult to conceive how the behavioral and social sciences could be simultaneously trivial, useless, unscientific, and threatening. Be that as it may, these attacks surface from time to time, and as such they constitute a source of embarrassment and difficulty for the leadership of the National Science Foundation and other funding agencies. To them the behavioral and social sciences appear as a minor part of their operation from an organizational and budgetary point of view, but as a major source of criticism and trouble from those quarters that matter.

It follows from this account that the main temptations generated by these pressures on the behavioral and social sciences are two: first, to maintain as low a profile as possible, to avoid political notice and to survive thereby, and, second, to present themselves as respectably and undangerously as possible and thereby to curry political and budgetary support. The main response to these temptations, according to my observations, is for the spokesmen of the behavioral and social sciences to represent themselves as adhering to the model of positive science, as using methodologically sound techniques, and as, therefore, supportable on the grounds that they are legitimately scientific. This strategy emerges — whether it is, in the end, effective or self-defeating — as the one that is most likely to blunt criticism both within the donor agencies and on the part of other government officials. In the end, of course, this response emerges as a victory of the positive-science emphasis and as a kind of marriage of convenience between the behavioral and social scientific investigators in the academy on the one hand and the Washington social science establishment on the other — a marriage that encourages those in the academy to support "hard" behavioral and social scientific investigations as such a policy encourages funding agencies to give research grants to such investigators because it provides evidence that their own standards are strictly "scientific." The only cautionary qualification to this diagnosis is to note that, if the liberal voice in the Democratic Congress presses, and the accommodative voice of the Bush administration responds, a more supportive stance toward a greater diversity of social science research — including research that has politically more critical implications — may resurface.

This "sociology-of-knowledge" diagnosis has perhaps gone on too long, but its implications are clear. Unless we witness major changes in the structure and prestige systems of universities, and/or major changes in the politics affecting the behavioral and social sciences, the model of the social sciences — including, of course, sociology — as sciences will be the dominant voice of the future. Empirical-science models of social study and explanation will be center stage and will call the tune, as it were, for those voices that will continue to reassert the concern with philosophical, moral, and social problems that has occupied a salient past in sociology. The content and tone of the dominant voice in counterpoint with subordinate protesting voices will change with changing times, but I would predict that it will be the main melody of the future.

REFERENCES

Blau, Peter and Otis D. Duncan 1967. *The American Occupational Structure.* New York: John Wiley.
Booth, Charles. 1892, 1902. *Life and Labour of the People of London.* New York: Macmillan.
Burawoy, Michael. 1979. *Manufacturing Consent.* Chicago: University of Chicago Press.
Gouldner, Alvin Ward. 1970. *The Coming Crisis in Western Sociology.* New York: Basic Books.
Habermas, Jürgen. 1973. *Theory and Practice.* Boston: Beacon.
Mayo, Elton. 1949. *The Social Problems of Industrial Civilization.* London: Routledge & Kegan Paul.
Mills, C. Wright. 1956. *The Power Elite.* New York: Oxford University Press.

Mullins, Nicholas C. 1973. *Theories and Theory Groups in Contemporary American Sociology.*
    New York: Harper & Row.
Parsons, Talcott. 1937. *The Structure of Social Action.* New York: Macmillan.
————. 1951. *The Social System.* Glencoe, IL: Free Press.
Reynolds, Larry T. 1977. *The Sociology of Sociology.* New York: McKay.
Roethisberger, Fritz and William Dickson. 1944. *Management and the Worker.* Cambridge, MA:
    Harvard University Press.
Rowntree, Benjamin C. 1922. *Poverty: A Study of Town Life.* London: Longman, Green.
Sorokin, Pitirim. 1928. *Contemporary Sociological Theories.* New York: Harper.
Tocqueville, Alexis de. 1941. *Democracy in America.* New York: J. & H. G. Langley.
Williams, Robin. 1963. *American Society: A Sociological Interpretation.* New York: Knopf.

4

The Curious Importance of
Small Groups in American Sociology

Allan Silver

The small group occupies a distinctive position in American sociology, past and present. To show this requires sustained comparisons with other Western nations, but an essay of this scope can offer only indicative illustrations. The story involves a conjuncture of two strands in the Anglo-American heritage — one religious, the other secular — which came together with far more force in America than in Britain. First, the core religious culture in America during its formative period was uniquely dominated by congregational doctrines and forms of church government. The congregational churches have long not been majoritarian, but their cultural and doctrinal influence continues, usually as unspoken cultural and intellectual assumptions. Second, the secular Anglo-American idea of "social control" has been biased in favor of face-to-face relations rather than control by institutional authority, religious or secular. The confluence of these two currents in America, as nowhere else, endowed the small group with a sociological significance in America that elsewhere it has largely lacked. I discuss, first, the impact of congregational forms of religion and, second, of the secular notion of social control.

It is widely said that the meliorist tendencies of American sociology were much influenced by reformist Protestant impulses, one evidence of this being the number of early American sociologists who began as clergymen or were the sons of clergy. This is true, but insufficient. Religion has constituted a "deep structure" influencing the assumptions of secular sociologists, even as they sought to offer a scientific account of the moral order (see Vidich and Lyman 1985). In the American case the most influential religious "deep structure" — for

AUTHOR'S NOTE: *This chapter has benefited from comments by Hal Benenson, Rogers Brubaker, William Martin, Hilary Silver, Marcel Teitler, and Alan Wolfe.*

the culture and for sociological thought — has been congregational doctrine and church government. In congregational doctrine, there is something sacred and irreducibly ultimate about the moral texture of face-to-face relationships organized as local congregations. In religious language — for example, that of the Constitution of the Congregational Churches of the United States of 1871 — the idea sounds like this: "The right of government resides in local churches, or congregations of believers, who are responsible directly to the Lord Jesus Christ, the One Head of the church universal and of all particular churches" (Walker 1960, p. 573). On this view, the church is composed of compacts made among freely choosing persons; there is no valid distinction between the personal and the institutional aspects of religious life. Thomas Hooker's *A Survey of the Somme of Church Discipline*, published in 1648, makes the point concisely:

> Amongst such who . . . have power each over other, *there must of necessity be an engagement*, each of the other by their free consent, before [in] any rule of God they have any right or power, or can exercise either, each toward the other. (Quoted in Morgan 1966, p. 26; emphasis in the original)

This perspective is not limited to rejecting the radical distinction in Catholicism and other hierarchical churches between office and person, priesthood and laity, *ecclessia* and the world. For hierarchical churches, marriage is in essence a sacrament — an expression of the church's action on the world. The congregational perspective considers personal emotions key to marriage (Morgan 1966, pp. 29-64; Schücking 1970). Personal affinities between spouses, accidental to the sacramental conception, are essential to the congregational view of marriage as a voluntary relationship. Husband and wife are doctrinally commanded to love each other (Leites 1982), but doctrine also provides a legitimate role for elective affinities in drawing them together and contributing toward marriage as a sacred arrangement.

In congregational relationships, face-to-face relationships are simultaneously ideological and personal: They are constituted both by the voluntary consent of particular persons to enter into relationships — marriage, congregation, local polity — and by the idea of communion in Christ. Despite vicissitudes in congregational theology, and the emergence in America of other religious traditions on a very large scale, this "deep structure" defining the linkages among person, community, and larger society has persisted as a model in American society and social theory. In the language of a churchly commentator:

> True *koinonia* [communion] occurs when the local church has the same authority as the communion as a whole [so that] the two, in deep mutual respect, maintain continual dialogue with one another . . . [L]ocal churches do not create the communion any more than the communion creates the local churches. . . . Christ gives the

Church power, feeding strength to the local church through the whole company of churches and to the whole company through the local church . . . [T]he whole is not itself except as it is made up of free and autonomous parts with direct access to Christ, but the parts are not themselves except as they belong to the whole which is also informed by Christ. (Walker 1960, p. ix; see also Atkins and Fagley 1942, pp. 340-392)

Projected as secular social thought: Small groups of interacting persons are both constituted by the larger society and, in turn, constitute it. It follows that the small group, like the congregation, is essential to understanding society as a whole.

This is not true of French sociology — neither of the passionately secular Durkheim nor of the foremost sociologist of French Catholicism, Gabriel Le Bras. Durkheim's account of the normative order accords causal priority not to the interacting small group but to impersonal dynamics constituting the secular moral order and to the administrative governance of the lay state. Le Bras's sociology of Catholicism drew a clear distinction between social interaction and the formal aspects of the church. A short passage gives the flavor of his approach.

The parish is something other than living men . . . [and] individual souls. . . . A church is not a parish, a people is not a parish. But if the church is bound [est affecté] to a people, a parish exists. The parochial bond is . . . the essence of the parish. . . . This bond is constituted by all the judicial obligations, spiritual or temporal, of the parishioner toward his church. (Le Bras 1955, p. 107; my translation)

Obviously, Le Bras's sociology is cast in theological terms: The parish, the smallest unit of the church, is understood not as the product of its human interactions, nor solely as an aspect of the church, but as a distinct phenomenon constituted by the relationship of individuals to the parish, not to each other. In contrast, the American Catholic sociologist Joseph H. Fichter's analysis of the parish (Fichter 1964) treats it precisely as constituted by what Le Bras called "living men . . . [and] individual souls" — as the sum of social interactions with its bounds.

What I have called the characteristically American, or "congregational," sociology of face-to-face relationships provides simultaneously for individualism and community. The view that America in particular normatively provides for individualism but not community derives from incomplete historical and theological assumptions. Joining in the constitution of congregations by personal interaction is not religiously valid unless based on individual choice. In the congregational perspective, community is constituted by individualism; the congregation is created by the consent of individuals not merely to join it but to create it continuously by their continuous consent.

In the Old World, community was sustained by hierarchical churches, intricate systems of patronage and clientage, the powers of landlords and princes, and the imperatives of collective life in town and country. In the European setting, neither freewill theologies nor notions of political agency and consent were understood to create the structures of sacred and secular community; rather, they signified participation in structures constituted by "tradition." With the important exception of merchant cities and artisinal and merchant guilds, these did not require the consent of participants for continued existence. Churches based on hierarchy and sacrament understood themselves as constituted by divine decree and apostolic succession; and the necessitous imperatives of community among aristocrats, artisans and peasants, rather than personal volition, accounted for communal ethos and practices.

Translating this into sociological terms means that a purely Lockean view of America as a liberal and capitalist society par excellence overlooks its indigenous theory and practice of community, one that has had a strong and continuing impact on American sociology. This theory of community, unlike that of the Old World, is based on interaction at the face-to-face level of an essentially voluntaristic character. To be sure, the coexistence of community and individualism in the congregational model does not imply romantic or "antisocial" forms of individualism, but an individualism consistent with—indeed, constituting—consensual values. It is precisely this idea that informs the idea of the primary group, the face-to-face community and socialization as they appear, variously elaborated, in the foundational work of Charles Horton Cooley, E. A. Ross, George Herbert Mead, Mary Parker Follett, and later in that of Robert Park and W. I. Thomas. For all these seminal figures, part and whole simultaneously constitute each other, as in congregational theology, endowing the small, face-to-face group with a strategic significance it lacks in the European tradition. No major tradition in European social thought and theory, whether inspired by the class-oriented left, market-oriented liberalism, or the organicist right, has accorded so causally decisive a role to small groups in understanding the larger society and the total polity.

The self-understanding of the American polity has also been shaped by these conceptions. Writing in 1915, Herbert Croly—an influential publicist for Progressive liberalism—drew on the work of "recent social psychologists [who] give a concrete account of the way social minds are formed, and consequently . . . bring the idea of social minds into relation with the fundamental idea of society as a process." Croly's writing illustrates how the congregationalist view of social structure sustains a sort of political pluralism distinctive to America and also evokes the emphasis on the germinal role of small-scaled groups characteristic of American reform movements:

A society is not made up primarily of individuals . . . [but] of an innumerable number of smaller societies . . . [each of which] . . . constitutes a society, whose reality is determined by [its] . . . purposes. Every church, every club, every political and military association, every labor union, every family, even every temporary social gathering, constitutes a society of a kind. . . . They acquire joint responsibilities and seek the realization of common purposes . . . [out of which] a social ideal gradually emerges. (Croly 1915, p. 197)

Congregationalists have long claimed that their theology and church govern-ment are seminal not only for religious but for political democracy (Heermance 1906). American social psychologists made an analogous claim, proposing that proper socialization in interpersonal relations of small scale is key to the development of democratic citizens; the idea is pervasive in Cooley, implicit in Mead, and reaches its fullest development in John Dewey. But while Croly drew such political consequences in Wilsonian America, contemporary British social psychologists like Wilfred Trotter and William MacDougall advanced theories of instinct, including that of the "herd," unconcerned with the small group and its distinctive attributes, and at odds with the texture of democracy (Soffer 1978, pp. 217-51).

Obviously, to take the small group as central for understanding society diminishes the interpretive force both of class and tradition. Less obviously, it also diminishes the dominance of market individualism. The congregational concept of social structure involves a form of individualism-in-solidarity that does not uncritically celebrate the utilitarian or self-regarding individualism of classical market theory. Illustratively, consider a passage of Cooley's:

It is . . . not my aim to depreciate the self-assertive passions. I believe they are fierce, inextinguishable, indispensable. Competition and the survival of the fittest are as righteous as kindness and cooperation, and not necessarily opposed to them . . . [because] the normal self is moulded in primary groups to be a social self whose ambitions are formed by the common thought of the group. (Cooley [1909] 1962, pp. 35-36)

To take as a model of "community" an image based on tradition and imperative necessity — as in peasant villages, manors, merchant guilds, clientalism, endemic war — rules out an appreciation of American models of community and, in particular, of the central role played in them by voluntaristic small groups.

I have already turned to the second, and secular, aspect of the story — the idea of "social control" and its sociological flowering in America. Especially in discussions and polemics in and after the 1960s, "social control" has been taken to refer to authoritative control from above, as by state bureaucracies. The assumption is that "control" is necessarily exercised by powerful authorities — emphasizing the noun, *control.* However, the original emphasis of "social control" lay rather in its adjective, *social.* It reflected the celebration by nineteenth-century liberal thought of moral self-regulation rather than gover-nance from above, despotic or traditional. I know no earlier appearance of the phrase than in John Stuart Mill's *On Liberty* ([1859]) 1956, p. 8), which applauds the possibility of normative regulation emerging from within civil society through mutual influence among citizens, replacing the historic governance of clergy, landlords, guild masters, and princes.

The classical idea of social control arose in Britain but came to flourish in America as the prevalence of both social and religious hierarchy, and classical market theory in Britain accorded it less intellectual space. It has few and weak counterparts in continental Europe, where principalities and absolutist monarchies were succeeded by strong administrative states. Two assumptions are key to the social control perspective. The first is that social relationships generated by price systems are insufficient in both fact and value as an account of social structure and the moral order. The second is that small-scale, face-to-face groups are of crucial interpretive importance in any account of modern societies (Janowitz 1975). These ideas—key to the formative American sociology of Cooley, Mead, Ross, Baldwin, and John Dewey—are rooted in the moral social psychology of the earliest secular social psychology to emerge in the setting of a thoroughly commercial society, that of the eighteenth-century Scottish Enlightenment, of which Adam Smith and Hume are the preeminent figures (see Bryson 1945).

The Scots and Americans both sought an empirical basis for the moral order, for the genesis of a restraining but not oppressive morality, in an arena that, until the emergence of market and liberal society, had been merely residual or interstitial: face-to-face, informal, small-scaled relationships. Families, churches, schools, and formal associations are understood essentially as "sites" of personal relations; the socializing and moralizing effect of institutions are understood to derive not from their formal properties and claims but from the personal relationships found within them.

The anti-institutional idea that the moral order is constituted essentially by the effects of personal relations emerges clearly in changing conceptions of the family. That the family is the "basic unit" of the moral order has become a platitude. But what this idea sought to overcome when it was new were two historically dominant notions of the family: first, that the father's domination of the family expresses the principle of social and political hierarchy, and, second, that the family was a solidary unit in alliance or conflict with others in a pervasively contestatory world, in which family resources were indispensable to collective defense and advancement (see Alberti [1935] 1969, and Giesey 1977, for illustrations, respectively, from the Italian Renaissance and eighteenth-century France). In their place was put the idea of the family as a small group constituted by interaction. For example, here is Adam Ferguson, the eighteenth-century Scottish moralist and social theorist, showing how family loyalty—which in the Scottish Highlands contributed to the pervasive antagonisms of clan society—could provide the basis of a universal and pacific moral order:

The fortunes of men are sometimes involved in those of their kindred. Although we distinguish therefore the specific principle of consanguinity from indiscriminate [general] affection and good will to mankind, yet it appears, that nature in planting the instinctive affections which united the members of a family together, and which may extend to a numerous kindred, has in this manner sown the seeds of a boundless society. Or seeming only to connect individuals of a narrow circle together, has formed a chain, whose links being continued in every direction, extend far beyond where personal acquaintance or choice would reach. (Ferguson, 1792, Vol. 2, p. 364)

Cooley undertakes a similar project in ascribing "primary ideals" to a reformed America: "Americans may surely claim that there was never before a great nation in which the people felt so much like a family, had so kindly and cheerful a sense of a common life" (Cooley [1909] 1962, p. 196). John Dewey's language in his early textbook in psychology, published in 1889, is directly descended from Ferguson's:

Sympathy is the sole means by which persons come within the range of our life. It is thus an extremely universal feeling. . . . It may be limited at first to those of our own family, our own rank in society, our own neighborhood, but this is because of a defective sympathy . . . [for] as our nature widens and becomes developed there must be a corresponding increase of sympathy. . . . Such a sympathy can, of course, recognize no distinction of social rank, wealth, or learning, or anything that tends to cut off one person from another. (Dewey, [1889] 1927, p. 332)

On this view, the morality of the small group, socialized in persons and extended over the polity, is key to democracy. The localism of the American polity, never the threat or obstacle to nationhood that it was in Europe, encouraged this outlook. Indeed, in the American case, the decline of localism has often meant the decline of a vigorous concept of nationhood; as illustrated by John Dewey's pessimistic meditation on these themes in *The Public and Its Problems*, published in 1926, this concern — today the province of conservatives — characterized American liberalism as well.

The morality of small groups is often contrasted with that of market society, but both are expressions of liberal society. The social control perspective assigns central importance to small-scale interactions in a manner paralleling the postulate of classical market theory that a multitude of small exchanges in the market results in a general order. In both cases, the unmediated governance of institutions such as religions and states is irrelevant, inefficient, or harmful. The moral order is constantly being re-created, on this view, by an indefinitely large number of encounters between people who meet in an arena defined not by institutions but by their own sentiments and interactions. Thus the web of social interaction, of which small groups are pulsing nodes, resembles the classical notion of the market: It is not regulated but re-creates itself; its indefinitely many transactions occur between people who are formally and juridically equal, all of whom may therefore "influence" each other.

Indeed, the democratization of "influence" is a central feature of the sociology of the small group and, in general, of a social world constituted by interaction. In principle, all may influence everyone else; the sources and distribution of influence are understood as the results of interaction and taken as phenomena for social science to explain. It had not always been thus. In the English language, *influence* was reserved for patrons and power brokers and, like its origins in astrology, was intrinsically vertical, describing the power of the mighty to exercise "influence" over others. Thus, until the electoral reforms of the 1880s, an English landlord might exercise what the political language of the time called "legitimate influence" over his enfranchised tenants (Davis 1972; Hanham 1978). In that setting, "influence" is not constituted by interaction but by status—the privileges associated with the ownership of landed property, and the obligations of tenants toward a landlord who, for example, does not always seek the highest possible rent. From the moment that the social world was conceived in terms of interaction, or mutual influence, best observed in the small group and small-scaled interaction, a profound transformation in a democratic direction is effected. It becomes possible to imagine society *as if* it were continuously created by an uncountable number of small-scaled interactions among persons of equal jural status; one task of empirical sociology becomes to investigate the varieties of interpersonal influences and their sources within such a world—according to some contemporary "micro-sociologists," its distinctive task.

These ideas are current in modern sociology. In *Union Democracy*, Lipset, Trow, and Coleman (1956) interpret their data to mean that optimal forms of personal groups among printers are vital to a democratic labor union. The spontaneous relations of neighbors and friends, according to Litwak (1985), may be integrated with the provision of public services in ways that enhance both efficiency and community. Fischer (1977, 1982) holds that the pattern of face-to-face relations in American cities largely contributes to urban community. These, and many other instances, manifest the continuity of the "congregational" model.

I have yet to address the familiar notion that the texture of face-to-face life in America is distinctively characterized not by latent "congregationalism" but a pervasive market orientation. Here is a recent statement of this idea:

> Social life is mutual negotiation and society, social order, relies on this mutual negotiation between individuals; this represents both creed and particular reality in American society. In no other society is this creed and the corresponding reality as prominent as the United States. (Münch 1986, p. 43)

Münch argues that, both in reality and in theory, "exchange and competition are thus in the United States the basic forms of interaction not only in economic life but in social life as a whole" (Münch 1986, p. 44) and traces their impact on the American preference for accounts of interaction in terms of exchange relations.

However, attributing exchange and competition solely or largely to market relations is ahistorical. European notions of instrumental exchange in personal interaction were deeply formed by practices and institutions that preceded the modern market — for example, deference, clientilism, honor — and are, therefore, embedded in nonmarket practices, though, of course, no less driven by instrumental imperatives. Many of La Rochefoucauld's *Maximes*, first published in 1665, seek to unmask such behavior as love and faithfulness in such terms; two examples of many:

> What men have called friendship is only a partnership, only a reciprocal managing of interests, and an exchange of services; it is after all only a transaction [*commerce*] in which self-love always seeks to gain something.

> The loyalty that most men show is only a device of self-love to gain trust; it is a means of surpassing others and to make us agents in the most important affairs. (La Rochefoucauld [1665, 1678] 1964, nos. 83, 247; my translation)

The *Maximes* are sometimes cited by exchange theorists as striking anticipations of scientific hypotheses (for example, Blau 1964) but without considering the historical setting to which they refer. Consider only a passage from Norbert Elias's analysis of the court of Versailles:

> The whole bustle of activity had a certain resemblance to a stock exchange. In it, too, a society actually present formed changing assessments of value. But at a stock exchange what is at stake is the value of commercial houses in the opinion of investors; at court it was the value of the people present in each others' opinion. And while at the former even the slightest fluctuation can be expressed in figures, in the latter a person's value was expressed primarily in the nuances of social intercourse. (Elias 1983, p. 91)

At Versailles, the competition for advantage and power was not only expressed but conducted through the dynamics of interaction rather than markets based on price systems; but it was hardly the less instrumental in its time and place. Capitalism, markets, or a "Lockean" America are not necessary for highly developed exchange or instrumental orientations in interpersonal relations, although, to be sure, the instrumentalism of premarket societies is profoundly different in cultural meaning from that prevailing in modern market society. If Old World notions of status, dignity, honor, loyalty, and "tradition" sometimes appear incompatible with instrumentality and exchange, it is because they have, with modernization, "floated free" from their historical settings and also, in retrospect, have become vulnerable to ahistorical or sentimental interpretations.

Every culture has its own way, in life and theory, to express and understand instrumentality; of these, the rational concept of interest intrinsic to market society (Hirschman 1977) is but one.

The continuing distinctiveness of the sociology of small groups and personal interaction in American does not lie only in its alleged propensity to project market relations onto personal ones — as in the American taste, which Münch well documents, for exchange theories. Rather, it lies in a vision of personal interaction that separates the utility of persons for each other from their worth as individuals engaged in the continuous creation with others of a multitude of small moral worlds. This vision endows small moral worlds with an ultimate significance in creating, sustaining, and improving the nation. In the statist regimes of continental Europe, the possibilities for moral reform flowed from the idea that the state represents a higher form of social organization — an idea held alike by reactionary nationalists like Treitschke, reformist liberals like Jules Ferry, and socialists like Jean Jaurès. All in varying ways were statists because they understood a properly constituted state to be the key source of reform and improvement, an idea shared, among other European sociologists, by Durkheim.

The American way was different. The Progressive reformers to whom the formative sociologists, among many others, supplied congenial ideas, largely understood the reformist and moral possibilities of the state to reflect the noblest values of relationships of small scale, because these were distinctively the basic source of social values. What made the state a worthy and effective agent of reform was its capacity to absorb and reflect, as it were, moral aspirations stemming from the social relations of small scale in which they are created at their source and, therefore, in their purest form.

To be sure, the small group perspective is not the only way in which sociology in America has addressed the significance of face-to-face relationships for the moral order; three others, of varying age and provenance, can be distinguished. The Parsonian "theory of action" sought to develop the counterpart of a Durkheimian sociology of social control, taking as its object the American polity conceived of as a "society," as Durkheim conceived of Republican France. Here, the "congregationalist" aspect of small groups is not essential; "action theory" does not denote a process of mutual moral control among persons creating and sharing a moral history, as does the small group perspective, but among anonymous and interchangeable citizens, reflecting the move from a nation of communities to a national polity — a comparatively recent event in the United States. Analogously, in what I will call, in an undiscriminating phrase, the "California school" — symbolic interaction, conversation analysis, ethnomethodology — the creation and sharing of a moral history with others is not a core problematic; this is, rather, symbolic and cognitive processes shaping behavior in interaction. Issues of social control centering on problematics of the moral order are replaced by those of mutual adjustment in symbolic and cognitive dynamics. Network analysis continues the impulse to construct the larger society out of small-scale interactions but does so in terms of structures generated by interactions, not in substantive, much less in moral, terms. The "subtext" underlying these perspectives is the irreducibility and ultimate significance of individual experience, whether in its subjective, interactional, or structural aspects:

> Everyone's life, experientially, is a sequence of microsituations, and the sum of individual experience in the world would constitute all the possible sociological data. . . . *Sociological concepts can be made fully empirical only by grounding them in a sample of the typical micro-events that make them up.* (Collins 1981, pp. 987-88; emphasis in original)

In all these literatures, an American strain continues in varying, even incompatible ways, to emphasize the fundamental character of the small. In each case, the claim is made that central features of total societies are best or uniquely understood by investigating properties of small-scale interaction between persons, albeit that those properties are differently conceived. The study of small-scaled interaction, now "micro-sociology," in relation to the larger society, now "macro-sociology," has clearly entered a new phase, as the "linkage" between the two has become a defined problematic—it being assumed that such a "linkage" is a central problematic for sociology (Alexander, Giesen, Münch, and Smelser 1987; Knorr-Cetina and Cicourel 1981).

The "congregational" sociology of small groups assumes that their members come to know and to deal with each other over time, forming groups with moral histories, which, cumulatively, are crucial for the moral order. Approaches appearing after Parsonian "action theory" do not take as central the problematic of moral order, and all are indifferent to a categorical distinction between strangers and those whose knowledge of each other informs their interactions. The Parsonian concern with an impersonal morality, micro-sociology's with interactional nuance, network theory's with the logic of structure—all, in varying ways, reflect massive changes in American society and culture intervening in the near century since the discipline shook free of religion and philosophy. The "congregational" tradition, deeply grounded in American culture as well as sociology, persists. In these respects, as in so many others, America both is and is not what it was a century ago, when sociology was born in the new world.

REFERENCES

Alberti, Leon Battista. [1435]. *I Libri della Famiglia*. Translated by Renée neu Watkins (1969) as *The Family in Renaissance Florence*. Columbia: University of South Carolina Press.
Alexander, Jeffrey C., Bernhard Giesen, Richard Münch, and Neil Smelser, eds. 1987. *The Micro-Macro Link*. Berkeley: University of California Press.

Atkins, Gaius Glenn and Frederick L. Fagley. 1942. *History of American Congregationalism.* Boston: Pilgrim.

Blau, Peter. 1964. *Exchange and Power in Social Life.* New York: John Wiley.

Bryson, Gladys. 1945. *Man and Society: The Scottish Inquiry of the Eighteenth Century.* Princeton, NJ: Princeton University Press.

Collins, Randall. 1981. "On the Microfoundations of Macrosociology." *American Journal of Sociology* 86:984-1015.

Cooley, Charles Horton. [1909] 1962. *Social Organization.* New York: Schocken.

Croly, Herbert. 1915. *Progressive Democracy.* New York: Macmillan.

Davis, Richard W. 1972. *Political Change and Continuity 1760-1885.* Hamdon, CT: Archon.

Dewey, John. [1889] 1926. *The Public and Its Problems.* New York: Holt.

———. 1927. *Psychology.* New York: Harper.

Elias, Norbert. 1983. *The Court Society.* New York: Blackwell.

Ferguson, Adam. 1792. *Principles of Moral and Political Science.* 2 vols. Edinburgh: Creech.

Fichter, Joseph H. 1964. *Parochial School: A Sociological Study.* New York: Anchor.

Fischer, Claude. 1977. *Networks and Places: Social Relations in Urban Settings.* New York: Free Press.

———. 1982. *To Dwell Among Friends: Personal Relations in Town and City.* Berkeley: University of California Press.

Giesey, Ralph E. 1977. "Rules of Inheritance and Strategies of Mobility in Prerevolutionary France." *American Historical Review* 82:271-89.

Hanham, H. J. 1978. *Elections and Party Management: Politics in the Time of Disraeli and Gladstone.* Sussex, United Kingdom: Harvester.

Heermmance, Edgar. 1906. *Democracy in the Church.* Boston: Pilgrim.

Hirschman, Albert O. 1977. *The Passions and the Interests.* Princeton, NJ: Princeton University Press.

Janowitz, Morris. 1975. "Sociological Theory and Social Control." *American Journal of Sociology* 81:82-108.

Knorr-Cetina, Karen and Aaron Cicourel, eds. 1981. *Advances in Sociological Theory and Methodology: Toward an Integration of Micro- and Macro-Sociology.* Boston: Routledge & Kegan Paul.

Le Bras, Gabriel. 1955. *Etudes de sociologie Religieuse.* Tome Premier. Paris: Presses Universitaires de France.

La Rouchefoucauld. [1665, 1678] 1964. "Maximes". In *Ouvres Complètes.* Paris: Éditions Gallimard.

Leites, Edmund. 1982. "The Duty to Desire: Love, Friendship and Sexuality in Some Puritan Theories of Marriage." *Journal of Social History* 15:381-408.

Litwak, Eugene. 1985. *Helping the Elderly: The Complementary Role of Informal Networks and Formal Systems.* New York: Guilford.

Mill, John Stuart. [1859] 1956. *On Liberty.* Indianapolis: Bobbs-Merrill.

Morgan, Edmund S. 1966. *The Puritan Family: Religion and Domestic Relations in Seventeenth Century New England.* New York: Harper.

Münch, Richard. 1986. "The American Creed in Sociological Theory." *Sociological Theory* 4:41-60.

Schücking, Levin. 1970. *The Puritan Family.* New York: Schocken.

Soffer, Reba N. 1978. *Ethics and Society in England: The Revolution in the Social Sciences 1870-1914.* Berkeley: University of California Press.

Vidich, Arthur J. and Stanford Lyman. 1985. *American Sociology: Worldly Rejections of Religion and Their Directions.* New Haven, CT: Yale University Press.

Walker, Williston. 1960. *The Creeds and Platforms of Congregationalism.* Boston: Pilgrim.

Part III
Sociology and American Public Policy

5

Witnesses, Engineers, or Storytellers? Roles of Sociologists in Social Policy

Peter Marris

What makes sociology influential? Let me take for granted that social research produces knowledge that is generally more reliable — more accurately observed, more systematically collected, and more representative — than the prevailing assumptions about social problems. Yet knowledge itself cannot determine policy, apart from some shared moral understanding to which it is connected; and in this essay I want to explore the nature of that connection, as I have observed it over thirty years of applied social research in Britain, America, and Africa.

In my experience, at least in Britain and America, this relationship has characteristically been conceived in one of two ways: either as the giving of evidence, by analogy with a court of law; or as problem solving, by analogy with research and development in engineering. I want to propose also a third analogy, to storytelling, where the resolution of the drama carries an explicit or implicit moral message. These conceptions of the role of sociology in policymaking do not refer to alternative kinds of research: Nearly all accounts of research give evidence, arrange that evidence to tell some story, and many offer solutions to problems. But it makes a difference how that account is conceived to be articulated with the debates about policy it seeks to influence. If it is primarily evidence, then there must be independently acknowledged principles of social justice by which to interpret it, and the most crucial virtue of the research will be its robustness as evidence — its ability to withstand hostile cross-examination. If research is conceived in terms of social engineering, its crucial virtue will be its ability to demonstrate successful solutions, given some independent definition of the problem. From either point of view, the sociologist is not responsible for the principles of policy by which the research is interpreted, and that detachment is seen as reinforcing the integrity of the findings. By contrast, if research is mostly persuasive as storytelling, the researcher *is* responsible for the moral interpretation of the findings, because the structure that organizes the findings — the beginning and ending, the issues chosen as central and the way they are resolved — are no longer merely conveniences of marshalling evidence, or steps toward demonstrating a solution, but the unfolding of a drama whose moral implications are crucial to the persuasiveness of the research.

Giving evidence and demonstrating solutions to problems are legitimate forms of scientific influence, while we do not usually think of stories as the way to present scientific knowledge. Yet even in situations that seem to be structured like a judicial hearing or an experiment, this appearance of an independent framework of principles or problem definitions often turns out to be illusory. The research itself has to incorporate principles and problems in order to organize its observations, and the working out of the tension between them constitutes the drama and the moral of the story. When social research is influential, it is, I suggest, nearly always because this dramatic structure catches the public imagination rather than the evidence itself. Yet the authority of social research still rests in its evidence. If it is to be influential, therefore, it has to meet at least two requirements: It has to demonstrate its credentials, as a source of impeccable, systematic social observation, and, at the same time, it has to arrange the findings of that observation into a convincing narrative. In addition to these, it is often required to fit into some academic tradition of discourse, whose concerns may be intellectually introverted and remote from policy. Social research has been less influential than it deserves to be largely because these three demands are extraordinarily difficult to reconcile. The storytelling aspect of sociology has been typically transposed into theoretical argument, often too arcane for the lay reader to grasp. Yet many cultures use stories to express generalizable social understanding, and they suggest a model for the way sociological understanding can be used persuasively in forming policy, without compromising its integrity.

The work of the Institute of Community Studies in London, where I began my research career in 1955, illustrates many of these tensions. In one respect, we simplified the problem because we were independent of any university. We saw ourselves as following Charles Booth, the Webbs, Seebohm Rowntree: men and women who had defined their research by their social purposes, without regard for any academic context.[1] We were indifferent to, if not contemptuous of, the Parsonian grand theory that was beginning to become fashionable in the rapidly growing sociology departments of British universities. Academic sociologists scorned us in return, as mere reporters. But we had the attention of a much wider and more influential audience; we had a theme, the importance of family ties; and a set of policy issues, such as slum clearance schemes and pensions to which it applied. The early books of the Institute — Michael Young and Peter Willmott's *Family and Kinship in East London* (1957) and Peter Townsend's *The Family Life of Old People* (1957) — were both widely reported on the day of publication, in the press, as important news. Because of our work, many assumptions about the disintegration of family ties, the loneliness of old people, and the nature of slums came to be questioned, and that put in doubt the policies that arose from them.

We were influential partly because books like ours, which gave readable accounts of systematic social research, were still something of a novelty. And each book told a compelling story — about kinship and community, being old, the nature of grief — which at once brought the facts to life and interpreted their meaning. But we were also influential because we were connected to the leadership of the Labour Party. Michael Young had been the party's research director; Peter Willmott, his chief assistant. Peter Townsend worked closely with Richard Crossman on revising old age pensions. Richard Titmuss, the party's chief adviser on social welfare policies, chaired our advisory committee. We were all Fabians, at least in spirit — we believed in a comprehensive welfare state with a genuinely progressive tax structure, sustained by a well-regulated mixed economy of public and private firms that would become more and more egalitarian. So I think we largely took for granted a consensus about the nature of social justice, broad enough to enable us to think of our reports as evidence — often accusatory evidence — in the trial of government policy. And we expected them to be influential as evidence rather than as stories. Peter Townsend, especially, became increasingly concerned with amassing incontrovertible evidence, assuming that the reliability of research findings was a critical issue in policy debate.

That confidence in providing knowledge to people who could both understand it and use it lasted only a few years. By the 1960s the Labour Party was becoming mired in economic difficulties that repeatedly undermined its social welfare program. It listened more to its civil servants and less to its intellectual advisers and I began to see that our work lacked a political analysis to match its insight into everyday life. We had taken the context of moral persuasion too much for granted.

It was about this time when I began to visit America — at first to examine urban renewal — and confronted a society where political power seemed too diffuse and inhibited to articulate any straightforward relationship between knowledge and action. Herbert Gans's *The Urban Villagers* (1962) — a story with a moral, like the work of the Institute — had more influence on public opinion than anything we wrote at the Institute. But connecting the makers of sociological insight to the makers of policy was a more artificial and self-conscious endeavor in the United States than in Britain. Leonard Duhl at the National Institute of Mental Health organized his "space cadets" (a group of policy researchers) and spoke of the "invisible college" of like-minded policy influentials. Paul Ylvisaker of the Ford Foundation's National Affairs Program traveled tirelessly up and down and across the country, linking mayors, community activists, journalists and newspaper editors, enlightened administrators and researchers in a personal inventory of mutually sympathetic, progressive thinkers and doers. I was impressed then — as I am today — with the time and energy that Americans must spend simply to create, and continually re-create, the context of shared understandings and purposes that we had taken for granted in Britain. The business of building coalitions to support reform — of drawing researchers, advocates, administrators, and politicians into a shared sense of mission — seemed to begin each time from scratch, as if nothing held people together but the purpose in hand.

It takes so much time and effort to organize the conferences and networks, where knowledge can be marshalled into a consensus of argument before a responsive audience of political actors, that Americans have been more impatient than the British, I think, with the limitations of sociology as moral witness. Science promises the kind of demonstrable truths that cut through ideological debate to assured results. Why should not social science provide the same, demonstrable solutions to social problems that physics or chemistry brought to the problems of engineering? In a pragmatic culture, social engineers with a fix are more attractive than moralists with a message, however well informed. So for all their extraordinary skill and aptitude at political networking, reformers like Paul Ylvisaker, when they turned to sociology in their own endeavors, used it with surprising indifference to the context of its interpretation, as if demonstrating a solution was enough to assure its adoption.

The idea of an experimental demonstration program is simple. You can diagnose a problem, select or invent a treatment, and test its effectiveness against a control group. It is the model of scientific method taught to every graduate student: Define your hypothesis and then devise a precise method to confirm or refute it. This is usually taken to mean quantifying the difference in outcome attributable to the factors hypothesized. If the hypothesis is confirmed, it then has the authority of a true statement. Translated into the terms of policy, you evaluate the outcome of an experimental intervention to see if it is demonstrably more effective than current practice. And the strategy assumes that more effective policies will then be chosen in preference to less.

The Ford Foundation Grey Areas Program, the President's Committee on Juvenile Delinquency, and other demonstration programs of the 1980s all adopted this experimental model as a strategy for change (Marris and Rein 1982). The President's Committee, especially, was enthusiastic about applying the method of social science to social problems. At first sight, it looks promising: Clearly defined goals and rigorous evaluation ought to rescue policy from the whims of fashion, ideological wishful thinking, and bureaucratic complacency. In practice, the appearance of evading all the conflicts and uncertainties turns out to be an illusion.

Take preschool learning programs, for instance. The Ford Foundation team believed that carefully structured learning for disadvantaged children below school age would prepare them for first grade. Once their first-grade performance improved, they should hold their own in school, and in the long run this should result in fewer dropouts, better employment opportunities, and less delinquency. These initiatives helped to inspire the Head Start program, one of the most thoroughly evaluated of the programs introduced by the Economic Opportunity Act of the Johnson Administration, and one of the most durable. In practice, the first-grade performance of the preschoolers did improve, compared with similar children who did not take part in the program. But by the third grade the difference seemed to have disappeared. Much later, however, as the children approached maturity, the preschoolers showed the kind of benefits that the reformers had hoped for. Although there was no difference in their grades, fewer of them dropped out of school, fewer were unemployed, and fewer were in trouble with the law than other comparable children (McKey et al. 1985).

This experience suggests how little, in practice, the relationship between sociological understanding and action resembles hypothesis testing or the methods of research and development. In the first place, the idea being tested was not a hypothesis but a set of interrelated ideas about child development. It referred to Piaget's studies of cognitive development, but it also reflected the belief that a child's performance was reinforced by his or her teachers' expectations — so that children who began poorly would not be much encouraged to do well. At the same time, it drew implicitly on attachment theory, emphasizing the importance of involving parents in their children's learning. Under all this lay the assumption that experiences in the first few years of life were profoundly consequential. Taken together, these ideas represented a prevailing progressive educational philosophy in which structured play, emotional security, and equal opportunity were all crucial. The experiments were not intended to put this philosophy in question; and because it was so widely accepted, the preschool programs continued even though the children's performance failed to confirm their predictions. When, much later, benefits from the programs began to appear again, these outcomes have been treated as if they confirmed the original idea, although they are inconsistent with them. The experimental model assumes that we know what we're doing, so that all we need to measure is the outcome: it worked, or not. But in the complex human behaviors that make up social interventions, we can rarely assume that what happened is simply what the intervention intended should happen, or that we know how relationships will affect people. Do preschool programs benefit children because, in paying more attention to their early learning, we make them feel better loved? Do the programs prepare them to be better behaved in school, so that teachers treat them more supportively? Do their parents continue to take more interest in their education, encouraging them to persevere? Measuring outcomes does not answer any of this.

The situation is even worse when the outcomes are simply negative. If a training program does not lead to more employment, the finding does not tell us whether training is irrelevant to employment, or that it was the wrong kind of training, or that the training was not carried out as intended, or perhaps that the advantage of training was overwhelmed by some factor, such as a recession, which masked its effect. At its crudest, evaluation by outcome leads to an impatient dismissal of every reform that does not at once produce results, and from this we learn very little. I have recently been talking with a foundation that is trying to promote new inner-city interventions against poverty, very similar to the experimental demonstration programs of a quarter century ago. Yet for all the resources that went into evaluation, what can be learned from these earlier endeavors except that, on the whole, they did not often seem to work? Why did they not work, and how might we make them work? That is what we need to understand, because our ideas of how to intervene to reduce poverty have changed very little. We still have no better proposals than preschool programs, education, job training, community development, and job creation.

For an experimental model of social policy development to work, we would have to assume that we already know so much about human behavior and relationships that we can infer from the outcome of an intervention what the process was that brought it about, and replicate it. The situations in which we want to intervene are usually so complex and so variable as to make this assumption untenable unless we make the circumstances so artificial that they no longer tell us anything much about everyday life. It follows that any useful interpretation of the outcome of an experimental program has to assume a great deal of prior understanding of human behavior; and these assumptions, rather than the findings themselves, usually determine what is believed to have happened. So the experimental model, so far from cutting through prejudice and moral persuasion to more certain knowledge only provides more, often poorly explained, material for ideological debate.

The experimental model is also politically intractable. It demands precisely stated goals, consistent procedures, an uncontaminated control group, and impartial analysis. By contrast, political actors thrive on ambiguity, responsiveness to events, spreading benefits to the largest possible constituency, and control over the interpretation of outcomes. An experiment constrains them, inhibiting their political skills: and the result is likely to be both a botched experiment and clumsy politics. For all these reasons, I believe that we should treat the testing of innovative policies as an exploration rather than an experiment. And the knowledge gained from exploring is characteristically presented not as an outcome but as an account of where we have been and what we have found. The case histories of antipoverty programs, which presented such accounts, contributed more to our understanding than all the elaborately structured measurements.

Policies are influenced much more by the stories we tell each other than by experimental findings, if only because the findings usually appear after the crucial decisions have been made. The Ford Foundation Grey Areas Program, the President's Committee on Juvenile Delinquency, and later the community action programs of the War on Poverty were all, for instance, shaped by a set of stories that were eloquently presented and often repeated. One was the story of how poverty was handed on from generation to generation through educational neglect and demoralization; another, the story of how all bureaucratic institutions tended, over time, to drift into rigidity and irrelevance; and a third story of how young people, deprived of opportunities for legitimate success, turned in compensation to the rewards of delinquency. The experimental programs were not designed to confirm the truth of these stories but to test the success of interventions that took them for granted, and so did not refute them if they failed. Instead, disappointment with these programs has encouraged another set of stories, equally influential, told by another group of actors. The poverty programs showed that you can't solve the problems of poverty by throwing money at them, one story runs; another tells how welfare encourages dependency, creating the very condition it was intended to relieve; and another, how hardworking citizens are being taxed to care for the lazy and immoral. President Reagan, a good storyteller, had his own, sometimes improbable, versions — like the man who used his food stamps to buy vodka.

Liberal or conservative, mean-spirited or generous, where do these stories come from? And why are they so persuasive? Storytelling is the natural language of persuasion, because any story has to involve both a sequence of events and the interpretation of their meaning. A story integrates knowledge of what happened with understanding of why it happened and a sense of what it means to us. If it fails to do all this, we say things like "but I still don't understand why he did that," or "why are you telling me this?" or "so what's going to happen?" Stories organize knowledge around our need to act and our moral concerns; and the finest stories do this with a subtlety and depth unmatched in any other way of communicating understanding.

We tell stories to each other all the time, about ourselves, our friends, the world we live in, and we listen to them everyday on television and in the cinema, and read them in newspapers, novels, and magazines. How stories about society are invented, begin to circulate, and become influential depends partly on what happens, and needs to be told, partly on discoveries (like the greenhouse effect), partly on ideological prejudices, on changes in perception. But sociologists, I think, have not usually been the inventors of new stories. Cloward and Ohlin's *Delinquency and Opportunity* (1960) inspired David Hackett of the President's Committee on Juvenile Delinquency. That conception of delinquency can be found also in Robert Merton's writings (1968) as well as the idea of bureaucratic dysfunction, which Paul Ylvisaker emphasized at the Ford Foundation.

Merton's conceptions, in turn, look back to Émile Durkheim and Max Weber. But sociologists surely did not discover the great themes that have dominated our understanding of society for the last hundred years — the rise of capitalism and class struggle; the loss of community; alienation and anomie; the search for equality, social justice, and a stable, secular social order. Rather, they have tried to give precision and coherence to these themes, to ground them in accurate and comprehensive observation, refuting false tales and correcting others. The stories sociologists tell are influential not because they are original but because they are authoritative. (Though the most memorable, like *Family and Kinship in East London* or *The Urban Villagers*, have the distinction of being both.) In 1961, for instance, I published a book about a slum clearance scheme in Lagos, Nigeria, where I tried to show that slum clearance did more physical and social harm than good (Marris 1962). The book was influential not because I was the first to see this but because men like Charles Abrams and Otto Koenigsberger, who advised the governments of developing countries on housing policies, had already seen it and welcomed an authoritative study that confirmed their point of view.

I suggest, then, that sociologists concerned with policy have to be storytellers, if they want to be persuasive, because storytelling is the language of persuasion. Much social research is a contemporary or retrospective following of events, a collection of autobiographies, for which storytelling is the most natural form of presentation. But sociologists are a distinctive kind of storyteller. They challenge or complement other stories we tell because their work can claim to be grounded in systematic, comprehensive, accurate records of events. Their characters are real, not invented. Unlike fiction, they do not depend on drawing the reader empathically into the characters' point of view, with all the moral ambiguity and tension that follows from that divided perception. But if the characters are less fully drawn, they are more representative. Sociologists are tellers of exemplary stories, whose moral represents a general truth.

All sociological interpretation has to contend with the difficulty that the events that constitute its data are arranged and defined by an observer and uniquely determined by a great many factors. So no interpretation can be sure to predict or explain another situation. One answer to this difficulty is to look for underlying, abstracted patterns, which are held to be generally influential, even if their effects are overwhelmed in a particular instance. Sociology then becomes the discovery and study of these patterns.[2] The alternative is to tell stories that preserve some of the complexity and uniqueness of actual events yet at the same time claim to be typical. They represent understanding that can be generalized to throw light on other apparently similar situations.

In this, sociological insights resemble proverbs — which are exemplary stories condensed to a single sentence — and, like proverbs, they can contradict each other without being untrue. "Too many cooks spoil the broth" and "many hands make light work" both represent common, useful knowledge. The question is not which is true but which is relevant to the situation in hand. The application of proverbial wisdom is a matter of matching the present against a store of examples of what is likely to happen in given circumstances. That process of matching makes us examine the present from different points of view, discriminating what is familiar and what is unique, to understand what recurring patterns of human behavior it represents. When I worked among the Kikuyu of East Africa, many years ago, I was struck by the way they used proverbs in public debate, much as we would use references in a paper, to establish the authority for an observation or a judgment. The Kikuyu culture is rich in proverbs, many of them similar to our own (for instance, "the wise man is not listened to on his own ridge" or "the thief and the thief-catcher are alike"). Debate sets proverb against proverb, testing the meaning of the present situation against an accumulated wisdom of experience, until everyone is satisfied. Similarly, Keith Basso (1987) describes how the Apache use stories of historical events as exemplary moral tales embedded in the landscape.

If sociological knowledge resembles proverbial wisdom, its insights, like proverbs, are only predictive if they fit the case; and because every situation must in some respect be different from any other, the question of fit is always debatable. And fit is not just a matter of whether the present situation resembles the situation whose interpretation is being held up as a model. If also depends on whether the interpretation is useful to the present possibilities of action.

In the 1970s, for instance, the British government introduced a dozen experimental community action programs modeled partly on American precedent. By then, American experience of evaluating social programs had made some of us skeptical of the rigorously experimental model. And, as I suggested earlier, the British are perhaps content to make less ambitious claims for social science, because they are more confident of a consensus about how to interpret its findings. At all events, the evaluation of these community development projects gave way to a more pragmatic interaction between interpretation and strategy. One of these projects, in the Midlands industrial city of Coventry, went through an especially self-conscious, reflective evolution. The project team began with the idea of relieving inner-city social deprivation by cooperative planning between local government and community. Disillusioned with cooperation, they turned to a conception of community advocacy, and, finally, to a structural explanation of inner-city decline as an aspect of international capitalist development (*Coventry CDP Final Report* 1975; Marris 1987, chap. 2). Each of these stages drew on a different account of what was happening in the inner city. In the first, the story concerns the failure of many inner-city residents to adapt to changes in the economy of their city, and the failure of government to help them. In the second, the competition between the claims of these inner-city families and the claims of big business on local government becomes the central theme. Finally, both of these gave way to an account of how the changing structure of international capital has turned the inner city into a marginal buffer zone. By then, the project was drawing to the end of its appointed five-year term. However, the shift in attention from local "social pathologies" to economic restructuring influenced the approach of subsequent national inner-city policies and helped to inspire several cities — including London — to attempt alternative, employment-generating development plans.

These shifts did not reflect changes in sociological understanding so much as changes in the actors' sense of their situation. They had always known that the inadequacies of families' coping strategies or of public services were aspects of greater and more powerful causes. The question was whether experimenting with neighborhood advice services, community newspapers, or local services alleviated the problems or only obscured their true nature. The structural account was adopted by most of the projects and publicized in a series of joint publications, because it satisfied the project leaders' need to set their work in a context broad enough to explain their frustrations. But it also compounded the sense of helplessness, which it analyzed so powerfully.

The metaphor of a structure — the structure of international capitalism — served to show how local consequences were related to changes in economic relationships of the largest scale, effectively criticizing the superficiality of much government policy. At the same time, the metaphor itself — the idea of relationships as a building — implied that these relationships were monolithic and determined. The relationship between the elements of a structure are all present at the same time: this beam rests on that beam, which rests on a foundation — and so on. Structure as a metaphor is appealing because it enables relationships that happen over time, such as producing goods and reinvesting profits, to be represented in a picture or diagram like the parts of a building, as if they were simultaneous, making their connections clear. But in doing so, it takes for granted that these relationships will continue to be reproduced according to the model that the structure represents. It seems then that change means dismantling structures; and this seems to pit the local community actor against the whole structure of capitalism in a hopelessly unequal struggle. Because the metaphor cannot represent the sequence of actions by which relationships are reproduced, it overlooks the possibility that an actor — any actor — can at any moment refuse to reproduce an expected pattern of behavior, provided he or she is prepared to accept the consequences. Once you think in terms of reproduction rather than structure, people become powerful again. Rosa Parks, refusing to take her expected place at the back of the bus, launched a movement that overwhelmed the institutions of racial segregation. That is another kind of story, with its own limitations. Centered upon the actor, it ignores the web of circumstance beyond the actor's reach. When it is time to act, we need to think of people like Rosa Parks; to understand the consequences, we need to see the larger structure in which our actions are contained. To be persuasive, then, the stories we tell must fit the need as well as the situation.

But as storytellers, sociologists compete with everyone else who has a story to tell. Their special claim on public attention lies in the quality of their observation and the sophistication of the accumulated understanding by which they interpret this data. But this truthfulness is not, in itself, necessarily persuasive, partly because we are reluctant to believe stories that do not fit our expectations, whatever the evidence, and partly because the appearance of sociological method is easy to fake well enough to take in a lay reader. Compare, for instance, three works each of which tells a different story about welfare and poverty, and each presented with the tables and statistics that typify sociological reporting — Greg Duncan's *Years of Poverty, Years of Plenty* (1984), William Julius Wilson's *The Truly Disadvantaged* (1987), and Charles Murray's *Losing Ground* (1984). The first two interpret carefully gathered and analyzed evidence to tell contradictory stories. In Duncan's story, people usually turn to welfare when misfortunes like the breakup of a marriage or unemployment befall them, and recover their economic independence in a year or two: welfare, then, is primarily a form of insurance against the kinds of misfortune that could push many of us into poverty. In Wilson's story, poor blacks and other minorities are locked into destitute inner cities, abandoned by their own middle class, unemployed and even unemployable: and this 'truly disadvantaged' underclass constitutes the public burden of welfare. But the contradiction, like the contradiction between proverbs, is productive, because each story represents an important insight, and in debating which story is most relevant to a particular situation or policy, we come to see the issues more sharply, in greater depth, and discover more clearly what we do not know.

By contrast, Charles Murray's story of how welfare policies have created dependency only borrows the trappings of sociological method. Figures are used misleadingly and tendentiously to support a story whose central characters are fictitious (Jencks 1985). The invented motives and behaviors of this stereotypical couple are then drawn out implausibly to demonstrate the moral. Debating Murray's story does not get us anywhere, except into untangling its errors and misconceptions. Yet of the three, Murray's story has been the most widely quoted, and probably the most influential, partly because it told what many wanted to hear, partly because it was expensively promoted by a conservative foundation, but partly also because it was the most readable: lively, amusing, with a well-dramatized moral. Good stories have qualities like dramatic timing, humor, irony, evocativeness, and suspense, in which sociologists are untrained. Worse, they have taught themselves that to be entertaining compromises the integrity of scientific work. But ugly and obscure language, humorless monotony, and failure to bring out the dramatic sequences inherent in human interactions surely cannot enhance the truth of any understanding. Sociological writing may be inescapably more laborious than fiction: It is hard to tell a good story while simultaneously displaying conscientiously the evidence on which it is based. But the more we attend to the storyteller's craft, and the more we honor it in the work of our colleagues and students, the more influential I believe we can be.

By comparing sociologists to expert witnesses, engineers, and storytellers, I have tried to explore different senses of how the findings of social research become articulated with policy debates. Evidence may take the form of a story; a story may be told largely by presenting statistical tables; the account of an experiment is itself a story. But each implies a different kind of responsibility for interpreting what is being said, and a different kind of authority. We give evidence in court, where the law provides the authoritative framework of interpretation, and the responsibility for that interpretation rests with the advocates, the judge, and jury. Correspondingly, sociologists can only present themselves as expert witnesses when there is a consensus about the moral objects of policy to which their evidence can relate and a responsible forum of debate — the kind of consensus that briefly informed the Labour Party in Britain after World War II. Once you have to assert your own framework of interpretation, you are no longer giving evidence, but telling a story — for storytelling, in the full sense, is not merely recounting events but endowing them with meaning by commentary and dramatic structure. Similarly, interpreting the findings of an experiment depends on a preestablished body of understanding that determines what it means to confirm or refute a hypothesis. But, as I have tried to show, in the context of social policy, such preestablished theories represent ideologies rather than an accepted body of social laws. In any particular situation, unique as it must be, the interpretation of the relationships that gave rise to the findings of a social experiment can rarely be taken for granted. And so, again, in asserting your own interpretation of what you have found, you become a storyteller.

Sociological stories, I have suggested, act like proverbs, in that a particular work becomes a reference for understanding a whole class of situations, for which it stands as an exemplary interpretation. Like proverbs, these stories offer diverse and conflicting insights. But in referring a question of policy to one such story, or challenging its relevance by reference to another, we come to understand better both what the policy is about and each other's sense of it. In doing so, the policy debate becomes more and more articulated with the best of our social understanding, exposing and discrediting the sentimental, shallow, wishful accounts that so often trivialize and mislead the discussion of policy. But this can only happen if sociologists are willing and able to tell their stories skillfully enough to capture the imagination of a broader and more political audience than their colleagues alone.

NOTES

1. Booth's *Life and Labor of the People in London* was published in 17 volumes between 1891 and 1903. Beatrice Webb, who worked with him on his monumental study, published studies of cooperatives, the trade union movement, and local government: Beatrice and Sidney Webb's 9-volume *English Local Government* appeared between 1906 and 1926. The Webbs were influential in the growth of the Labour Party, the Fabian Society, and the London School of Economics. Seebohm Rowntree's most famous work was his study of poverty in York, *Poverty: A Study of Town Life* (1901). He published a second study of poverty in *Poverty and Progress* in 1941.

2. Roy Bhaskar develops this approach in Bhaskar (1979).

REFERENCES

Basso, Keith H. 1987. "Stalking with Stories: Names, Places and Moral Narratives Among the Western Apache." In *On Nature, Landscape and National History,* edited by Daniel Halpern. San Francisco: North Point Press.

Bhaskar, Roy. 1979. "On the Possibility of Serial Scientific Knowledge and the Limits of Naturalism." In *Issues in Marxist Philosophy,* edited by John Mepham and David Ruben. Hassocks: Harvester.

Cloward, Richard and Lloyd Ohlin. 1960. *Delinquency and Opportunity: A Theory of Delinquent Gangs.* Glencoe, IL: Free Press.

Coventry CDP Final Report: Part I, Coventry and Hillfields: Prosperity and the Persistence of Inequality. 1975. Coventry: Home Office and City of Coventry in association with the Institute of Local Government Studies.

Duncan, Greg J. 1984. *Years of Poverty, Years of Plenty.* Ann Arbor: University of Michigan, Institute of Social Research.

Gans, Herbert J. 1962. *The Urban Villagers.* New York: Free Press.

Jencks, Christopher. 1985. "How Poor Are the Poor?" *New York Review of Books* 32(8):41-49.

Marris, Peter. 1962. *Family and Social Change in an African City.* London: Routledge & Kegan Paul.

————. 1987. *Meaning and Action.* London: Routledge & Kegan Paul.

Marris, Peter and Martin Rein. 1982. *Dilemmas of Social Reform.* Chicago: University of Chicago Press.

McKey, Ruth Hubbell et al. 1985. *The Impact of Head Start on Children, Families and Communities: Final Report of the Head Start Evaluation, Synthesis and Utilization Project.* Washington, DC: U.S. Department of Health and Human Services.

Merton, Robert K. 1968. *Social Theory and Social Structure.* New York: Free Press.

Murray, Charles. 1984. *Losing Ground.* New York: Basic Books.

Townsend, Peter. 1957. *The Family Life of Old People.* London: Routledge & Kegan Paul.

Wilson, William J. 1987. *The Truly Disadvantaged.* Chicago: University of Chicago Press.

Young, Michael and Peter Willmott. 1957. *Family and Kinship in East London.* London: Routledge & Kegan Paul.

6

Sociology and Nuclear War

William A. Gamson

Read the question both ways. How has the pervasive threat of nuclear war affected what we do as sociologists? And what relevance has sociology had, if any, to diminishing this pervasive threat? The first question is easier and seeds the answer to the hard one.

For better or worse, the sociology of peace and war is part of the peace movement.[1] There have been two major periods of mobilization during the nuclear age — 1957-63 and 1980-84. I'll refer to these, respectively, as the "fifties" and the "eighties" mobilizations. During each of these mobilizations, a minimobilization occurred within sociology.

Both broad mobilizations were heavily reactive to periods of heightened cold war. The context for the fifties mobilization included sharp Soviet-U.S. conflict over West Berlin and the wall; cold war rhetoric with widely publicized images of a shoe-pounding Khrushchev proclaiming, "We will bury you;" a Cuban missile crisis that made the unthinkable very thinkable; and repeated nuclear test explosions by both sides, culminating in a 50-megaton contribution by the Soviet Union spewing radiation across the planet. No wonder Dr. Spock was worried.

The signing of the Limited Test Ban Treaty of 1963 ushered in a long period of détente, which, in shaky fashion, managed to survive even the Vietnam War. That part of the fifties mobilization that had become institutionalized continued to operate after 1963, but the mobilization around nuclear issues was over for the time being. The movements we associate with the sixties — particularly the civil rights and anti-Vietnam War movements — gave little thought to the threat of nuclear war.

While this is understandable enough for the civil rights movement, it is surprising for an antiwar movement. We know now that real risks of nuclear war were present during the Vietnam era. In 1968, the Joint Chiefs of Staff advised

President Johnson that he might have to order the use of nuclear weapons to free U.S. troops who were surrounded at their mountain base at Khe Sanh, just south of the demilitarized zone. General William Westmoreland, former commander of U.S. forces in South Vietnam, notes in his memoirs that this was almost an ideal occasion for using tactical nuclear weapons. "If Washington officials were so intent on 'sending a message' to Hanoi, surely small tactical nuclear weapons would be a way to tell Hanoi something."

In 1969, with negotiations under way with North Vietnam, President Nixon sent a July 15 message to Ho Chi Minh that, unless some "serious breakthrough" was achieved by a November 1 deadline, he would regretfully find himself "obliged" to have recourse "to measures of great consequence and force," a threat that Henry Kissinger repeated to Vietnamese negotiators in Paris. Nixon actually reviewed possible targets for nuclear attack — one of them a railhead in North Vietnam a mile and a half from the Chinese border. The anti-Vietnamese war mobilization was at its height in the fall of 1969. While nuclear war was not on the minds of the challengers, the anti-Vietnam war movement was on Nixon's mind and he elected to let the November 1 deadline pass without action.

From Kissinger's memoirs, we learn that, in 1973, during the October Israeli-Arab War, a Defcon III nuclear alert — the highest since the Cuban missile crisis — was issued to all U.S. forces. Soviet and American warships were, as Kissinger puts it, "milling around" together in the Mediterranean in situations where they could easily have become engaged through accident or miscalculation. Sixty B-52 nuclear bombers were moved from their Guam base to the United States to join the Strategic Air Command alert of American strategic forces.

Nor were Vietnam and the Middle East the only potential flash points for a nuclear war during this period. Schwartz and Derber (1990) carefully document a whole series of close calls during this period including not only those above but superpower confrontations in Cuba in 1970 (the "second Cuban missile crisis" involving an alleged Soviet submarine base at Cienfuegos) and the India-Pakistan war of 1971 (in which Soviet and U.S. naval forces, nuclear capable, squared off in the Bay of Bengal). And all of these incidents took place during a period of relative détente.

Beginning in the mid-1970s, opponents of Soviet-American détente began a major mobilization effort to discredit it. This campaign, led by the Committee on the Present Danger (CPD), took special aim at the laboriously negotiated SALT II arms control agreement, urging a major U.S. nuclear arms buildup as an alternative. They succeeded in putting the Carter administration increasingly on the defensive. By 1979, ratification of the SALT II treaty by the Senate was in serious doubt and public opinion polls showed an increasing majority for those believing too little was being spent on military defense rather than too much.

In this atmosphere, the Soviet invasion of Afghanistan provided the decisive event in the successful CPD mobilization effort. The Carter administration threw in the towel, withdrawing its effort for ratification of SALT II and initiating sharp increases in military spending. In effect, supporters of détente within the political establishment conceded the foreign policy ground and presaged their own defeat in the next election.

The Reagan administration accelerated the buildup of nuclear forces—just saying yes to each new offering. Tired old cold war rhetoric was spruced up to space-age standards and given a bizarre twist with high government officials discussing nuclear warning shots and the ease with which we could survive a nuclear war with enough shovels. Finally, counterinsurgency dreams that we thought had been buried in Vietnam turned out to be alive and well at the Central American desk, the National Security Council, and the CIA for starters. The eighties mobilization was a response to this second cold war and the collapse of plausible opposition to it within the polity.

Sociology as a profession and a discipline responded to both of these peace movement mobilizations as did many other fields. The fifties mobilization spawned the peace research movement, with sociologists playing prominent roles in a thoroughly interdisciplinary effort. Peace studies programs, courses, research centers, and journals were established, some of which survived the period between the cold wars.

Institutionalization within the sociology profession though remained weak and marginal. The section on the Sociology of Peace and War, begun in the mid-1970s as the section on World Conflicts, hovered for many years near the minimum numbers necessary for survival, quickly overtaken by many newer sections. Courses on society and nuclear war, world conflicts, or the sociology of peace and war rarely became standard parts of the sociology curriculum in colleges and universities. Boulding (1984) found only four articles directly related to issues of peace and war in the *American Sociological Review* from 1960 through 1977. Funders for peace research programs and centers turned to other issues and few universities were willing to use internal money to keep these going in the absence of strong departmental support.

The sociology response to the eighties mobilization does not seem that greatly different. As Nusbaumer (1989) has documented, another minimobilization did take place. Examining 53 major social problems texts for the 12-year period of 1976-87, he found a substantial increase in the inclusion of war and peace as a topic. Only one-sixth of the texts published through 1982 covered it but, in the period from 1984 through 1987, over 70% (12 of 17) of the texts included war and peace among the problems considered. Several new editions of older texts added the topic for the first time. Nusbaumer also noted the sharp increase in "peace-oriented educational programs" with sociology department participation in half of them by 1988.

Nevertheless, the weak institutionalization within sociology remains, even after this eighties mobilization. The impact on our teaching activities has not been matched by a corresponding increase in research activities on war and peace. Nusbaumer (1989) shows very little increase in ASA annual meeting sessions devoted to the topic. The section on Peace and War is still the smallest among the 26 ASA sections although, at least, it is no longer in imminent danger of going under.

I have argued that sociological interest in issues of nuclear war reflects our participation in a more general peace movement mobilization. A significant number of sociologists reflect this mobilization in their own work by turning their attention to nuclear issues in their teaching and research; many, as we will see shortly, also contribute to the movement effort in important ways.

Our response to peace movement mobilizations is appropriate and commendable but it contains a major peril. As we saw above, the absence of a mobilization against the threat of nuclear war is no evidence at all for the absence of risk. The peril of nuclear war was not necessarily diminished in the period between the two cold wars. A number of Soviet-U.S. military incidents and confrontations occurred that plausibly could have led to the use of nuclear weapons; the United States gave serious consideration to using them in Vietnam and made implicit threats to use them on more than one occasion. These matters were deliberately not made public at the time nor were they accompanied by a heavy dose of cold war rhetoric; hence, they failed to spark a general mobilization and stimulated little concern about the issue within sociology. But the need for whatever sociologists can contribute to the prevention of nuclear war did not diminish.

I write in the aftermath of the 1988 Moscow summit with Reagan retracting his evil empire portrayal of the Soviet Union. This is public acknowledgment of a cease-fire in the second cold war. No one needs reminding of the fragility of such a state and the possibility of another change, but, for now, it seems safe to predict that we are in for a period with less saber rattling and with luck, less saber using. No new peace movement mobilization around issues of preventing nuclear war is likely in such a climate, but the problem will not disappear. If we are so dependent on the peace movement for our continuing concerns about this issue, how will we sustain a sociological interest without its energy to propel us?

HOW SOCIOLOGY AFFECTS THE
THREAT OF NUCLEAR WAR

Sociology has responded to the threat of nuclear war but has the threat responded to us? My first reaction is to recall a story that a former president of the ASA tells about a conversation with his wife following a tiring meeting of the governing council. The council had spent a long afternoon debating a resolution to condemn the government of West Germany for some reprehensible practices against one of its universities. "Well, what did you decide?" his wife asked with mock suspense. "We decided not to condemn this," he answered. To which she responded, "Boy, they must have been relieved!"

In terms of direct political influence on U.S. nuclear policy, sociology and sociologists have not been significant actors. If they have had any contacts with policymakers, it has tended to be with those in politically neutered enclaves such as the Arms Control and Disarmament Agency or the U.S. Institute for Peace. Granted that this could change as the political climate changes, but humility about our direct political impact is certainly in order.

Nevertheless, there are indirect ways in which sociology seems to have had considerable impact: first, through the spread of sociological discourse on war and peace into other arenas and, second, through a variety of interactions and involvements with political groups that challenge U.S. military and foreign policy.

The Spread of Discourse

We are accustomed to thinking of power and influence in institutional rather than cultural terms. The conceptual tools for a political analysis in which actors bring resources of one sort or another to bear on other actors are relatively well developed. This is less true for cultural power and it is worth pausing to consider some of the mechanisms by which it's exercised.

Nuclear policy, like any other policy issue, is contested in a symbolic arena. Advocates of one or another persuasion attempt to give their own meaning to the issue and to events that may affect its outcome. Their weapons are metaphors, catchphrases, and other condensing symbols that frame the issue in a particular fashion. This is not to deny the clashes of material interests that may underlie the struggle but simply to highlight another, complementary level of analysis.

This symbolic contest is especially complicated in the case of nuclear arms issues. Discourse on declared nuclear policy takes place in a quasi-public arena dominated by strategists and defense intellectuals — what Kenneth Galbraith calls a "nuclear priesthood." They speak a language laced with acronyms and neologisms that exclude the laity. The language is not, in the end, that complicated to learn — as one must in order to participate or be "taken seriously" in this arena. But entering into this linguistic world has a hidden cost, as Cohn (1987, 1988), Chilton (1988), M. Schwartz (1984), and others have argued so provocatively. The language implies a framework with a host of taken-for-granted assumptions and premises; it's part of a package.

To complicate matters further, there are large gaps between discourse on nuclear policy — that is, declaratory policy — and what is actually being done about the acquisition, deployment, and targeting of nuclear weapons. While the priesthood carries out arcane debates about counterforce versus countervalue, massive retaliation versus flexible response, and the meaning of deterrence and how it is enhanced, the weapons are bought, built, and targeted, largely untouched by such discourse. Indeed, in the case of the nine-lived MX missile, its proponents have been quick to shed old justifications, adopting new and sometimes contradictory ones for each new budget skirmish. Under the circumstances, one can legitimately ask whether it is worth any effort trying to influence this protean and serviceable strategic discourse. Sociologists should let it be and worry about the symbolic contest in other arenas.

If the strategic discourse is something of a red herring, the need for appropriate symbolism to sustain a more general foreign and military policy remains. Proponents and opponents of particular policies are engaged in a framing contest, using metaphors, catchphrases, and other condensing symbols to give meaning to relevant events. Much of the relevant symbolic work for proponents of official nuclear arms policy centers on threat enhancement and the maintenance of a larger cold war belief system. Debates about how a weapon should be based to make it less vulnerable to surprise attack take place within this larger shared frame. To be drawn into a debate on these terms is to take for granted the very premises and assumptions that need to be contested. Indeed, removing such assumptions from scrutiny is the ultimate achievement of successful ideological work.

Symbolic contests, then, are first and foremost framing contests. To the extent that a given frame is unchallenged in a discourse arena, the policies that stem from it will remain extremely difficult to challenge. The challengers will be forced to narrow their objections to fit the frame — arguing about the excessive cost of a particular weapon or the type and amount of contra aid needed, for example. Without attempts at reframing, even the occasional victory will be fleeting.

To make the framing concept clearer, examine the dominant frame on preventing nuclear war, *Soviet Expansionism*. It is difficult to be fair in the statement of a frame that is not one's own. An adequate statement should meet the following fundamental ground rule: it should be accepted as fair by an advocate. If an advocate says, "I wouldn't put it quite that way," this rule has not been met and the frame is being refracted through the lens of another frame. In stating the frame below, I use the language of its advocates as much as possible:

> The issue is what's the best way to deal with an expansionist Soviet Union so that it will eventually change its ways. The United States doesn't start fights but we can't be pushed around either. Nor are we willing to see our friends bullied — we have a moral responsibility to protect the weak to the extent that we can. The Soviet Union is a classic expansionist power seeking to extend its control whenever it can make or exploit an opportunity. The best way to deal with a bully like that is to be strong but

not provocative. The danger of war comes when, by appearing weak, the bully is encouraged to take advantage and then we can't avoid fighting back. Keeping U.S. nuclear forces equal or superior to Soviet nuclear forces will deter Soviet adventurism and best keep the nuclear peace.

This general frame contains other assumptions that equate strength with weapons in general, and with nuclear weapons in particular, that interpret Soviet actions and motives in a particular fashion, and that provide a justification for military intervention in Central America, Vietnam, and elsewhere. The frame itself need not be stated but can be invoked by such handy condensing symbols as "the lessons of Munich," which implicitly equates the Soviet Union with Hitler's Third Reich.

What has all this to do with sociology? There are several streams of work within sociology that have contributed to a discourse that challenges this dominant frame and seeks to develop alternative frames on preventing nuclear war. These streams are not subfields of sociology but interdisciplinary subfields; sociological contributions are thoroughly merged with and not easily distinguishable from other social science disciplines. The journals that serve as forums for this discourse draw on many disciplines, some of them even bridging the humanities and social sciences.

I will focus on three such streams where sociologists have been prominent contributors: (1) conflict resolution, (2) political cognition and imagery, and (3) frame-critical nuclear discourse. My intent is not to review this work but to use examples from it to make the argument that it both challenges the *Soviet Expansionism* frame and has spilled over from the academic arena to other arenas and influences more general political discourse on preventing nuclear war—albeit in a modest way.

Conflict Resolution

Conflict theory within sociology has emphasized the pervasiveness and reality of conflict. James Laue, one of those sociologists who carries this discourse to other arenas, was asked by an interviewer for the *U.S. Institute of Peace Journal,* what was meant by conflict resolution. "We start in the field of conflict resolution," Laue explained, "with the assumption that conflict is normal and natural and an inevitable part of human social relations. So the aim of conflict resolution is not to stop or to repress conflict, but to try to deal with conflicts which will naturally arise." Conflict is a natural part of social life, not an aberration. It does not necessarily reflect misunderstanding among those with no objective differences to fight about, although misunderstanding can complicate conflict resolution. The problem for the analyst becomes one of figuring out how conflicts can be carried on in some regulated fashion, limiting the means to prevent costly side effects for the conflicting parties and third parties.

Applied to the problem of preventing nuclear war, this perspective necessarily implies an alternative frame to *Soviet Expansionism*. The frame difference can be seen most clearly by examining what Wertsch (1987) calls the "scope of identification." He notes that, in any discourse on nuclear war, there is an implicit "we" with whom the speaker or writer identifies. This can range from a very narrow or particularistic "we" as in the case of survivalists who stock food and weapons in fortified fallout shelters to a universalistic "we" that includes all of humanity.

The scope of identification in *Soviet Expansionism* is typically the United States, "the West," or the "United States and its allies." It is the perspective of one partisan in a conflict. This is fundamentally true in both simpler and more sophisticated versions. The simple version accepts a world of good guys and bad guys, of a peace-loving America and an expansionist Soviet Union. The more sophisticated version recognizes a certain symmetry but it nevertheless remains a contest with "our side" and "their side."

Wertsch contrasts this nationalist scope with a more universalistic scope. The conflict resolution tradition suggests that this can be expressed in a number of different ways. First, there is a large body of work that emphasizes the constructive role of third parties. The techniques that these third parties use — mediation, arbitration, conciliation — are the techniques of the good broker who is fair, sympathetic to the legitimate concerns of the conflicting parties, and in some sense above the battle. The search, as Laue puts it in his interview, is for a "win-win" outcome "in which nobody loses but everybody gains something." This third-party scope of identification differs fundamentally from the partisan one implicit in *Soviet Expansionism*.

Another body of work emphasizes the strengthening of integrative ties, thereby allowing conflicting parties to sustain a greater amount of conflict in their relationship without resort to war. This work encourages economic and cultural interdependencies and the development of transnational ties. Then, when a serious disagreement arises, the long-run interest in maintaining the relationship will outweigh the short-run interest in getting one's way and will promote compromise and a mutual interest in utilizing conflict resolution techniques. Again, the scope of identification is universalistic — in this case, an implicit systems perspective. The concern is with stability in an interdependent system of state actors, not with the best ways for a particular coalition or a nation to maximize its outcomes in this system.

If the universalistic scope of identification in the above work is implicit, it becomes explicit in work that focuses on global consciousness. The power motives of national actors are contrasted with the common interests of ordinary people in all countries in preserving the planet and leading their lives with peace and justice. While neither a third party nor a systems perspective, this frame contrasts even more sharply with the *Soviet Expansionism* scope of identification. If there is an "our side" and "their side," it is not the United States versus the Soviet Union but the people versus the state managers.

Explore any rivulet of the conflict resolution stream and one finds a fundamental contrast to the national scope of identification that is central to the dominant frame. Hence, conflict resolution work attempts to reframe the dominant political discourse on nuclear war, challenging it on a taken-for-granted, core assumption; it is both critical and proposes alternative frames.

Political Cognition and Imagery

This tradition is less clear in its implicit assumptions about the reality and pervasiveness of conflict. It assumes that at least some significant part of conflict is the result of distorted images of an enemy that both sides share; their beliefs frequently form a mirror image. Sophisticated versions concede that significant parts of the conflict may be real but emphasize that their resolution is made more difficult by false perceptions, faulty communication, and misunderstanding.

Within sociology, it is social psychological traditions that are best represented in this work. Some writers emphasize the psychodynamic functions served by an externalized bogeyman or scapegoat (see Fellman 1989). We are psychologically receptive to a frame that portrays us as defenders of the good, besieged by an evil empire. Child-rearing practices and other socializing agents prepare us to receive it in a variety of ways, many of them indirect. These images of an enemy help to maintain a degree of international tension that makes it easier to gain support for heavily nuclearized armed forces and for U.S. military intervention in the Third World to combat the enemy.

The interactionist tradition in sociology emphasizes malignant processes that increase the possibility of nuclear war. Countries become locked into situations, becoming more concerned about losing face than achieving an outcome that has meaning and worth in its own right. To reverse the arms race — an example of one such malignant process — unilateral initiatives to reduce tension are suggested, inviting reciprocation from the adversary. Under the right conditions, its advocates argue, a benign arms race in reverse may be set in motion. Similar advice would apply to major power confrontations in regional conflicts.

Again, the challenge to *Soviet Expansionism* assumptions is clear and unequivocal. Far from taking for granted the assumption of a peace-loving United States and a Soviet bully, it is precisely this assumption that is called into question. The scope of identification is always universal, never national. This discourse again presents a reframing challenge to the dominant frame for understanding nuclear war.

Frame-Critical Nuclear Discourse

Work on cognition and imagery emphasizes the decoding process and the receiver of messages; discourse analysis emphasizes the encoding process and the sender. This chapter, with its arguments about taken-for-granted assumptions and organizing frames, reflects this new interdisciplinary subfield. In addition to *frame analysis,* some of the mouth-filling code words to invoke it include *hermeneutics, deconstruction, critical theory,* and *genealogical post-structuralism.*

I feel at home in only a few parts of this forest and will confine most of my attention to those parts, but there are some common landmarks that I recognize in the stranger parts. There is typically a close attention to language, metaphor, and symbolism. There is a concern about subtexts, about what is between the lines, with unintended messages. There is a broad definition of what constitutes a text for analysis — an architectural arrangement, a visual image, a mode of dress or hairstyle can all qualify.

My own version of it represents what Rein and Schon (1977) call "frame-critical analysis." The purpose is to develop concepts and techniques that will help in surfacing the taken-for-granted assumptions in dominant frames. Its critical purpose is demystification and its reframing purposes are self-conscious and open.

There are, by now, a substantial number of sociologists who make framing processes central in their work. This includes those who focus on media frames (for example, Tuchman 1978, and Gitlin 1980), those who focus on social movements (for example, Snow et al. 1986, and Snow and Benford 1988), and those who focus on policy analysis (e.g., Rein 1986). Some draw their inspiration from Goffman's *Frame Analysis* (1975), but there are multiple sources for these ideas, inside and outside of sociology.

The idea of a frame contest implies that frames succeed in any given arena in part because of the activities of their sponsors. Hence, Nathanson (1988) documents the construction and maintenance of the "Soviet threat," providing perfect complementarity to social psychological work on images of the enemy. Sanders (1983) documents the success of the Committee on the Present Danger in reframing the discourse on Soviet-American relations for the second cold war.

Other sociologists have focused on the mass media as the critical arena for discourse on nuclear war, analyzing the ways in which media practices reinforce or, less frequently, undercut dominant frames. Analysts of popular culture have examined the framing process in films, television dramatizations, and other texts with implications for nuclear war. Much of the burgeoning body of work on nuclear discourse is comparative and, again, heavily interdisciplinary.

All of this work, with its attention to the construction process and the message that lies beneath manifest content, is inherently critical and challenges the dominant *Soviet Expansionism* frame. In principle, it could be applied to challenger discourse as well and sometimes is. But it is dominant frames that benefit by allowing their premises to remain invisible and beyond scrutiny. An assumption that must be defended is no longer hegemonic; once contested, it runs the risk of being discredited. For challengers, this risk is already an inevitable and unavoidable part of their task.

To summarize, virtually all of the discourse relevant to nuclear war where sociology has been an important contributing discipline challenges the dominant frame and presents an alternative. The alternative is so normative in sociological discourse that even those sociologists who study institutions like the military are likely to reflect it. They focus their attention on the role of peacekeeping forces and antinuclear thinking within the military rather than on how the United States can best maintain its international power.[2]

In the case of conflict resolution and imagery work, the scope and identification at the core of *Soviet Expansionism* is rejected. In the case of discourse work, the dominant frame itself is critically analyzed; scope of identification is only one of many assumptions to be scrutinized. In effect, sociological work on peace and war lends itself to groups who are actively engaged in this reframing process in other arenas.

SOCIOLOGY AND THE
PEACE MOVEMENT REVISITED

To what extent has discourse from this academic arena spilled over into other arenas? The question returns us to sociology's relation to the peace movement. Substantial parts of the peace movement became institutionalized during the fifties mobilization and earlier. Part of this institutionalization consisted of establishing forums for challenger discourse on nuclear war. *The Bulletin of Atomic Scientists* goes back to the scientists' movement of the late 1940s, described so well in Boyer (1985), and continues to provide a forum for critical analysis of nuclear policies. *Nuclear Times*, a product of the eighties mobilization, offers itself as a forum for a wide variety of peace organizations and analysts. By including sections that discuss current research, it self-consciously attempts to act as a bridge between academic and challenger discourse.

The institutionalization includes independent think tanks such as the Institute for Policy Studies, the Institute for Defense and Disarmament Studies, the Institute for Peace and International Security, and the World Policy Institute. Such centers frequently provide forums of their own — publications and conferences — for an alternative nuclear policy discourse. In addition, their members write and speak in other forums as specialists on nuclear and foreign policy.

In addition to the think tanks, there is an infrastructure of organizations going back to the fifties mobilization or, in some cases, to the prenuclear age. SANE is perhaps the best known of the survivors of the fifties mobilization and its merger with the Nuclear Freeze symbolizes the uniting of these two mobilization waves.

But the eighties mobilization spawned or revived a great many other peace movement organizations beyond SANE/FREEZE. These include the various professional groups such as Physicians for Social Responsibility, the Union of

Concerned Scientists, and Educators for Social Responsibility; women's groups such as Women's Action for Nuclear Disarmament (WAND) and Mothers Embracing Nuclear Disarmament (MEND); and economic conversion groups such as Jobs with Peace.

Eighties peace discourse has emphasized the "deadly connection," the important link — so ignored during the Vietnam era — between military intervention in the Third World and the threat of nuclear war. Increasingly, the alternative policy arena blends anti-interventionist and antinuclear discourse in a seamless web. Hence, organizations whose primary focus is Central America frequently share the same forums with groups focused on nuclear arms policy.

Think of this alternative discourse arena as a halfway house. It is one step removed from the academic arena but still not quite the real world. But the actors in this arena — the professional staff of the organizations and institutes — play an important bridging role. On the one hand, they speak in seminars with legislators and their aides and in other ways participate in an oral policy discourse among members, as opposed to challengers. It's true that the members they have access to have had minimal influence during the Reagan/Bush years, but this may change.

These alternative discourse actors also provide a bridge to another critical arena: the world of the mass media. Many maintain routine relationships with sympathetic journalists and help to meet their news needs by providing interviews, op-ed articles, and as panelists for radio or television shows. "In the Public Interest", for example, provides tapes of pithy, well-written public service commentary by movement professionals; these are made available, free of charge, to a list of radio stations who have agreed to run them. In sum, these actors have acquired the kind of communication skills one needs to participate in many general-audience media forums.

The good news is that many of them are aware of and influenced by the discourse on conflict resolution, imagery, and framing described above and by a lot of additional sociological work that doesn't directly address issues of peace and war. The ranks of executive directors of peace organizations and think tanks have many Ph.D.s or A.B.D.s in the social sciences. They don't read our journals, of course, but they are eager for ideas that are addressed to their continuing concerns. In short, they are receptive to sociology when it is expressed in a mode and style that is appropriate to their forums, not our forums.

If sociologists are going to have an impact on a more general media or policy discourse on nuclear war, they will do so by first having an impact in this alternative policy arena. Traveling between discourse arenas is a special skill, but not all of us need to learn it for sociology to have an impact. But we must recognize and value those who do it effectively.

At the moment, we are fortunate in having a number of sociologists who are effective bridgers, many of them veterans with years of practice. James Laue and Elise Boulding come to mind as exemplars, articulate spokespersons for sociological ideas in the alternative discourse arena. And they are not alone. *The Bulletin of Atomic Scientists* and *Nuclear Times,* for example, have published a number of articles by sociologists and other social scientists drawing on the traditions described above. Others appear in symposia and conferences that bring academics together with peace movement professionals.

It's worth emphasizing, though, that a great deal of sociology of interest to the movement arena goes beyond what we have to say about peace and war. Much of political sociology, especially resource mobilization theories of social movements and research on the operation of power in American society, is highly relevant. So is organizational theory on the problems of maintaining commitment and motivation by members, on managing internal conflicts, and on the benefits and problems of decentralization; on the centrality of social networks in recruiting; on how ordinary people think about issues of war and peace and public affairs more generally.

To be most useful, we should ask not only what sociology has to contribute to thinking about nuclear war but what it has to contribute to the full range of problems experienced by those who are professionally engaged in reframing efforts and public mobilization. Sociology and the peace movement have the same interest. We will serve ourselves best by addressing the full range of issues that makes it easier for them to do an effective job and increase their chances of success in our common reframing purpose.

CONCLUSION

I have argued that sociology is indelibly linked to the peace movement. When it mobilizes, we mobilize with it. Unfortunately, mobilization is less a response to changes in the risk of nuclear war than to the cold war rhetoric that is used to gain public support for foreign and military policies. Many of the riskiest policies, however, thrive on secrecy rather than overt public support.

The second cold war is apparently ending and we approach a period in which there will be no external mobilization to sustain our interest in these issues. But the institutionalized peace movement sector will continue and parts of it may move inside the polity if a more sympathetic administration is elected.

Inside or outside, this is sociology's natural constituency. Our contributions on the sociology of peace and war are only a small fraction of what we can offer them. Sociologists who have never thought of themselves as specialists on peace and war but share the concern with reframing nuclear discourse might well ask themselves how they can help the peace movement sector. Indeed, they had better ask themselves because, in the absence of a new mobilization, no one is likely to prod them.

NOTES

1. I will focus on the U.S. peace movement and how it relates to American sociology but the arguments hold, with different particulars, for many European countries. In using the term *peace movement,* I'm talking about a movement sector with many actors, not a single collective actor such as an advocacy network or a movement organization.

2. For example, military sociologist David Segal became interested in the U.N. peacekeeping force in the Middle East, studying the conflict between normal military socialization and the peacekeeping mission assigned to it.

REFERENCES

Boulding, Elise. 1984. "The Participation of Sociologists in the Nuclear Debate." Paper presented at the American Sociological Association meetings, San Antonio.

Boyer, Paul. 1985. *By the Bomb's Early Light.* New York: Pantheon.

Chilton, Paul. 1988. *Critical Discourse Moments and Critical Discourse Analysis.* Working Paper #7. San Diego: University of California, Institute on Global Conflict and Cooperation.

Cohn, Carol. 1987. "Nuclear Language and How We Learned to Pat the Bomb." *Bulletin of Atomic Scientists* 43(5):17-24.

————. 1988. *Sex and Death in the Rational World of Defense Intellectuals.* Working Paper #8. San Diego: University of California, Institute on Global Conflict and Cooperation.

Fellman, Gordon. 1989. "Immortal Adversaries: Eros, Destructiveness, and the Threat of Nuclear Death." Mimeo. Waltham, MA: Brandeis University, Sociology Department.

Gitlin, Todd. 1980. *The Whole World Is Watching.* Berkeley: University of California Press.

Goffman, Erving. 1975. *Frame Analysis.* New York: Harper & Row.

Kissinger, Henry. 1979. *The White House Years.* Boston: Little, Brown.

Nathanson, Charles E. 1988. *The Social Construction of the Soviet Threat.* Working Paper #10. San Diego: University of California, Institute on Global Conflict and Cooperation.

Nusbaumer, Michael R. 1989. "Changes in Scholarship and Higher Education: The Case of Sociology." In *Peace Movement Dynamics,* edited by John Lofland and Sam Marullo. New Brunswick, NJ: Rutgers University Press.

Rein, Martin. 1986. *Frame-Reflective Policy Discourse.* Working Paper #3. Berlin: Leyden Institute for Law and Public Policy.

Rein, Martin and Donald A. Schon. 1977. "Problem Setting in Policy Research." In *Using Social Research in Public Policy Making,* edited by Carol H. Weiss. Lexington, MA: Lexington.

Sanders, Jerry W. 1983. *Peddlers of Crisis.* Boston: South End Press.

Schwartz, Morris. 1984. "The Social-Psychological Dimension of the Arms Race." In *Search for Sanity,* edited by Paul Joseph and Simon Rosenblum. Boston: South End Press.

Schwartz, William and Charles Derber. 1990. *The Nuclear Seduction.* Berkeley: University of California Press.

Snow, David A. and Robert D. Benford. 1988. "Ideology, Frame Resonance, and Participant Mobilization." In *From Structure to Action: Comparing Social Movement Research Across Cultures,* edited by Bert Klandermans, Hanspeter Kriesi, and Sidney Tarrow. Greenwich, CT: JAI.

Snow, David A., E. Burke Rochford, Jr., Steven K. Worden, and Robert D. Benford. 1986. "Frame Alignment and Mobilization." *American Sociological Review* 51:464-81.

Tuchman, Gaye. 1978. *Making News.* New York: Free Press.

Wertsch, James V. 1987. "Modes of Discourse in the Nuclear Arms Debate." *Current Research on Peace and Violence* 10(2-3):102-12.
Westmoreland, William. 1976. *A Soldier Reports*. New York: Doubleday.

Part IV
Sociology and Critical American Issues

7

Sociological Foundations of the Civil Rights Movement

Charles U. Smith
Lewis M. Killian

Sociology's influence on the civil rights movement has necessarily been limited in comparison with other factors — and in small part also because of a historic and continuing division in the discipline itself.

From the beginning of sociology as an accepted academic discipline in the United States, there was disagreement as to how societal change would occur. One school of thought, led by Lester F. Ward, believed that, in a democracy, social change could and should be deliberately planned and executed. The other school, influenced by William G. Sumner, believed that social change could and would occur only through natural evolutionary processes.

Sumner staunchly advocated a laissez-faire approach to social change. He felt that there was a natural strain of consistency and improvement in social institutions. Conscious efforts by man to alter the mores and intervene in the pristine evolutionary process would be "mischievous," doomed to ineffectiveness, and "the greatest folly of which a man can be capable." (Sumner 1906, pp. 97-98).

The theoretical positions of these two pioneers have had an enduring impact upon American sociology. The Sumnerian doctrine remains pervasive in much sociological, political, and economic thought today. It has contributed to the "pure science, knowledge for its own sake," idea that has permeated much of mainstream sociology. The Ward view, reflected in Robert Lynd's *Knowledge for What?* (1939), persisted, however, and is presently favored by many sociologists, especially blacks. Nevertheless, while the civil rights movement may constitute one of the best historical tests of sociological theories of social change, it emerged from a complex of social forces, not from the theories of sociologists, even though opponents of the movement have often denounced sociologists as being among the chief conspirators in it, and the critical decision of the U.S. Supreme Court concerning school segregation has been called a "sociological decision." These forces included conscious efforts to bring about reform, fortuitous events, and a number of social trends tangential to race relations.

SOME EVENTS AND TRENDS LEADING TO
THE CIVIL RIGHTS MOVEMENT

World War II (1941-45) is widely regarded by social scientists and the general public as one of the most important factors that heightened the consciousness of blacks about their plight. Although, for the most part, blacks in the armed forces were restricted to racially segregated service units, large numbers of them on foreign duty experienced interactions with whites and an acceptance by them that contrasted starkly with the racial segregation and institutionalized discrimination in the United States. Upon returning home after the war, black veterans, in attitude, rhetoric, and action, manifested an increasing discontent with their status quo.

James L. Bruton, a World War II veteran who served in France, stated in an interview on April 26, 1988, that

> several things became apparent to me during my foreign military service and greatly influenced my attitude towards American whites and race relations in the U.S. First, I discovered that the generally assumed superior intelligence of whites was a myth, because I had to instruct many of them, higher in rank, just how things should be done; second, I felt less fear of white authority and treatment by whites upon returning home to Florida, and third, I knew, along with thousands of other black World War II veterans, that things must change and that racial discrimination must be fought at all levels.

Historically, the black press was the chief advocate for the race. Although the overwhelming majority of America's whites did not read and/or were unaware of these publications, they waged an unremitting campaign against racial discrimination that began with John Russwurm's *Freedom Journal* (founded in 1827) and 24 others established before the Civil War, including the most famous of the period, Frederick Douglass's *North Star* (Myrdal 1944, pp. 912-13). Virtually all blacks who could read (and many of those who could not) were kept abreast of incidents, patterns, trends, and editorial opinions regarding the never-ending array of racial discriminations and efforts to ameliorate them.

The black church and the black school, historically, had little direct effect in advancing the protest ideology espoused so ardently by the black press. Both of these institutions contributed, however, to an enhanced collective awareness of racial discrimination and greater social consciousness among blacks. As Myrdal (1944, p. 877) stated, "The Negro church fundamentally is an expression of the Negro community itself, and within it the Negro has a sense of freedom."

The black church was a self-contained, independent institution generally beyond direct control or manipulation by whites. Although, historically, its efforts on behalf of civil rights were modest and moderate, its very existence became the solid base from which the leadership of the civil rights movement was to emerge. Because it was operated, sustained, and managed entirely by blacks, its ministers were largely immune from direct economic and political reprisals by white state and local officials and citizens.

Two black educational institutions kept and published reports that kept interested persons and agencies informed about racial victimization and relations with whites. For years, Tuskegee Institute (now University) through its Bureau of Records and Research, published annual reports on lynchings in the United States. Likewise, the Department of Social Sciences at Fisk University under the leadership of Charles S. Johnson (a sociologist) published the *Monthly Summary of Events and Trends in Race Relations*. Though no longer issued, these publications significantly contributed to racial consciousness among blacks.

One of the highly significant educational thrusts that black children and youth experienced in the all-black schools in the South was the study of black life and culture. Carter G. Woodson, who founded the Association for the Study of Negro Life and History and edited its *Journal of Negro History*, also wrote the widely used textbook *Negro Makers of History*, which was the standard instructional source in southern black secondary schools. The discovery and learning of the achievements of blacks by southern black students may very well have contributed to a racial consciousness and desire to succeed that resulted in the fact that most of the civil rights litigation of the National Association for the Advancement of Colored People was on behalf of blacks in the South and border states.

While black colleges and universities in the South were historically not on the "cutting edge" of civil rights activism and protest, most had college-level courses in Negro history, the Negro family, and race relations. Such formal learning experiences, combined with the wide use of visiting Negro speakers, Negro library collections, and the advent of television, produced a state of "readiness" among these students to act when the "time was right," even though they had no protest strategies or any real notion of resource mobilization. As Smith wrote in 1961 (p. 224) in the *Journal of Intergroup Relations:*

The struggle for greater civil rights came at a time when, because of radio, television, and other communications media, changing educational philosophies and higher educational attainments, and certain fortuitous events, the Negro college student was beginning to develop a new conception of himself as a significant element in the population of America.

It is almost impossible to overestimate how the publication of Gunnar Myrdal's *An American Dilemma* refocused America's thinking about its racial problems and helped to create a climate for political, educational, and judicial changes in race relations and civil rights for blacks in the United States. Published in 1944 during World War II, this two-volume, 1330-page work was discussed, reviewed, praised, criticized, and vilified; but rarely was it ignored. It received great attention, in the United States and abroad, which was remarkable because much of the world was at war. Myrdal laid a solid empirical base for future civil rights activity and public policy for race relations — as well as for sociological research on race.

By far the most solid and consistent foundation for the civil rights movement was laid by the NAACP with the successful litigation of civil rights court cases extending as far back as the 1930s. Although the NAACP acted on behalf of blacks as early as 1910 (Finch 1981, in Smith 1984, p. 92), it was in the 1930s that it began to systematically seek equity, justice, and access for Negroes/blacks under provisions of the Fourteenth Amendment. After 1935, with Charles Houston as its chief legal counsel, soon to be assisted by his successor Thurgood Marshall, the NAACP posted a solid record of civil rights victories in the areas of voting, education, public accommodation, administration of justice, employment, and housing.

National and international actions and policies of several U.S. presidents from the 1930s to the early 1950s were also significant in the continuity of forces and activities that formed the foundation for the civil rights movement. In the 1930s, President Franklin D. Roosevelt's New Deal economic recovery program, though reviled by Republicans, demonstrated that problems of the human condition need not be left to chance.

To accomplish his goals, Roosevelt also reconstituted and reoriented the U.S. Supreme Court to his philosophy and frame of reference. This philosophical conception is still present in the Court and it has maintained its receptivity to pleadings on behalf of citizens under the "equal protection" clause of the Fourteenth Amendment. President Roosevelt also led the United States into World War II, thereby expanding and enhancing the perceptions of black military personnel regarding civil rights and racial discrimination.

In the 1940s and early 1950s, President Harry Truman continued the pattern of national concern for the needs of American citizens, including blacks. In 1947, he pushed through the U.S. Congress the Fair Employment Practices Act to achieve greater equity in the workplace for disadvantaged groups. He also appointed a Committee on Equality of Treatment and Opportunity in the Armed Forces that recommended the "rapid and complete" integration of all military units. As a result, the armed forces were substantially desegregated between 1949 and 1954, and completely so by 1960, at least officially. A federal civil rights act giving some support to voting rights was also passed in 1957 during the Eisenhower administration.

Truman also involved the United States in the Korean War in 1950. Black servicemen operated for the first time in a fully desegregated U.S. military force in the full range of units from combat to support to service. The Korean experience of black military veterans and civilians alike contributed greatly to a growing foundation for the civil rights movement.

The presidential and national actions were important parts of the events and developments that converged with patterns and trends in institutions, organizations, and the courts to produce a growing consciousness, convergence, consensus, continuity, and climate for the civil rights movement. The question remains, however, "What part did sociologists have in the creation of this climate?" To what extent were the social foundations of the civil rights movement also sociological?

SOCIOLOGY AND THE
CIVIL RIGHTS MOVEMENT, 1896-1960

The deepest roots of the civil rights movement and the beginnings of sociology as a discipline in the United States lie in the same historical stratum. The time was around the turn of the century; sociology is the older of the two. It is not clear, however, to what extent sociology has been an important part of the foundations of the movement, in either the earliest stages or the later, more crucial phases.

Students of the civil rights movement have never agreed on just when it began. Certainly, the date was no later than the day blacks took to the streets of Montgomery in mass action. Perhaps, though, it was May 17, 1954, when the Supreme Court gave black Americans the hope that an ancient injustice would at least be righted. Yet, as has been seen, the decision itself was the culmination of many social trends and of a concerted legal attack on segregation resumed by the NAACP just after the conclusion of World War II.

The earliest stirrings of the twentieth-century movement to secure full citizenship rights for blacks are found in the short-lived movement organization of 1905-9, the Niagara Movement. Out of it grew, of course, the NAACP. From its inception, the goals of this, the oldest black protest organization, have been the goals of the civil rights movement. Both of these movement organizations arose at a time when blacks and their white liberal allies realized that, with the disenfranchisement of blacks and the passage of Jim Crow laws, protected by the *Plessy* decision, the freedom promised by the Thirteenth, Fourteenth, and Fifteenth Amendments had been almost wiped out.

It is ironic that the one person most often acclaimed as the founder of both of these organizations was a sociologist, but one who was kept outside the mainstream of the profession. While W.E.B. DuBois was a very active research sociologist from 1897 until 1910, he had become convinced by the end of the decade that scientific investigation was not enough to bring about social reform. He declared that he stepped out of his "ivory tower of statistics and investigation" (Green and Driver 1978, p. 19).

Although between 1896 and 1914 DuBois published, among other things, the still current *The Philadelphia Negro* (1899), *Souls of Black Folk* (1903), and 18 sociological monographs, he was not recognized as a sociologist by the profession. He had only one article in the *American Journal of Sociology*; in 1938 E. B. Reuter characterized him as an agitator, an author, and an educator — not as a sociologist (Green and Driver 1978, p. 41). While DuBois was amassing data that could have destroyed many of the stereotypes of blacks, sociologists in the white mainstream were debating whether blacks were even assimilable. Even the most liberal, reformist founders such as Small, Ward, and Cooley had difficulty breaking free from popular conceptions of instinctive racial antipathies. Thomas, in one of the earliest attacks on this hypothesis, wrote in 1904 (p. 593), "But for all its intensity, race-prejudice, like other instinctive movements, is easily dissipated or converted into its opposite by association, or a slight modification of the stimulus."

More typical of the sociology of the first decade of this century, however, were the ideas of Franklin Giddings, with his "consciousness of kind"; Edward A. Ross, with his belief in a hierarchy of races; and U. G. Weatherly, who believed that there was a natural, organic aversion to biological assimilation. Even more significant than outright racist theories was, as has been shown, the pervasive influence of Sumnerian thinking. The laissez-faire philosophy was later reinforced by the objectivist view of sociology as a value-free, noninterventionist science. In his 1929 presidential address to the American Sociological Society, William F. Ogburn, a dominant figure in the study of social change, declared, "Sociology as a science is not interested in making the world a better place to live. . . . Science is interested in one thing only, to wit, discovering new knowledge" (Pettigrew 1980, p. xxii). Even Robert E. Park, an early leader in the sociological study of race relations, was noted for his disdain of the "do-gooder." "The first thing you have to do with a student who enters sociology," he declared, "is to show him that he can make a contribution if he doesn't try to improve somebody" (Rausenbush 1979, p. 97).

Ironically, however, another theoretical strain in the approach to race relations had developed largely out of Park's early work. In 1913 he joined forces with W. I. Thomas at Chicago. That same year Park gave a paper titled "Racial Assimilation with Reference to the Negro," and the next year he introduced what was probably the first course in race relations in a sociology department, other than the one at Atlanta University. The "immigrant studies" of the Chicago department, combined with the abandonment of biological analysis, led to serious and optimistic examination of the possibility of eventual assimilation of blacks as well as other minorities. In 1919 Charles S. Johnson, under Park's sponsorship, completed *The Negro in Chicago*, the study of the Chicago race riot. Although DuBois had left sociology for social action, by 1920 the discipline had begun to take black Americans seriously both as citizens and as colleagues.

Yet race relations still did not rank high on the agenda of mainstream sociology. Between 1895 and 1915 only 2.2% of the articles appearing in the *American Journal of Sociology* were on the subject. The proportion of articles on race in sociology journals increased somewhat after the inauguration of *Social Forces* in 1922. Between 1922 and 1929 this journal carried 50 articles as compared with only 22 appearing in the *American Journal of Sociology* between 1916 and 1929 (Pettigrew 1980, p. xxvii). A growing number of articles were written by black sociologists.

During this same period few courses were apparently being taught centering on the subject of race relations. It was not until 1932 that there appeared the book *American Minority Peoples*, by Donald S. Young, generally considered to be the first major text in race relations.

At the same time the NAACP, still under the leadership of DuBois, was pursuing a notably activist legal, educational, and political strategy. By 1917 it had won its first significant civil rights victory in *Buchanan v. Warley*, outlawing residential segregation by legislative action. By 1924 it had won its first token victory in the South, the Texas white primary case. In 1930 it was successful in blocking the nomination of Judge John J. Parker, a North Carolina segregation-ist, to the Supreme Court. DuBois continued to be ignored by the sociological profession, however. As late as 1949 even Arnold Rose, in *The Negro's Morale*, referred to him as a scholar and social scientist but not as a sociologist (Green and Driver 1978, p. 41).

Still, the interest of mainstream sociologists in race relations did grow somewhat during the 1930s. More significantly, there was a growing body of scholars for whom minority relations constituted a specialty. Many of them were black. Most of the black sociologists were teaching in black institutions, however, for the profession was still almost as segregated as was the rest of white America. But when Gunnar Myrdal came to the United States in 1939, he was able to call on a wealth of sociological talent to assist in the most comprehensive study of black-white relations every to be undertaken. While the Swede was an economist and did not always follow his sociological adviser's guidance, *An American Dilemma* can be properly classified as a sociological enterprise. Arnold Rose was coauthor of the final draft and Samuel Stouffer took over the duties of director of research when Myrdal was forced by the war to return to Sweden. In lesser roles the staff included Guy and Guion Johnson,

Arthur Paper, and T. J. Woofter. T. C. McCormick and Charles S. Johnson prepared independent memoranda in support of the project. Johnson's study resulted in *Patterns of Negro Segregation*, published in 1943. Louis Wirth and Herbert Goldhamer prepared a memorandum on the problem of miscegenation, published as a chapter in Otto Klineberg's *Characteristics of the American Negro* (1944). Myrdal turned to sociologists Louis Wirth, E. Franklin Frazier, and Donald S. Young for critical reviews of the work (see Southern 1987, pp. 29-48).

Whatever the value and the effect of *An American Dilemma*, sociologists played a major role in it. Yet one would not have predicted the black insurgency of the 1950s and 1960s from Myrdal's massive work, from the numerous courses in minority problems being taught in American universities in the 1940s, or from the rapidly growing body of race relations literature in sociology. In 1963 Everett Hughes asked, "Why did social scientists — and sociologists in particular — not foresee the explosion of collective action of Negro Americans toward immediate full integration into American society?" He added, "It is but a special instance of the more general question concerning [lack of] sociological foresight of and involvement in drastic and massive social change and extreme forms of social action" (1963, p. 879).

The sociological approach to race relations had indeed become liberal in contrast to the radical laissez-faire, sometimes racist, approaches of the early years, yet liberal sociology remained essentially evolutionary and was often aloof from societal needs. Even the Southern Sociological Society, started in 1936 with a focus on social problems of the region, soon began to shift its focus to more disciplinary and conceptual concerns (Simpson 1988). The change is illustrated by the contrast in titles of presidential addresses: Topics such as "Race Relations and Developmental Change," "Negroes, Education and the Southern States," and "Public School Desegregation and the Law," had been replaced in the 1960s by such titles as "Process-Orientation in Sociological Theory and Research," "Beyond Rational Bureaucracy: Changing Values and Social Integration in Post-Industrial Society," and "The Status Attainment Process: Socialization or Allocation."

Many sociologists concurred that this was the proper course for the discipline, but others, especially blacks, felt that it made for a sterile sociology, too irrelevant and conservative to have any ameliorative effect on human problems. The black pioneers in the discipline maintained, from the beginning, their consistent priority for applied research on the problems of blacks in America.

The protest theme is inescapable in all of the following classics:

1934, Charles S. Johnson, *Shadow of the Plantation*, and
1941, *Growing Up in the Black Belt*;
1899, W.E.B. DuBois, *The Philadelphia Negro*;
1932, E. Franklin Frazier, *The Negro Family in Chicago*,

1939, *The Negro Family in the United States*, and
1940, *Negro Youth at the Crossway*;
1940, Ira DeA Reid, *In a Minor Key*;
1945, St. Clair Drake and Horace Cayton, *Black Metropolis*;
1948, Oliver C. Cox, *Caste, Class and Race*; and
1955, Hylan Lewis, *Blackways of Kent*.

One black sociologist other than DuBois laid a plank in the foundation of the civil rights movement by social action. Charles G. Gomillion, of Tuskegee Institute, led the fight for black voter registration in Macon County, Alabama, during the 1940s and 1950s. His efforts were climaxed by the defeat in the U.S. Supreme Court of Alabama's gerrymandering of Macon County to exclude all but seven blacks from voting (*Gomillion v. Lightfoot*, 1961).

In 1947 another black sociologist isolated on the fringes of the profession challenged both the reality of democracy in the United States and sociological theories. Oliver C. Cox (1948, p. xxvii) wrote, in *Caste, Class and Race*,

> Such men as Senator Bilbo, in both the North and the South, should not be thought of as insane or diseased. The tremendous political power and influence which they possess did not come to them simply by accident or chance. Their politics reflect significantly the wishes and interest of that class which holds the actual power of the nation.

In his massive attack on "orthodoxy in theories on race relations," Cox condemned what he called the "caste school of race relations," Robert E. Park's theory of accommodation and the gradual shifting of the color line to permit assimilation, and what he called Myrdal's "mystical approach." He said of the American creed, "The crucial circumstances, then, are not the presumed universal acceptance of the 'creed' but rather the interests which make its peculiar and divergent interpretations inevitable" (Cox 1947, p. 513). He called Myrdal's theory of cumulation, with its evolutionary premise, a mystical, capitalist rationalization of race relations because it assumed that beliefs are the prime movers in prejudice and discrimination rather than the vested interest that they serve. Unlike mainstream sociologists he predicted that only a revolution could bring about fundamental change in the status of black Americans. Yet Cox was also lacking in sociological imagination concerning race relations. He insisted that the revolution must be a class-based, socialist one and that the Lenin of this revolution would have to be a white man.

Liberal, mainstream sociology in the 1940s and 1950s failed to anticipate the movement for several reasons. One was the evolutionary assumptions that pervaded most of sociological theory. As late as 1972 Stanford Lyman called attention to the persistence of this assumption in Talcott Parsons's theories even after the civil rights movement. He wrote,

In Parsons' later discussions of the prospects for blacks in American there is no mention of revolutionary change. Rather, in line with Myrdal's conception of a social system moving in accordance with it's own dynamic, Parsons perceives American society as about to embark on the final phase of what he terms the "inclusion process" of the black minority. (Lyman 1972, p. 158)

A second premise, strongly influenced by the important work of social psychologists such as Gordon Allport, was reinforced by Myrdal's assumption that the problem of race relations was essentially a white problem, a problem of conflicting valuations in the minds of whites and of white prejudices. In 1958 Herbert Blumer charged that a large proportion of race relations research consisted of "accounts of various minority groups, characterizations of discriminatory relationships, and reports on the distribution of attitudes" (1958, p. 431). Studies of change were largely concentrated on variables related to changing individual white attitudes, such as on education, contact, and various forms of psychotherapy.

A logical companion to this premise was the treatment of blacks as passive victims of prejudice and discrimination rather than as a dynamic force. In acknowledging the long historic existence of black protest leaders, later highlighted in the work of Herbert Aptheker (1943), Myrdal (1944, p. 736) observed, "These race martyrs can be said to have laid the foundations, not only for the tradition of Negro protest, but also — because of their regular and conspicuous failure — for the 'realistic' theory of race relations." To Myrdal and to most sociologists, the NAACP, with its legalistic approach, represented the contemporary acme of black protest.

The civil rights movement challenged these dominant sociological assumptions. First, the black lawyers who were the early leaders chose to disregard both the Sumnerian thesis that law cannot change the mores and also the social psychological assumption that changing white attitudes should be the first point of entry into Myrdal's "vicious circle." When white southerners did not obey the new law and the federal government, under President Eisenhower, did not come forth with the firm enforcement of the changed policy that Kenneth Clark (1953, p. 54) had concluded was necessary for the accomplishment of efficient desegregation, blacks demonstrated the vitality of the protest movement. Not only did the lawyers expand their legal attacks on various forms of segregation but new leaders appeared to shock the nation with direct, nonviolent mass action initiated by them, not by whites.

It was in the first, courtroom, phase of the movement that sociologists did begin to take part in intervention, but then only in a supporting role. Opponents of the *Brown* decision denounced it as a "sociological decision," yet Franklin Frazier was the only sociologist mentioned by the court. Myrdal was, of course, demonized by segregationists as being both a sociologist and a socialist. Yet how important social science testimony was to the decision remains a matter of controversy. Richard Kluger, in *Simple Justice*, identifies as the key factor in the decision the conclusion of the Court that the first Justice Harlan's dissent in 1896 — dissent from the reasoning that enforced separation did not stamp the colored race with a badge of inferiority — had been correct. Footnote 11 to *Brown v. Board of Education of Topeka,* citing works by contemporary social scientists, was added "to buttress such a brisk dismissal of Plessy's essence," Kluger (1976, p. 705) contends. Whatever its actual importance, Footnote 11 remains a symbol of the participation of social scientists, including many sociologists as well as anthropologists and psychologists (notably Kenneth Clark), in this initial phase of black insurgency in the 1950s. During the hearings in lower courts leading up to the momentous debate before the U.S. Supreme Court in the case of *Brown v. Board of Education* and related cases, sociologists were involved as advisers, researchers, and expert witnesses. The roll of honor includes the names of Wilbur Brookover, of Michigan State University; Johne J. Kane, of Notre Dame; Kenneth Morland, of William and Mary; Frederick Parker, of the University of Delaware; and Alfred McClung Lee, of Brooklyn College (Clark 1953, pp. 4-5). Yet it must be acknowledged that the elevated social consciousness of black Americans, the growing consensus that they would wait no longer for equality, the convergence of social trends that created a climate of readiness for action, and the courageous actions of blacks who protested first in the courtroom and then on the street provided far more stones for the foundations of the civil rights movement than did sociologists.

REFERENCES

Aptheker, Herbert. 1943. *American Slave Revolts.* New York: International Publishers.

Blackwell, James and Morris Janowitz. 1974. *Black Sociologists: Historical and Contemporary Perspectives.* Chicago: University of Chicago Press.

Blumer, Herbert. 1958. "Research on Race Relations." *International Social Science Bulletin* 10.

Clark, Kenneth B. 1953. "Desegregation: An Appraisal of the Evidence." *Journal of Social Issues* 9(4).

Cox, Oliver C. 1948. *Caste, Class and Race.* Garden City, NY: Doubleday.

DuBois, William E.B. [1899] 1967. *The Philadelphia Negro.* Reprint. New York: Schocken.

———. [1903] 1961. *The Souls of Black Folk.* Reprint. New York: Fawcett.

Green, Dan S. and Edwin D. Driver. 1978. *W.E.B. DuBois on Sociology and the Black Community.* Chicago: University of Chicago Press.

Hughes, Everett C. 1963. "Race Relations and the Sociological Imagination." *American Sociological Review* 28:879-90.

Johnson, Charles S. 1922. *The Negro in Chicago.* Chicago: University of Chicago Press.

———. 1943. *Patterns of Negro Segregation.* New York: Harper.

Klineberg, Otto. 1944. *Characteristics of the American Negro.* New York: Harper.

Kluger, Richard. 1976. *Simple Justice.* New York: Knopf.

Larson, Calvin. 1973. *Major Themes in Sociological Theory.* New York: David McKay.

Lyman, Stanford M. 1972. *The Black American in Sociological Thought.* New York: Capricorn.

Lynd, Robert S. 1939. *Knowledge for What?* Princeton, NJ: Princeton University Press.

Myrdal, Gunnar. 1944. *An American Dilemma*. New York: Harper.

NAACP Legal Defense and Educational Fund, Inc. 1972. *Report on Services to the People of the United States*. Author.

Pettigrew, Thomas F., ed. 1980. *The Sociology of Race Relations*. New York: Free Press.

Rausenbush, Winifred. 1979. *Robert E. Park: Biography of a Sociologist*. Durham, NC: Duke University Press.

Rose, Peter. 1968. *The Subject Is Race*. New York: Oxford University Press.

Simpson, Ida Harper. 1988. *Fifty Years of the Southern Sociological Society: Change and Continuity in a Professional Society*. Athens: University of Georgia Press.

Smith, Charles U. 1961. "The Sit-Ins and the New Negro Student." *Journal of Intergroup Relations* 2(3):223-29.

———. 1975. "Public School Desegregation and the Law." *Social Forces* 54:93-101.

———. 1984. "The Role of the NAACP in Public Education in the United States." *Negro Educational Review* 35(3-4):89-101.

Smith, Charles U. and A. S. Parks. 1957. "Desegregation in Florida: A 'Progress Report.' " *Quarterly Review of Higher Education Among Negroes* 22(1):54-60.

Southern, David W. 1987. *Gunnar Myrdal and Black-White Relations*. Baton Rouge: Louisiana State University Press.

Sumner, William G. 1906. *Folkways*. Boston: Ginn.

Taper, Bernard. 1962. *Gomillion v. Lightfoot: Apartheid in Alabama*. New York: McGraw-Hill.

Thomas, William I. 1904. "The Psychology of Race Prejudice." *American Journal of Sociology* 9:593-611.

Young, Donald. 1932. *American Minority Peoples*. New York: Harper.

8

Definitions of the Underclass: A Critical Analysis

Robert Aponte

The *underclass* concept has never been consistently defined despite three decades of sporadic use in the United States. Up to now, it appears the term has been used primarily as a rhetorical device to command attention or enhance interest in the situation under study. Rarely has it been used to describe a reasonably defined group, in keeping with prior usage of the term. However, as the term has begun to be widely utilized by both scholars and journalists in recent years, efforts at generating a consensually based and empirically grounded definition, reflecting currently popular usage, have begun to succeed. The central argument of this chapter is that the emerging definition, a behaviorally oriented one, is fundamentally flawed both methodologically and substantively. The attachment of behavioral criteria to the definition, it is argued here, necessarily sustains the ill-advised view that many of the poor are impoverished by their own hand. It is further argued that, if we are to codify a definition, one based on deprivation rather than behavior, this definition is far more appropriate for a number of reasons. Such a definition would be more in line with earlier uses of the term *underclass* as well as with both scholarly and lay notions of "class." More important, such a definition would encompass most of the

AUTHOR'S NOTE: *Financial support is gratefully acknowledged from the Ford Foundation, the Carnegie Corporation, the Chicago Community Trust, the U.S. Department of Health and Human Services, the Institute for Research on Poverty, the Joyce Foundation, the Lloyd A. Fry Foundation, the Rockefeller Foundation, the Spencer Foundation, the William T. Grant Foundation, and the Woods Charitable Fund. I gratefully acknowledge comments on an earlier draft of this paper by the following individuals, not all of whom agreed with the basic thesis but all of whom contributed toward improving the final product. They are Ken Auletta, Daniel Breslau, Carole Cloud, Stephen Esquith, Herbert Gans, Rosemary George, Richard Child Hill, Christopher Jencks, Matthew Lawson, Frank Levy, Joan Moore, Kathryn Neckerman, Frances Fox Piven, Lee Rainwater, Erol Ricketts, Raquel O. Rivera, and William J. Wilson. I would most especially like to thank Jeff Dean, Rita Ordiway, and Robin Pline for typing and editing numerous drafts of this manuscript, usually under quite difficult circumstances.*

population captured by the emerging behavioral model but would be easier to operationalize with clarity. In addition, a deprivational definition is more readily related to appropriate policy considerations. The major strength of a behavioral model of the underclass is its more closely resembling the image currently implanted in the public consciousness. In our view, however, adopting definitions on that basis must be resisted.

ORIGINS

Although proponents of a behavioral definition of the underclass contend that most observers have agreed with their basic premise, a careful review of the literature undermines that interpretation. The underclass concept was first used in this country by Gunnar Myrdal (1962, 1964), the distinguished Swedish scholar who wrote extensively on American social problems. Although he noted its virtual absence in American discourse, he nevertheless believed this term best captured the social phenomenon he wished to describe. While he neglected to give the term a rigorously precise definition, for him it encompassed those families and individuals in the lowest economic stratum of American society. These were the long-term poor, those experiencing little or no advancement in spite of the postwar economic growth that provided rapid mobility for so many others.

For Myrdal, the problem stemmed primarily from structural unemployment, particularly that resulting from the increasing levels of skill or education necessary for most employment. This tended to skew unemployment toward the least educated and skilled workers, those already likely to be poor. But those individuals were far less able to increase their skill or educational capacities because of their already precarious economic health and related handicaps. Moreover, argued Myrdal, the major governmental redistributive mechanisms of the day often totally or largely bypassed the poor while more generously benefiting the more advantaged (farm subsidies, urban renewal, unemployment benefits, and the like). The minority poor were even more constrained than others under these circumstances because of the additional burden of discrimination they faced, argued the author. In short, for Myrdal, the formation of an American underclass had little to do with behavioral orientations but much to do with material deprivation and a lack of reasonably accessible avenues to mobility for those at the very bottom.

A second use of the concept during the early 1960s was that by Tom Kahn (1964) of the League for Industrial Democracy. Although he cited Myrdal's work, Kahn's use of the concept differed somewhat. He applied it strictly to workers (or potential workers) and argued that the proportion of the unemployed who were long-term unemployed was growing and that these long-term unemployed were slipping into an "under-class" by virtue of the seeming permanence of their unemployment. He held that this group "is composed mainly of Negroes, males 65 and over, young men, farm laborers, those in unskilled occupations and those with less than 12 years of schooling" (Kahn 1964, p. 19). Like Myrdal, Kahn emphasized changes in the mode of production, the shift in demand for labor from low- to high-skilled workers, and the increasing use of automation as causes of rising long-term unemployment.

Joan Gordon (1965), in an obscure study of welfare families in New York City, actually used the term in the subtitle of her mid-1960s report. Like many subsequent works, however, her report provided little in the way of a definition for the term and, in fact, made scant use of the term beyond its prominent display in the subtitle. Acknowledging Myrdal's earlier use of the term, Gordon suggested it encompassed the unemployed, the casually employed, and the economically dependent, thereby including the "multi problem" families she studied (1965, p. 9). Interestingly, she found her sample of black, inner-city (Harlem), AFDC mothers to largely subscribe to such mainstream values as the importance of education, an orientation to work, setting higher goals for their children, and so on (1965, pp. 132, 134). This suggests that her use of the term was not meant to convey the idea that these families were normatively deficient.

A fairly extensive search through the 1960s literature yields precious few references to the underclass despite the great outpouring of poverty-related work at the time. Primarily used in passing, the term was seldom defined or linked to behavioral deficiencies. Michael Harrington (1969), for example, in the *second* edition of his classic work, *The Other America*, refers in passing to the potential for a "hereditary underclass" to emerge as a result of the predictably severe labor market crowding he foresaw for the coming decade (Harrington 1969, p. xxiv). A more prominent use of the term is found in an editorial by Lee Rainwater (1969) in the February 1969 edition of *Transaction*. The editorial addresses the theme of that issue, "The American Underclass," which appears prominently on the cover page. In the editorial, Rainwater makes a number of arguments emphasizing the societal causes of the underclass and the political mobilization necessary for effecting solutions, but refrains from defining the term. Nonetheless, from his remarks, it is clear that he refers to the poorest segments of society whom he saw as falling further behind the *average* American's standard of living in the decades since World War II. Interestingly, although the underclass was the theme for that particular issue, the term appears in not a single one of the six full-length articles in that edition, suggesting its use was still rather limited at that time. Additional passing references to the underclass during the period denoted the group as the socially immobile, least well-off segments of the population, but without the imputation of behavioral deficiencies (Billingsley 1968; Gans 1968; Miller and Roby 1968).

In the early 1970s, some four references to "the underclass" could be found in the literature (Liebermann 1973; "The Underclass" 1974). In three of these cases, the concept referred strictly to the economic dimensions of poverty. First

Lee Rainwater's important (1970) publication *Behind Ghetto Walls* used the term, as did his earlier work, to denote those among the poor experiencing little mobility. Second, a study by Liebermann (1973) reported a comparison of poor whites and native Americans in a predominantly rural area of central Michigan. It defined the underclass, in a footnote, as the "lower lower class" or the unemployed, part-time employed, and low-paid employed. The next of these, a short article in *Time* ("The Underclass" 1974) accompanying a large cover story on the black middle class, simply made reference to blacks under the poverty line with respect to their brief discussion of the underclass.

Only one of the early 1970s publications located for this essay utilized the term *underclass* to denote problem families or individuals (Moore et al. 1973). Appearing in *The Public Interest*, the article focuses on the devastation of a Chicago neighborhood largely from the perspective of housing. In the process, the article makes occasional rambling and disjointed references to problem elements among the poor, labeling them a "destructive" or "dangerous underclass" that is prone to, among other things, "incessant drifting." This latter characteristic is apparently the greatest barrier to rehabilitating the group, according to the authors (1973, p. 57). Perhaps because its main focus was elsewhere, the article does not provide any kind of systematic discussion denoting which elements among the poor constitute "the underclass," other than to blame failed welfare policies, along with poverty, joblessness, and other ineffectual social policies and institutions, for the emergence of the group. In any case, based on the paucity of references to this work by virtually all recent studies on the underclass, it would appear to have had little influence on any of the subsequent research on the underclass.[1]

Thus, up to the mid-1970s, while few references to the underclass could be found in the literature, when they appeared, they made reference to the poor generally, the persistently poor, or the poorest of those groups, almost without exception. In only one case did a published work employ residential, ethnic, racial, or behavioral criteria with respect to its definition of the underclass, and it appears to have had little influence on subsequent work in the field whether implied or explicit. It was mainly after the mid-1970s that such criteria began to be utilized.

Usage of the underclass concept to refer to groups suffering from more than a lack of money emerged in full force in the late 1970s. A *Time* magazine cover story in August 1977, probably stimulated by the arson and looting that hit several New York ghettos in July of that year, was titled "The American Underclass" (Russell 1977). Gone was the carefully crafted explanation for the phenomenon of Myrdal and Kahn, replaced by paragraph after paragraph of descriptive prose on the minority poor of large-city ghettos. All 11 accompanying photographs featured ghetto blacks or Hispanics, 10 of which were meant to capture intense deprivation or alienation among these groups. The article held that most members of the underclass were big-city blacks, particularly in the

North, although it noted that some whites and Hispanics were also among the group.

Although *Time*'s conceptualization of the underclass, like those cited earlier, was only vaguely defined, several key points were reasonably clear. For *Time*, the underclass was only a subset of the poor, specifically the long-term poor, consistent with earlier work. But, for *Time*, the underclass was explicitly, or at least overwhelmingly, urban, though the reasons for this were not specified. In addition, despite several vague references to underclass characteristics such as proneness to crime and violence, weak family structures, and deviant values, the article refrained from incorporating those elements into a definition. Indeed, it laid some emphasis on the lack of reasonably accessible jobs as a key component of the problem, noting, in particular, the movement of manufacturing jobs away from the inner cities of the North. Nevertheless, the *image* of the underclass emphasized in this work was one of a group resignedly crime and welfare prone as well as one holding values at odds with those of the mainstream. This marked a sharp turn away from earlier renditions of the phenomenon (including *Time*'s own of two years earlier).

Time's use of the term in association with problem elements of the poor was accompanied by at least one additional important work, an unpublished manuscript titled "How Big Is the American Underclass?" (Levy 1977). Both of these works suggest some association of the *underclass* term with *behavioral characteristics* of the poor, although neither cites any relevant literature on this, and each fails to offer any coherent reason for the attribution. The *Time* article merely implies the connection by numerous references to the dysfunctional behavioral or attitudinal characteristics of segments of their underclass. Levy (1977, p. 30) simply states at one point, "For most people the term 'underclass' says more about behavior then it does about income."[2]

Yet, in spite of the rather limited extent to which these works sought to establish a tradition, their combined influence seems to constitute the basic foundation for the emerging behavioral definition. The *Time* article, as a cover piece, was highly visual and widely circulated. Appearing on the heels of the widely reported looting spree during New York's blackout, the only major outbreak during the 1970s, it surely provided lasting and frightening first impressions of the concept for much of the public. The piece by Levy, on the other hand, while never published and thereby only of limited circulation when first written, nonetheless became an important historical document and continues to be widely cited by students of poverty. This is because Levy's paper was among the first to produce national estimates of the size of the nation's persistently poor population. Levy reported these estimates using the Panel Study of Income Dynamics (PSID) data, a longitudinal study, which was then just reaching a mature enough stage for such analysis. Thereafter, use of the *underclass* term increased briskly. Those utilizing a behavioral definition almost inevitably cited Levy's work, but, following the tradition of the *Time* piece, focused on the urban poor.

Increased use of the *underclass* terminology after 1977 included scholarly works (e.g., Wilson 1978, 1980; Norton 1979; Glasgow 1980; Kusmer 1980; Swinton and Burbridge 1981; Cottingham 1982; Lodge and Glass 1982), government-sponsored reports (President's Commission 1980; Salinas 1980; Committee on National Urban Policy 1982), and journalistic accounts (Auletta 1981a, 1981b, 1981c, 1982; Treadwell and Shaw 1981; Brotman 1982). Generally speaking, the scholarly accounts tended to vary the most with respect to what population groups were denoted by the underclass concept. Their usage of the term ranged from denoting simply those under the poverty line (Wilson 1978) to the vagabonds and tramps of the late nineteenth and early twentieth centuries (Kusmer 1980). For most of them, the term emphasized poverty rather than behavior and was used mainly, it appears, for its attention-getting value. Government-sponsored studies, on the other hand, dwelled upon the urban poor and advanced the term more cautiously, noting the lack of a precise definition for it. Journalistic accounts also varied on how the term was used but tended toward the notion that the underclass suffered from more than a lack of income. One such work, that by Auletta (1981), formulated a behavioral definition that became widely circulated and accepted, setting the standard for most subsequent work, as show below.

Among the more influential uses of the underclass concept was that in William Wilson's (1978) *The Declining Significance of Race*, a path-breaking but controversial work. In his first edition, Wilson (1978, p. 1) used the concept to refer simply to those "at the very bottom of the social class ladder," suggesting in a later footnote that this population could be approximated by those under the federal poverty line. However, in the supplemental chapter included in the second edition, largely a response to critics, Wilson states (1980, p. 157):

> The underclass concept embodies a reality which is not captured in the more general designation of "lower class." For example, in underclass families, unlike other families in the black community, the head of the household is, almost invariably, a woman. The distinctive makeup of the underclass is also reflected in the very large number of the adult males with no fixed address — who live mainly on the streets, roaming from one place of shelter to another.

Thus, while we're left with no significant change in definition, we are treated to a more disturbing *image* (female-headed families, unattached street-corner men, and so on). This not only helped firmly establish the term, it also facilitated associating the underclass image primarily with certain segments of the black poor, however unintendedly.

Another influential book, *The Black Underclass* (Glasgow 1980), appeared at the turn of the decade. Glasgow's use of the term was, by far, the most thoughtful up to that time in that he provided a reasonably elaborate explanation of the term that entailed few ambiguities. For Glasgow, the *underclass* term denoted the persistently and intergenerationally poor, and such persons could be found in many places and be of any racial or ethnic group. It was their lack of mobility that set them apart from other poor. Moreover, Glasgow was careful to point out (1980, pp. 8-9) that

> the term *Underclass* does not connote moral or ethical unworthiness, nor does it have any other pejorative meaning; it simply describes a relatively new population in industrial society. It is not necessarily culturally deprived, lacking in aspirations, or unmotivated to achieve. Many of the long-term poor, those who have been employed for most of their productive lives but who have never moved from the level of bare subsistence living, are essentially part of the underclass.

Thus Glasgow's definition, like earlier ones, stressed persistent poverty as the criterion distinguishing the underclass from others in poverty, along with advancing structural or societal sources for the phenomenon. Yet, his work, like Wilson's, could easily be misconstrued to imply that the underclass was largely limited to behaviorally deficient inner-city blacks, especially males engaged in various illicit activities, because Glasgow's study was limited to young inner-city black men, many of whom led such unconventional lives.

Among the less influential works utilizing the *underclass* term in the late 1970s to early 1980s, those by Norton (1979), the President's Commission (1980), Salinas (1980), and Cottingham (1982) also failed to tie their use of the term to dysfunctional behavior. The Committee on Urban Policy (1982) in their chapter on the underclass also stopped short of defining the underclass in such a manner. Rather, they approach the idea, along with related ones, as a hypothesis requiring more study. Kusmer (1980), in a dissertation, uses the term to denote the tramps and vagrants of an era preceding the Depression. Only Swinton and Burbridge (1981) suggest that the underclass is generally conceptualized as a group whose behavior contributes to its poverty. However, these authors appear to confuse the underclass concept with that of the "Culture of Poverty," implying that the two are related. Moreover, they are in fact strongly critical of the concept, referring to it as "the underclass theory of racial inequality" (Swinton and Burbridge 1981, p. 1) and concluding that it is empirically flawed. In spite of this, the view that the underclass label largely applied to the behaviorally handicapped gained in popularity. In part, this could have been facilitated by the ease with which such widely read works as those by Wilson (1980) and Glasgow (1980) were subject to misinterpretation. A more substantial boost, however, was undoubtedly provided by the various journalistic accounts that maintained the idea (Auletta 1981a, 1981b, 1981c; Brotman 1982).

The final and perhaps most influential of the early 1980s writers on the underclass was journalist Ken Auletta. Auletta first reported on the underclass in a series of widely read *New Yorker* (Auletta 1981a, 1981b, 1981c) articles that were followed by a full-length, critically acclaimed book, within a single year (Auletta 1982). Auletta traversed much literature and conducted numerous interviews in his attempt to nail down an understanding of what causes and defines the underclass. But, as he reported early on, "to attempt to discuss the origins of the underclass is to run smack into a ferocious political and ideological debate" (1981a, p. 91). His ability to nail down a precise definition also proved elusive. However, he ultimately concluded that most observers of the underclass believed that the group suffered from *behavioral deficiencies,* along with their poverty, and these were the distinguishing characteristics that separated this group from the rest of the poor.

Auletta's work almost certainly had the most significant impact on how the term would be used. Few subsequent works on the topic appeared without acknowledging him. But his suggestion that "most students" of the underclass believed the group suffered from more than poverty is debatable. Indeed, just four months before Auletta's first article appeared, a team of journalists for the *Los Angeles Times,* also working on a comprehensive story on the underclass, arrived at a different conclusion. Their research, which included interviews with Wilson and Glasgow, among others, led them to conclude that *staying below the poverty level* for any of a number of reasons was the essential criterion for "underclass" membership (Treadwell and Shaw 1981, p. 10). Nevertheless, after 1982, Auletta's suggestions would often be invoked to justify linking the term to behavioral deficiencies (e.g., Nathan 1983; Carson 1985, 1986; Ricketts and Sawhill 1986, 1988).

AN EMERGING DEFINITION

By 1983, the underclass designation had become well established. The Population Association of America, for example, held a session on the underclass at its annual meeting in the spring of that year, which featured, among others, a paper coauthored by Glasgow (Glasgow and Reid 1983). This would become a regular feature at subsequent meetings (as it has for such other scholarly groups as the American Sociological Association and the Association for Public Policy Analysis and Management). In addition, a symposium on the underclass, edited by Wilson (1983), appeared in the journal *Society* that year.

Despite the increased frequency of use, the underclass concept continued to be used differently by different writers. The papers in the *Society* piece, for example, continued the tradition of employing the term to denote various segments of the poor without regard to strict definitional criteria (e.g., Kasarda 1983; Whitman 1983; Wilson 1983). Other works suggested that persistent poverty, a measurable construct, would more appropriately define the underclass (Aponte 1986; Ruggles and Martin 1986), while some have used the term to denote concentrated urban poverty (Danziger and Gottschalk 1987; Wilson 1987). A number of observers wrote strongly worded critiques of the ongoing use of the term in general (Gilliam 1981; Sherraden 1984; Beverly and Stanback

1986; Marks 1987), while still others embraced a behavioral definition (Nathan 1983, 1987; Carson 1985; Chicago Tribune Staff 1986; Lemann 1986; Ricketts and Sawhill 1986, 1988). In the case of one of the more influential scholars, William Wilson, usage of the *underclass* term has evolved from denoting a general economic condition to a more elaborate situation that incorporates poverty concentration along with other features.

In his most recent work on the topic (Wilson 1989), Wilson has suggested using the criteria of weak attachment to the labor force in conjunction with residence in a "social environment" that reinforces the weak attachment as the most appropriate way to conceptualize "the underclass." He acknowledges the work of one of his colleagues (Van Haitsma 1989) with respect to the formulation and elaboration of such a definition. In previous works, however, Wilson has used the term differently (Wilson 1985, 1987) and without attaching strictly bounded definitional criteria to its use.[3] Hence, Wilson's work has been cited approvingly, in at least one case, by scholars espousing a behavioral definition of the underclass (Ricketts and Sawhill 1988) even though Wilson has been critical of this work (Wilson 1988).

However, by the 1980s, a number of observers had already begun lamenting the widespread, but inconsistent, use of the term (Muzzio 1983; Kornblum 1984; Sherraden 1984; Carson 1985). The dilemma is best captured by a passage in Muzzio (1983, p. 10, as cited in Carson 1985):

It may be appropriate to ask how much the study of the underclass concept has matured. The evidence is not very encouraging. The core concept — the underclass itself — has resisted definition, for no analyst has been impressive enough to impose his definition on the literature. . . . This means that writers on the subject cannot even always agree on what to write about. It also guarantees confusion and misunderstanding in the treatment of all subsequent questions — description, causality, social consequences, policy prescriptions — and thus has enormous practical as well as theoretical implications.

Efforts soon appeared that sought to move the field toward a consensual definition by distilling previous research, developing and operationalizing a definition, and subjecting the latter to empirically grounded analyses (Carson 1985; Ricketts and Sawhill 1986, 1988; Reischauer 1987; Ricketts and Mincy 1988). These efforts received a major boost in an important roundtable discussion by numerous scholars held in Washington, D.C., on March 5, 1987 (McFate 1987). Sponsored and hosted by the Joint Center for Political Studies (JCPS), a well-respected, black-oriented think tank and advocacy group, the meeting was called for the express purpose of achieving a definitional consensus on the underclass concept for research purposes.[4] While there were a number of research papers distributed to the participants as background material, the centerpiece of the meeting was a paper by Ricketts and Sawhill (1986). This work, subsequently published in the *Journal of Policy Analysis and Management* (Ricketts and Sawhill 1988), established the first empirically based, behaviorally oriented definition of the underclass. After much deliberation on the merits of the paper relative to competing interpretations of the concept, the panel emerged having, by virtue of majority opinion, endorsed a definition that differs only marginally from that of Ricketts and Sawhill.[5] Their work will, therefore, serve as the major object of this critique.

CRITIQUE OF RICKETTS AND SAWHILL

Ricketts and Sawhill (1986, 1988) determined, from their reading of the literature, that the underclass concept was meant to capture "the coincidence of a number of social ills including poverty, joblessness, crime, welfare dependence, fatherless families, and low levels of education or work related skills" (1988, p. 316). They further contend that previous works attempting to estimate the size of the underclass have tended to treat the underclass as a subset of the poor on the basis of the *duration* of their *poverty* or on the basis of their *residence* (e.g., areas of high poverty concentration). Such efforts, according to the authors, do not capture the population of concern to us because (Ricketts and Sawhill 1988, p. 318)

> while the poor and the underclass may be overlapping populations, it is unlikely that they are identical or that one is a simple subset of the other. The fact that some members of the underclass engage in illicit activities, such as drug trafficking, suggest that not all members of the underclass are poor. Similarly, many poor people — one thinks particularly of the working poor and of the many persistently poor people who are elderly or disabled — are not usually considered members of the underclass.

Therefore, they set out to capture or measure the *real* underclass, those individuals who *engage in behaviors* "at variance with those of mainstream America (such as joblessness, welfare dependency, unwed parenting, criminal or uncivil behavior, and dropping out of high school)" (Ricketts and Sawhill 1988, p. 317), with particular concern for behavior "likely to inhibit social mobility, to impose costs on the rest of society, or to influence children growing up in an environment where such behaviors are commonplace" (1988, p. 319). In addition, they sought to identify *areas* where such behavior is "commonplace" because such places are likely to be areas where such conduct may be (become) normative. They are also areas that may justify the used *targeted* aid formulas.

Due to the constraints of the available public use data, the authors were able to produce more findings with respect to the second goal, identifying "underclass areas," than with the first, identifying members of the underclass. Indeed, for reasons not fully apparent, their definition of underclass membership hinges on first establishing the so-called underclass areas. The underclass areas, in turn, came to be defined, using 1980 census figures, as census tracts with relatively high proportions (one standard deviation above the mean on all indicators) of the following (Ricketts and Sawhill 1988, p. 321):

(1) high school dropouts (16- to 19-year-olds)
(2) prime age males not working regularly
(3) households receiving public assistance (proxy for women not married/not working)
(4) households with children headed by women (proxy for early childbearing, potential for dependency, and fatherless rearing)

A member of the underclass was then defined as "someone in an underclass area who engages in various socially costly behaviors" (1988, p. 321) such as those that constitute (or can lead to) the indicators.[6]

On the basis of these constructs, the authors were able to ascertain the following: about 2.5 million persons lived in the 880 census tracts that constituted the underclass areas, or about 1% of the U.S. population. The tracts were overwhelmingly urban and were disproportionately located in the old industrial towns of the Northeast. The authors also found that, while there was a great deal of overlap between the "extreme poverty areas" (that is, those areas found by the census to contain more than 40% of the population in poverty) and their "underclass areas," the relationship was not perfect. Whereas 61% of the underclass areas were to be found in extreme poverty areas, only 28% of extreme poverty areas could be characterized as underclass areas. The authors go on to estimate, on the basis of statistical proxies, that about one-half million of the residents of these areas constitute the underclass. A more detailed methodological critique of Ricketts and Sawhill has recently been provided by Hughes (1988) and will only be touched on in passing here. Among other things, however, Hughes finds that one criterion of "underclass" membership used by these authors — that of dropping out of high school — is likely to be misspecified. This is because when Hughes looked at changes over time (1970-80) in the incidence of the four indicators of underclass behavior within the census tracts of the eight cities he studied, he found that, while most such behavioral indicators increased over that period, the prevalence of dropping out declined. The possible significance of this point to the arguments made here is subsequently shown.

A more fundamental question for us is just what is it that we are measuring? The authors claim to be measuring "behavior" rather than "poverty," repeatedly reminding the reader that the underclass and the poor are *not* one and the same and that neither is a mere subset of the other. Yet they end up zeroing in on areas that are overwhelmingly impoverished: 61% of their underclass areas are in the census-defined extreme poverty areas — an even higher proportion if one considers the standard poverty areas (those with at least 20% of the population in poverty). Moreover, they fail to show (or to argue) that any significant portion of their underclass is *nonpoor*. After all, these are persons with little or no employment and many are on public assistance, not to mention their high probability of living in a poverty area. Thus, for all intents and purposes, what they have essentially done is key in on a *subset* of the poor, particularly those living in areas of poverty concentration. Many of the impoverished in these areas are likely to be the long-term poor as well as in the underclass. And, while some of the "underclass" in these areas may in fact command relatively handsome incomes illicitly, there is little to suggest that any more than a small fraction of them are so fortunate. Moreover, it is hard to imagine that such individuals were nonpoor prior to entering the underground economy.

Another important issue concerns the problem of the dropout indicator. In Ricketts and Sawhill's own analysis, this variable stood out in an important way for our purposes. In the course of the authors' investigation of whether the "underclass areas" were similar to those tracts the census has designated as extreme poverty areas, they found that the prevalence of the *three other* indicators, (female headship, households on assistance, marginal male employment), in terms of their mean values across the two types of areas, were nearly identical. For example, the proportion of families headed by women was 60% in the underclass areas and 59% in the extreme poverty areas. The proportion of households receiving assistance in the areas were, respectively, 34% and 33%; those for marginal employment among men: 56% and 57%. However, the respective proportion of 16- to 19-year-olds who were out of school without diplomas was 36% in underclass areas and 19% in the extreme poverty tracts. Indeed, the similarities and the outlying discrepancy are not lost on the authors, who note:

> As shown in Table 2, the incidence of various social problems, with the exception of high school dropouts, in underclass areas is not significantly different from their incident in areas of extreme poverty.... This suggests that extreme poverty areas can reasonably be used as a proxy for concentrations of social problems. (Ricketts and Sawhill 1988, p. 322)

However, they go on to argue that the underclass areas are still distinct from poverty areas because they do not overlap any more than earlier noted. Because they do not present a replication of their findings without the dropout indicator, we do not know how much greater an overlap would obtain in its absence.

However, if, following Hughes (1988), the dropout variable were severed from the analysis, the extent to which the revised underclass areas overlap with the extreme poverty areas is likely to increase greatly. Moreover, there are reasons other than those raised by Hughes (though possibly related) for considering the dropout indicators as an unsatisfactory proxy for underclass behavior. For one thing, many who drop out return or obtain equivalent degrees. But more important is the fact that the *salience* of dropping out to both the individual and society hinges strongly on external conditions that are likely to vary across situations. For example, under conditions where lucrative unskilled employment is available, such as unionized bricklaying, and where dropouts move directly into such positions, the consequences of the reduction in schooling are minimally significant. A better proxy for dropouts that could more reasonably be related to social distress would be one that captured youths who were out of school, out of work, and lacked a diploma.

Following this, one must question whether the distinction between the underclass members and others in comparable situations is truly meaningful. For example, what is so special about the poor who reside in such areas and can be characterized as deviant that distinguishes them from their nondeviant *neighbors* in poverty, such that the former make up a separate "class" of persons? And what distinguishes them so importantly from other poor and nonpoor who also "deviate" but reside in "less deviant" areas? By the authors' definition, you can be in the underclass if you are characterized by one of the four "behaviors" (*statuses* might be a better term) in the typology and *reside* in an *underclass* area, but not if you are simultaneously characterized by several of the indicators of the deviance (an unwed mother who dropped out of high school, does not work, and receives public assistance) but reside in a less deviant, neighboring impoverished area.

A related question concerns the spouses, dependent children, and other cohabiting relatives of the underclass who are not characterized by any deviant behavior. Are they not also members of the underclass, or are we to accept the notion that related family members fully *sharing* residential facilities and economic resources can occupy a different social *class* from that occupied by a family head? And what of underclass "turnover"? As the authors note, they have no data on the relative "flows" of people into and out of their underclass. But can the distinctiveness of underclass membership really hold under conditions of high turnover? Does a working, married mother join the underclass immediately upon entering widowhood — and vice versa upon remarriage? Of course not, but the problem really isn't the methodological issue of whether sizing up the underclass cross-sectionally fails to capture an important component of its makeup over time. Rather, it is whether the status distinctions underlying underclass membership can remain meaningful in the face of potentially brisk turnover.

Nevertheless, singling out *areas* in which certain indicators of undesirable behavior are unusually high may well be justified under certain conditions. This could hold, for example, if there was reason to believe that concurrently high levels of particular behaviors in common areas entailed synergistic effects.

Indeed, the authors hypothesize just such a connection with regard to their underclass areas: the likelihood that high levels of deviance in an area may undermine normative socialization, particularly for the young. However, it is important to point out that this more reasonable argument is based on differences between *places*, not differences between *people*. As such, it would be far more appropriate to label such places "environmentally disadvantaged areas" or "zones of environmental distress" or even the less flattering "pockets of deviance," rather than underclass areas. Why tie the properties of a *place* to a *class* of people who can hardly be identified, even on the basis of their allegedly deficient behavior?

A final problem with the behavioral definition undermines even the area-level concept so long as it is tied to the concept of deviance. This concerns the essence of what is meant by deviant behavior. Much of what the authors operationalize as deviant behavior — including what they are trying to capture, not just what they are forced to use as proxies — may be far from what ought to be reasonably viewed that way. While able-bodied men eschewing available work might reasonably be deemed behaviorally deviant, those ready, willing, and able to work who *cannot find* work are deviant only in a highly artificial, statistical sense. Widows heading families and abandoned wives on welfare, as well, can hardly be deemed behaviorally deficient simply because of their current situations. Indeed, aside from the dropping out variable, the indicators corralled by the authors, as noted by Hughes (1988), are more suggestive of involuntary hardship than they are of willful deviant behavior, though both may prevail in the identified areas. This renders tying the spatial properties to behavior as problematic as tying them to an under*class*.

In summary, we have argued that the attempt by Ricketts and Sawhill to quantify an "underclass" is flawed for several reasons. First, they cannot justify distinguishing a "class" of people based upon their behavior, within certain areas, from others who behave similarly elsewhere or from those with whom they reside. They further cannot justify designating the behavior they measure as unambiguously deviant, though much of it may be so. While the *areas* they measure may indeed constitute places of particular social distress, these problems are as easily related to the impoverishment that characterizes the areas as to the indices of deviance that underlie their definition. Finally, even if these areas are uniquely demarcated by their high levels of deviance, the implicated environmental properties do not arise from the unique characteristics of a given set of people. Thus labeling such places as under*class* areas is intellectually inappropriate. However, the more fundamental issues and the broader implications of the definitional debate are more directly addressed in the next and final section, where we advance an alternative perspective.

AN ALTERNATIVE PERSPECTIVE

The word *underclass* is almost certainly among the most effective, attention-commanding terms in social science discourse. It is not surprising that it has often been used to designate various subgroups in the population without regard to conceptual clarity or conceptual consistency, though usually with reference to groups at the margin of society. As the term has recently captured the attention of policymakers, media, and the public, social scientists have been asked to codify a definition for research purposes. If the scholarly community is to attach the scientific seal of approval to the label, we argue, the underlying concept ought to be reasonably concrete and scientifically meritorious. We have argued that a definition linked to behavioral attributes falls far short of these necessities; we contend here that the more measurable and empirically validated concept of persistent poverty best meets these prerequisites. Along with this, it encompasses the major portion of the population designated as the underclass by those advocating behavioral definition. Finally, in this last section, we address the fundamental tension underlying the definitional debate on the underclass.

In place of the emerging behavioral definition, we suggest that the population in persistent poverty best exemplifies the underclass concept. We showed earlier that the term was first used to describe such a group. It would consist of that subset of the population that is impoverished year in and year out and that thereby constitutes the lowest stratum of the American class structure. This group can be quantified via existing data sets and constitutes a relatively concrete "class" of people. *Class* in American parlance has variously been defined to refer, in broad terms, to the various economic groupings of our population. In the more classical, usually Marxian, discourse, it is determined by one's relations to the means of production or, more simply, one's relative control over societal resources. Hence, it strongly determines and demarcates levels of living. A second, more popular or lay understanding of class, which is closer to the Weberian perspective (see Wilson 1978), stresses earnings capacities and levels of living—the standard "upper-class," "lower-class," "middle-class" typology. Such usages have never utilized behavior as a demarcating criteria. Rather, economic class membership has often been analyzed to predict and explain social behavior.

In addition to more resembling a class, the persistently poor, as was earlier shown, are likely to include those citizens in need of policy attention, who reside in Ricketts and Sawhill's "areas of multiple social ills." This group, however, is more readily quantified using well-established research techniques, such as the poverty index and a time dimension, which do not hinge on nebulous behavioral criteria. Such a population would include many that the behavioral school would reject, such as the elderly dependent and the impoverished disabled, along with the working poor, who remained impoverished for prolonged periods. Beyond their equally low standards of living, inclusion of these groups makes sense because full-time workers unable to rise above the barest levels of subsistence are surely as important an object of research and policy as the sporadically or never employed, even if the former are less likely to "hustle" on the side. In addition, low-wage employment and joblessness are two sides of the same coin. The elderly, infirm, and otherwise non-able-bodied persistently poor, on the other hand, are just as *dependent* on governmental goodwill as the despised AFDC families, though the policy prescriptions for the former (more generous assistance) may differ from those for the latter (jobs *and* child care). Though such groups may constitute different segments of the underclass, they are still, by most definitions, part of the same social or economic *class*.

With regard to targeting policy, aiming directly at the poor — individually or in concentrations — makes more sense than shooting for "areas of social ills" to the extent that the latter are not characterized by impoverishment, for important reasons. This is because the behavioral aberrations depicted by Ricketts and Sawhill are not always indications of need for policy intervention. As we earlier argued, dropping out of high school may be of little concern for policy if it is followed by employment prospects. Likewise, families led by women are not *necessarily* an object of public concern. It is the *poverty* often associated with these indicators that gives them their salience as an object of public policy and creates the risk factor of dependency and crime. Thus, whenever an older female celebrity desiring motherhood but unable to locate an acceptable spouse has a child out of wedlock it causes so little concern. In such a case, there is little to fear about the likelihood of dependency, delinquency, and so on. Likewise, the jobless living comfortably on early retirement pensions, intrafamily transfers, and so forth, even if seeking work, pose far less of a problem than the destitute, homeless, or otherwise desperate unemployed, precisely because of the material deprivation experienced by the latter and *its* implications for their potential behavior.

In the final analysis, however, the debate between the economic and the behavioral definitions of the underclass boil down to arguments about the causal linkages between structure, poverty, and behavior. On the one hand, there are those that see self-defeating attitudes and behavior — as in the long-discredited "culture of poverty" thesis — as the primary cause of poverty. On the other, there are those that argue that we must look to the structure of opportunities for the explanation of poverty and the often accompanying pathologies. A behavioral definition of the underclass inherently allies itself with the individual-as-cause thesis, no matter how strongly proponents may claim agnosticism. This is because the perspective seeks out and identifies as a "class" a subset of the poor who are admitted therein precisely on the basis of their acknowledged (by definition) self-defeating, dysfunctional behaviors — in effect, a class of the poor in poverty by their own hand.

Such a viewpoint woefully misdirects our attention from the vast structural problems giving rise to poverty more generally to the individualistic attributes of the most problem-ridden segments of the poor. In this framework, the object of scholarship is no longer the source of the poverty. Rather, the inquiry is directed toward the causes of the behavior. The source of the poverty is known. The source of the poverty is the *individual*; and there is a whole class of *them*. Because they are more dangerous (crime) and costly (welfare) than the non-aberrant poor, they are worthy of, and accorded, research and policy priority. And because their problem is behavior and not poverty, the solutions can be sought in rehabilitative strategies rather than in the reform of opportunity structures or in the redistribution of resources.

Indeed, as Harris (1982) insightfully suggests, a research agenda too narrowly focused on the individual can lead to excessive rumination on such questions as why some make it and others do not, as it did Auletta (1982), the person most responsible for the rise of the behaviorally based underclass thesis. But in the face of the thousands upon thousands of failures generated by the system, concluding, as Auletta did, that the problem is partly systemic and partly individualistic can be likened to what Harris termed (1982, p. 88)

> a streak of prurient yahooism such as one might find in Roman spectators defending the sport of throwing people to lions. Every once in a while *someone* manages to avoid getting eaten. Ergo, the reason that people get eaten is partly that the lion is hungry and partly that the victims don't try hard enough. (Emphasis added)

The one redeeming feature of the behavior-based definition of the underclass is its closer approximation to the image of the group held by the public at large, thanks to the often misguided but widely circulated work of some journalists (e.g., Auletta 1982; Lemann 1986). Reflecting the concerns entailed by these beliefs, scholars like Christopher Jencks have contended:

> If you don't believe pathological behavior is really a problem worth worrying about, the correct position to take is to stop worrying about the underclass and go back to talking about poverty, which is a perfectly feasible position to take. But it's a tactical error to import poverty back in under the rubric of the underclass. (cited in McFate 1987, p. 11)

But one could just as forcefully maintain that if you want to worry about pathological behavior — a perfectly feasibly position to take — then stop worrying about the underclass and go back to studying deviance, criminology, and so forth.

In fact, taking a broad perspective on the problems of poverty and/or the underclass, as we suggest, should in no way impinge on scholarly attention to such problems as dependency and crime. A broader perspective can accommodate hypotheses on the right (Murray 1984) as well as the left (Wilson 1987). Insights derived thereby have generated numerous hypotheses about poverty and the resulting problems associated with the underclass rubric such as joblessness, the rise in families led by women among the poor, and even street crime. For example, Sampson (1987) has recently established a link between violent crime among blacks and the rise in female-headed families, which indicates that these are strongly associated with rising joblessness. The recent rise in welfare dependency in the inner cities of the largest metropolises, in turn, have been shown to be highly associated with deindustrialization (Wacquant & Wilson 1989b).

It is probably true that the image of "the underclass" held by the public is as unflattering as the behavioral definition. But, as Wilson (1988) has recently pointed out, the American public, in sharp contrast to its counterpart in industrialized Europe, has consistently clung to the belief that the poor are impoverished by their own hand. Following this, should we modify the definition of poverty to include an element of self-infliction, such as redefining the poor as the "indolent indigent"? If social scientists put forth half the effort expended on individualistic theorizing about poverty toward more comprehensive analysis of the phenomenon, half-baked conceptualizations like the "deviant underclass" would be far more difficult to sustain.

NOTES

1. Not a single study of the underclass reviewed here cites Moore et al.

2. In a recent personal communication, Levy suggested that, while he could not recall precisely why he used "underclass" in the title of his work or why he felt the term symbolized the problem poor for many, he offered some suggestions. His own use of the term, he believed, was for its exclamatory or attention-getting value. He also suggested it has probably been picked up to refer to the inner-city minority poor because of the heightened concern over the rising crime and riots of the 1960s along with the widely noted welfare explosion of the late 1960s and early 1970s, all of which were thought to be largely a product of big-city poor minorities.

3. Wilson has, at times, relied upon descriptive prose to delineate his conception of the underclass (e.g., Wilson 1985a, 1985b, 1987), referring to the urban underclass at one point, as "that heterogeneous grouping of inner city families and individuals who are outside the mainstream of the American occupational system. Included in this population are persons who lack training and skills and either experience long-term unemployment or have dropped out of the labor force altogether; who are long-term public assistance recipients; and who are engaged in street criminal activity and other forms of aberrant behavior" (Wilson 1985a, p. 133). One unintended consequence of using this kind of a definition has been the ease with which readers can interpret the definition in ways inconsistent with that apparently intended by the author (see Ricketts and Sawhill 1988). More recently, Wilson has sought to incorporate the notion of *poverty concentration* (Wilson 1987) as a key element in the formation of an underclass. As of now, however, Wilson has strongly endorsed disattachment to the labor force as the major characteristic of the underclass, as articulated by his colleague Van Haitsma (1989).

4. In attendance at the meeting, as shown in McFate (1987, p. 11), were the following scholars: William J. Wilson and Robert Aponte, University of Chicago; Sheldon Danziger, Institute for Research on Poverty; Christopher Jencks, Northwestern University; Isabel Sawhill, Erol Ricketts, and Michael Fix, the Urban Institute; Sara McLanahan, University of Wisconsin; Robert Reischauer, Brookings Institution; Mark Hughes and Jennifer Hochschild, Princeton University; Peter Gottschalk, Boston College; Harry Holzer, Michigan State University; Mary Cocoran, University of Michigan; James Gibson, the Rockefeller Foundation; Joan Maxwell, the Greater Washington Research Center; Angela Blackwell, Public Advocates, Inc.; Milton Morris, Katherine McFate, Margaret Simms, and Emmet Carson, JCPS.

5. It should be noted that, while the majority of the participants agreed with the outcome, the resolutions were hardly binding. In addition, no "policy paper" by the center or any of the individual participants has appeared attempting to proclaim or codify the definition. Moreover, at least two (aside from myself) of the participants have written papers criticizing the Ricketts-Sawhill formulation (Hughes 1988; Wilson 1988).

6. Presumably, the lack of reasonably usable data on such additional "deviant" activities as drug use (abuse) or criminal acts prevents their incorporation into these behavioral operationalizations.

REFERENCES

Aponte, Robert. 1986. "The Urban Underclass: Measurement, Origins, and Prospects." Paper presented at the annual conference of the Association for Public Policy Analysis and Management, LBJ School of Public Affairs, Austin, Texas, October.

Auletta, Ken. 1981a. "A Reporter at Large (The Underclass I)." *The New Yorker* 57(39, November 16).

———. 1981b. "A Reporter at Large (The Underclass II)." *The New Yorker* 57(40, November 23).

———. 1981c. "A Reporter at Large (The Underclass III)." *The New Yorker* 57(41, November 30).

———. 1982. *The Underclass.* New York: Random House.

Beverly, Creigs C. and Howard J. Stanback. 1986. "The Black Underclass: Theory and Reality." *The Black Scholar* 17(5):24-33.

Billingsley, Andrew. 1968. *Black Families in White America.* Englewood Cliffs, NJ: Prentice-Hall

Brotman, Barbara. 1982. "Facing up to the Underclass in America." *Chicago Tribune*, September 26, sec. 2, pp. 1, 2.

Carson, Emmett D. 1985. "A Quantitative Analysis of the Underclass Concept." Ph.D. dissertation, Woodrow Wilson School of Public and International Affairs, Princeton University.

———. 1986. "The Black Underclass Concept: Self-Help vs. Government Intervention." *The American Economic Review* 76(2):247-50.

Chicago Tribune Staff. 1986. *The American Millstone: An Examination of the Nation's Permanent Underclass.* Chicago: Contemporary Books.

Committee on National Urban Policy. 1982. "The Urban Underclass." Chap. 3 in *Critical Issues for National Urban Policy: A Reconnaissance and Agenda for Further Study.* Report to the National Research Council. Washington, DC: National Academy Press.

Cottingham, Clement. 1982. "Introduction." Chap. 1 in *Race, Poverty, and the Urban Underclass,* edited by Clement Cottingham. Lexington, MA: D. C. Heath.

Danziger, Sheldon and Peter Gottschalk. 1987. "Earnings Inequality: The Spatial Concentration of Poverty and the Underclass." *American Economic Review* 77(2):211-15.

Gans, Herbert J. 1968. "Culture and Class in the Study of Poverty: An Approach to Anti-Poverty Research." In *On Understanding Poverty: Perspectives from the Social Sciences,* edited by D. P. Moynihan. New York: Basic Books.

Gilliam, Dorothy. 1981. "Underclass." *The Washington Post*, November 28, p. B1.

Glasgow, Douglas G. 1980. *The Black Underclass: Poverty, Unemployment, and Entrapment of Ghetto Youth*. San Francisco: Jossey-Bass.

Glasgow, Douglas and John Reid. 1983. "The Black Underclass." Paper presented at the annual meeting of the Population Association of America, Pittsburgh, April.

Gordon, Joan. 1965. *The Poor of Harlem: Social Functioning in the Underclass*. New York: Office of the Mayor.

Harrington, Michael. 1969. *The Other America*. 2nd ed. New York: Macmillan.

Harris, Marvin. 1982. "Why the Underclass Can't Type." *Psychology Today* 16(6):81-88.

Hughes, Mark Alan. 1988. "Concentrated Deviance or Isolated Deprivation? The 'Underclass' Idea Reconsidered." Report prepared for the Rockefeller Foundation. Princeton, NJ: Princeton University, Princeton Urban Regional Research Center, Woodrow Wilson School of Public & International Affairs.

Kahn, Tom. 1964. *The Economics of Equality*. New York: League for Industrial Democracy.

Kasarda, John D. 1983. "Caught in the Web of Change." *Society* 21(1):41-53.

Kornblum, William. 1984. "Lumping the Poor: What Is the 'Underclass'?" *Dissent* 31(Summer):295-302.

Kusmer, Leslie K. 1980. "The Underclass: Tramps and Vagrants in American Society, 1865-1930." Ph.D. dissertation, Department of History, University of Chicago.

Lemann, Nicholas. 1986. "The Origins of the Underclass." *The Atlantic Monthly* 257(6, June).

Levy, Frank. 1977. "How Big Is the Underclass?" Working paper 0090-1. Washington, DC: Urban Institute.

Liebermann, Leonard. 1973. "Atomism and Mobility Among Underclass Chippewas and Whites." *Human Organization* 32(4):337-47.

Lodge, George C. and William R. Glass. 1982. "The Desperate Plight of the Underclass." *Harvard Business Review* 60(4):60-71.

Marks, Carole. 1987. "The Specious Origins of the Black Underclass." Paper presented at the annual meeting of the American Sociological Association, Chicago, August.

McFate, Katherine. 1987. "Defining the Underclass." *Focus: Newsletter of the Joint Center for Political Studies* 15(6):8-12.

Miller, S. M. and Pamela Roby. 1968. "Poverty: Changing Social Stratification." In *On Understanding Poverty: Perspectives from the Social Sciences*, edited by D. P. Moynihan. New York: Basic Books.

Moore, Winston, Charles P. Livermore, and George F. Galland, Jr. 1973. "Woodlawn: The Zone of Destruction." *The Public Interest* 30(Winter):41-59.

Murray, Charles. 1984. *Losing Ground: American Social Policy, 1950-1980*. New York: Basic Books.

Muzzio, Douglas. 1983. "The Smell in the Urban Basement." *Urban Affairs Quarterly* 19(1):133-43.

Myrdal, Gunner. 1962. *Challenge to Affluence*. New York: Pantheon.

————. 1964. "The War on Poverty." *The New Republic* 150(6):14-16.

Nathan, Richard P. 1983. "The Underclass Challenges the Social Sciences." *The Wall Street Journal*, July 8, p. 20.

————. 1987. "Will the Underclass Always Be with Us?" *Society* 24(3):57-62.

Norton, R. D. 1979. *City Life Cycles and American Urban Poverty*. New York: Academic Press.

President's Commission for a National Agenda for the Eighties. 1980. "Social Distress and the Urban Underclass." Chap. 5 in *Urban America in the Eighties: Perspectives and Prospects*. Report of the Panel on Policies and Prospects for Metropolitan and Nonmetropolitan America. Washington, DC: Government Printing Office.

Rainwater, Lee. 1969. "The American Underclass: Looking Back and Looking Up." *Transaction* 6(4):9.

————. 1970. *Behind Ghetto Walls: Black Families in a Federal Slum*. Chicago: Aldine.

Reischauer, Robert D. 1987. "The Size and Characteristics of the Underclass." Paper presented at the annual conference of the Association for Public Policy Analysis and Management, Bethesda, MD, October.

Ricketts, Erol and Ronald Mincy. 1988. "Growth of the Underclass: 1970-1980." Discussion paper. Washington, DC: Urban Institute, Changing Domestic Priorities Project.

Ricketts, Erol R. and Isabel Sawhill. 1986. "Defining and Measuring the Underclass." Paper presented at the American Economics Association Annual Meeting, New Orleans, December.

————. 1988. "Defining and Measuring the Underclass." *Journal of Policy Analysis and Management* 7(2):316-25.

Ruggles, Patricia and William P. Marton. 1986. "Measuring the Size and Characteristics of the Underclass: How Much Do We Know?" Prepared for the Rockefeller Foundation. Washington, DC: Urban Institute.

Russell, George. 1977. "The American Underclass." *Time* 110(August 28):14-27.

Salinas, Patricia W. 1980. "Subemployment and the Urban Underclass: A Policy Research Report." NTIS #PB81-132219. Washington, DC: U.S. Department of Commerce.

Sampson, Robert J. 1987. "Urban Black Violence: The Effect of Male Joblessness and Family Disruption." *American Journal of Sociology* 93(2):348-82.

Sherraden, Michael W. 1984. "Working Over the Underclass." *Social Work* 29(4):391-92.

Swinton, Daniel H. and Lynn C. Burbridge. 1981. *Civil Rights and the Underclass*. Unpublished manuscript, Urban Institute, Washington, DC.

Treadwell, David and Gaylor Shaw. 1981. "Underclass: How One Family Copes." *Los Angeles Times*, July 5, pp. 1, 10-4.

"The Underclass: Enduring Dilemma." 1974. *Time* 103(24, June 17):26-27.

Van Haitsma, Martha. 1989. "A Contextual Definition of the Underclass." *Focus* (Institute for Research on Poverty, University of Wisconsin, Madison) 12(1):27-31, 42.

Wacquant, Loïc J.D. and William Wilson. 1989a. "The Cost of Racial and Class Exclusion in the Inner City." *The Annals of the American Academy of Social and Political Science* 501(January):8-25.

————. 1989b. "Poverty, Joblessness and the Social Transformation of the Inner City." Pp. 70-102 in *Welfare Policies for the 1990s*, edited by Phoebe H. Cottingham and David T. Ellwood. Cambridge, MA: Harvard University Press.

Whitman, David. 1983. "Liberal Rhetoric and the Welfare Underclass." *Society* 21(1):63-74.

Wilson, William J. 1978. *The Declining Significance of Race: Blacks and Changing American Institutions*. 1st ed. Chicago: University of Chicago Press.

————. 1980. *The Declining Significance of Race: Blacks and Changing American Institutions*. 2nd ed. Chicago: University of Chicago Press.

————. 1983. "Inner City Dislocations." *Society* 21(1):80-86.

————. 1985a. "The Urban Underclass in Advanced Industrial Society." In *The New Urban Reality*, edited by Paul E. Peterson. Washington, DC: Brookings Institution.

————. 1985b. "Cycles of Deprivation and the Underclass Debate." *Social Service Review* 59(4):541-59.

————. 1987. *The Truly Disadvantaged: The Inner City, the Underclass, and Public Policy*. Chicago: University of Chicago Press.

————. 1988. "The American Underclass: Inner City Ghettos and the Norms of Citizenship." The Godkin Lecture, delivered at the J.F.K. School of Government, Harvard University, April.

————. 1989. "Social Research and the Underclass Debate." Revised version of paper presented at the state meeting of the American Academy of Arts and Sciences, Cambridge, MA, April.

9

Political Dimensions of the Underclass Concept

Walter W. Stafford
Joyce Ladner

The resurgence of interest in problems of the poor, especially those of poor blacks with tenuous attachments to mainstream economic and social institutions, has rekindled debates among social scientists and policymakers about the interrelationship of race, poverty, and culture. Much of this current debate is reminiscent of the exchanges and claims of the 1960s, when social scientists argued the validity of the concept "culture of poverty" and its usefulness as an explanation of the persistence of poverty within the black community.

Some twenty years later, as we examine the conceptual basis of the underclass, and the political context in which it is being debated, it appears that some of the concepts about a culture of poverty that were dismissed earlier because of questions about their validity or usefulness are being used to conceptualize, define, and measure the underclass. For this reason, an indication of similarities and dissimilarities between the content and context of current studies and discussions of the underclass and those of the culture of poverty are in order. Such a comparison provides a useful backdrop for this chapter, which will focus on the political context of present assessments and debates concerning the conceptualization of the underclass.

There is nothing in this review that suggests that the similarities and dissimilarities between the culture of poverty and the underclass counterbalance each other. As we shall point out, there are some differences, such as those having to do with the force of culture and power relationships that have led to differences in formulations and receptivity even if not necessarily in validity or usefulness.

Similarities in Formulations

There are four similarities in the formulations of the culture of poverty and the underclass; they are as follows: (1) An assumption that existing institutions can absorb low-income groups — particularly African Americans — if they alter their behavior; (2) an assumption that cultural and behavioral traits associated with poverty are transmitted from one generation to another; (3) a body of broad generalizations about patterns of deviant behavior among certain population groups that are developed and circulated by social scientists and journalists, which are generalizations based upon limited observations and data; and (4) each of the concepts has achieved prominence and has been promoted during periods when relations between the races were relatively unstable and were being reexamined.

Neither concept emphasizes the institutional practices and characteristics that limit the access and participation of groups and lead to inequalities in resources. This lack of emphasis has led in both periods to acute concerns about meaning and definitions, particularly in discussions about African Americans. The term *culture of poverty* came to the fore during the 1960s when the demands on institutions by blacks led to new perspectives of power relationships between minorities and established majorities. Twenty years later, as the reshaping of power relationships continues, culture bids to assume a different and possibly more powerful role. The projected rise of African Americans, Latinos, and Asian Americans as the fastest-growing groups in the population and the labor force provides added meaning and force to varied cultural heritages. The consequences of this new "rising tide of color" has become a matter of interest if not urgency in some quarters.

Dissimilarities in Formulations

Major differences related to the respective formulations are as follows: (1) Structural variables, particularly economic changes, are given more attention in the formulation and use of the underclass concept; (2) there are more conscious and rigorous efforts to shape and to use the concept by social scientists associated with institutions that have decided political goals; (3) there is now more emphasis on class differences within the black community; (4) there is more emphasis on "dependency" as a political concern; (5) more explicit assumptions about the nature of racism, and its relation to poverty, are being made in the formulation of the underclass concept; and (6) blacks are playing a more prominent role in the promotion of the underclass concept.

Much of the policy debate about the concept of the underclass is associated with major "think tanks," which did not exist or figure strongly in the debate about poverty and racial discrimination during the 1960s. These include the

American Enterprise Institute, the Heritage Foundation, the Manhattan Institute, the Urban Institute, and the Joint Center for Political Studies. The Rockefeller Foundation is the leading funder of research studies on the underclass.

Public policy is increasingly being influenced by institutes funded by foundations and business corporations, and less by unattached, individual social scientists. The interest of these groups in the underclass is part of a recent trend. Their interest has given the concept a high visibility in policy debates at a time when blacks and Latinos are becoming a more prominent concern of politicians as voters and a concern of businesspersons as future workers.

Concomitant with the shift in the institutional base of research has been a redefinition of the analytical focus. Most notable has been the shift from conventional comparisons of whites and blacks to comparisons of middle- and low-income groups within the black community. This shift from inter- to intragroup comparisons has reduced discussions about racism in the conceptualizations and the policy recommendations to a minimum. The institutions and some of the analysts, who are the leaders in reformulating the issues around the underclass, are often as interested in building an acceptable political agenda as they are in defining a problem. Discussions about racism have been minimized to make the political solutions more palatable (Lowi 1988).

PURPOSE AND AIMS

This chapter examines the conceptual basis of the underclass and the political context in which it is being debated. This decision is based upon the recognition that the concept has gained political sanction and a large measure of public acceptance in the absence of rigorous examination of assumptions and testing of hypotheses.

We maintain that the function and the value of concepts and labels that gain widespread acceptance as descriptions of group behavior and that lack anchoring in an integrated body of knowledge are as much political as heuristic. Whereas the perceived problem groups cannot be ignored, neither can the interest groups that define their membership and deviance.

The specific aims of this chapter are to examine (1) the "claims-making" process by which a concept like the underclass gains sanction and public acceptance; (2) the reasons for the acceptance and popularity of the concept; (3) the politics of definition, including views of critics and proponents; (4) the measurement of the underclass, and its problems; and (5) selected assumptions that characterize, which include concentration and isolation, intergenerational dependency, crime, marriage and family, and the labor market.

THE CLAIMS-MAKING PROCESS

Interest groups concerned with social problems, especially those involving deviancy, are often involved in a claims-making process in which the control of definitions engenders control of expertise, diagnosis, and data analysis (Lewis and Salem 1988).

Wolfson (1984) has noted that the claims-making process for medical discoveries is the principal mover in the emergence of new deviance designations. First, public claims are made about a new treatment for a problem; then information, in a highly dramatic form, begins to filter to the public about the discovery. Following this stage, legitimacy is sought through validation in legislative committees and by the body politic. Finally, the terminology is institutionalized as a result of being codified and bureaucratized. The medical discoveries process provides a useful analogy for the underclass phenomenon. In the case of the underclass, newspapers and magazines highlighted the concept, foundations funded the research even before the critical parameters were clear, social scientists promoted the claims in congressional committees, and it eventually underwent a trial of inclusion within institutions.

Our concern with the implications of this type of process involves its long history in the social sciences. When poorly defined terms and concepts are the basis for policy decisions, the results can be catastrophic. This is illustrated by the use and misuse of the concept of the "learning disabled." When Congress passed legislation in 1975 for special education programs, it assumed there was consensus about the research results as well as the existence of a well-trained pool of teachers capable of referring students to appropriate programs and providing assistance to them. In fact, the relevant research was inadequate, the findings were contradictory, and the proposed solutions were a subject of controversy among educators. The subsequent implementation of "special education" programs in schools has been fraught with cultural bias, and "resource rooms" as often as not are used as a strategy for classroom control rather than promoting learning. Evaluation research since the 1980s shows widespread negative effects of these programs on lower-income youth, especially blacks (Tucker 1980; Edgar 1987). Poorly defined concepts foster and reinforce labeling and the use of stereotypes. Once a concept is incorporated in general perceptions and becomes a guide to program development, it is almost impossible to eradicate. Social scientists, who are often active members of the labeling professions, may show sensitivity to the maintenance of values but at the same time exhibit insensitivity to political consequences. The result of their giving the intellectuals' imprimatur to a concept is often the creation of a convenient terminology that unwittingly reinforces existing stereotypes and prejudices of laymen, professionals and agencies, and journalists. The history of the concept of a "culture of violence" affords a good example of this process. The initial argument for the existence of a "culture of violence" was that groups, especially blacks, were more violent in certain regions of the country partly because of the legacy of violence and conflict in these areas. The concept was later easily integrated into views of lower-income blacks regardless of geographical area. Even after the basic premises were refuted by social scientists, the concept and its attendant prejudices persisted in the literature and in the courts.

The above examples suggest that the promotion of concepts or theories by social scientists and others can have serious consequences, even if the assumptions are weak and if the propositions are untested. To the extent that social scientists' accountability is only to their peers, they are "protected": Their legitimacy is not dependent on the prescriptions or recommendations they present or support. Practitioners, unlike social scientists, usually have a limited interest in theory building. Once a concept is "sanctioned" in the public realm, however, they have an interest in deferring to presumed authority and in resisting changes in the basic premises of the accepted formulation. Practitioners maintain power and control by claiming to comprehend social science formulation and to be able to solve problems that they fit into their value framework.

REASONS FOR POPULARITY

There are three reasons why the "underclass" concept has gained widespread popularity. First, it is a broad term that easily stratifies disparate groups who appear to be deviant. It provides a convenient "net" for social scientists, journalists, and practitioners. A summary of the research on the underclass published by the Urban Institute (1987) notes that the behavior-based definitions of the "underclass" are not limited by considerations of income or wealth: "Neither an underclass member with a lot of money — like some criminals and 'hustlers' — nor one with the behavior of the underclass and a small amount of money, is excluded from consideration."

Second, in a period when the media were giving considerable attention to conservatives — notably Murray (1984) — for their views on poverty and race, the "underclass" provided a conception that enabled liberals to become actively involved again in the debate about behavior, civility, and dependency. Early on in the assertions about the underclass, a small group of conservative journalists, social scientists, and theologians dominated much of the discussion on the behavior of the poor. Conservatives gained a broad audience unavailable to them before, and at the same time liberals saw an important opportunity to reestablish the legitimacy they had lost in the 1960s as interpreters of broad change in the black community. With the revival of familiar characterizations under the rubric of the *underclass,* liberals had a way of regaining prominence in the discussion of behavioral characteristics of blacks without offending black social scientists, advocates, and community leaders. The concept permits liberals and conservatives to promote their values relating to race and ethnicity without racism being the dominant focus of analyses and policy prescriptions.

Wilson, for example, has argued that there is something uniquely different about the "ghetto underclass." His use of the term *ghetto* signaled a turn against the political definitions of community favored by most black analysts and public figures. He has tried to make the appeal of the concept broader by arguing that it is not black/white but intragroup comparisons that are being made. Class, not race, is the central problem of the "ghetto underclass." According to Wilson, what is needed now are universal policies for the poor that would assist all groups, including the "ghetto underclass." Thus many of the race-specific programs, notably affirmative action, are not as important as they had been before, because they have primarily assisted only the black middle class.

Third, the "underclass" concept has encouraged wider participation by researchers, policy analysts, politicians, and journalists in discussions about the norms and values of the faster-growing nonwhite populations. Blacks and Hispanics are among the nation's fastest-growing population groups and there are labor shortages in many areas of the nation.

There is a growing concern about how blacks and Latinos, who have been left behind during expansions and retractions, will respond to an economy that is generating a large number of low-wage jobs with little opportunity for upward mobility (Greenstein 1986). This concern provides an interesting paradox. While there is a reluctance to incorporate problems of race in the conceptualizations of the underclass, race is a major consideration in the viability of the market.

THE POLITICS OF DEFINITION

Definitions play critical roles not only in the analysis of problems but in the determination of power relationships among groups. In the field of race relations and poverty, the determination of definitions *is* a key issue. Demographic changes among blacks and Latinos have the possibility of altering long-established practices of key public and private institutions, if not altering traditional and existent values. As Novak (1987) has noted, values are the cutting edge of much of what happens in the political arena in the 1980s.

There is a decisive move, mirrored in our politics as well as in our intellectual life, from issues to values. This means looking at reality and at problems, not solely in terms of issues, as we often used to do, but in terms of some of the underlying values that are there or that we think ought to be there and that we would like to encourage and support, if they are missing there.

In this context, we examine some of the proponents and critics of the concept and some of the definitions and hypotheses associated with it. Most of the recent definitions (earlier definitions have been developed by Myrdal, Levy, Glasgow) of the "underclass" relate primarily to lower-income blacks, even though the concept includes whites and Hispanics. Glasgow (1980) provided the earliest of the underclass formulation of the 1980s, proposing that the underclass has emerged from a combination of institutional racism and structural changes in the economy that have produced and reinforced a cycle of poverty in the black community.

Since Glasgow, the underclass definitions have moved away from a consideration of racism and institutional barriers to a focus on attitudinal and behavioral deficiencies (Carson 1986). With a few notable exceptions (Ricketts and Sawhill 1988; Ruggles and Marton 1986), researchers have also tended to define the underclass concept loosely.

In 1982, Auletta defined the underclass as the passive poor — usually long-term welfare recipients, street criminals, hustlers, traumatized drunks, drifters, homeless shopping-bag ladies, and released mental patients who frequently roam or collapse on city streets.

Other definitions appeared shortly afterward. Clark and Nathan (1982) stressed education, experience in the labor market, literacy, and stable family relationships; a group of researchers at the Joint Center for Political Studies stressed criminal activities (McFate 1987); Carson (1986) focused on deviant behavior and deviant attitudes toward that behavior; Landry's (1987) definition included unskilled day workers along with the unemployed, people on permanent welfare, and those living off illegal activities.

Wilson (1987), who has received most of the credit for popularizing the concept, is also imprecise in the definition he offers. In one of his earliest definitions, he defined the underclass as

> individuals who lack training and skills and either experience long-term unemployment or are not a part of the labor force, individuals who engage in street criminal activity and other aberrant behavior, families who experience long-term spells of poverty and/or welfare dependency.

Ricketts and Sawhill (1988), writing after Wilson's main publication, attempted to develop a definition that could test some of the key assumptions. Their definition is based on what they assume to be a clear consensus around values and norms and deviation from them. They note:

Behavioral norms are not invariant. But in American society, circa 1980, it is expected will attend school and delay parenthood until at least 18, that adult males (who are not disabled or retired) will work at a regular job, that adult females will either work or marry, and everyone will be law-abiding.

McLanahan, Garfinkel, and Watson (1988) have attempted to bring the concept into line with current thinking in economics and with established sociological traditions. For them, the underclass comprises family units with no readily salable labor power or other factors of production.

In 1989, Wilson narrowed his definition to focus on the weak attachments of underclass members to the mainstream labor market while maintaining that the aberrant behavior should remain a focus (Wilson 1989). He also gave greater importance to the role of racial discrimination in the creation of the underclass (Wacquant and Wilson 1989) after minimizing its importance in the modern economy in *The Truly Disadvantaged* (1987).

Despite Wilson's adjustments in his definition, our review of the assumptions about and definitions of the underclass over the last seven years suggests that the definitions remain value-laden, concerning behavior, and difficult to measure.

MEASURING THE UNDERCLASS

The principal problem researchers have faced in attempting to measure the underclass has been distinguishing its membership from those people who are simply poor. The question of size of the underclass ultimately depends upon the definition being used. In general, the tighter the definition, the smaller the number of people encompassed; conversely, the looser the definition, the larger the number. For example, Gottschalk (1987) provides two estimates; one is loose, the other is more refined. By his looser definition, he estimates that, in 1987, for every three people in the underclass, one was poor. Using the tighter definition, there was one poor person for every 33 in the underclass.

If the Ricketts and Sawhill definition is used, there were 2.6 million people living in underclass areas in 1980. Because Ricketts and Sawhill are defining areas, rather than solely estimating populations, they are cautious to note that not all of the people living in underclass areas are poor. Further, not all of them engage in underclass behavior, even though they all live in neighborhoods where such behavior is common. A profile of the population of the tracts, in comparison with the U.S. population by groups, is interesting. Most of the underclass tracts, as specified by Ricketts and Sawhill, are in older industrial cities in the Northeast. Within these tracts, 59% of the residents are black, 28% are white, and 11% are Hispanic. Nearly two-thirds of the adults have not completed high school and few in the population are foreign-born. The number of disabled in the tracts is much higher than that in the nation as a whole.

Keeping in mind the assumptions promoted by other researchers and analysts, it is important to note what Ricketts and Sawhill's profile did not show. It did not show that a high proportion of children 18 or under or 6 or under resided in underclass tracts. Because a significant proportion of black children under 6 resided in female-headed households that were poor in 1980, this fact would imply that most of them did not reside in underclass tracts. Further, the Ricketts-Sawhill definition tells us very little about the turnover of the population, the location within cities, and whether public housing is included within the tracts. The location of public housing could be important because it represents a special case in which turnover rates would be different, the percentage of blacks would be high, and welfare would be highly concentrated. Overall, according to the Ricketts-Sawhill count, there were approximately 450,000 adults living in underclass tracts who had no regular attachment to the labor force.

The studies of the empiricists suggest that the probable number of individuals in the underclass is small (Ruggles and Marton 1986). Even when definitions and working hypotheses are tightened, there remain questions about the skill and concentration of the underclass. Hughes (1988), utilizing the same definition as Ricketts and Sawhill, found that underclass tracts had declined in many cities, and he argued that the Ricketts and Sawhill description of the underclass is probably more reflective of a larger aggregate population within cities.

SELECTED PARAMETERS AND ASSUMPTIONS ABOUT CLASS AND RACIAL CONTACT

Concentration and Isolation

One underlying assumption of the underclass argument is that the aberrant values/norms of its members are reinforced by their limited contact with the larger middle class. In general, we assume that the proponents of the underclass concept are referring to the norms of the larger middle class. (This is only an assumption on our part, because none of the writers is explicit.) Here, Wilson is an exception in that his argument largely employs an intragroup comparison with emphasis on place and role of the black middle class. Wilson makes many allusions to the black middle class, but they are general and difficult to follow, especially because his account ignores the 1960s, a key catalytic period. Essentially, he argues that during 1940 through the 1950s, even though blacks were poor, they did not exhibit the "deviant" behavior found in certain areas today. He attributes much of the increase in deviancy to the exodus of the black middle class from older black communities.

In making his argument, Wilson relies essentially on one book, *The Black Metropolis* by Drake and Cayton. His argument is an inverse of the prototypical argument that blacks suffer in terms of educational and economic gains from lack of contact with whites. As interesting as his thesis may be, it suffers because it fails to explain how contact between poor blacks and the black middle class could be diminishing if residential segregation of blacks in most of the large cities is increasing (or at least remaining steady). If residential segregation in most of the large cities (including Chicago, where most of Wilson's material comes from) is increasing, or remaining at the same level, how far removed is the black middle class? Massey and Denton (1987) show that blacks, regardless of income, remain more spatially isolated than whites, Hispanics, or Asians. According to these authors, in Chicago, the level of black isolation has changed little over the last decade; and, moreover, by measures of acculturation and rising socioeconomic status, black suburbanization remains low in all cities. They write:

> If the black middle class has abandoned the black poor, it has not been by moving to Anglo neighborhoods, at least on a significant scale. Most blacks continue to reside in predominantly black neighborhoods, even in cities with relatively large and affluent black middle classes, such as New York, Chicago and Philadelphia.

The reality is that blacks in the suburbs remain only a fraction of the black population, and a sizable proportion of this population resides in poverty.

Wilson's argument concerning isolation and contact, as well as those of other proponents, also fails to consider changes in perceptions about contact between races and classes, the greater sophistication of the media in providing all groups with images of middle-class life-styles, and the role of "fixed units" of public housing. These omissions weaken their premise concerning the effects of concentration. Residents of public housing, especially in Chicago, have for decades been isolated from all groups. This was the result of intentional planning and purposive site selection; and these had little if anything to do with the ebb and flow of migration; rather, the result was based on the politics of Chicago and the Chicago Housing Authority. If blacks in these thousands of apartment units are being counted among those who lack contact with whites and middle-class blacks, then it is not a recent phenomenon, as Wilson contends.

Another question that Wilson's argument concerning contact fails to satisfy has to do with the relationship of capital to poverty. The argument can be made that one of the reasons for the persistent poverty of many blacks is that blacks have not built a significant base of capital that has a flow within segregated communities. This argument has merits, because it recognizes the importance of the control of capital in achieving goals in the political economy. Wilson does not make this argument; if he did, it would alter many of his basic concepts about behavior and would focus the argument on the effects of discrimination.

The historical reality is that the black middle class has been so small and fragile that its differentiation from the poorer blacks is neither that significant nor that clear-cut. It did offer "role models"; however, they were not necessarily based on contact, even in the most segregated of communities. The existence of class biases in the black community has long been recognized. A more sensitive observation about the contemporary black middle class might be that, unlike the black middle class of prior generations, its contacts with the poor in the present generation are as representatives of the "welfare state."

Several studies document the narrow growth of the black middle class through the public sector in the last decades (Moss 1988). A reformulation of Wilson's observations would show that the black community has become involved in a new class dynamic. Blacks are often the teachers for lower-income blacks, the social workers, the police officers, the probation officers, and the upper-level administrators of social welfare and social control agencies. It is the interaction between a middle class, which continues to have limited options outside of government, and a lower-income group, with even fewer options, that deserves attention. It is particularly important in the nation's central cities.

Intergenerational Welfare Dependency

A critical assumption among some theorists of the "underclass" is that dependency is translated from one generation to the next; that is, it persists through pathological linkages in which traits such as autonomy, independence, ambition, and coping are not reinforced during childhoods spent on welfare (Hill et al. 1985).

The dependency assumption emphasizes the motivations and the attitudes of parents; however, neither the findings of studies on blacks nor the findings of studies on whites support these "motivational" hypotheses. Researchers have not found any conclusive evidence that welfare leads to changes in the attitude of recipients or their offspring. These groups have lower self-esteem and show lower self-efficacy, but there is nothing in the findings to suggest that welfare is the cause rather than the consequence of these negative self-attitudes (Garfinkel & McLanahan 1986). Further, there is substantial evidence to show that the poor can and do move out of poverty and that dependency is not transmitted.

Hill and colleagues (1985), using the Panel Study of Income Dynamics (PSID), found that the majority of youth from poor families move out of poverty as adults. However, young adults from poor families are much more likely to be poor as adults than those from nonpoor families. Similar patterns emerged for welfare status. While children from welfare-recipient parental homes are somewhat more likely to be welfare recipients themselves, the degree to which children as young adults depend on welfare as their main source of income is largely unaffected by the degree to which their parents depended on welfare. Hill and colleagues found that parental attitudes play little role in whatever transmission of welfare status does occur. Importantly, in terms of the thesis of the "ghetto underclass" proposed by Wilson, Hill and colleagues found that black males and females from welfare-dependent families were no more likely to become welfare dependent than were similar blacks and families who had never received welfare. By contrast, Hill notes that the lack of intergenerational welfare dependency was more equivocal among whites.

In regard to aspirations, researchers have consistently found that lower-income black families have high aspirations for their children (Rodman and Voydanoff 1978); this is true even though institutional barriers within schools may lower aspirations as the children mature. McLanahan (1985) has suggested that being on welfare may enhance the long-term educational attainment of black children, at least at the earliest stages.

CRIME

The researchers who use crime as a variable are extremely vague in their definitions. Wilson includes "street crime" in his description of the underclass. Street crime has various manifestations that he does not identify. The other proponents simply cite criminal activities.

The inclusion of crime in definitions of the underclass is confounded by a variety of methodological and conceptual problems. Wilson cites arrest figures for only one year. This is very misleading because arrest rates have vacillated significantly in many of the larger cities. More important is the fact that none of the proponents of the crime variable provides an analysis of the issues and the relationship of crime to economic variables.

There is continuous debate among sociologists, especially criminologists, about the use of arrest, self-report, and victimization statistics. Much of the arrest data is a reflection of only a small proportion of those who commit crimes. In fact, the figures may reflect as much about police behavior as they do about the commission of offenses. The disproportionate number of arrests of lower-income blacks may be related in part to their demeanor and/or their place of residence (Smith and Visher 1981). The data on self-reported criminal activity reveals that, although black youth report more predatory and property crimes, the relationships are not significant for crimes against persons (Elliott and Ageton 1980). Recent self-report surveys show that serious involvement of black youth in personal crimes has declined (Elliott et al. 1983). Among adults, there are few studies of criminal activity and propensities based upon self-reports. However, those that have been completed (among men who have been incarcerated) do not show any significantly higher involvement in crime (Petersillia 1985).

Finally, the emphasis on street crime ignores those poor communities that have low crime rates and disregards the importance of resources and social agencies. Studies by criminologists (Fagan 1987; Curtis 1987) in high-crime inner-city communities show that the lack of income and the absence of funds from public and private organizations limit both the formal and the informal control of delinquency.

Marriage and Families

The inclusion of marriage rates and family characteristics in the formulations of the underclass concept is also problematic. Following Moynihan's lead, Wilson and others argue that one of the reasons for the persistence of poverty in black families is that black males cannot find jobs. Novak (1987) has gone further than most other analysts in promoting the new focus on black males and the deterioration of the black family. In congressional testimony, he reinforced the focus on black males and their families by saying that "never in American history, and not often in the history of civilized societies anywhere, has there been such widespread abandonment of women by young men."

Joblessness among black males is certainty a principal consideration in any analysis of race and poverty. An increasing number of black males began to drop out of the labor market in the 1960s and this has continued into the 1980s. Once these men are jobless, they often do not return to the labor market (Smith and Welch 1987). Even for black men who find work, income parity with white males remains illusive. In a review of the earnings of white and black men between 1953 and 1985, Vroman (1987) notes that nearly all of the gains in black men's relative earnings since World War II occurred between 1964 and 1974. For Wilson and others to be right, the proportion of blacks married should increase during the period in which black males gained the greatest relative earnings. However, McLanahan, Garfinkel, and Watson (1988) have found that the association between unemployment and single motherhood was closer in the 1950s, during a period in which Wilson argues that black behavior was closer to the norm.

Black female earnings are also of crucial concern. The earnings of black women are lower than those of white women. Moreover, their unemployment rates have been double those of white women in the 1980s. The degree to which black females improve their earnings is important, because black couples are more likely than whites or Hispanics to have a wife in a primary earning role.

Equally important in formulating the underclass concept are trends in black marriages. It is misleading to use the marriage patterns of lower-income blacks when blacks as a group have lower rates of marriage (Garfinkel and McLanahan 1986). Unpublished data from the Current Population Survey for 1986 show that the proportion of married black males in professional and managerial occupations was virtually the same as that in lower-level occupations, while there was a much higher proportion of married white males in upper-level occupations.

Simply stated, marriage in the black community is not an underclass problem but one related to a complex set of cultural and economic forces that transcend the data of most empirical studies in the social sciences. These forces call for a broader and more sensitive interpretation.

Labor Markets

McLanahan, Garfinkel, and Watson (1988) present one of the few formulations of the underclass concept that incorporates current thinking in economics and sociology about the interaction of employers with lower-income blacks and Latinos in the labor market. Wilson and other proponents usually describe trends in employment without providing a theoretical framework.

The trend data are only part of the picture. At best these data show that many cities have lost manufacturing jobs that provided lower-income blacks with employment. However, this has a weak application for many cities, especially New York, which, according to the Ricketts-Sawhill definition, would have the largest concentration of underclass tracts. In New York City, blacks never had a substantial base in manufacturing, thus their underclass status could not be attributable to these losses. The other finding of the trend analysis is that blacks and Hispanics lack the skills to get hired within the faster-growing service industries. This is also misleading: A college degree is often a screening device for jobs in the service industry, but many of these jobs do not require much more than a high school degree. Historical exclusion from jobs and industries that provide on-the-job training is also a critical problem for blacks and Latinos.

The "skill and spatial mismatch" arguments have flaws as well. According to conventional economic theory, the market adjusts to gains in skills, and persons with limited skills make adjustments by taking lower pay. However, in the case of blacks, the market has traditionally not adjusted without intervention. Blacks have had high unemployment rates in periods of growth as well as decline. They have failed to gain jobs, even if the employers were in their neighborhoods, and they have been unable to get jobs where distances were greater (Ellwood 1986). Many of the lower-paying white-collar service industries are close to the residences of blacks; however, their access to these jobs is limited. Moreover, while members of the black underclass have more problems in the labor market than members of the white underclass, Carson (1986) has found that, when all other characteristics are equal, minority members who are not a part of the underclass are treated the same as whites who are part of the underclass.

The limitations of trend analysis in explaining the underclass has led McLanahan, Garfinkel, and Watson (1988) to apply segmentation theory and incorporate the concept of dual labor markets into their definition. This concept divides labor markets into primary/core and peripheral/secondary. Core industries are characterized by stable, often high-wage employment with job ladders and opportunities for training. By contrast, peripheral industries are cyclical, have a high turnover, and provide low wages and virtually no training. While Garfinkel, McLanahan, and Watson build an important dimension into the discussion, they delimit its value by focusing on salable labor power (human capital) as a supply consideration without focusing on the institutional barriers (demand) that receive most attention from economists and sociologists (Cain 1976; Pomer 1986). Studies show that blacks have limited access to primary jobs and industries (Pomer 1986) and that blacks and Latinos tend to be concentrated in a narrow range of industries and jobs (Stafford 1985). When there is economic growth, their employment often expands within the industrial base where they already have employment. When there is economic contraction, they find it difficult to shift industries.

SUMMARY AND CONCLUSIONS

When the claims of the proponents of the underclass are given close scrutiny and related to research findings in various fields, they provide only tenuous explanations of the persistence of poverty among blacks. They have provided very little information that was not known before the research started. They are especially weakened by the intraracial comparisons among blacks, the failure of the proponents to account for historical barriers such as public housing and urban renewal, the absence of a theoretical focus on crime, the failure to acknowledge continued discrimination in the labor market, and an unwillingness to examine the discriminatory allocation of resources by institutions.

The decisions to minimize or to ignore studies that show institutional barriers help corroborate our earlier observation that the proponents of both the underclass and the culture of poverty have tended to accept and endorse the framework and structure of existing institutions. According to these formulations, the problem resides in the attitudes and behavior of the poor rather than in institutions.

In rebuttal to the claims of the proponents of the underclass, this chapter has documented studies, particularly of the labor market, that clearly show extensive barriers to opportunities for blacks in all status groups. If institutional barriers did not exist, blacks would be more randomly distributed in housing and employment than they are.

In the main, we only hypothesize as to why the claims made by the proponents of the underclass have gained wide attention. Part of the answer is found in the involvement of research and policy institutes, especially in the ways they have influenced the formulation of the questions and definitions and the promotion of studies. Part of the answer lies in the fact that vigorous claims have been made about the underclass in Congress and in the media. Further, foundations and policy institutes have provided the resources that have enabled writers and analysts to promote research and assertions before hypotheses and assertions were tested and corroborated. Finally, the concept is palatable to those who are seeking answers about the growing rates of poverty, homelessness, and unemployment of blacks in an economy that has generated large numbers of new jobs in the 1980s. The underclass formulations do not require an examination of institutional barriers but allow both conservatives and liberals to focus their prescriptions on behavior and attitudes.

This review and the assessments lead us to reject the argument made by some proponents of the underclass concept that they are providing a liberal alternative to conservatives' claims and prescriptions. In the late 1970s, conservatives promoted themselves and many ideas without a popular mandate from the populace (Ferguson and Rogers 1986). Their ideas about poverty and inequality gained headlines in the course of this overall promotion. A key conclusion of this chapter is that some of the proponents of the underclass concept are not presenting liberal alternatives to the conservatives but are largely reinforcing the conservatives' assumptions on and conceptualizations of the poor and their behavior. Their main contribution has been to expand the base of the discussion of poverty, status, and behavior and, ironically, to provide new insights into reasons why institutional change is so important for understanding the persistence of poverty.

We suggest that the most difficult theoretical and practical analyses are to be found in understanding how economic, social, and political institutions limit black and Latino access and mobility despite their growing numerical presence. This type of research is less likely to receive funding, because it raises questions about the network of decision making that maintains or fosters racial inequalities. However, anything short of understanding how racial and ethnic discrimination operates in the post-1980s political economy is unlikely to contribute significantly to an understanding of the relationship between poverty and race.

REFERENCES

Auletta, Ken. 1982. *The Underclass.* New York: Random House.

Cain, Glen G. 1976. "The Challenge of Segmented Labor Market Theories to Orthodox Theory: A Survey." *Journal of Economic Literature* 14:1215-17.

Carson, Emmett. 1986. "The Black Underclass Concept: Self-Help vs. Government Intervention." *The American Economic Review* 76(2):247-50.

Clark, Kenneth and Richard Nathan. 1982. "The Urban Underclass." In *Critical Issues for National Urban Policy: A Reconnaissance and Agenda for Further Study.* Washington, DC: National Research Council.

Curtis, Lynn. 1987. "The Retreat of Folly: Some Modest Replications of Inner-City Success." *The Annals of the American Academy of Social and Political Science* 494:71-89.

Duncan, Greg, Martha Hill, and Saul Hoffman. 1988. "Welfare Dependence Within and Across Generations." *Science* 239:467-71.

Edgar, Eugene. 1987. "Secondary Programs in Special Education: Are Many of Them Justifiable?" *Exceptional Children*, April, pp. 555-61.

Elliott, Delbert and Suzanne Ageton. 1980. "Reconciling Race and Class Differences in Self-Reported and Official Estimates of Delinquency." *American Sociological Review* 45:95-110.

Elliott, Delbert, D. Huizinga, B. A. Knowles, and R. J. Canter. 1983. *The Prevalence and Incidence of Delinquent Behavior: 1976-1980.* Boulder, CO: Behavioral Research Institute.

Ellwood, David. 1986. "The Spatial Mismatch Hypothesis: Are There Teenage Jobs Missing in the Ghetto?" In *The Black Youth Employment Crisis,* edited by R. B. Freeman and H. J. Holzer. Chicago: University of Chicago Press.

Fagan, Jeffrey. 1987. "Neighborhood Education, Mobilization, and Organization for Juvenile Crime Prevention." *The Annals of the American Academy of Social and Political Science* 494:54-70.

Ferguson, Thomas and Joel Rogers. 1986. *The Decline of the Democrats and the Future of American Politics.* New York: Hill and Wang.

Garfinkel, Irwin and Sara McLanahan. 1986. *Single Mothers and Their Children.* Washington, DC: Urban Institute.

Glasgow, Douglas. 1980. *The Black Underclass.* New York: Random House.

Gottschalk, Peter. 1987. "Statement: Poverty, Hunger and the Welfare System." Hearings before the Select Committee on Hunger, House of Representatives, 99th Congress (99-23:9-34). Washington, DC: Government Printing Office.

Greenstein, R. 1986. "Statement: Poverty, Hunger and the Welfare System." Hearings before the Select Committee on Hunger, House of Representatives, 99th Congress (99-23:99-35). Washington, DC: Government Printing Office.

Hill, Martha et al. 1985. *Motivation and Economic Mobility.* Ann Arbor, MI: Survey Research Center.

Hughes, Mark Allen. 1988. *Concentrated Deviance or Isolated Deprivation? The "Underclass" Idea Reconsidered.* Princeton, NJ: Woodrow Wilson School of Public and International Affairs.

Interagency Committee on Learning Disabilities. 1987. *Learning Disabilities: A Report to the U.S. Congress.* Washington, DC: Department of Health and Human Services.

Landry, Bart. 1987. *The New Black Middle Class.* Berkeley: University of California Press.

Lewis, Dan and Greta Salem. 1988. *Fear of Crime: Incivility and the Production of a Social Problem.* New Brunswick, NJ: Transaction.

Levy, Frank. 1977. "How Big Is the American Underclass?" Working Paper 0090-1. Washington, DC: Urban Institute.

Lowi, Theodore. 1988. "The Theory of the Underclass: A Review of Wilson's 'The Truly Disadvantaged.' " *Policy Studies Review* 7:852-58.

Massey, Douglas and Nancy Denton. 1987. "Trends in the Residential Segregation of Blacks, Hispanics, and Asians: 1970-1980." *American Sociological Review* 52:802-25.

McFate, Katherine. 1987. "Defining the Underclass." In *Focus: Newsletter of the Joint Center for Political Studies.* Washington, DC: Joint Center for Political Studies.

McIntrye, Lonnie and Eugene Pernell. 1985. "The Impact of Race on Teacher Recommendations for Special Education Placement." *Journal of Multicultural Counseling and Development,* July, pp. 112-19.

McLanahan, Sara. 1985. "Family Structure and the Reproduction of Poverty." *American Journal of Sociology* 90:873-901.

McLanahan, Sara, Irwin Garfinkel, and Dorothy Watson. 1988. "Family Structure, Poverty, and the Underclass." Pp. 102-48 in *Urban Change and Poverty,* edited by Michael McGeary and L. Lynn. Washington, DC: National Academy Press.

Moss, Philip. 1988. "Employment Gains by Minorities, Women in Large City Governments, 1976-83." *Monthly Labor Review* 110:18-24.

Murray, Charles. 1984. *Losing Ground: American Social Policy, 1950-1980*. New York: Basic Books.

Novak, Michael. 1987. "Statement: Poverty, Hunger and the Welfare System." Hearings before the Select Committee on Hunger, House of Representatives, 99th Congress (99-23:9-34). Washington, DC: Government Printing Office.

Patterson, J. T. 1981. *America's Struggle Against Poverty, 1900-1980*. Cambridge, MA: Harvard University Press.

Petersillia, Joan. 1985. "Racial Disparities in the Criminal Justice System: A Summary." *Crime and Delinquency* 31:15-34.

Policy and Research Report. Fall, 1987. "The Underclass Dilemma." Policy and Research Report. Washington, DC: Urban Institute.

Pomer, Marshall. 1986. "Labor Market Structure, Intergenerational Mobility, and Discrimination: Black Male Advancement out of Low-Paying Occupations, 1962-1973." *American Sociological Review* 51:650-659.

Ricketts, Erol and Isabel Sawhill. 1988. "Defining and Measuring the Underclass." *Journal of Policy Analysis and Management* 7:316-25.

Rodman, Hyman and Patricia Voydanoff. 1978. "Social Class and Parents' Range of Aspirations for Their Children." *Social Problems* 25:333-44.

Ruggles, Patricia and William Marton. 1986. *Measuring the Size and Characteristics of the Underclass: How Much Do We Know?* Washington, DC: Urban Institute.

Smith, Douglas and Christy Visher. 1981. "Street Level Justice: Situational Determinants of Police Arrest Decisions." *Social Problems* 29:167-77.

Smith, James P. and Finis Welch. 1987. "Race and Poverty: A Forty-Year Record." *American Economic Association Papers and Proceedings* 77:152-58.

Stafford, Walter. 1985. *Closed Labor Markets*. New York: Community Service Society.

Tucker, J. A. 1980. "Ethnic Proportions in Classes for the Learning Disabled: Issues in Nonbiased Assessment." *Journal of Special Education* 14:316-25.

Urban Institute. 1987. *Policy and Research Report* 17:2-5. (Washington, DC)

Vroman, Wayne. 1987. *Labor Supply and Black Men's Relative Earnings Since 1964*. Washington, DC: Urban Institute.

Wacquant, Loïc and William Wilson. 1989. "The Cost of Racial and Class Exclusion in the Inner City." *The Annals of the American Academy of Social and Political Science* 501:8-25.

Wilson, William. 1985. "Cycles of Deprivation and the Underclass Debate." *Social Science Review* 59:541-59.

———. 1987. *The Truly Disadvantaged*. Chicago: University of Chicago Press.

———. 1989. "Social Research and the Underclass Debate." Paper presented at the American Academy or Arts and Sciences, Cambridge, MA.

Wolfson, Charles. 1984. *Social Deviance in the Human Sciences*. Springfield, IL: Charles C Thomas.

10

The Wrong Stuff:
Reflections on the Place of Gender in
American Sociology

R. W. Connell

Women's studies, masculinity/femininity, the sexual division of labor, the gender order: Here is newly minted or freshly polished terminology, and an area of intellectual excitement and research activity. In the last twenty years, this has been one of the growth points of American sociology. I would argue that it is the most important recent development in social science as a whole.

This is not to say that either the issue or the research interest is new. The field has a long history and its history matters, as we found on looking into the research on masculinity and the male "sex role" (Carrigan, Connell, and Lee 1985). The idea of a science of sex and gender goes back to the nineteenth century: to the later work of Darwin in evolutionary biology, to early anthropology, to the forensic psychopathology of Krafft-Ebing, to the socialist idea of a science of social conditions and its application to the "woman question" by Engels and Bebel. Though much of this literature ran into dead ends, it had the net effect of problematizing gender, of making social arrangements about sex and sexuality appear in need of explanation. At the same time, a practical demand for a critical study of gender built up, especially through late nineteenth- and early twentieth-century feminism in both its "suffragist" and socialist forms.

Early American research on the question, around the turn of the century, thus emerged in a context where the "naturalness" or "socialness" of gender was already at issue, and where political and social consequences hung on the conclusions reached. Rosenberg's (1982) fascinating historical study shows that the question was taken up by a new group in the American intelligentsia, university-trained women — the first generation of researchers to come out of the opening of higher education to women. The studies of sex differences they launched came to a clear and revolutionary conclusion. Contrary to the assumptions of doctors, academics, and popular opinion, there were very limited differences in intellectual powers or in other psychological traits between women and men. This psychological finding opened the way to a critical sociology of gender. If the subordination of women was not based on natural difference, it was just as subject to critique and accessible to reform as the subordination of the working class was. On both sides of the Atlantic, this prospect was opening up by the second decade of this century. It can be seen, in different forms, in the writings of Jessie Taft in America and Alexandra Kollontai in Russia.

It is a historic fact that the possibility of a critical sociology of gender was not realized at this time. The reasons were complex: One was the disintegration of "first-wave" feminism as a political force; another was the purge of the American left during and after World War I, in which critical sociologists like W. I. Thomas (himself a theorist of gender) were targeted. Research on "sex differences" continued; indeed, has continued to this day. As Maccoby and Jacklin (1975) show, it has continued to return the same results. If it were not for the strong cultural bias about the matter, we should long ago have been calling this "sex-similarity" research.

The sex-difference research lost its power to shock because it was gradually drawn into a new and shock-proof container, the theory of "sex roles." This was the decisive turn in the American sociology of gender. The concept of a "social role" as the building block of social structure was virtually created in the 1930s (though the stage metaphor, of course, is older). By the 1950s, the role concept was institutionalized in sociological theory as well as in research. The role model was rapidly adopted in work on gender. The 1940s saw theoretical and speculative papers about "sex roles," notably by Parsons and Komarovsky; by the 1950s, "sex role research" was effectively the name of the field. The actual research was often indistinguishable from the old style of sex-difference research. What had happened was a renaming, the insertion of that tradition into a new intellectual and moral framework.

It is no news that the general framework of social theory that developed in the United States in the 1940s and 1950s was socially conservative. It is worth considering how sex-role theory works as ideology. I have developed a technical critique of the theory elsewhere (Connell 1987, pp. 47-54, 167-71); the argument is too long to recite here, but a key point can be recalled. Sex-role theory, like role theory in general, appears to be social in the sense that it locates the determinants of people's action in the expectations of others, in role prescriptions or "norms." However, this sociality is an illusion. The ultimate determinants of action in role analysis are actually individual choices. In the language of modern social theory (e.g., Giddens 1979), role theory dissolves structure into action. In sex-role theory, the missing element of "structure" is covertly supplied by biology, by the natural difference of sex. Paradoxically, the very movement of thought that asserts the socialness of gender, that talks of "expectations," "stereotypes," and "norms," at the same time naturalizes these arrangements. The socialization of people into these norms becomes the natural means by which the well-being of society is preserved.

Thus the social analysis of gender—at the turn of the century, a disturbing and radicalizing force — by the 1950s and 1960s had become entirely compatible with a technology of social control. I do not know if there has been any systematic study of the reception and application of American social research in this period. My impression, from such clues as the journals in which minor contributions to the literature appeared, is that sex-role research had a readership in the rapidly developing areas of professional practice concerned with social training, minor pathology and adjustment, marriage guidance, counseling, social work, some areas of teaching (especially early childhood teaching), and the like.

This is not to suggest that sex-role theory was an academic branch of the Billy Graham organization, or even Norman Vincent Peale's. The best American sex-role research—and some was very good indeed, such as Komarovsky's *Blue-Collar Marriage* (1964) — threw up lots of evidence of tension and trouble in the ordinary conduct of gender relations. Sex-role theory was also able to register change in norms, and some of the most interesting American contributions were on exactly that theme. Parsons tackled it, at a high level of abstraction; a more concrete example is Hacker's "The New Burdens of Masculinity" (1957). Indeed, we might say that the practical agenda of sex-role discussions in this period was a question of modernization, of how traditional norms could or should be adjusted to the new pressures of the space age by new normative choices made in the face of rapid technological change.

That such modernization need not require any change in gender basics was a given already in the public culture. One has only to think of the exemplars of American modernity in this period—John F. Kennedy, or the "astronauts" of Project Mercury and Project Apollo — and focus on the social position constructed for their wives, a position of conspicuous marginality (Wolfe 1980). In terms of sociological theory, sex-role theory evaded the question of fundamental change in two ways. The first has already been mentioned, the lack of a substantive concept of social structure in sex-role analysis. This meant it had no way of grasping the questions of interest formation or social dynamics within the realm of gender. (When sex-role theory talks about change, as it often does, it is always change in response to pressures from something outside gender itself—from technology or economics or whatever.) Most noticeably lacking from sex-role theory, as from role theory generally, was a sense of the structure of social power.

Second, the sociology of "sex roles" failed to live up to its own promise of providing an account of gender as a pattern of reciprocity, for its treatment of the male role and the female role was not symmetrical. In practice, the female role was — and is — its central concern. Given that the definition of sex roles was constructed (from Parsons on) around a normative standard case, and given that the American public culture defined the normative position of an adult woman as that of a wife-and-mother, the central concern of sex-role analysis in actuality was *woman in the family*. Other topics (e.g., women's paid work) were interpreted in relation to this one (e.g., "women's two roles," the "working mother," "latch-key children"). Even a strenuously realistic study like *Blue-Collar Marriage* is focused on the wives and their accounts of the marriages, and not equally on the husbands.

This had two interconnected consequences. The sociology of sex roles had fallen into the classic trap of "studying down" rather than "studying up," of focusing on the less powerful and taking for granted the activities of groups with power. The question of masculinity was a muted theme in sex-role literature. Of course, most sociology was in actual fact about men, but its authors hardly registered the point. The cast of characters in *The Power Elite*, to take just one example, was almost exclusively male, but Mills did not concern himself with this fact.

Masculinity was a doubly muted theme in sociology, a subfield of a marginalized area. "Women in the family" was not the right stuff on which an ambitious young male sociologist, with his way to make it in an academic scene where grants and promotions were mostly controlled by other men, would be likely to focus. There were more important, more testing, things to do: methodology, modernization, urban, military, political, comparative. So sex-role research, despite the aura of Parsons, remained an academic backwater. And a backwater that men avoided. Like the "child development" field in psychology, and for much the same cultural reasons, "sex-role" research became an area of concentration for women.

This was shortly to have dramatic consequences, but the stimulus to change came from outside academic social science. The advent of "second-wave" feminism and gay liberation at the end of the 1960s not only put sexual politics vehemently on the public agenda, it also changed the terms in which the issue was discussed. The moment of change can be seen exactly. Friedan's *The Feminine Mystique* was still about women-in-the-(bourgeois)-family, still about norms and expectations. That is to say, it was within the conceptual envelope of sex-role theory — even if it was articulating discontents that pushed at the limits of this envelope. Millett's *Sexual Politics*, Firestone's *The Dialectic of Sex*, Morgan's *Sisterhood Is Powerful*, Altman's *Homosexual: Oppression and Liberation*, all published within a couple of years of each other at the beginning of the 1970s, were about power. All stood outside the framework of sex-role theory — though it took some time for this to register.

The concept of "patriarchy" came to sum up the feminist (though not the gay) emphasis on power. It stood for the observation that men were socially dominant and women socially subordinated, that this was a matter of social arrangements — an institutionalized subordination, not an emanation of natural differ- ence — and that it was an extremely pervasive institutional arrangement, in different spheres of society, in different societies, and in different periods of history. These facts proved to be spectacular examples of the things-everybody- knows-but-nobody-noticed, and almost as soon as pointed out they were unde- niable. By the time conservative men made serious efforts to retrieve the ideology of naturalness, they were arguing against a trend: Goldberg's *The Inevitability of Patriarchy* (1973), for instance, already had the flavor of a rearguard action.

This is not to say that a grand theory of patriarchy suddenly appeared and swept all before it; on the contrary. The *concept* of patriarchy was easy to state, but a *theory* of patriarchy, an account of its workings as a social structure, proved surprisingly hard to develop. The most sustained and impressive attempt to do so was the work of socialist feminists in Britain, especially Mitchell. Her *Woman's Estate* (1971) was the most sociological of the first crop of women's liberation texts, and her *Psychoanalysis and Feminism* (1975) was the most sophisticated structuralist attempt to theorize patriarchy. On one line of thought, "patriarchy" was theorized as the structure of the ideological realm, "class" being the structure of production. On another line, patriarchy was seen as a phenomenon of domestic life (an idea derived from sex-role theory's focus on women-in-the-family), and a "political economy of housework" emerged, focusing on the way women's subordination was functional to the economic interests of capital. In both lines of argument, patriarchy survived through history because it secured the reproduction of the relations of production. Already, in an eerie way, the theory of patriarchy was following the course of sex-role theory, shrinking into a restricted — and subordinated — place in a more comprehensive social theory. By the end of the 1970s, Marxist feminists themselves were alarmed by what was happening (Hartmann 1979).

Another strand of feminism cut the connection and steered off in a different direction from socialist social theory. Here the transhistorical character of patriarchy was emphasized, and it was pictured as a structure of domination pure and simple. Though this also happened in other parts of the world, American feminism led the move and provided its most prominent theorists, such as Daly (1978) and Dworkin (1981). But as this development unfolded, a strange reversal became apparent (traced in Eisenstein 1984, and Willis 1984). An emphasis on sexual "difference," on men's violence, on women's mothering, and on universal patriarchy, led away from a concern with social structure and the issue of social inequality, back to a kind of essentialism. Whatever its language, in practice much of this was indistinguishable from biological deter- minism. And though it satisfied the need for a movement rhetoric for feminism, it provided no grip on the interplay between gender and class, or between gender and ethnicity, that were increasingly important *practical* concerns of feminism.

By the early 1980s, the main attempts to construct a coherent theory of patriarchy had failed. The public face of feminism was increasingly provided by a discourse of sexual difference that was disconnected from issues of political economy and social structure (Segal 1987). The spectacular growth of American academic research on women (and, to a lesser extent, on masculinity) was framed not by a developing feminist theory of power, still less by the alliance of feminism and gay liberation foreshadowed around 1970, but by a residual sex-role theory and by the concept of "women's studies."

The popularity of the "women's studies" framework is often taken as a measure of the strength of feminism. Certainly it has been the vehicle for a great deal of feminist work and has sustained a feminist presence in academia even in the darker days of the 1980s. But in terms of social analysis, the concept of "women's studies" is a measure of the marginalization of feminism, its inability so far to put the inequalities of sex and the problem of oppression at the top of the agenda in sociology, history, and economics. In effect, the "women's studies" concept allows feminist research to continue in the absence of a social theory of gender.

Nevertheless, over the last fifteen years or so, this work has transformed the factual basis of the analysis of gender. We now have an extensive historiography of the social position of women, which gives substance to the idea of a large-scale social dynamic of gender (e.g., Davidoff and Hall 1987). We have a sociology of income, occupations, and workplaces that provides a picture of the sexual division of labor in industrial societies and some understanding of gender as a dimension of organizations (e.g., Game and Pringle 1983). We have the makings of a social psychology of gender that is sensitive to the construction of femininity and masculinity under conditions of social inequality (e.g., Haug 1987). I have cited British, Australian, and German instances of this work to indicate that the movement of thought is international. Given the massive predominance of American higher education in world scholarship, more has been done in the United States; but it is not different in kind.

So far as the sociology of gender has had an impact on social practice in this period, it has not been because of new concepts. Progressive inflections of sex-role theory, as represented in the United States by the liberal feminism of NOW, have had most practical influence. Such ideas have framed "equal opportunity" programs in workplaces and antisexist programs in schools; and this framing is one reason why these programs characteristically fail to do much for working-class women. Social research has fed in facts (e.g., from surveys of the occupational distribution of women, or the "career" choices of children) that professional practitioners wanted but has had little to say either about ultimate purposes or about strategies of social change.

Yet those were the issues broached by the radical theorists of the early 1970s, and the promise can now be made good. The research of the last two decades has transformed the knowledge base: We are no longer guessing about most of the big issues. Some lines of theoretical argument have been tried and found inadequate. We have much clearer criteria for what an adequate social theory of gender would contain. It must deal with the question of bodily difference without falling for biological determinism. It must focus on, and theorize, institutionalized power. It must give an account of other dimensions of gender, notably economic process and emotional relationship. Its domain is the full scope of social process — it must not be a truncated theory. It must deal with gender in its fullness, for instance, being informed by the concerns of gay liberation as well as feminism. It must be capable of illuminating the interplay of gender and class, gender and ethnicity. It should see gender on a global scale and abandon the startling ethnocentrism of most English-language writing about these issues.

That sounds like a tall order; yet constructive theoretical developments are now taking place on all these fronts. I think the most promising overall approach is to bring the theory of gender into relation with the practice-based analysis of social structure, and that is the basis of my own attempts at theoretical synthesis. But I could also point to very significant developments that are using semiotics, discourse theory, and the like under the influence of French poststructuralism.

I am arguing that a historic possibility now exists for a development in social theory that would consolidate the intellectual gains made in the wake of the women's liberation and gay liberation movements and carry through the revolution in the social sciences that these movements call for. Sociology, as the social science that has been most hospitable to the new sexual politics and that makes the largest claims as an integrating science of society, is the most likely academic site for this to occur.

Whether it does occur is another question. Here we have to think about both the sociology of the intelligentsia and the historical conjuncture we are in. I remarked earlier that the construction of the "sex-role" field as a kind of academic "women's work" initially marginalized it but then took on a different significance. The concentration of women in this field became, in the 1970s and 1980s, a basis for the growth of women's studies, for the development of support networks, and for the excitement that was generated both by the sense of exploring new conceptual worlds and by the recognition suddenly being given to a new group of intellectuals. Had the "sex-role" field been as dominated by men as, say, political sociology was in the 1960s, the impact of feminism would have been more muted and the outcome, I suspect, much more conventional. Being outsiders, the new academic feminists were less respectful of disciplinary boundaries, of conventions about talk and teaching, of established hierarchies of prestige (see Bunch 1979).

But the first brave days are gone; there is even talk about living in a "postfeminist" period. I hardly need to remind Americans of what it is like living under an ultraconservative government, or of the impact on educational institutions of the political and religious campaigns of the new right. The strength of conservative sexual ideology has been displayed in the AIDS issue, with a difficult public health problem being quickly transformed in the media into a "gay plague" and among fundamentalists into a display of the wrath of God (Altman 1986). There is a dialectic in sexual politics as much as in class politics, and we are now well acquainted with the moment of negation. There are even fresh-made stereotypes for the researchers: academic feminists as man-eating dykes and their male supporters as quiche-eating wimps, if not faggots.

I jest — but not very merrily. A lot of pressure has built up in the intelligentsia of Western countries against the realization of the opportunity I have just been outlining. The pressures include direct opposition, such as the "moral" campaigns by the religious right (which has attempted to dismantle one university gender studies program in Australia, and I presume has made similar attempts in the United States), and the attacks on equal opportunity programs by the political right. More important within the intelligentsia is the structuring of academic climates of opinion, and research funding priorities, by the global ascendance of economic rationalism. We face demands from both government and business for the social sciences to reorganize themselves around the task of economic recovery and forget the "soft" issues of the 1970s.

Further, it should not be forgotten that, despite two decades of feminism, most senior positions in universities and colleges remain in the hands of men, and most research funding bodies continue to be controlled by men — for most of whom "feminism" represents at best a minor academic interest group. The AIDS crisis excepted, the idea of academic work around issues raised by gays is even more exotic. In short, the space for critical social theory in the world of the late 1980s is not great; and the space for a critical sociology of gender is even narrower.

Yet it can be produced, and parts of it are being produced. If the overall political climate is wintry, the underlying problems remain, and some kind of concern about them is widespread. Feminist writing is still one of the more buoyant areas of the academic book trade. I am not an enthusiast for Foucault's theorizing, but one must acknowledge the wide attention gained by his *The History of Sexuality* (1980) as a sign of the actual need for paradigms in this area. There is a growing attention to the problem of masculinity, which suggests a new willingness to "study up" in relation to gender. (This literature is ambivalent, more often concerned with modernizing masculinity than analyzing dominance; but there is nevertheless a critical sociology of masculinity emerging; Kimmel and Messner 1989.)

It seems unlikely that any one of the groups currently working on the social analysis of gender can sustain its whole promise in the current political and economic climate. The transformation of the field, if it comes, is likely to come from the interplay of a number of projects: liberal feminist reform and the statistical and descriptive research it sponsors; socialist and radical feminist concern with power and the critique of institutions; gay men's and women's investigations of sexuality and of the state; heterosexual men's work on masculinity; and the urge to theorize that can spring up anywhere across this spectrum. Above all, it will come because there is a social and intellectual need for it.

It is easy to think of the sociology of gender as a "new field" within sociology, something that gets added on to the other sections, forums, and themes at an annual conference. It would be quite possible to contain the promise this way. A few specialist journals, a few specialist conferences, someone appointed as the "gender specialist" (or the token feminist) in each department, and the job is done.

The social sciences need better than that. On a wide range of issues, they will remain stultified until they have taken on board the issues of sexual politics and the results of the last two decades' work on them. Social science cannot understand the state, the political economy of advanced capitalism, the nature of class, the process of modernization or the nature of imperialism, the process of socialization, the structure of consciousness or the politics of knowledge, without a full-blooded analysis of gender.

This is a strong claim and I cannot hope to make it good here, though each of the items on this list can be defended in detail. I will try to make the claim plausible in the case of the first item on the list, an issue I have been particularly concerned with recently. (See Franzway, Court, and Connell 1989, for documentation of all the points below.)

The state is one of the key objects of social theory. The class dimension of state power is central in socialist analyses of advanced capitalism; themes of citizenship, rights, and development are familiar in liberal social theory; the structure of the modern state is directly at issue in Weberian accounts of modernity. In none of these theoretical traditions is the dimension of gender explicit, but in all of them it is not far below the surface. The gendered public/private division is implicit in the Marxist distinction of the state from civil society; the "social contract" in the liberal theory of citizenship is implicitly a compact among men (as heads of households); the Weberian model of bureaucracy is a model of a gendered form of organization that presupposes a sexual division of labor.

Similarly, no empirical study of the state can go far without encountering the facts of gender. It is familiar that state elites are almost wholly composed of men, in almost all countries. The gender patterning is highly systematic and goes right through the state structure. A textbook case is the link between sex and salary level among public sector employees in the Australian state I come from, New South Wales (see Table 10.1). There are, in addition to the overall connection of gender with income and rank, clear sectoral distinctions. There are concentrations of men in police, military, and infrastructural sectors, as well as in the state directorate; concentrations of women in certain "service" areas (e.g.,

TABLE 10.1:

Sex and Salary Among NSW State Employees, 1985

Salary	Percentage of Women
$44,601+	6%
$35,201-44,600	8%
$27,001-35,200	14%
$21,101-27,000	18%
$18,601-21,100	30%
$13,701-18,600	42%
up to $13,700	68%

early childhood education, nursing) as well as in occupations such as cleaner and secretary.

The internal structuring of the state revealed by personnel statistics is also found in organizational practice, culture, and ideology. The masculinized ideology of the military apparatus is familiar enough; it becomes obsessive in certain forms (*Rambo*; "the right stuff" among Tom Wolfe's flyer jocks). In a different inflection, it appears in the state directorate too. Those who have followed the cultural history of the American presidency from Kennedy through Johnson and Nixon to Reagan will recognize themes of threatened masculinity in a number of forms. Getting down to brass tacks, the political economy of the welfare state is also gendered. The state structures its welfare services around particular models of the family and thereby creates powerful economic pressures on households. The "feminization of poverty" in recent decades has dramatized a pattern of gender relationships that has always been there. "Social" policy across the board is deeply implicated in the regulation of gender relations.

In these ways, we may say that the state is gender structured and is an agent in sexual politics. Inevitably, the state is also a stake and object of sexual politics. Much of the activity of liberal feminism has been directed either to lobbying or to entering the state apparatus. The long American campaign for the ERA, and the Australian "femocrats," are conspicuous examples of this. Socialist and radical feminism have been more ambivalent about the state but have been quite unable to avoid an engagement with it, through a range of issues from sexual violence to women's employment rights. Gay politics has been centered on relationships with the state, from the first campaigns for homosexual law reform to the current embroilment around AIDS. Nor has the new right, for all its ideology, turned away from the state. Anita Bryant's opening antigay campaign was directed at repealing a local government antidiscrimination ordinance, and many others have followed in her tracks.

We are now at the point where this kind of data, together with theoretical arguments about the state developed by socialist feminists, gays, and radical feminists, can be developed into a substantial analysis of the state as an institutionalization of gender relations and a presence in sexual politics.

I would suggest that a parallel job can now be done for each of the fields of social analysis listed above. The analysis of gender is intellectually in a position to transform the social sciences. Whether the job gets done partly depends on struggles between social forces outside academia. But it will also be a test of the maturity and capacity for critical renewal of the social sciences themselves.

REFERENCES

Altman, D. 1972. *Homosexual: Oppression and Liberation*. Sydney: Angus & Robertson.
———. 1986. *AIDS in the Mind of America*. New York: Anchor.
Bunch, C. 1979. "Feminism and Education." *Quest* 5(1):7-18.
Carrigan, T., R. W. Connell, and J. Lee. 1985. "Toward a New Sociology of Masculinity." *Theory and Society* 14(5):551-604.
Connell, R. W. 1983. *Which Way Is Up?* Sydney: Allen & Unwin.
———. 1987. *Gender and Power*. Stanford, CA: Stanford University Press.
Daly, M. 1978. *Gyn/Ecology*. Boston: Beacon.
Davidoff, L. and C. Hall. 1987. *Family Fortunes*. London: Hutchinson.
Dworkin, A. 1981. *Pornography: Men Possessing Women*. London: Women's Press.
Eisenstein, H. 1984. *Contemporary Feminist Thought*. London: Unwin Paperbacks.
Firestone, S. 1971. *The Dialectic of Sex*. London: Paladin.
Foucault, M. 1980. *The History of Sexuality*. Vol. 1. New York: Vintage.
Franzway, S., D. Court, and R. W. Connell. 1989. *Staking a Claim: Feminism, Bureaucracy and the State*. Sydney: Allen & Unwin.
Friedan, B. 1963. *The Feminine Mystique*. New York: Norton.
Game, A. and R. Pringle. 1983. *Gender at Work*. Sydney: Allen & Unwin.
Giddens, A. 1979. *Central Problems in Social Theory*. London: Macmillan.
Goldberg, S. 1973. *The Inevitability of Patriarchy*. New York: Morrow.
Hacker, H. M. 1957. "The New Burdens of Masculinity." *Marriage and Family Living* 19(3):227-33.
Hartmann, H. 1979. "The Unhappy Marriage of Marxism and Feminism." *Capital and Class* 8:1-33.
Haug, F. 1987. *Sexualization of the Body*. London: Verso.
Kimmel, M. S. and M. A. Messner, eds. 1989. *Men's Lives*. New York: Macmillan.
Komarovsky, M. 1964. *Blue-Collar Marriage*. New York: Vintage.
Maccoby, E. E. and C. N. Jacklin. 1975. *The Psychology of Sex Differences*. Stanford, CA: Stanford University Press.
Millett, K. 1972. *Sexual Politics*. London: Abacus.
Mills, C. W. 1956. *The Power Elite*. New York: Oxford University Press.
Mitchell, J. 1971. *Woman's Estate*. Harmondsworth: Penguin.
———. 1975. *Psychoanalysis and Feminism*. New York: Vintage.
Morgan, R., ed. 1970. *Sisterhood Is Powerful*. New York: Vintage.
Rosenberg, R. 1982. *Beyond Separate Spheres*. New Haven, CT: Yale University Press.
Segal, L. 1987. *Is the Future Female?* London: Virago.
Willis, E. 1984. "Radical Feminism and Feminist Radicalism." Pp. 91-118 in *The 60s Without Apology*, edited by S. Sayres et al. Minneapolis: University of Minnesota Press.
Wolfe, T. 1980. *The Right Stuff*. New York: Bantam.

Part V
Sociology and Its Constituencies

11

The Cultural Contradictions of Teaching Sociology

Paul J. Baker
William C. Rau

This chapter opens with two quandaries. First, the largest and most enduring audience for sociology is undergraduate students. They are the chief source of employment for the profession. Yet there is an ambivalent relationship between sociologists and those who come to hear their message for college credit. We need the students to survive, but they offer negligible opportunities for professional advancement and often are a source of academic embarrassment for the profession. On the local campus, sociology majors are often perceived as inferior students. This perception is confirmed by nationally normed exams that rank sociology majors among the lowest-scoring groups in undergraduate education (Figure 11.1 and Table 11.1). When we reflect on our largest perennial audience, we acknowledge our need for undergraduate students; but, too often, they bring neither intellectual stimulation to individual sociologists nor academic acclaim to the profession.

The tension between dependency and embarrassment is also related to a second quandary. The typical undergraduate sociology program is a poor field in which to receive rigorous training for graduate study. How could an academic discipline that has evolved over the past century reach such a circumstance? Why is there such discontinuity between undergraduate and graduate training in the field of sociology? Why does the undergraduate curriculum seem to have so many thinly constructed courses that minimize intellectual achievement or critical reasoning? We respond to these questions by examining various aspects of the undergraduate sociology curriculum. Our first task is to explore some of the cultural and structural forces that shape most undergraduate sociology programs.

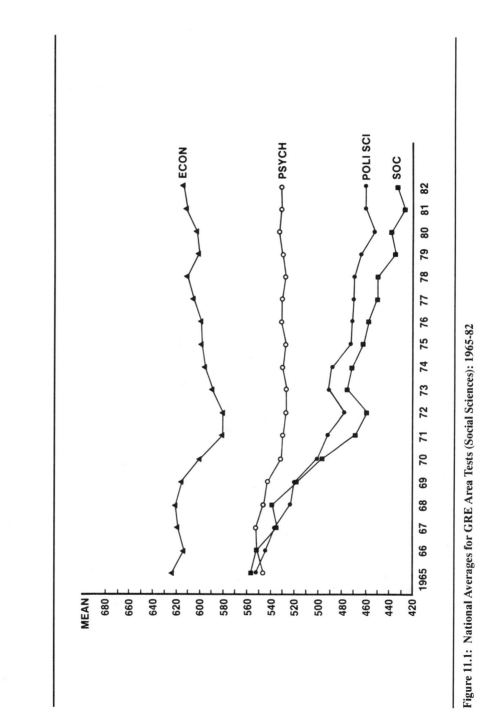

Figure 11.1: National Averages for GRE Area Tests (Social Sciences): 1965-82

TABLE 11.1: Undergraduate Majors Rank Ordered by 1977-82 Test Performances on the GRE, LSAT, and GMAT

RANK	GRE/VERBAL	GRE/ QUANTITATIVE	LSAT	GMAT
1	Philosophy	Physics	Mathematics	Mathematics
2	English	Mathematics	Economics	Philosophy
3	Anthropology	Engineering	Philosophy	Engineering
4	History	Computer Science	Engineering	Chemistry
5	Foreign Language	Chemistry	Chemistry	Economics
6	Physics	Other Science	Other Humanities	English
7	Other Humanities	Economics	Foreign Language	Computer Science
8	Journalism	Biology	English	Foreign Language
9	Political Science	Philosophy	Anthropology	History
10	Biology	Anthropology	Biology	Other Humanities
11	Psychology	Business	Other Science	Biology
12	Chemistry	Psychology	History	Other Science
13	Other Science	Foreign Language	Psychology	Political Science
14	Mathematics	Other Humanities	Journalism	Psychology
15	Art/Music	Political Science	Art/Music	Other Social Science
16	Economics	Other Social Science	Other Social Science	Art/Music
17	Computer Science	History	Political Science	*Sociology*
18	Other Social Science	English	Speech	Education
19	*Sociology*	Art/Music	Business	Business
20	Engineering	Journalism	*Sociology*	
21	Speech	Speech	Education	
22	Social Work	*Sociology*	Social Work	
23	Business	Education		
24	Education	Social Work		

SOURCE: Adleman (n.d., Table F-13).

While we examine various quandaries in the sociology curriculum, we also suggest new directions for improving the academic credibility of undergraduate programs. Further, we offer a framework for deliberation on a central challenge in our discipline: the development of academic programs that provide sustained rigor and intellectual continuity in a loosely ordered curriculum dominated by bread-and-butter courses.

ORGANIZING THE LEFTOVERS: THE SOCIOLOGY CURRICULUM

Sociology was first organized as academic work for students and professors in the 1880s and 1890s. During the first several decades, sociologists struggled against considerable odds to develop a field of study and gain academic respectability. Sociology was driven by the spirit of social amelioration and attempted to make the study of all kinds of social problems academically credible. There was a tendency to add courses to the curriculum around the fringes of economics and the practical concerns of social welfare. While early founders were defensive about organizing the leftovers in the social sciences (Small 1915; Wirth 1947), they kept busy establishing a curriculum and finding jobs for newly trained sociologists, many of whom were converts from economics or the ministry. The founders enjoyed making pronouncements about the "science of society," but the rhetoric of science did not help create a coherent academic discipline or a well-organized curriculum.

In the 1920s and 1930s, the issue of cultural purity for the new field of sociology became more pronounced. The preachers and reformers were dismissed and academic warfare broke out between the positivistic methodologists (George Lundberg, William Ogburn) and antipositivistic theorists (H. Becker, R. MacIver, F. Znaniecki). By the 1950s, sociology had established national networks of methodologists and theorists who had local representatives in virtually all large sociology departments in the country. Two cultural traditions had emerged as competing worldviews for the study of an array of interesting topics that sociology claimed as its teaching domain. Name a topic in the curriculum (marriage and the family, race relations, juvenile delinquency, social inequality) and sociologists would quarrel immediately over the most respectable way to study it.

The debates of the 1940s and 1950s did not lead to any resolution of curricular matters for undergraduates. But everyone seemed to benefit from a famous and fortunate friendship in sociology — Paul Lazersfeld and Robert Merton (Merton 1979). A distinguished methodologist and a distinguished theorist joined forces in the name of middle-range sociology that relied on both theory and methods in the complex task of advancing science. Merton and Lazersfeld ushered in an era of good feelings. In the 1950s and 1960s, sociologists were optimistic about building a stronger academic discipline and their optimism was fueled by an enormous expansion in undergraduate enrollments.

Undergraduate enrollments grew not because of left politics and the political turmoil of the 1960s but because of the rapid expansion of the social service sector. Mushrooming numbers occurred prior to establishment of undergraduate programs in social service fields, especially bachelors programs in social work and criminal justice. During the 1960s, sociology was still the logical choice for many students who liked people or wanted to work with the dispossessed. Much to the students' surprise, they would learn in literature, such as Berger's *Invitation to Sociology*, that sociologists have little interest in working with people. The 1960s can be described as the decade in which sociology continued to advance its cultural purity and unwittingly became further alienated from its undergraduate student constituency.

This contradiction surfaced in the 1970s when the enrollment bubble burst. At the same time, the discipline moved into an era of fragmentation and intensive specialization. The new pluralism featured many methods, theoretical paradigms, areas of inquiry, new vistas of applied work, and arcane quarrels among the experts on such topics as ethnomethodology and the proper way to measure status attainment. With no new intellectual giants to integrate the field, Gouldner's (1970) "coming crisis in sociology" came, would not go away, and now haunts scholars and teachers alike. The resulting incoherence is particularly difficult for college teachers who are expected to present a coherent and stimulating view of sociology to undergraduates.

This brief historical overview suggests that the sociology curriculum has been loosely structured from the beginning. In its American form, sociology has evolved as a cultural entity with three distinct legacies.

(1) The theoretical legacy. Building on the founding giants of the nineteenth and early twentieth centuries (Marx, Weber, Durkheim, Simmel, Mead), several generations of scholars have written a rich literature of commentary on the theorists and theories of sociology.

(2) The methodological legacy. Building on the social survey movement of the progressive era, a variety of attitude studies, important work in demography, and major developments in statistics and computer software, sociologists have acquired a special claim to analyze all kinds of social data that can be quantified. Another group of researchers are responsible for significant advances in qualitative field methods.

(3) The civic legacy of substantive topics. Sociologists have had a long-standing interest in selected topics as distinctly "sociological" for purposes of curricular content — family, crime, delinquency, race relations, community, gender, death and dying, deviance, complex organizations. In each case, a group of sociologists who did important pioneering work can be identified in the family tree of sociology. But another group of scholars from other fields (psychology, anthropology, political science, history, economics, journalism) has contributed to the core literature of the specialized fields in sociology. The subfields are in fact multidisciplinary in character, but sociologists often claim the privilege of teaching them to undergraduates as "sociology."

Given these three legacies, the undergraduate curriculum has been structured around two core professional subcultures — theory and methods — that are loosely grafted onto an array of civic topics. The Venn diagram in Figure 11.2 suggests a pattern of seven distinct combinations of these three legacies.

Figure 11.2 depicts one of several ways to portray the culture of the sociology curriculum. It does not present the persisting ideas of the discipline that often appear in popular and scholarly writings (social inequality and conflict, private troubles and public issues). Nor does it recognize the analytical themes that distinguish sociology from other fields. For example, examination of introductory texts suggests that most key words in the discipline can be classified under one of four global concepts: culture, social self, social structure, social process. These four global terms can be viewed as a shared framework loosely integrating

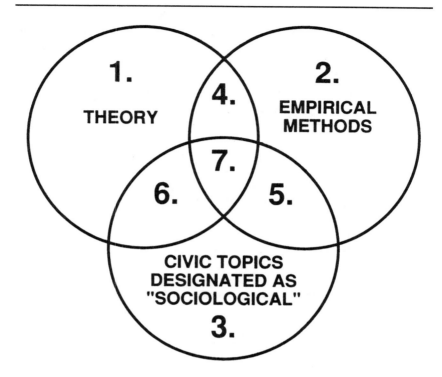

Figure 11.2: Core Components of the Undergraduate Sociology Curriculum and Their Interrelationships

NOTE: (1) Theory = classical writings in paperbacks and text readers; textbooks review contemporary theory. (2) Methods = statistics textbooks and methodology textbooks; statistics and methods are rarely covered in the same book. (3) Civic topics = textbooks for such courses as social problems, family, criminology, race relations; these books are expository and descriptive with little theory and no methods. Also, original literature widely read by civic-minded citizens (Mills 1951, *White Collar*). (4) Theory-methods = formal theory building (Cohen 1980, *Developing Sociological Knowledge*) and areas in which formal theories are being tested empirically (for example, social psychological research and formal models in demography). (5) Methods-civic topics = empirical methods are used to investigate a civic topic. There is minimum theory but significant insightful information in this literature (Whyte 1981, *Street Corner Society*; Farley 1984, *Blacks and Whites*). (6) Theory-civic topics = self-conscious use of theory to analyze a civic topic (Wirth 1938, "Urbanism as a Way of Life"; Gans 1972, "The Positive Functions of Poverty"). (7) Theory-methods-civic topics = middle-range work in which sociologists integrate theory and empirical research to better understand a civic topic (Bellah et al. 1981, *Habits of the Heart*; Perrow 1984, *Normal Accidents*).

the three legacies. Certainly these broad concepts are employed within any of the seven combinations presented in Figure 11.2. Trained sociologists see these global concepts (generally in the background) at work in just about any task of social analysis they undertake. But can students see them at work in the various courses they take? Without a carefully thought-out curriculum, this analytic foundation will remain beyond the grasp of all but a few students who have a passion for searching out the connections.

THE LOCAL CULTURE AND STRUCTURE OF
THE DISCIPLINE: THE SOCIOLOGY DEPARTMENT

Each sociology department represents a unique combination of the three core components of the curriculum. In extreme cases of small departments with one or two sociologists, there is full-time work covering theory, methods, and several civic topics. In the largest departments, some sociologists have the privilege of working inside one or two circles only, with little contact with the rest of the discipline. The most typical pattern requires a bicultural commitment from the college teacher. Theorists are expected to teach one or two topical fields as well as theory; methodologists are expected also to extend their interests to one or two topical areas. There are important exceptions, but, as a rule, theorists do not teach methods and vice versa. In many departments, the theorists and methodologists remain completely separated despite occasional claims that theory and methods are integrated meaningfully in the discipline. In like fashion, some teachers develop topical interests with little or no self-conscious interest in either theory or empirical methods. At one hypothetical extreme, one can imagine professors who teach courses that integrate theory, research, and civic topics as a coherent expression of the discipline. At the other hypothetical extreme, one can envision professors who stay in one of the three subcultures in self-contained isolation. Theory, methods, and substantive civic topics remain mutually exclusive domains of teaching interest. Students shuttle from one course to another with little or no awareness that sociologists have anything in common.

We have suggested some of the patterns that represent the subcultures of sociology. Our next concern is the delivery system that transforms the ideas of the discipline into college courses. The most striking feature of the sociology curriculum is the loosely structured nature of the course offerings. Most courses in the sociology curriculum have no prerequisites other than the nominal and basically irrelevant requirement of introductory sociology. It is a curriculum of free choice. Sociology is packaged as an open-ended cafeteria of survey courses offered in the marketplace of student tastes. Sociology programs have minimal focus for majors and no sense of coherence for nonmajors. How can one account for this organized anarchy?

First, one must recognize the general patterns in which students are recruited to various departments. Some highly vocational fields are structured from day one by a prescribed battery of courses closely knit together by outside credentialing agencies (for example, nursing, accounting). In contrast, most disciplines in the arts and sciences are less prescriptive. But there are fundamental differences among disciplines in the arts and sciences, because some fields offer courses that are defined as "essential knowledge" for students pursuing various career interests (for example, chemistry and biology for premeds, economics for business majors).

Sociology does not offer a set of courses that are essential for any professional field in the United States. And unlike history or political science, it is not considered essential for the broader purposes of citizenship education. Historically, sociology enjoyed a close relationship with social work; and many sociology courses were considered highly desirable, if not essential, for the helping professions. But in the past decade, many sociology prerequisites have been replaced by undergraduate social work courses that cover many of the same ideas. At one time or another, various academic programs have required a particular sociology course for majors; for example, nursing students are sometimes required to take introduction to sociology. These kinds of requirements still exist, but there is no evolving consensus in the academic world about the unique and indispensable contribution sociology courses have to offer. The fundamental issue is that sociology has not generated a body of knowledge that others in the academy see as "essential knowledge" for undergraduate education. Most courses in the sociology program are offered as "optional knowledge" in a wide range of general education courses in the social sciences or as electives in the curriculum at large.

In essence, the sociology curriculum is designed for students who will have limited exposure to the discipline. Most introductory students never take another course in the field; and many others will take two or three courses at most. There is little likelihood of linearity in these courses. Therefore, most sociology teachers introduce the field from "scratch." Because most sociology courses are not attached to other courses in any meaningful linear fashion, many professors often complain about the need to teach some aspect of their field as a self-contained introduction to a given topic.

WHERE SOCIOLOGISTS MEET
UNDERGRADUATES: THE CLASSROOM

Despite the dilemmas that an unstructured curriculum often creates in the classroom, sociologists have failed to generate meaningful empirical literature about this, their own social problem. For most teachers of undergraduates, it remains a private trouble. We appreciate the diversity in American higher education that precludes sweeping generalizations about all sociology classrooms, but some general characteristics can be mentioned about many contemporary teaching environments. It is also important to keep in mind that our observations are made for the purpose of better understanding the intellectual anemia of much undergraduate instruction in sociology. We limit our comments to characteristics of undergraduate students, the typical content of courses, and widely adapted procedures for testing students.

First, most students come to sociology classrooms with a thinly constructed understanding of society. This point has been made repeatedly in recent years and we want to avoid the heedless bashing of students for their lack of knowledge of history, geography, civic affairs, literary works, or the scientific method. The point to be made is that, because students have such limited contextual knowledge of societal affairs, it is often difficult for sociology teachers to know where to begin. Mention "Third World" countries and one-half the students may be lost. The teacher faces a critical moment, "Do I stop here for a minilecture on the cold war, decolonization, and the emergence of First, Second, and Third World countries? Or do I push on and hope that students at least have a general understanding of the topics?"

Most students also have dualistic views of the social world. Their thinking is often concrete and categorical, yet they already appear cynical and difficult to shock with such titilations as NACIREMA (Miner 1956). Once again, the teacher faces choices. "Should I pour on a heavy debunking message and concentrate on the few who seem genuinely interested in my critical views? Or should I be more sympathetic to the worldviews of young people who pretend to be worldly but have little sense for their naïveté?" These questions never seem to be resolved, but they challenge sociology teachers every time they walk back into the classroom.

If teachers face a serious problem with the intellectual paucity of their student audience, the typical reading assignment from mass-marketed textbooks hardly offers encouragement for improving the academic climate of the classroom. Most textbooks in the core courses of sociology (introduction, social problems, family, criminology, juvenile delinquency, social psychology) perpetuate the very problems that disturb many teachers. The repeated complaint that students have poor vocabularies and cannot think critically is often made by teachers who assign college textbooks with a ninth-grade reading level and no consideration for the serious tasks of critical reasoning. Typically such texts are works of encyclopedic exposition in which an author attempts to cover an array of topics along with a hodgepodge of concepts, theories, famous names, statistical graphs, and dozens of marginally appropriate photographs. Textbooks typically follow a standardized formula that is driven by the curse of coverage. And teachers dutifully comply; "If this is Tuesday, it must be social roles." Such literature provides limited opportunities to generate authentic intellectual interest in the themes of sociology.

Our criticism of sociology textbooks is not intended as a blanket indictment. We applaud a small number of high-quality textbooks in the field of sociology, but such books are the exception (Baker 1988). More often, mass-marketed textbooks undermine the integrity of sound teaching by distorting the meaning of sociological ideas and the process of sociological inquiry.

Mass-produced textbooks create a watered-down exposition that oversimplifies complex and subtle ideas. Another problem is the instructor's manual and its supplementary bank of test questions. High-tech publishing firms now provide the test questions on computer discs; teachers can generate exams in a few minutes. Many instructor's manuals also contain a lecture outline for each chapter of the book. Everything is now complete for a teacher-proof educational system: Adopt the book, use the lecture outlines, and create multiple-choice exams from the test bank. From beginning to end, teaching is made convenient and problem-free for the teacher. Textbooks are promoted as trouble-free products, much as one would promote automobiles and refrigerators.

One of the problems with the publishers' technical routinization of the sociology curriculum is the kind of questions it asks of students. Each year, publishers produce thousands of multiple-choice exam questions that are written at low levels of cognitive reasoning (Baker 1981). This proliferation of materials designed to ritualize and reinforce mechanical thinking is a major force contributing to the trivialization of the discipline. Publishers insist that test banks are necessary for sales; "A book without a test bank will never sell." If the publishers are correct in this assertion, then the final responsibility rests with teachers who choose to weigh the worth of the discipline's ideas in small and meaningless fragments. The process of learning sociology becomes little more than a fast lesson in memorizing italicized words.

We argue that the sociology curriculum consists of two cultural centers (theory and methods) surrounded by a variety of topical courses that are rarely offered with depth or sequential linearity. What are the consequences of this system? All too often, teachers of sociology have trivialized the discipline's civic tradition in order to maintain a large audience of nonmajors who take a few sociology courses as electives. This expedient compromise has the unanticipated consequence of producing majors who lack serious understanding of the discipline.

The curriculum shapes the kinds of sociology majors found in colleges and universities. The kinds of majors can vary according to the areas of concentrated study. What are the implications if students choose to emphasize or avoid rigorous work in theory and methods? Figure 11.3 outlines the logical possibilities of educating majors with differing emphasis on theory and research methods. Given the limited capacity of undergraduates to engage in serious social inquiry and the shallow coverage of disparate, self-contained topics as sources of the discipline, the end result frequently is a semiliterate major who lacks depth in a topical area, has little understanding or appreciation of the classical theoretical writings as humanistic literature, and has meager technical skills for sophisticated empirical analysis. Unfortunately, few students are

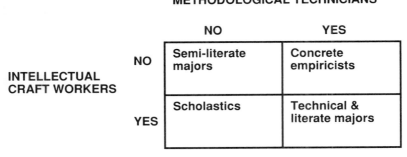

METHODOLOGICAL TECHNICIANS

		NO	YES
	NO	Semi-literate majors	Concrete empiricists
INTELLECTUAL CRAFT WORKERS			
	YES	Scholastics	Technical & literate majors

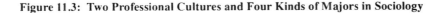

Figure 11.3: Two Professional Cultures and Four Kinds of Majors in Sociology

educated in sociology departments to become both humanistically literate and methodologically sophisticated.

Consequently, most sociology majors can best be described as dilettantes who are ill-prepared for graduate programs in sociology. There is a sharp discontinuity between the consumption of numerous topical undergraduate courses presented in a highly descriptive fashion and the demand for analytical skills to pursue the subtleties of research as well as the philosophical and historical understanding essential for the critical appreciation of sociological theory.

This discontinuity between undergraduate and graduate programs creates a persisting paradox: Many distinguished faculty in doctoral programs complain about the quality of sociology graduate applicants and are pleased to consider nonsociology majors who are better equipped for advanced work. If the teaching of undergraduates rarely leads to the preparation of serious scholars in the field of sociology, what can be said about the intellectual worth of sharing one's field with college students? We respond to this question in the next section.

REFORMULATING THE PROBLEM: BASIC QUESTIONS AND A NORMATIVE FRAMEWORK

We acknowledge one of the fundamental problems facing teachers of under-graduate sociology: the realization that the vast majority of their students have little or no interest in sociology when the course is over. Teachers face an audience that has very little interest in the discipline, yet they must sustain a sense of intellectual integrity about their field in the face of this indifferent and skeptical attitude. Typically there are two ways to respond to such circum-stances: (1) Defend sociology by stressing its claim to academic purity or (2)

		WHAT WE TEACH: CONTENT	
		Disciplinary Knowledge	Knowledge of Everyday Life & Civic Affairs
HOW WE TEACH: THINKING SKILLS OF THE TEACHING-LEARNING PROCESS	High Level Reasoning Skills: Analysis, Synthesis, Application, Evaluation, Dialectics	**A** HIGH CULTURE OF ACADEMIC SOCIOLOGY	**B** CIVIC SOCIOLOGY OF THE WELL INFORMED CITIZEN
	Low Level Reasoning Skills: Memorizing Discrete Items of Information	**C** WATERED DOWN SOCIOLOGY	**D** POP SOCIOLOGY

Figure 11.4: Undergraduate Courses: What We Teach and How We Teach

yield to the pressures of the undergraduate culture and prove the worth of sociology by demonstrating its relevance for everyday affairs. The first option takes the lofty position of the priestly role and makes its claims through esoteric language of the high culture. The second option assumes the common ground of the audience and takes the role of the popular preacher who knows how to speak the vernacular.

Both of these typical responses to the marginal interests of students are unacceptable. They are posited on a false dichotomy of keeping the purity of the discipline versus pandering to the masses. These popular positions often fail to explore various instructional patterns that connect the content of sociology (what we teach) with the reasoning processes expected of students (how we teach). We examine alternative combinations in Figure 11.4.

What we teach. The content of sociology taught to undergraduates is highly diverse. At one end of the continuum, much emphasis is given to teaching those ideas (historical and contemporary) that have been generated within the profession by academic sociologists. Teachers in this tradition want to share the work of major thinkers (Marx, Weber, Durkheim, Goffman), important theories (symbolic interactionism, world systems), and the most recent research findings. They take great interest in teaching an analytical vocabulary and solid content.

At the other end of the continuum, one finds an open-ended invitation to an undisciplined interest in all that is relevant to the everyday world of students: contemporary politics, social movements of all kinds, and the fads and fashions of popular culture. The commitment to relevance is attached to the belief that sociology can relate to anything. Once one learns such ideas as *social roles, deviance,* and *primary groups,* one can apply these terms to an endless list of illustrative cases. Often students become confused with the case materials teachers use and the key concepts being taught with the case materials. The story of Anne Sullivan and Helen Keller overshadows the analytical issues of language, socialization, and social self. In the extreme, the everyday life approach to sociology is little more than an elaborate description of the commonsense world already familiar to the student.

How we teach. A wide range of intellectual traditions (Socrates, Marx, Whitehead, Dewey) has identified the mental processes of critical thinking as being crucial to the full development of human thought. More recently, philosophers, psychologists, and educators have codified this hierarchical commitment as higher-order reasoning in contrast to lower-order reasoning. We are especially indebted to Dewey (1933) for distinguishing between reflective-critical thinking and unreflective-routine thinking. The teachers of sociology conduct their work along this continuum. But the commitment to critical reasoning is more often a statement of ideal intentions rather than of common practice (Baker 1981).

The cross-tabulation of the dichotomies of content ("what we teach") and instructional method ("how we teach") creates four constructed types of the sociology curriculum. Brief comment will be made on these distinct approaches to sharing the discipline with undergraduates.

(A) The high culture of sociology. Cell A represents a strong commitment to emulate graduate school standards in the undergraduate program. The required reading is solidly academic. In theory courses, it might be a study of the classics (Durkheim's *Suicide*). If a textbook is used, it would be highly reputable (Perrow's *Complex Organization*). Students would be expected to demonstrate the same kind of reasoning strategies that experts in the field would use if they responded to essay questions or wrote a paper on a given topic. In some elite schools, a few undergraduate teachers have earned high acclaim for their exemplary work in this tradition (John Pock, Reed College; Robert Merton at Harvard, Tulane, and Columbia; Everett Wilson at Antioch College and UNC-Chapel Hill; Milton Yinger, Oberlin). These master teachers are able to communicate the excitement of sociology to bright undergraduates without sacrificing either the content of the discipline or the rigor of reasoning for its full appreciation.

(B) Civic sociology of the well-informed citizen. Two terms are developed in Cell B. The first term, *civic sociology,* refers to an extensive body of literature

on the critical appraisal of civic affairs that has been written throughout the twentieth century by both sociologists and journalists. Journalistic sociology includes works of scholarship intended for both sociology and the general reading public (E. A. Ross, *Sin and Society*; Mills, *White Collar*; Bellah et al., *Habits of the Heart*). Sociological journalism is written by journalists and appreciated by academic sociologists as well as the general public (J. Riis, *How The Other Half Lives*; W. Lippmann, *Public Opinion*; S. Terkel, *Working*). This literature is highly accessible to college teachers, students, and ordinary citizens who want to be well informed about the society in which they live.

The second term, *the well-informed citizen,* was coined by Alfred Schutz. He offered the following definition:

> The well-informed citizen . . . stands between the ideal type of the expert and that of the man on the street. On the one hand, he neither is, nor aims at being, possessed of expert knowledge; on the other, he does not acquiesce in the fundamental vagueness of a mere recipe knowledge or in the irrationality of his unclarified passions and sentiments. (Schutz 1970, p. 240)

Literature of civic sociology is highly appropriate for "the citizen who aims at being well informed" (Schutz 1970, p. 240). But this literature was never designed for the rote mechanics of multiple-choice exams. It was written for thoughtful deliberation and is ideally suited to cultivate reflective thinking essential for well-informed citizenship. Many service courses taken by non-majors might be considered for Cell B. The accent is on both relevance and rigor.

(C) Watered-down sociology. There are several ways to water down sociology for undergraduates. Perhaps the most common approach is to rely heavily on a mass-marketed textbook with an accompanying support system. "I am Professor Doinglittle who represents Bottomline Publishing House this semester. They provide the book, my lecture outlines, suggested films, and text questions. Your education is in good hands. It has been arranged carefully for maximum coverage of the field in 17 weeks." The formula for coverage in the textbook may include 150 action photos, a dozen portraits of famous sociologists, and 450 sociological terms in the glossary.

(D) Pop sociology. This teaching configuration is driven by the urgency to be relevant without concern for analytical rigor. Priority is given to making sociology interesting to the student. And, in the name of interest, attention turns to descriptive accounts of topics that are currently popular in the media. This transformation of sociology into uncritical journalism is apparent in some of the text readers on the market. The "sociological" works selected by some editors are more likely to be from the field of journalism than sociology (see, for example, *Annual Sociology: 1987-1988*). Yet no effort is made to clarify the distinction between journalism and sociology. And no consideration is given to the important tasks of critical reflection. The irony of the situation is that many

sociologists have strong disdain for journalism, yet teachers often assign reprint materials from *Time, Newsweek, USA Today,* and *Redbook* as "sociology." Students never know the difference.

The constructed types are illustrated easily in sociology classrooms and publisher's exhibits at sociology meetings. Our concern in this chapter is not to verify the types empirically but to see them as a way to redesign the sociology curriculum in order to overcome the current cultural contradictions that face many teachers of sociology. This leads to our concluding section on designing the curriculum.

RESOLVING THE CULTURAL CONTRADICTION
THROUGH CRITICAL THINKING

We conclude this chapter with suggestions for redesigning the curriculum. Our recommendations are guided by David Perkins's concept of design. According to Perkins (1986, p. 36), "A design refers to a structure adapted to a purpose". The design question that follows from Perkins's definition concerns the extent to which the purposes of the curriculum are aligned to appropriate structures.

The question of design begins with purpose. And questions about redesigning the sociology curriculum begin with the acknowledgment that sociologists often face a dual audience with two seemingly contradictory purposes: (1) preparing majors for further study in the discipline and (2) providing ideas and factual information to students who have no intention of becoming sociologists. How can the sociology teacher help some students become experts while sharing expert information and abstract theories with other students who do not want to be experts? How can the same structure serve such differing purposes? We believe the answer lies in a reexamination of the central meaning of sociology: an intellectual institution of social reflection. To write sociology books is to help readers think about their society. In like fashion, to teach sociology is to help students think about their society. The act of scholarship in writing sociology should serve the same central purpose as the act of teaching sociology.

The fundamental purpose of sociology is to help all kinds of people (fellow experts, policymakers, fledgling graduate students, novice undergraduates, well-informed citizens) gain a critical understanding of the society in which they live. This premise has been expressed by several sociologists for several decades. Lynd (1939) asked the question, *Knowledge for What?* And Mills (1959) saw a promising answer in the *Sociological Imagination.* Gouldner (1970) argued that sociology must be reflexive. In Janowitz's (1972) terms, the purpose of sociology is best served through a commitment to enlightenment. Shils (1980) expressed similar views in his essay "The Calling of Sociology." Stanley warns that contemporary technological mystification "must be met with social criticism" (1979, p. 250). And, finally, Bellah et al. (1985) have expressed the need for renewing the enlightenment tradition of sociology as thoughtful "public conversation." These scholars and many others recognize the close relationship between sociology and public discourse about numerous social issues. Sociology is one of the public institutions dedicated to open debate in a democratic society.

Sociology is part of the enlightenment tradition. In our judgment, the great literature of the discipline since the writings of Tocqueville and Marx has been works of critical reasoning about the structures and processes of modern society. In terms of the Venn diagram in Figure 11.2, this literature is most likely to be found when civic topics are joined to theory or research or both. The purpose of teaching sociology is to share and cultivate the same kinds of critical reasoning found in the distinguished writings of the discipline. Not all sociological literature is adaptive to the purposes of undergraduate teaching. In recent years, some aspects of sociology have become increasingly technical and esoteric. The discipline seems designed only for experts who want to communicate among themselves; sociology seems to be drifting into specialized communities of expertise. Put differently, the three legacies of Figure 11.2 are becoming specialized enclaves. It becomes increasingly difficult for undergraduates to receive a coherent sense of the discipline when theory, methods, and civic topics become uncoupled. Undergraduate teachers have no control over these macro-cultural trends, but they must renew their own academic work by identifying sociological literature that remains true to the enlightenment tradition. They must also create opportunities for undergraduates to conduct research on topics that are meaningful to the interests of a well-informed citizenry.

If the purpose of teaching sociology is to foster critical reasoning about all things social, the next task is to determine appropriate structures for this work. This requires careful attention to structuring all learning experiences around various aspects of critical thinking. It is not a question of whether critical reasoning should be used in some situations and not in others. To the contrary, all teaching that does not foster critical reasoning is inappropriate to the field of sociology. Just as Shakespeare must be appreciated on the stage, sociology must be studied as thoughtful public conversation. One can never start to appreciate sociology by memorizing watered-down fragments of information; the literature was never written to be disembodied in such fashion.

The framework for designing the sociology curriculum is found in Figure 11.4. The purpose of sociology as enlightenment cannot be met in the instructional configurations found in Cell C (watered-down sociology) or Cell D (pop sociology). Cell C promises academic purity without rigor; Cell D promises relevance without rigor. Cell A (high culture and academic sociology) and Cell B (civic sociology of the well-informed citizen) provide the meaningful points of departure for the reconstruction of the sociology curriculum. The crucial issue is determining the kinds of critical thinking tasks that are appropriate for the full range of courses found in the four-year college curriculum.

Designing the sociology curriculum around crucial critical thinking tasks is a big order. The work has hardly begun. One helpful building block in the reconstruction of the undergraduate program is the concept of "thinking frames" (Perkins 1987). David Perkins (1987, p. 47) defines the thinking frame as "a guide to organizing and supporting thought processes." Thinking frames include a wide range of instructional tactics that have been used to sharpen reasoning processes, for example, Aristotle's enumeration of syllogistic forms, Dewey's problem-solving cycle, methodologists' basic rules for interpreting cross-tabulated data, and C. W. Mills's distinction between private troubles and public issues. Thinking frames do not provide the content of one's thoughts but, instead, how to organize one's thoughts in order to study the content.

Sociologists must select and develop appropriate thinking frames for different sociology courses. For those courses in the curriculum that are designed for well-informed citizenship (Cell B), we argue for the self-conscious development of thinking frames that can be applied to civic sociology. Accepting Gans's (1979) assertion that sociology and journalism have common interests in looking at American society, we offer a corollary to this assertion: Literature in both fields can be studied with the same critical frames by teachers and students who are interested in the substantive topics of the civic culture traditionally found in the sociology curriculum. The same critical frames can be used because both fields share the same general rules of civic discourse: rules of evidence, causal inference, definition, and logical consistency. Baker and Anderson (1987) have developed a systematic set of thinking frames that allow critical assessment of sociological journalism and journalistic sociology. This critical thinking model is only one of many thinking frames that have been developed for sociological instruction (Toulmin et al. 1979; Logan 1976).

The kinds of thinking frames used in advanced sociology courses (Cell A, high culture of academic sociology) are more self-consciously sociological. For example, students in a theory class might be asked to read a novel and interpret it from the perspectives of symbolic interactionism, functionalism, and conflict theory. Students in complex organizations might read Bolman and Deal's *Understanding and Managing Modern Organizations*. They would study the four frames of the book: structural approach, human resources, political, and symbolic. Once they have acquired and internalized these frames, they might transfer their understanding to case materials or a field investigation from a local organization where they have gained firsthand information. In methods courses, numerous opportunities exist to apply various statistical approaches (which can be used as thinking frames) to all kinds of data sets (Babbie 1989).

The emphasis on critical thinking is appropriate for students at all levels of instruction and can be taught with varying degrees of technical sophistication. It is, therefore, possible to challenge many of the weak students who currently major in sociology with sterner stuff. At the same time, the accent on critical thinking can appeal to stronger students who will take sociology more seriously as a thoughtful field of study. In short, teaching sociology through strategies of critical reasoning fosters a sense of excellence for both students and teachers at all levels of the undergraduate curriculum.

Purpose and structure are integrated through the self-conscious use of appropriate thinking frames that enable students to become active learners in a wide variety of settings: (1) new capacities to become critical consumers of social information, (2) new capacities to transfer various theoretical paradigms into insightful understanding of complex social issues, and (3) new capacities to use the tools of research to transform raw data into meaningful social information. Entry-level courses (introduction, social problems, American society) that are well designed for critical thinking can serve both majors and nonmajors with full integrity. Because the larger goal of well-informed citizenship is part of the enlightenment tradition, basic courses provide a meaningful foundation for majors and a valuable educational experience for nonmajors. There is no necessary discontinuity between Cells A and B of Figure 11.4. The curriculum can be seen as a graduated continuum that begins with the reflective literature of civic sociology and moves toward a deeper understanding of the specialized fields of the discipline. But the basic commitment to better understanding the structures and processes of the complex social order will not change.

We conclude this chapter on an optimistic note. There is no need to accept the current cultural contradictions as inevitable. We can do something about our current state of affairs if we have the vision and commitment to teach large numbers of nonmajors to be well-informed citizens as well as the small minority of majors who want to be the next generation of professional sociologists.

REFERENCES

Adelman, Clifford. 1987. *Annual Sociology 1988-1989*. Guilford, CT: Dushkin.
———. n.d. *The Standardized Test Score of College Graduates, 1964-1982*. Washington, DC: National Institute of Education.
Babbie, Earl. 1989. *The Practice of Social Research*. Belmont, CA: Wadsworth.
Baker, Paul. 1981. "Learning Sociology and Assessing Critical Thinking." *Teaching Sociology* 8:325-63.
———. 1988. "Sociology Textbooks: Managing Clones or Writing Works of Distinction." *Teaching Sociology* 16:381-83.
Baker, Paul and Louis Anderson. 1987. *Social Problems: A Critical Thinking Approach*. Belmont, CA: Wadsworth.
Bellah, Robert, Richard Madsen, William Sullivan, Ann Swidler, and Steven Tipton. 1981. *Habits of the Heart*. New York: Harper & Row.
Berger, Peter. 1963. *Invitation to Sociology*. New York: Doubleday.
Bolman, Lee and Terrance Deal. 1985. *Understanding and Managing Modern Organizations*. San Francisco: Jossey-Bass.
Cohen, Bernard. 1980. *Developing Sociological Knowledge*. Englewood Cliffs, NJ: Prentice-Hall.
Dewey, John. 1933. *How We Think*. Chicago: Henry Regnery.
Durkheim, Émile. [1897] 1966. *Suicide*. New York: Free Press.

Farley, Reynolds. 1984. Blacks and Whites. Cambridge, MA: Harvard University Press.

Gans, Herbert. 1972. "The Positive Functions of Poverty." American Journal of Sociology 78:275-89.

————. 1979. Deciding What's News. New York: Vintage.

Gouldner, Alvin. 1970. The Coming Crisis in Western Sociology. New York: Basic Books.

Janowitz, Morris. 1972. "Professionalization of Sociology." American Journal of Sociology 78:105-35.

Lippmann, Walter. 1922. Public Opinion. New York: Macmillan.

Logan, Charles. 1976. "Do Sociologists Teach Students to Think Critically?" Teaching Sociology 4:29-48.

Lynd, Robert. 1939. Knowledge for What? Princeton, NJ: Princeton University Press.

Merton, Robert K. 1979. "Remembering Paul Lazersfeld." Pp. 19-22 in Qualitative and Quantitative Social Research, edited by Robert K. Merton, James S. Coleman, and Peter Rossi. New York: Free Press.

Mills, C. Wright. 1951. White Collar. New York: Oxford University Press.

————. 1959. Sociological Imagination. New York: Oxford University Press.

Miner, Horace. 1956. "Body Ritual of the Nacirema." American Anthropologist 58:503-7.

Perkins, David. 1986. Knowledge as Design. Hillsdale, NJ: Lawrence Erlbaum.

————. 1987. "Thinking Frames: An Integrative Perspective on Teaching Cognitive Skills." Pp. 41-61 in Teaching Thinking Skills: Theory and Practice, edited by Joan Boykoff Baron and Robert Sternberg. New York: Freeman.

Perrow, Charles. 1979. Complex Organizations: A Critical Essay. Glenview, IL: Scott, Foresman.

————. 1984. Normal Accidents. New York: Basic Books.

Riis, Jacob. 1957. How the Other Half Lives. New York: Sagamore.

Ross, E. A. 1907. Sin and Society. New York: Houghton Mifflin.

Schutz, Alfred. 1970. On Phenomenology and Social Relations. Chicago: University of Chicago Press.

Shils, Edward. 1980. The Calling of Sociology and Other Essays. Chicago: University of Chicago Press.

Small, A. W. 1915. "Fifty Years of Sociology in the United States." American Journal of Sociology 21:721-864.

Stanley, Manfred. 1978. The Technological Conscience. Chicago: University of Chicago Press.

Terkel, Studs. 1972. Working. New York: Avon.

Toulmin, Stephen, Richard Rieke, and Allan Janik. 1979. An Introduction to Reasoning. New York: Macmillan.

Whyte, William. 1981. Street Corner Society. Chicago: University of Chicago Press.

Wirth, Louis. 1938. "Urbanism as a Way of Life." American Journal of Sociology 44:1-24.

————. 1947. "American Sociology – 1915-47." American Journal of Sociology. Index to Volumes 1-52, pp. 273-81.

12

Organizations and Sociology

Marshall W. Meyer

This chapter focuses upon the role of organization studies in sociology rather than the internal organization of sociology, but it carries some important implications for the latter. The specific question I wish to address is whether sociology is about to lose organization studies and, if so, why. I think there is some danger that organizations will become disconnected from sociology, despite its prominence in several major sociology departments and in the major sociological journals. The loss would not be a unique occurrence. In a recent article, James Coleman (1987) notes the decline of two key schools of socio-logical thought — the Chicago school, which focused on urban problems during the 1920s and 1930s, and the Columbia school, which focused on the study of public opinion and the mass media during the 1940s and early 1950s. Coleman's point, which I do not dispute, is that the rise and decline of these schools is due in some measure to the rise and decline of the problems they addressed: urban issues in the case of the Chicago school and the development of mass media and their implications for democratic governance in the case of the Columbia school. Coleman argues further that absent a core set of problems relevant to contem-porary society, and hence absent research carrying implications for policy, sociology faces a danger, like eighteenth-century natural philosophy, of "having its more vital areas peel off, one by one, with the remaining core becoming defined as 'that in which no one else is interested' " (1987, p. 132).

The decline of the Chicago and Columbia schools of sociology notwithstand-ing, the study of urban problems and of mass communications have not disap-peared from the academic landscape. They have merely diffused beyond the

AUTHOR'S NOTE: *This chapter was originally an address to the thematic session "Sociology and Its Constituencies" at the 1988 meetings of the American Sociological Association. Many thanks to Jitendra Singh and Lynne Zucker for their comments on earlier drafts. They are forgiven for any flaws remaining in the text.*

borders of sociology, their sociological origins all but forgotten in many instances. Specialized institutions of social work, urban design, and criminology now address urban problems; specialized schools of communication and, importantly, marketing departments in business schools, teach material formerly in the exclusive domain of public opinion and mass communication. Some, to be sure, would argue that urban studies and mass communication remain vital within sociology. There are sociologists doing outstanding work in both fields. Diana Crane's co-citation analysis (1988), however, shows mass media studies to be unconnected to any of the three core specialties of sociology identified as of 1987. Urban sociology remains within one of these core specialties (which otherwise consists of class issues from a Marxist perspective, social movements, industrialization, and revolution), but the urban subfield is classified as "low interdisciplinary sociology" by Crane because sociology constituted less than a third of its citing sources.

The same co-citation analysis suggests that the field of organizations, like mass communication, may already have exited sociology. Organizations, according to Crane (1988, p. 22), does "not appear on the basis of citation data to be even peripherally related to the sociology literature." Given the weakening intellectual ties of organizations to sociology, which I shall illustrate presently, and given the history of exit, or partial exit, of other subfields from the discipline, the exit of organizations from sociology would not be surprising. I do not advocate this outcome, but I think it likely unless we do something about it.

No field of inquiry, I submit, could be more closely tied to core sociological concerns and more policy relevant than the study of organizations. In the last decade, the organizational landscape of the United States has changed dramatically. The most important change has been the emergence of an active market for mergers and acquisitions of large business firms. This has created organizational volatility and vulnerability of unprecedented proportions, as documented by Paul Hirsch (1987). A second change, of almost equal importance, has occurred in organizational labor markets. Employment is high. But many new jobs are less than full-time and/or are temporary. Most new employment is in the service sector, which is notoriously labile. And contractual relationships have displaced employment relationships in many instances (Pfeffer and Baron 1986). The M&A market has done for managers what the decline of permanent employment in core industries has done for workers: attachment to organizations has been weakened. To use David Riesman's language, people now tend to view their ties to organizations as transactional (what's in it for me — today?) rather than institutional (what future can we build together?). This may or may not be a good thing. What we think we know about recent Japanese experience suggests that the transactional model does not promote competitiveness in international markets. In almost all respects, core Japanese firms are more stable than their U.S. counterparts. The Japanese M&A market is weak to nonexistent (in part because firms are financed through debt rather than equity shares).

Moreover, employment relationships as well as customer and supplier relations in Japan are normally long term. Sociologists, I believe, should be thinking about problems of this magnitude but are reluctant to do so.

I shall approach the relationship of organizations to sociology from several perspectives. The first argument I shall pursue is that the basic intellectual stance of sociology (or, at least, contemporary sociology) renders the study of organizations suspect. Organizational studies are, therefore, rendered marginal to sociology and vulnerable to inroads from other disciplines, especially economics. A second argument is that organizational sociology is partly to blame for the separation of organizations from sociology. Organizational sociologists have become somewhat solipsistic — we have a language that no one else, our sociological colleagues included, understands — and narrow in their focus. A third argument is that the study of organizations needs sociology, and very badly. Sociology is needed to supply research talent to the field of organizations. But this kind of talent is not likely to be cultivated in settings where there is hostility toward business (particularly big business), bureaucracy, and concepts of utility maximization.

THE INTELLECTUAL STANCE OF SOCIOLOGY

Let me start with the intellectual stance of sociology — to the extent that one can speak of sociology having a single intellectual stance — and its relationship to organizations. I believe that several elements are common to the various perspectives on social life represented in sociology. These elements include what Peter Berger (1963) calls the debunking motif, sympathy if not outright advocacy for the underdog, and a preference for structural as opposed to volitional explanations for action. This intellectual stance, I shall argue, renders organizations peripheral to sociology. It also renders sociology of marginal significance to the study of organizations. Contemporary thinking about organizations assumes rather than debunks rationality. It also takes for granted ownership and managerial prerogatives, often (I think too often — see below) ignoring the preferences of other actors in organizations. And it emphasizes strategic choice rather than structural constraint. Many sociologists find contemporary thinking about organizations to have too much of a managerial cast. And organization theorists often find sociologists reluctant to address outcomes that are of interest to managers, and performance and survival outcomes in particular.

The Debunking Motif

Sociologists take pride in exposing unexpected or unanticipated patterns of action, especially when these patterns run counter to official stories. Concepts of unanticipated consequences and dysfunction, articulated most eloquently by Merton (1958), are as central as any to our vocabulary. These concepts were applied with some success to organizations through the early 1960s. The case studies of bureaucracy conducted by Merton's students exemplify applications of the debunking motif: Selznick's (1957) notion of informal co-optation, Gouldner's (1954) discussion of mock bureaucracy, and Crozier's (1964) statement of the vicious circle of bureaucratic dysfunctions powerfully convey the message that not all organizations operate according to plan.

From the mid-1960s onward, however, ideas about unanticipated consequences and dysfunction have served organizational sociology less well. The utility of these concepts declined as the focus of organizational studies shifted from the behavior of the individual persons in organizational settings to whole organizations and as quantitative methods displaced case analyses. Whereas it was possible and plausible to identify dysfunctional behavior of individual persons and groups within organizations, particularly when dysfunction took the form of resistance to official goals, dysfunctional *organizational* patterns were not so easily described by sociologists. For this reason, a rather remarkable intellectual shift occurred: Whereas through the 1950s and mid-1960s, organizational sociology was skeptical to agnostic with respect to the efficiency properties of organizations, from the mid-1960s through the late 1970s, it reversed position and assumed extant organizational patterns to be on balance more efficient than inefficient (or dysfunctional). This shift was signaled in the theoretical work of Thompson (1967) as well as in the empirical studies of Lawrence and Lorsch (1967), Blau and his colleagues (see Blau, 1970), and the work of the Aston group of researchers. Blau, for example, explained persistent effects of size on structural differentiation largely in efficiency terms (e.g., differentiation permits economies of scale in administration to be realized).

I want to point out that the language of economics is much more supple (if not more precise) than sociology in dealing with efficiency outcomes in organizations, partly because economists have been discussing efficiency much longer than sociologists. Economists make two seemingly inconsistent assumptions about efficiency in organizational settings. On the one hand, economics in general has a bias toward efficiency whereas sociology in general does not (only recent organizational sociology does). Extant patterns and, therefore, extant organizations nowadays are believed efficient. Interestingly, economists have not always treated organizations as efficient. Traditional (i.e., pretransaction-cost) industrial organization economics held that organizations were aberrations in markets, that industry structure, by which was meant concentration, determined the conduct and performance of individual firms. This view has been challenged successfully by Ronald Coase and Oliver Williamson, who developed the language of transaction-cost economics to transform a monopoly explanation of organization into an efficiency explanation, bringing organizations within the ambit of orthodox neoclassical economics. (See especially

Williamson 1985, chap. 6.) On the other hand, economics attributes departures from the ideal of efficient conduct to utility-maximizing behavior on the part of individuals. The basic thrust of agency theory (Jensen and Meckling 1976) is that owners cannot expect managers always to act in the interest of owners. Stratagems ranging from the extraction of "rents" of office to manipulation of short-term profitability benefit managers at the expense of their employers. Sociology has yet to challenge this two-edged sword of economic reasoning — extant organizations are efficient, yet utility maximization on the part of individuals yields inefficient conduct on the part of organizations. Sociologists could exploit this inconsistency in economics, but a much more differentiated view of organizations as amalgams of diverse interests will be required. In particular, we should ask what groups or interests within organizations establish efficiency criteria and subsequently pursue these efficiency outcomes, what groups or interests pursue other outcomes, and what conditions shift the balance of power in favor or in opposition to efficiency outcomes? Lynne Zucker and I have explored organizations as collections of interests in *Permanently Failing Organizations* (Meyer and Zucker 1989). We argue that interests are more likely to diverge under conditions of low performance than when performance is high; specifically, we argue that sustained low performance, an impossibility under the assumption that extant organizations are efficient, occurs when dependent actors, who prefer maintenance of existing organizational patterns to performance outcomes, effectively challenge managerial initiatives intended to restore high performance. For the most part, however, sociologists have preferred not to exploit the obvious contradictions of economic reasoning. Quite the opposite, rather than studying organizations more microscopically in order to unravel the efficiency assumptions with which economics is laden, we have mimicked economists and, indeed, outdone them by studying ever-larger aggregates, such as organizational populations and entire industries. Advantage economists.

Sympathy (Read Advocacy) for the Underdog

Having largely abandoned the debunking motif, possibly to its detriment, the field of organizations is further removed from sociology by sociology's orientation to issues of poverty, gender, race, crime, revolution, and the like. These are not unimportant problems. But, for the most part, they are problems affecting the underdogs, the dispossessed, and sometimes the pariahs of society. Not so with organizational studies. Contemporary organizations, especially the large ones, are not normally creatures of the dispossessed. When they are, we call them social movements and, if large enough, revolutionary forces. Instead, organizations are creatures of capitalism or of the state. As such, their purposes derive from the interests of capital or the state, the elites rather than the underdogs in modern societies. I hasten to add that the interests of capitalism and the state are not always the same. As Richard Hofstadter (1955) points out, the regulatory apparatus of the federal government is mainly a product of antibusiness sentiment, sentiment driven by the interest of the middle classes rather than the lower classes.

The opposition of interests between underdogs and elites may be sufficient to set organizational studies apart from the intellectual stance shared by large numbers of sociologists. Given its identification with underdogs, sociology at its best questions the obvious. It asks why, for example, housewives still outnumber househusbands. Contemporary organizational research does not do this. It takes for granted official organizational goals. Sometimes organizational research asks unabashedly how best to achieve these goals; sometimes it explores why goals are subverted; and sometimes it merely ignores official goals. But non-Marxist organizational research rarely questions goals. And even when organizational researchers have attempted to take a critical stance, they have succeeded only partially. The study of directorial interlocks is illustrative. Interlocking has increased over time, especially in core industries, but there is little strong evidence that direction of the economy lies in the hands of a small coordinated elite. To paraphrase Beth Mintz and Michael Schwartz (1985), bank hegemony is exercised only indirectly.

I want to point out that organizations have not always operated in the interests of elites. As Reinhard Bendix (1956), Vernon Dibble (1965), and Arthur Stinchcombe (1985) have pointed out, the principles of stratification and of organization have historically been in competition with one another. Organizations, of course, have won the competition, but only after a protracted struggle against traditional elites whose power derived from inherited wealth. Only recently have organizational rewards (salary and other forms of compensation) risen to the point that substantial wealth could be accumulated from them. Thirty years ago, C. Wright Mills (1955) observed that corporate executives were not among the very rich; only ten years ago, few if any CEOs earned $1 million a year. Given this historical transformation, the continued preeminence of organizations as sources of wealth and power cannot be guaranteed. Developments sketched at the beginning of this chapter — the emergence of an active M&A market, the separation of careers from organizations — suggest that new elites are already challenging entrenched organizational elites. How serious this challenge is remains to be seen.

A Preference for Structural Explanation

Alongside identification with the underdog, the core of modern sociology contains a preference for structural as opposed to volitional or agency explanations for behavior. Sociologists are weaned on Durkheim (1951), who taught that suicide is due to suicidogenic currents at the societal level rather than individual predilection or pathology. Structural determination permeates other subfields of sociology, sometimes providing convenient targets for conservative critics of the discipline. James Q. Wilson and Richard Herrnstein (1985) have argued that the kinds of causal explanations used by criminologists have all but absolved criminals of responsibility for their acts.

The theme of structural constraint is still prevalent in organizational theory. The maintained hypothesis is still environmental determination of organizations. But this hypothesis is losing influence, in part because ideas about environmental determination have been stretched beyond reasonable limits. More important, there is a rapidly growing field of organizational strategy, which assumes organizations to be volitional rather than passive, shaping rather than shaped by their environments. The study of organizational strategy has moved rapidly, paralleling developments in business firms from a focus on product strategy to diversification strategy to survival strategies in the global marketplace (Bowman 1988). The field of strategy lacks the strong theoretical foundation of organizational sociology and is often criticized on that account. But it opens possibilities that are not available under the older assumptions of structural or environmental constraint.

SOLIPSISM IN ORGANIZATIONAL SOCIOLOGY

The foregoing discussion suggests some intellectual currents driving sociology and organization studies apart. But intellectual currents do not account fully for the separation of sociology from organizational studies. I believe that a set of interrelated social and political influences, both social and political broadly conceived, have conspired to separate organizational sociology from core sociological concerns. These factors include a surprising concentration of people and resources and, correlatively, the emergence of ideas and language in organizational sociology that are for the most part inaccessible to outsiders.

Organizational sociology has been highly concentrated in the United States, until recent years almost entirely on the West Coast. An affinity of interests brought together a number of organizational sociologists at Stanford and the University of California, Berkeley business school. These people, in turn, generated large grants and large numbers of doctoral and postdoctoral students. The simple demographic facts of concentration may explain why two recent and distinctive schools of organizational sociology, population ecology and institutional theory, originated on the West Coast. Each of these schools offers interesting alternatives to the efficiency assumptions embedded in organizational sociology of the 1960s and 1970s. However, their quest for distinctiveness may have obscured their most important contributions and may, therefore, have contributed to the separation of organization studies from sociology.

Population Ecology

Let us consider, first, organizational population ecology. The population ecologists have been consistently critical of efficiency thinking about organizations and have posed an interesting alternative to it. In their early work, widely cited but not sufficiently understood, both Hannan and Freeman (1977) and Aldrich (1979) distinguished static efficiency from dynamic survival outcomes and argued that the two need not be closely linked. Hannan and Freeman argued, additionally, that the link between efficiency and survival is especially tenuous for generalist organizations in "coarse-grained" environments where change occurs slowly. This alternative to the standard efficiency model has not been pursued sufficiently in research. It should be.

Rather than focusing on differences between efficiency and survival outcomes and the concomitants of both, population ecologists, until recently, have been preoccupied with arguments about inertia in organizations. The initial argument was as follows: Because organizations are inertial and, therefore, resistant to internal change, change in organizations occurs at the population level through processes of death and replacement. Put somewhat differently, a lack of adaptive capacity renders organizations progressively less fit over time; at some point, extant organizations are replaced by new ones whose fit to the environment is greater. This core argument of population ecology seemed inconsistent with many sociologists' understandings of organizations, particularly understandings developed from studies of big business and government, which have always seemed to be remarkably resistant to selection pressures (see Kaufman 1976). But the argument did contain a refutable implication, namely, that organizational inertia in conjunction with changing external circumstances would cause organizational death rates to increase with age. Let me express this somewhat differently. The population ecologists claimed that organizations are essentially nonadaptive. Once formed, they cannot be changed, at least not easily. Environmental changes occur regardless. The logical implication is that the fit of organizations to the environment will diminish over time and that, therefore, death rates of organizations will increase correspondingly with age.

Research conducted by population ecologists has failed to confirm the core argument that organizations were incapable of internal change or adaptation. Most population ecology studies, in fact, did not even gather the data needed to estimate rates of internal change (an exception is Singh, House, and Tucker 1986). This is understandable, given that most, although not all, studies in the population ecology tradition have relied on archival data, which include birth and death dates but normally contain few data on organizational arrangements. However, data on mortality rates were gathered in abundance. These data showed organizational mortality to decrease rather than to increase with age (Freeman, Carroll, and Hannan 1983), inconsistent with declining environment-organization fit, which is the logical implication of the inertia argument and consistent with most sociologists' perceptions of the capacity of organizations, particularly large ones, to resist dissolution. Rather than conceding the point and reworking their model to take account of organizational power or dominance, population ecologists have labeled declining organizational death rates with age as indicative of a "liability of newness," whereby existing organizations are favored over new ones. In a recent theoretical statement, Hannan and Freeman (1984) maintain that selection at the population level rather than adaptation within individual organizations determines organizational forms. But the argument has shifted somewhat. Population ecology now claims that the "liability of newness" is evidence that selection pressures favor organizations that are stable and accountable for their actions and hence organizations exhibiting tendencies *not* to change over time. The environment, in other words, prefers continuity and reliability rather than change in organizations.

To some, the circularity or near circularity of the argument that selection processes favor organizations that tend not to change is an indictment of the entire population ecology subfield of organizational studies. I think this too harsh an assessment. Indeed, some recent research on organizational birth frequencies, as yet unpublished, may help to unravel the mystery of why organizational death rates decline with age. This research shows that the density of organizations at time of birth has subsequent effects on death rates regardless of age: The lower the density of organizations of a given type at the time of formation, the lower their death rates throughout their life spans (Carroll and Hannan 1988). In other words, what was understood earlier as a "liability of newness" may in fact be a first-mover advantage: The earliest and hence the oldest organizations of a given type have the lowest mortality. Somewhat differently, established organizations squeeze out new competitors. This interpretation, if corroborated, would be of some appeal to the wider community of sociologists.

The contributions of organizational population ecology should not be overlooked. The ecological argument offers one of the few sensible alternatives to the economic model of organizations, although I believe that it will ultimately have to be reconciled with economic models. Sociologists cannot overlook organizational performance forever. I also think that the ecologists are recognized as having pioneered the use of methods needed to explore an alternative model. But I also believe that had the population ecologists been more open to conventional sociological thinking, that is, less willing to attribute observed patterns to natural selection and more willing to think of organizations as controlling their environments rather than being controlled by their environments, the significance of their work would have been more apparent to all.

Institutional Theory

Institutional theorists have also been critical of efficiency thinking about organizations. The basic thrust of the institutional school is that some organizations (some, not all) are more like social institutions driven by internal and largely self-confirming logics than rational organizations driven by technological imperatives and performance constraints. Organizations-as-institutions is, therefore, like population ecology, an important alternative to the efficiency model of organizational conduct.

Although there is a high level of activity in institutional theory, there is as yet little agreement among institutionalists as to what their theory is. To be certain, institutional theorists agree as to what the theory is not — it is not the efficiency model. Technical organizations, which are expected to be efficient, are clearly distinguished from institutional organizations, which are relieved from efficiency constraints. As W. Richard Scott (1987) has noted, there are several varieties of institutional theory, ranging from the older Selznickian (1957) notion of organizations as instilled with noneconomic value, to the Berger and Luckmann notion (1967) of organizations as socially constructed realities, to the Meyer and Rowan (1977) idea of organizations as products of rationalized myths, to the more recent conception of organizations as products of highly differentiated institutional logics generated at the societal level.

One problem with diversity in the institutional school is that almost no refutable propositions remain. There is no disconfirming evidence. (By contrast and as noted above, the population ecologists have tended to ignore disconfirming evidence.) Institutional arguments are supported by null correlations of external events with organizational changes (Tolbert and Zucker 1983, who treat a declining correspondence of city characteristics with adoption of civil service procedures as evidence of *increasing* institutionalization of civil service) and by strong correlations (Meyer, Scott, and Strang 1987, who treat correlations of federal Elementary and Secondary Educational Act funds with administrative ratios and costs as evidence of institutional effects). Institutional effects are gauged by cognitive effects (Zucker 1977, who showed cultural persistence to be greater in groups labeled as organizations than in other groups), by shifts in organizational structure (Strang 1987, who showed consolidation of school districts to be a function of state funding), and even by rates of organizational mortality (Singh, House, and Tucker 1986, who found listing in an official community directory and receipt of tax-exempt status to decrease mortality rates of voluntary social service organizations).

But there is an even deeper problem with the institutional approach. The problem lies in the assumption that order exists in institutions (i.e., social templates of what organizations ought to be) but not at all in extant organizations. This is especially the case for the third (organizations as rationalized myth) and fourth (organizations as institutionalized logics) kinds of institutionalization discussed by Scott. Richard Ingersoll's (1988, p. 14) review of Meyer and Rowan's work on schools is quite pointed in this regard:

> When [Meyer and Rowan] do discuss what goes on in classrooms, they emphasize dissensus, diversity and lack of standardization. Their earlier studies looked at how

some teachers had developed more complex structures than others for coordinating class assignments, etc. What they miss, however, are the enormous similarities in classroom culture.

. . . although they acknowledge that teachers both instruct and socialize, the institutionalists assume classroom instruction is the primary goal of school cores. As a result, their emphasis on dissensus, ambiguity, and lack of control all revolve around difficulties of rationalizing such an activity. But what if technical instruction is not the primary task of schools?

Taken-for granted cultural transmission, reproduction, and socialization are ignored. Beginning with Emile Durkheim, continuing through Talcott Parsons and functionalist theories of education and on through to current revisionist and critical theories of schools, the major roles of classroom education have been seen as socialization, instruction, and differentiation . . . a great deal goes on in classrooms that is not particularly characterized by dissensus.

Ingersoll's critique might be extended to domains other than education, including much of government. Where cultural transmission, reproduction, and socialization are principal objectives of organizations, order is to be expected (and is usually found) in the organization's normative climate rather than in its instrumental activities.

The quest for distinctiveness, then, has led population ecology and institutional theory in entirely different directions, both away from core sociological issues. Population ecology has focused, at least until recently, rather narrowly upon the issue of inertia in organizations and has wrestled with evidence showing entire organizations, not just their component parts, to resist change, contrary to predictions. Institutional theory has had a much broader purview, so broad that its boundaries remain ill-defined and its hypotheses, in many cases, incapable of disconfirmation. Even so, its assertion that social institutions penetrate many organizations (which is of some interest to nonorganizational sociologists) is not readily reconciled with its assertion that "decoupling" and nonrational conduct thereby result. Institutional theory continues to wrestle with the problem of defining and finding operational measures describing institutional environments, which are hypothesized to account for many organizational phenomena. Both population ecology and institutional theory remain important alternatives to efficiency models of organizational conduct. But their importance lies in observations that would not surprise most sociologists and that could easily be cast in conventional sociological language. For population ecology, the key observation is that many organizations are inertial and, therefore, resistant to environmental pressures (which, presumably, tend toward efficiency). For institutional theory, the key observation is that many organizations, particularly those whose purposes are normative or cultural, are exempt from the rules of the efficiency game.

Please understand the spirit of these comments. Much has been accomplished in organizational sociology. Indeed, the growth of the subdiscipline, and particularly of population ecology and institutional theory, has been one of sociology's notable success stories of the last decade. But theoretical distinctiveness sometimes shades into solipsism. Solipsism in organizational sociology, to the extent it exists, can serve only to isolate organizations further from sociology in the coming years. And it cannot help but isolate organizational sociology from the kinds of policy concerns sketched at the beginning of this chapter.

THE NEED FOR ORGANIZATIONAL SOCIOLOGY

Aside from growing intellectual differences between organizational scholars and sociologists, an institutional transformation of substantial magnitude is removing organizational studies from sociology departments. This is the movement of business schools from the periphery to the center of university life and, concomitantly, the development of identifiable business disciplines. One of these disciplines is organizational behavior, which usually (but not always) encompasses organizational sociology. Business schools are in the business of teaching accounting, finance, marketing, and operations research. They are not eleemosynary institutions (and, indeed, are regarded by some administrators as profit centers, whose net revenues should be made available for general university purposes). Organizational behavior is included in the curriculum out of several impulses. One is the belief that organizational psychology (particularly motivation and leadership) may somehow prove important to managers. Another is the perception that organizational politics is ubiquitous, especially important for senior managers, and overlooked entirely in the technical curriculum. Finally, there is the matter of ethics. The accountants and finance faculty, having reinvented the wheel (see Noreen 1988) by proving as Talcott Parsons (1937) demonstrated a half century ago that a moral or ethical (read normative) basis is required for successful cooperation in business, have become receptive to explicit instruction in ethics. Ethics is usually taught under the rubric of general management or organizational behavior.

A role for organizational sociology is perceived to exist at the intersection of motivation/leadership, politics, and ethics. Organizational sociology is perceived to be concerned with matters of organizational design, because of its focus on structure and environmental influences, and hence a useful complement to motivation and leadership. Because organizational sociology is more tolerant of departures from the rational model than, for example, organizational economics, it is also considered to be a favorable location for research and teaching on politics in organizations. And although organizational sociologists are not professional ethicists, their familiarity with cross-cultural research enables them to discuss values more fluently than staff from other disciplines traditionally represented in business schools. As a consequence of these tendencies, business schools are hiring organizational sociologists in record numbers and perhaps in greater numbers than sociology departments.

The shift of organizational sociologists into business schools will affect organizational sociology profoundly. The most noticeable impact will not be in the production of research but in the production of Ph.D.s. Few business schools have large doctoral programs. And business school students in organizational behavior doctoral programs do not learn the same organizational sociology as their counterparts in sociology departments because sociology is only one of several disciplines represented. There is much more emphasis on current journals and correspondingly less on the classics. The movement of organizations from sociology into the business schools, then, not only potentially shrinks the pool of Ph.D.s in organizational studies, but it also shifts the training of doctoral students somewhat away from theory as it is taught in the disciplinary social science disciplines.

The changes notwithstanding, an important role potentially remains for organizational sociology, whether in business schools or elsewhere. This role, as I see it, extends beyond joining other areas of sociological inquiry with the study of organizations (as in the recent work on organizational labor markets, organizational demography, organizational networks, and organizational culture). Rather, the role of organizational sociology is to bring the unique intellectual stance of sociology to bear on organizations. The basic elements of this stance — again, the debunking motif, sympathy for the underdog, and a preference for structural as opposed to volitional explanation — need not be antithetical to the study of organizations, provided they are utilized as tools for challenging prevailing orthodoxies rather than as means of constructing a new orthodoxy. Organizational sociology succeeds best when it focuses relentlessly on the behavior of organizations and the people in them. It succeeds less well when it reduces complex patterns of behavior to abstractions such as efficiency, inertia, or institutionalization. And it succeeds poorly or not at all when it attempts to draw specific inferences from highly aggregated data, which admit of alternative interpretations.

Whether or not organizational sociology as we know it will survive the movement of organizational scholars into business disciplines is unclear. I am not optimistic. I believe that sociology, in order to reclaim the field of organizations, must do three things. First, it must seriously engage ideas about productive efficiency without accepting them uncritically. We do not know, for example, what happens to day-to-day conduct when divisionalization, decentralization, and stringent financial controls are imposed upon units within large firms. The economists argue that efficiency benefits accrue, but there is reason for skepticism. Sociology must, second, treat businesses and business people as worthy if not always admirable subjects of study. This means putting aside prejudices and returning to the study of executives' careers as well as executive activity and authority. Sociology must, third, place volitional explanations for action on an equal footing with ideas about structural constraint. This means observing organizations firsthand and gathering data about intentions as well as on outcomes. Unanticipated outcomes of purposeful social action — and organizational action is preeminently purposeful action — cannot be gauged absent data about intentions. At the same time, I believe that organizational sociologists should be more attentive to other sociologists' inclination to view organizations as powerful entities and as agents of acculturation, socialization, and, indeed, societal action rather than as passive actors whose purpose is to perform reliably and to mirror the larger social order. The study of power, of course, has proved one of the most elusive problems of our discipline. The ubiquity of large organizations in contemporary society practically compels that questions of power be addressed in organizational contexts.

Finally, I believe that sociologists may choose to ignore the movement of organizations and organizational scholars into the business schools, but only at their peril. Economics is firmly ensconced in schools of management, and so are some areas of psychology. History and political science have strong toeholds. Sociology should be represented also, if only to render the full range of social science disciplinary perspectives available to business students. The tension between sociology's organic view of relations between individuals, organizations, and society and the more instrumental perspectives of the established business disciplines cannot help but be a source of intellectual energy and creativity over the coming decades.

REFERENCES

Aldrich, Howard. 1979. *Organizations and Environments.* Englewood Cliffs, NJ: Prentice-Hall.

Bendix, Reinhard. 1956. *Work and Authority in Industry.* Berkeley: University of California Press.

Berger, Peter. 1963. *Invitation to Sociology.* Garden City, NY: Doubleday.

Berger, Peter and Thomas Luckmann. 1967. *The Social Construction of Reality.* New York: Doubleday.

Blau, Peter M. 1970. "A Formal Theory of Differentiation in Organizations." *American Sociological Review* 35:201-18.

Bowman, Ned. 1988. *Strategy Choices.* Unpublished manuscript, University of Pennsylvania, the Wharton School, Reginald Jones Center.

Carroll, Glenn R. and Michael T. Hannan. 1988. "The Role of Density Delay in the Evolution of Organizational Populations: A Model and Five Empirical Tests." Paper prepared for the Wharton Conference on Organizational Evolution, Philadelphia.

Coleman, James S. 1987. "The Role of Social Policy Research in Society and in Sociology." *American Sociologist* 18:127-33.

Crane, Diana. 1988. "Sociology as a Discipline Since the Seventies: A Co-Citation Analysis." Paper presented to the conference, "Sociology and Institution-Building," Wickenburg, AZ.

Crozier, Michel. 1964. *The Bureaucratic Phenomenon.* Chicago: University of Chicago Press.

Dibble, Vernon. 1965. "The Organization of Traditional Authority." Chap. 21 in *Handbook of Organizations,* edited by James G. March. Chicago: Rand-McNally.

Durkheim, Émile. 1951. *Suicide.* Glencoe,IL: Free Press.

Freeman, John H., Glenn Carroll, and Michael T. Hannan. 1983. "The Liability of Newness: Age-Dependence in Organizational Death Rates." *American Sociological Review* 48:692-710.

Gouldner, Alvin W. 1954. *Patterns of Industrial Bureaucracy.* Glencoe, IL: Free Press.

Hannan, Michael T. and John H. Freeman. 1977. "The Population Ecology of Organizations." *American Journal of Sociology* 82:929-64.

———. 1984. "Structural Inertia and Organizational Change." *American Sociological Review* 49:149-64.

Hirsch, Paul. 1987. *Pack Your Own Parachute.* Reading, MA: Addison-Wesley.

Hofstadter, Richard. 1955. *The Age of Reform.* New York: Vintage.

Ingersoll, Richard. 1988. *The Rationality of School Ritual: Beyond Institutional Theories of Education.* Unpublished manuscript, University of Pennsylvania, Department of Sociology.

Jensen, Arthur and William Meckling. 1976. "Theory of the Firm: Managerial Behavior, Agency Costs, and Ownership Structure." *Journal of Financial Economics* 3:305-60.

Kaufman, Herbert. 1976. *Are Government Organizations Immortal?* Washington, DC: Brookings Institution.

Lawrence, Paul S. and Jay W. Lorsch. 1967. *Organization and Environment.* Boston: Harvard University, Graduate School of Business Administration.

Merton, Robert K. 1958. *Social Theory and Social Structure.* 2nd ed. New York: Free Press.

Meyer, John W. and Brian Rowan. 1977. "Institutionalized Organizations: Formal Structure as Myth and Ceremony." *American Journal of Sociology* 83:340-63.

Meyer, John W. and W. Richard Scott. 1983. *Organizational Environments: Ritual and Rationality.* Beverly Hills, CA: Sage.

Meyer, John W., W. Richard Scott, and David Strang. 1987. "Centralization, Fragmentation, and School District Complexity." *Administrative Science Quarterly* 32:186-201.

Meyer, Marshall W. and Lynne G. Zucker. 1989. *Permanently Failing Organizations.* Newbury Park, CA: Sage.

Mills, C. Wright. 1955. *The Power Elite.* New York: Oxford University Press.

Mintz, Beth and Michael Schwartz. 1985. *The Power Structure of American Business.* Chicago: University of Chicago Press.

Noreen, Eric. 1988. "The Economics of Ethics: A New Perspective on Agency Theory." *Accounting, Organizations & Society* 13:359-69.

Parsons, Talcott. 1937. *The Structure of Social Action.* Glencoe, IL: Free Press.

Pfeffer, Jeffrey and James Baron. 1986. "Taking Workers Back Out: Recent Trends in the Structuring of Employment." Research Paper No. 926. Stanford, CA: Stanford University, Graduate School of Business.

Scott, W. Richard. 1987. "The Adolescence of Institutional Theory." *Administrative Science Quarterly* 32:493-511.

Selznick, Philip. 1957. *TVA and the Grass Roots.* Berkeley: University of California Press.

Singh, Jitendra, Robert House, and David Tucker. 1986. "Organizational Legitimacy and the Liability of Newness." *Administrative Science Quarterly* 31:171-93.

Stinchcombe, Arthur. 1985. *Stratification and Organizations.* New York: Cambridge University Press.

Strang, David. 1987. "The Administrative Transformation of American Education: School District Consolidation, 1938-1980." *Administrative Science Quarterly* 32:352-66.

Thompson, James D. 1967. *Organizations in Action.* New York: McGraw-Hill.

Tolbert, Pamela and Lynne G. Zucker. 1983. "Institutional Sources of Change in the Formal Structure of Organizations: The Diffusion of Civil Service Reforms 1880-1935." *Administrative Science Quarterly* 23:22-39.

Williamson, Oliver. 1985. *The Economic Institutions of Capitalism.* New York: Free Press.

Wilson, James Q. and Richard Herrnstein. 1985. *Crime and Human Nature.* New York: Simon & Schuster.

Zucker, Lynne G. 1977. "The Role of Institutionalization in Cultural Persistence." *American Sociological Review* 42:726-43.

Part VI
Sociology and Social Criticism

13

The Virtues of Dissent in Sociology

Lewis A. Coser

Max Scheler once defined human beings as dissatisfied animals. While one may doubt this broad characterization in an age of narcotizing mass media catering to apparently satisfied viewers, Scheler's definition seems to hold for some social philosophers and social scientists, who can indeed be seen as dissatisfied men and women who forever seem to question the wont and use of their societies and their times.

The political theory of Plato and Aristotle arose amidst the turmoil and rapid shifts and changes in the political affairs of the Athenian polis, where tyrants were overthrown by republican institutions only to be followed again by despotic rulers. Under these circumstances, the political state of affairs, the *res publica*, could no longer be taken for granted. It needed the scalpel of analysis in order to be understood properly. Such an understanding, on the other hand, was not sought for knowledge's sake alone but was meant to provide guidelines that opened vistas through criticism of the present state of affairs toward a truly humane condition in which citizens overcoming present crises would find themselves fully at home in the polity.

Machiavelli, the originator of modern political thought, wrote in the age of the crisis and decline of the Italian Renaissance city-state, menaced by French or Spanish invasion and the usurpation of princes such as the Medici. One fails to understand *The Prince* but above all the *Discourses* if one does not perceive them as responses of the author to the crisis and problems of his age and as attempts to overcome current decay by the cultivated virtue of participant republican citizens.

Much the same can be said about the great seventeenth-century British classical political thinkers, especially Hobbes and Locke. Whatever major differences there be in their orientations and in the remedies they proposed for the disordered condition of Britain in the throws of revolution and civil war, they were at one in addressing their thought to an audience that was anxious and afraid in a revolutionary world that, most of them felt, they had never made. Their critique of present disorders as well as their depiction of the ravages of revolutionary crises were meant to provide securer foundations for a more stable and more acceptable polity.

As to sociology, it is almost a commonplace to say that it was the child of the transformation of Western society in the wake of the industrial revolution and the rise of capitalism. Saint-Simon distinguished normal and critical periods in the history of humankind and was ever ready to demonstrate that the early nineteenth century and its immediate antecedents were critical periods par excellence. The sociological thought of his onetime disciple Auguste Comte was likewise infused with an almost panic sense of the sickness of the age. Whatever denotations and connotations the term *positivism* may have acquired later on, the positivist sociology that Comte put on the map was never intended to be pure description of what is but a blueprint of what the world could be if men and women would learn how to change the shape of their collective lives in the light of critical rejection of what had heretofore been the case. *Savoir pour pouvoir*, to know in order to act, was the major slogan inscribed on the Comtean banner. And the knowledge that he propagated was nothing if not critical knowledge.

I shall not bore you with a history of sociological thought since the days of Comte, but I feel justified in arguing in broad strokes that almost all major sociological figures of the past took their point of departure from felt misgivings about the master trends of their day and age. This is so not only for those who can be located on the left of the political spectrum. It applies to Max Weber as well as to Marx, to Simmel, to Durkheim, to Veblen as well as to William Graham Sumner.

On the contemporary scene, even though I have no hard data, apart from reading biographical materials of contemporary sociologists, I feel justified in asserting that the majority of them decided to become sociologists because of felt dissatisfaction with the working of their society. While in college, they were dissatisfied animals; they were drawn to sociology because they perceived it as a medium not only for a better understanding of their society but for its radical or reformist reconstruction. Even the young Talcott Parsons joined a student socialist society at Amherst College.

What is so perturbing in the present state of sociology, however, is the fact that a high proportion of generous, hopeful, critical undergraduates are being influenced in graduate school into relegating their critical impulses into half-forgotten liminal layers of their mind. When exposed to the influence of teachers fascinated by the continuous growth of methodological refinement, they are too often trained to become sophisticated computer specialists rather than critical thinkers. To them, the methodological tail wags the substantive dog. In their highly skilled hands, sociology is in danger of abandoning its critical birthright.

While they may mightily contribute to the growth of sophisticated research techniques, they fail to enhance the critical bite of sociological ideas. Lacking this bite, their work is too often dull, as tedious as a laundry list.

The weakness of critical thought among so many sociologists is especially salient when, as Norman Birnbaum (Birnbaum, 1988, pp. 39-40) has recently observed, "natural scientists have been far more critical of existing institutions, for more open to new possibilities of social organization, far more historical and even visionary in their outlook than social scientists." More important contributions to the study of the social impact of genetic manipulation, or biological engineering, to the degradation of the environment, or to the problems of the public control of scientific innovations, have come from the camp of the natural rather than the social sciences.

We live in times of crisis arguably at least as deep as those to which our social and political scholarly fathers responded, but one would hardly gather that this is the case if one peruses the latest issues of the *American Sociological Review* and the other major journals of the discipline. In fact, even though there are honorable exceptions, when it comes to critical thought, we are often constrained, just like in electronic technology, to rely on imports: Habermas, Giddens, or Bourdieu serve as substitutes for missing native critical products.

It is not only the hypertrophy of empiricist methodology that accounts for the lack of critical dimensions in current sociological thought. Of late, our conceptual vocabulary has also suffered from a depletion of critical bite. Two examples, with which I have dealt in greater detail elsewhere (Coser, 1988), will have to suffice: the redefinition of the term *social movement* and the indiscriminate uses of the concept of deviance.

The term *social movement* was coined, by analogy to Newtonian mechanical movements, in the beginning of the nineteenth century by Saint-Simon and his disciples in France and, a bit later, by Lorenz von Stein in Germany. It was meant to denote the movements of social protest that had arisen in France, and soon elsewhere, against the impact of the industrial revolution on artisans, handicraft workers, journeymen, and the emergent industrial working class. It was seen as a movement of protest against novel forms of exploitation, immiseration, and proletarianization. Those who propagated the new terminology were intent upon documenting that the new world of industrial capitalism could no longer be understood in terms of the old political categories. What was now on the order of the day was no longer developments in the body politic, the moves of government and parliaments, or bureaucratic manipulation, but new phenomena in the body social. In other words, the term intended to draw attention to revolutionary structural developments, demonstrations, protest marches, strikes, and the like that could no longer be comprehended by reference to antiquated political notions. Those who talked of social movements, those who favored them, like Saint-Simon and the Saint-Simonians, but also those who opposed them, like Lorenz von Stein, intended to speak of new social forces that had arisen in opposition to the status quo and in reaction to the waste and exploitation of human energies and strivings that had come about in the wake of capitalist industrialism.

The term *social movements*, as used in current sociological thought, has almost completely lost its earlier critical bite and resonance. It is now used indiscriminately for movements of Mothers Against Drunk Driving, Hare Krishnas, and various West Coast cults intended to replenish the depleted egos of Yuppie devotees, as well as for, say, the women's movement, the civil rights movement, or the Communist party. The term has been so emasculated that it has been used for movements abetted and even financed by the powers that be and not only for movements of protest and revolt against the status quo. The case against drunken driving is surely worthwhile, but it is senseless to put it into the same category as the civil rights struggle.

It might be objected that definitions are of no importance and that what counts are novel sets of data no matter what definitions have been used in order to bring them to awareness. This, however, is an egregious mistake. Definitions and concepts are guideposts to what is to be investigated, ways of pointing to what is being looked for. A way of seeing some facets of reality is always a way of not seeing others.

The history of the term *social deviance* is rather different, but, in this case also, whatever critical meaning may once have been connoted by the term has by now been excised or put on a back burner. Originally the term had some limited usefulness; it pointed to similarities in various phenomena that seemed otherwise to have little in common. It seemed of use in pointing to the fact that various types of activities that otherwise had little in common, say, juvenile delinquency and check forging, had the common characteristic of rejecting middle-class norms and values. But such limited heuristic utility has long been overshadowed by what has become a shockingly uncritical way of thinking.

As Robert Merton was the first to point out (Merton, 1976, pp. 29 ff.), and as I have argued in his wake, the current usage of the term *deviance* fails to make distinctions between the actions of men and women intent upon changing the current state of affairs to reach superpersonal societal goals contributing to the collective welfare, and actors who are intent only on reaching their personal goals by way of "innovations" that enhance their chance to maximize their individual well-being. The current usage of the term puts Socrates and Al Capone, Martin Luther King and a common highway robber, into the same conceptual category. By putting the disinterested springs of action of a guide to a more desirable human condition and the interested activities of various types of criminals into the same bracket, the term *deviance* has served conservative — nay, reactionary — purposes, even though most of those who use the term are probably unaware of such mischievous uses.

To repeat, self-centered deviance and innovating social deviance have in common that they involve breaches of norms. But the former centers on the enhancement of the goals of the norm-breaker while the latter is motivated by attempts to enhance the welfare of the community of which the norm-breaker is a part. To confound actions that aim at enhancement of the self and actions that aim at increasing community benefits is a mischievous enterprise. Moreover, the wide and inclusive definition of *deviance* that is so often propounded today quite obviously redounds to the benefit of reactionary or conservative political trends by asserting that all those who fail to conform are necessarily enemies of the good society. It is a preferred and choice weapon of the enemies of promise.

Before I attempt to delineate at least some of the virtues of critical thought in sociology, let me briefly mention a set of phenomena that have in the last few decades characterized not only sociology but the other social sciences as well. I refer to the decline of Utopia and the rise of distopian images. In the past, as Mannheim pointed out a long time ago, utopias served as guideposts for critical dissections of current conditions and as measuring rods for the emancipatory potential of human collective action. To be sure, utopia was literally nowhere, but utopian visions served to indicate present deficiencies in the light of future goals and aspirations. At present, however, utopian thought has either receded completely or has taken refuge in socially innocuous science fiction. There has also arisen a flourishing cottage industry peddling the distopian consequences that allegedly would follow if attempts were made to tamper with the beneficial working of free markets and free enterprise. Do not undermine the received verities as expounded by Milton Friedman, so the distopians assert, lest you prepare the road to the Gulag. Even the most timid extensions of the welfare state, so they argue, may lead straight to the hell of totalitarian domination. To them, behind the apparently innocuous social welfare official, there lurks the shadow of Big Brother.

To be sure, not all social scientific endeavors have to be critical. I do not want to denigrate the achievements of an approach that limits itself to describing the social scene. We surely need accurate road maps if we are to navigate successfully amidst the complexities of the current scene. Sociography is a worthwhile, even necessary, vocation, but it is not sufficient. Sociology that limits itself to taking account of what is, serving as a kind of sociological Richter counter or seismograph that registers the problems and issues that are raised in public opinion or in the mass media, is not enough. Critical sociological thought is needed in order to pinpoint and locate social problems and issues of which ordinary men and women are not yet aware. Here again Merton did pioneering work when he stated a while ago that one needs to distinguish manifest and latent social problems. "It has sometimes been proposed," he (1976, p. 13) argues,

> that sociologists should confine their attention to the conditions generally regarded as undesirable . . . [This] would result in sociologists adopting the subjective judg-

ments of the groups or individuals under study . . . while believing that they maintained the objectivity of the scientific observer. . . . It is . . . a function of sociologists to study not only manifest social problems — those widely identified in the society — but also latent social problems [that appear only in the light of the analytical and critical apparatus that is the birthright of the sociological calling].

The critical sociologist has developed a trained vision, discerning fissures in the social fabric that are not easily discernible by people on the street. Critical sociologists do not want to force ordinary people to give credence to their visions, but it is their mission to identify and put into the limelight what is undesirable and destructive in what seems acceptable to the conservative and the unaware. Critical sociology should see it as its task — to put it in the vernacular — to point out that there are many ways in which the fish may stink.

Critical sociologists leave it to others to sing the praise of current achievements and to point to the glories of present successes. They focus instead on the worm in the apple, on the rot behind the glittering facade of the current scene. What is more, whereas the consensus-oriented sociologist sees in such phenomena as demonstrations, riots, racial disturbances, and the like symptoms of pathology, the critical sociologist is able to point out that what may appear as sickness may be more of the nature of the sign or signal of deep-seated maladjustments in the social structure that can only be remedied through thorough reconstruction of basic societal premises.

Social violence, manifestations, demonstrations, acts of disobedience are not only protests: They are claims to be considered. They are weapons of last resort for those who are ordinarily excluded from the forum of public opinion and from action in the public arena. Just like a fever, distressing as it may be, is a sign of some bodily malfunctioning, and is a diagnostic clue for the physician, so what appears to be the pathologies of the inner city may be seen by the critical sociologist as a visible sign of the sickness of an acquisitive society and the decay of communal bonds in the vortex of clashing self-interests.

It is likely that, as in the past, there will be no ideological consensus among sociologists when it comes to, for example, social problems. While for some of us, a public protest may be a problem, for others, the issue is public apathy. All one can hope for, or so it would seem to me, is that the voice of critical sociologists that has become so muted of late be again heard loud and clear. They should not monopolize the sociological forum, but they must be heard. I hope that younger sociologists will not be intimidated into lowering their voices. They should not be prevented from getting the encouragement they deserve. They will be to the benefit of our discipline as a whole. Without the bite and stimulus of critical thought, we are likely to lose the small measure of public attention we have heretofore enjoyed.

Had it not been for a small band of critical social scientists like Michael Harrington, the war against poverty would most likely not have been fought in the 1960s. The defenders of the status quo were not even able to perceive that poverty was indeed a problem. It was only when critical voices began to assault middle-class complacency that the powers that be were prodded into action — insufficient as it turned out to be.

In addition, it is not only the merit of critical social scientists to alert the common conscience and to stimulate a sense of outrage over injustices, they also serve as role models for younger and aspiring sociologists. When Herbert Gans, S. M. Miller, Lee Rainwater, or Hylan Lewis, to mention just a few, were moved to point at the indignities and the deprivations and humiliation suffered by millions of underprivileged men and women, they served as role models for younger sociologists and contributed to their realization that alternatives to the currently dominant style of sociological thought are readily available.

What was true then is true now. Only if complacent and sluggish public opinion and the powers that be are prodded into action through critical vision will there be a chance to revitalize a regimented and bureaucratized society that has come increasingly to resemble, as Max Weber already argued, the Egypt of the Pharaohs. Without the sting of critical thought, the body of our discipline, and also the entire social fabric, are likely to congeal into frozen conformity. As John Dewey taught us a good while ago, "Only a hitch in the working of habit occasions emotion and provokes thought." It is mainly critical vision that provides such a hitch. Three cheers for its continued vitality within and without sociology.

REFERENCES

Birnbaum, Norman. 1988. *The Radical Renewal: The Politics of Ideas in Modern America*. New York: Pantheon.

Coser, Lewis A. 1988. "Sociological Theory and Social Movements." Paper read at the workshop, "Social Movements," University of Michigan, Ann Arbor, June 8-10.

Merton, Robert K. 1976. "Introduction." In Robert K. Merton and Robert Nisbet, *Contemporary Social Problems*. 4th ed. New York: Harcourt Brace Jovanovich.

14

Sociology for Whom?
Criticism for Whom?

Todd Gitlin

SOCIOLOGY AS FOOTING FOR SOCIAL CRITICISM

This is an auspicious moment for thawing out the question: What do sociology and social criticism have to do with one another? The question was not born yesterday. It dates to the early nineteenth century at least, when intellectuals recognized themselves as intellectuals. This was Marx's and Engels's question, in a sense: What is the social base and warrant for practical criticism — the opposite of idle exhortation? Where does criticism get its traction? Engels's ([1880] 1975) idea was that where the utopian spirit of social criticism was literally baseless — it was founded on the premise that thought could have its way in the world unimpeded — so-called scientific socialism was to be different: It was to be aligned with an agency of change. Brawny Marxism set itself to work; by comparison, free-floating criticism was idle. Marx and Engels not only proposed that serious criticism was automatically interested (it had a "class basis") but, *contra* utopianism, they proposed that, to become effective, criticism must not dangle in social space, it must extend "real" interests, must have cut at the joints of a society in being. Marxism was not only (or, by some accounts, not at all) a theory but a mode of theorizing that would rationalize, and thus advance, the claim of one class (the knowing proletariat) to rule. Communists, guided by proper understanding, would instruct the revolutionary class in its destiny — the realization of a logic already at work in its social relations.

Saint-Simonian theory and positivist method had already entered the lists as modes of thought with comparable objects: to equip a class (in their case, scientists and other intellectuals) with a knowledge that would rationalize — make rationally defensible — their own ascendant power. It was left to Weber to generate doubts, supply a cautionary answer to the question of what sociology had to do with criticism — intellectuals might be a class, yes; one must attend to their embeddedness in society, yes; under certain circumstances, they might even make history (as in the famous case of the Protestant ethic); but, in the rational-legal order, the price they paid for the heroic pursuit of ideas and ideals was steep: perhaps all their huffing and puffing amounted to nothing more than growling and pacing within the iron cage. Moreover, Weber's social scientist was duty-bound to separate his or her commitments as a critic from his or her calling as an analyst of society; criticism was to be performed after hours if at all. But notice that Weber himself thought that sound sociology made for good criticism, even if a division of intellectual labor was required to keep the second from contaminating the first. Mannheim, a more ambitious rationalist, hoped that free-floating intellectuals could not only free themselves from cages of all sorts but reason their way to social reconstruction.

I am acutely aware that these historical sketches are sketchy in the extreme. But I hope to have suggested that the question of the relation between sociology, a way of knowing, and social criticism, a way of acting, richly deserves to be a perennial. It is never resolved so much as it is negotiated to a provisional settlement. It surfaces again when that settlement breaks down — especially when a new cohort discovers that its angle of vision has been discounted or dealt out. After the political, generational, racial, and gender-based insurgencies of the 1960s and after, the question has in recent years been frozen — largely because of an inhospitable social and political climate. If it is now thawing out a bit, perhaps this is partly because of a larger climatic shift — a shift of the larger culture and polity to which sociology and social criticism contribute, which shapes them in turn.

THE USES OF BAD WRITING

If sociology and social criticism have been coupled historically, surely one thing that has rent them asunder is the recent self-insulation of professional sociology. And no factor has contributed to that self-insulation more than the quality, if that is the right word, of academic writing. Which raises the question of why academics, in particular sociologists, write routinely, hermetically, in clotted prose, ridden with jargon and the passive voice, crossing the line from complexity to obscurity. The alarm has been sounded by Russell Jacoby, whose ill-tempered clavier in *The Last Intellectuals* (1987) perhaps prematurely presumes that the public intellectual is an endangered species. It is easy enough to make sport of bad writing as Jacoby does. But I wish to climb Jacoby's ladder and to inquire into the causes and social uses of bad writing. This is not to say that bad writing automatically incapacitates sociology for social criticism: Marx himself is the counterexample, although when he set his head to pamphleteering he was the most lucid of polemicists. But most sociological writing, unlike Marx's, fails to spawn social criticism on the part of the less brilliant but more writerly. It does not spawn criticism at all. Failing to speak to a public, it is ill-equipped to mobilize itself into criticism. Accessibility is not sufficient but it is necessary for a social critic. Consider economics. Economists have usually become influential with larger publics (regardless of their influence with Washington, a separate question) to the degree that they are well positioned at elite universities and write clearly if not elegantly, even at times when they have had no direct influence on Washington — consider the very different contributions of John Kenneth Galbraith and Milton Friedman or, in the next rank, Paul Samuelson, Lester Thurow, and Robert Reich. (Under special circumstances, however — that is, in the Reagan administration — it is possible to gain influence on policy without the highest academic standing *or* any remarkable prose style: namely, Arthur Laffer.) Books establish quotability and lead to newspaper-certified expertise, syndicated columns, lecture tours, television interviews, and the like.

Why bad prose? There is, in the first instance, an institutional explanation: Bad prose flourishes because academic institutions and professional gatekeepers tolerate, even encourage, it. My impression is that graduate students are rarely encouraged, let alone required, to write more accessibly, let alone more clearly, elegantly, subtly, or excitingly. Teaching those arts is difficult in the best circumstances; as it is, there is no premium for trying. Nor, in general, are students necessarily rewarded for it. Bad writing is plainly no impediment to publication in the profession's journals. (There is a good case to be made for the contrary.) There are even penalties for writing well — one can be tarred with the brush of "journalism," which can even result, as in the case of Paul Starr at Harvard, in dismissal. (What a misunderstanding this anathema of journalism is, by the way, most of which is badly written in other ways than the academic — simplistic, obvious, cliché-ridden, short-sighted, historically thin, repetitious, condescending — and polices its own boundaries by branding superior work as, what else, sociology.) Sociology is sanctified by profaning what sociology is not — a move familiar to sociologists of deviance. The sociology/journalism either/or impoverishes both.

The self-reproducing, closed-in, professional tendencies of academic life are part of the story, then. But inward-turning, hard-to-decipher prose also has a larger functional reason. It is the mystery that enshrines the authority of the clerisy — frowned upon in recent years (in which case the mystery compensates the profession for its sense of futility). The cipher can be broken, but that takes a specialist in cryptology. The existence of the cipher certifies that the specialty has a point. The aura of mystery may go so far as to insulate the work from any immediate social impact (consider the example of Talcott Parsons), but it may, if suitably located at prestigious institutions, attract — or at least not repel — generations of students who proceed to widen the circle of influence via further generations of students, at least until countercircles organize and disciples free themselves of the grip and regroup. Whatever else quasi- and pseudoscientific, poststructuralist, and other specialist languages are about, they are united in self-regard.

Not all styles of self-regard have the same sweep and function, of course. The master form, the resurrected totalist project of the last twenty years is what has been called, modestly, "theory" — the imitation Parisian varieties of poststructuralist, especially deconstructionist, literary and social theory. While breaking academic literary study away from the literature that is ostensibly its object, and apparently downgrading literature to one among many types of "text," "theory" proclaims the centrality, indeed the supremacy, of the theorist as not only interpreter but master of ceremonies and even director of the entire critical enterprise — even as the theorist loudly proclaims that no master discourse exists. Theory's clotted but occasionally elegant and currently ambitious form of discourse has one distinct virtue: it breaks down parochial boundaries. Like psychoanalysis and Marxism before it, the poststructuralist avant-garde makes its mark across the boundaries of history, philosophy, political science, sociology, anthropology, women's studies, law, and film as well as literary studies. It attracts some of the brainier and intellectually more ambitious students to a common academic culture and an aura of currency that literature itself can no longer provide. It radiates subversion, interdisciplinary span, and international reach at once. It flatters itself for deep insurgency and promises international conferences. Insisting that interpretation is intrinsically political, its writing style largely incapacitates its practitioners for political and intellectual action that extends beyond the protected grazing fields of academe. Wonder of wonders, this subversion requires not the slightest engagement in the polity. Breaking the spell of literature, identifying the authority of texts with their methods of crystallizing power, "theory" gathers authority through its own texts and their miracle, mystery, and deauthorizing authority.

TWO STYLES OF BAD WRITING

The kind of bad writing that concerns me is not just a succession of careless mistakes. Nor am I concerned with *difficult* writing that conveys intricate thought. The academy now spawns bad writing that is bad not because the argument traced is intrinsically difficult but because the expression is ungainly, tangled, and hermetic — full of rhetorical flourishes, high on cloistered display, and low on the conveyance of meaning. Dependent clauses pile up not because the quality of mind is baroque, as in Henry James, but because the writer cannot be troubled to clarify matters for readers who are not adepts — though they may become so by dint of their reading of the arcana. The voice is passive either because the writer has bowed before a society he or she sees as so formidable and adamant it seems beyond human power to change or because the writer abdicates responsibility for observing what he or she has observed, and wishes to engrave his or her perceptions in stone. In this sort of bad writing, the jargon does not convey elusive concepts but the writer's pleasure in neologism or club membership. This sort of bad writing is, indeed, a "discourse." It has its audiences, its subtexts, its assurances. It has its reasons. By now, it also has its traditions. Not incidentally, this sort of bad writing has become a credential that proves to crusty academia that the Marxist or poststructuralist scholar is a safe acquisition — safely enclosed within the charmed circle of those who are comprehensible only to each other and incapable of rousing any rabble at all.

In sociology I am concerned with two principle types of obscurantist writing. I want to suggest that the two, whose motivations are very different and even appear to be diametrically opposed, share complementary flaws and, indeed, a common model of the relation of ideas to action.

The first obscurantism is the style of research and writing that C. Wright Mills (1959) called "abstracted empiricism." Thirty years after he savaged it, abstracted empiricism has become normal procedure in most of our social science departments. Computers and statistical advances have multiplied the means of obfuscation. If you read Mills's essay with care, you see he is not objecting to empirical research. He has such a healthy respect for "fact" that he could even be accused of making a fetish of the concept. The nature of Mills's objection is that empiricism has become abstracted from general ideas about social structure. It has tended to restrict study to that which can be measured. It has lost what ought to be its motives in larger, historically based studies of the drift and thrust of social life. It is a collection of means that have become end. To which, more than a quarter century after the publication of Thomas S. Kuhn's *The Structure of Scientific Revolutions* (1962), one should add that abstracted empiricism takes for granted an impoverished and in many ways misleading model of progress in the natural sciences.

Why the rise of abstracted empiricism? As Norman Birnbaum points out in his provocative book *The Radical Renewal* (1988), during the postwar period (1946-64 by his dates) when abstracted empiricism swept through the social sciences, its dominance stemmed not so much from its pseudoscientific language but from its utility to centers of power in an era of presumably manageable problems:

> The American social sciences constituted a social technology, and [I would say elements of — T. G.] a legitimating ideology, for the larger society — more precisely, for many of its elites. Connected to the corporate structure, to the foundations, and to government by intermediaries recruited from the university not despite but because of their utter absence of critical distance from the distribution of power, the social sciences in the end delivered much of what was required of them. (Birnbaum 1988, p. 13)

But the rise of abstracted empiricism is behind us, and the situation today is different. Government spending on the social sciences has declined considerably, yet the hegemony of abstracted empiricism continues — challenged here and there, yet scarcely undermined. The "social technology" of abstracted empiricism evidently has a life of its own, even as its market value has declined. As faith in government-sponsored reforms dwindled after the 1960s (though not so much as the Reaganite right has argued), so did funding for ambitious, potentially unsettling empirical studies. As Christopher Jencks (1988), an empiricist of a decidedly antiabstracted sort, has recently written:

> The main reason we don't know the answers to [various questions about race, class, and ghetto culture] is that research of this kind requires many false starts, gradual improvements in measurement and data analysis, and lots of replications. Getting reliable answers takes several decades. Unfortunately, those who pay for such research want quick results. When the first results turn out to be inconclusive, they either shift their attention to another problem or conclude that all social science is a waste of money. (Given the way we organize and fund social science, that is largely true.) (Jencks 1988, p. 30)

One might have looked to a so-called critical sociology, and in particular to critical-minded, ambitious, overarching theory, to counter the abstractedness of sociology's empiricism. But theory has, in many ways, betrayed the hopes that critics (especially of my generation) reposed in it. In place of the Parsonsian Grand Theory, which Mills attacked, our theorists have gone in for self-enclosure — self-enclosure of a peculiarly defeating sort, namely, theorizing that presupposes a directive model of ideas. Promethean effort has built theoretical ghettos — elaborate Marxisms, poststructuralisms, Franco-feminisms, recondite deconstructionisms. Granting fruitful ventures among them, I detect method in the obscurantism. For one thing, there is sheer pleasure in belonging to the club whose collective insight enables it to pierce all veils. The private language and parochial tone become, in effect, elevating. More troubling, smug and parochial tones and vocabularies carry an implied politics. The unspoken and perhaps unthought premise is that once the happy few arrive at a correct class map (or a determination of the composition of surplus value, or a theory of imperialism or of housework or of the male gaze), they will bring it to the attention of the plebes, who will, if they know what is good for them, snap to attention. Plebes, after all, are the recipients, not the makers, of history. History, if it belongs to anyone, belongs to specialists in theory. The unstated (even unfelt) premise is that the theorists will stand in good stead once their party comes to power. The impenetrability of the writing is acceptable because the proprietors of the discourse situate themselves as insiders in training to be managers: in effect, a party of the right-minded. The point of the self-insulating discourse is vicarious mastery of an otherwise intractable world.

In this spirit, the theorist has a rationale for refusing to indulge in a deep social criticism that would also have practical use. Two rationales, actually. On the one hand, there is always work to be done perfecting the theoretical model. Practical criticism would distract. It would also threaten the accommodation one has made, however reluctantly, with an inhospitable society — scholastic radicalism, in other words, can serve the theorist as a shield against practical resignation. (The prototype is T. W. Adorno's style of burrowing away beneath the social quicksand.) Second, from an absolutely radical theoretical viewpoint, practical criticism taints itself by trafficking with the real political structures that have the power to implement criticism.

The curious and interesting thing is that, for all their differences, abstracted empiricism and Promethean theory share a commitment to a management model of knowledge. To exaggerate: Abstracted empiricism wants to be on top — wants to roll up its sleeves and go to work for management — and Promethean theory wants to be on top — wants to be management itself. But at a deep level, the two tend toward the same structural model of the relation between knowledge and power. In both cases, the ideal is that knowledge moves into the world by serving a center of power. In the case of abstracted empiricism, the center is an institution that actually exists: government, corporation, or foundation. In the case of abstracted, Promethean theory, the center is hypothetical: a revolutionary class. In either case, obscurantist language masks a commitment to a model in which knowledge serves power.

But social criticism cannot be left to dance attendance upon power. Social criticism requires a public that does not depend upon the largess of power either actual or anticipated. That is, it requires — or aims to bring about — a democratic domain where ideas contend. That domain is its audience, its raison d'être. Criticism checks power; it instigates and goads; it is impertinent. Whoever is in power, criticism would be impious. The decline of social criticism is, therefore, part of a larger crisis. It is inseparable from the decline of a public at large.

THE MISSING PUBLIC

One of the striking things about sociologically informed postwar social criticism is its commitment to engaging, animating, provoking its publics. In sociology, the exemplary figures are David Riesman and C. Wright Mills.[1]

The commitment to a public could even be inadvertent. David Riesman (1969, p. xi) has written that he and his coauthors "had no expectation" when *The Lonely Crowd* was published in 1950 that it "would be widely read outside the relevant academic fields" — which goes to show that writing for the academy need not have been incapacitating, at least before the professional language became refined to the present extent. It also goes to show the force of the paperback revolution ushered in by Jason Epstein at Doubleday Anchor, where

The Lonely Crowd was an early beneficiary. The book must have tapped widespread middle-class anxiety with the affluent, suburbanizing 1950s; as did, in different ways, William H. Whyte's *The Organization Man* (1956) and John Kenneth Galbraith's *The Affluent Society* (1958). All three were highly accessible, knowledgeable about disciplinary "literatures," yet written for "attentive" (Riesman's word) outsiders. Riesman's style, by turns chatty and approachably awkward, graceful and warm, nuanced and colloquial, served him and his critical strategy well — a fellow-feeling critic by temper, his tone was that of a man who wanted to counsel society, not lecture it.[2] It is probably not irrelevant that Riesman wrote unconfined by the Ph.D., as did another of the most readable sociologists of the postwar period, Daniel Bell — not until he was granted one for the already published *The End of Ideology* (1962).

C. Wright Mills's political passions have been amply appreciated, but, what is more striking, a quarter century after his death, is that he wrote with a passion *for sociology's reconstructing mission* — a passion hard to imagine or reconstruct in more jaded and suspicious decades.[3] Mills, the chief inspiration to scores of young intellectuals in the early 1960s, published more than his famous and accessible books — he published not only in professional journals and books but in journals directed toward intellectual elites (*Politics, Partisan Review, Commentary, Dissent, The Nation*) as well as popular magazines open to critical ideas (*Pageant, The New York Times Magazine, Saturday Review of Literature, Esquire, Harper's*). Working by elimination through American institutions, one after the other, he had concluded by the late 1950s that the main agencies in American life were hopelessly corrupted, committed to their private brands of irresponsibility and unreason. At a high pitch of despair, in a revolutionary leap, Mills proclaimed that intellectuals might be their own agents of change. If most of the academy had reconciled itself to the main structures of American power, the students of the New Left were aborning as the intimation of a new force — internationally, too.

Sometimes these publics already exist to be approached — namely, Mills's young New Left, Robert Bellah's liberal churches, Harry Edwards's black middle classes, or, for that matter, Allan Bloom's cultural monarchists. Sometimes they discover themselves in the process of eavesdropping on work done for a professional audience — namely, Riesman's anxious middle classes. Powerful work can always, to some degree, make its way against institutional barriers to an audience it helps usher into existence. But the self-enclosure of university culture remains an obstacle to public intellectual life — as the erosion of public intellectual life renders self-enclosure comfortable.

For more than two centuries, magazines have been pipelines for the public circulation of social criticism. Thus Thomas Paine in 1775:

> It has always been the opinion of the learned and curious, that a magazine, when properly conducted, is the nursery of genius; and by constantly accumulating new

matter, becomes a kind of market for wit and utility. The opportunities which it affords to men of abilities to communicate their studies, kindle up a spirit of invention and emulation. An unexercised genius soon contracts a kind of mossiness, which not only checks its growth, but abates its normal vigour. Like an untenanted house it falls into decay, and frequently ruins the possessor.

As culture goes specialized and professional, general-circulation magazines and intellectual journals decline. General thought is so distinctive a taste, now, as to qualify as a special interest alongside personal computing, running, and so on at the serious newsstand.

In the 1980s, public intellectual verve has been most conspicuous on the right, although the situation is probably changing. The gravitation of *Partisan Review* and *Commentary* into the neoconservative camp (using the latter word in both senses) and the editorial alignment of *The New Republic* (though by no means the entirety of the magazine, especially the back of the book), suggest, among other things, that the neoconservative right believed in general criticism as the left — stronger in the social sciences — did not. The rise of the right-wing "counterestablishment," to use Sidney Blumenthal's (1986) term, was in no small degree the rise of an intellectual infrastructure: foundations subsidizing right-wing books for general readerships (Charles Murray's *Losing Ground* 1984, George Gilder's *Wealth and Poverty* 1981, as well as publications like *National Review, The Public Interest, The American Spectator, The New Criterion, Public Opinion* as well as the neoconservative journals already mentioned). The journals of the right have offered more than proximity to power and money; they associate money, glamor, style, energy, and public-spiritedness with conservative social criticism and in the process become a magnet for talented writers who are then channeled into the more general press (via the weeklies as well as newsmagazines and the op-ed pages and columns of major dailies). Public television has been arid, though there are oases dotted here and there — recently, Bill Moyers's forays into intellectually serious interviews and for two decades William Buckley's *Firing Line*, which has made a pass at intellectual seriousness from time to time, serving, in the process, a legitimizing function for the right. Public radio's daily *Fresh Air* is stronger on cultural criticism than social; indeed, it cedes topics smacking of politics to *Morning Edition* and *All Things Considered*, which hew closely to the conventionally defined news but do tilt toward asking liberal questions.

Where have the journals and magazines gone? They have been segmented by specialty. Journals of film, feminism, Marxism, theory, and on and on abound, but my sense is that the number and circulation of *general* journals of analysis and opinion have shrunk in relation to the college-educated public. The length of articles and pieces of fiction have also shrunk — Saul Bellow (1989) was recently driven to publish a novella as an original paperback for a lack of a magazine to publish it; essays over 7,000 or 8,000 words regularly go begging.

In the commercial magazines, formats are confining; shortness and slickness is the norm. When the left adapts — as with the celebrity covers of *Mother Jones* and *Ms.* — some of the muckraking strengths remain but the weaknesses on institutional analysis, theoretical conundrums, and programmatic alternatives stand out all the more starkly. Part of the left's problem, of course, is money. Postal increases, the rising cost of paper, and so on have hurt. Left-wing philanthropy, in the wake of the 1960s and the promise of mobilization at the grass roots, has concentrated on practical political and social payoffs — community projects and the like. Only *Dissent*, of the long-running journals, has been able to sustain, even increase its circulation — without benefit of an angel-in-charge; it struggles to distribute more than 10,000 copies. But the problem is more than financial. The more accessible weeklies on the left — *The Nation* and *In These Times* — are erratic, awkwardly stapling the agendas of activists to the agendas of academics. *The New York Review of Books* is apparently allergic to the social sciences, and most of all to writers under fifty. The success of the political-cultural bimonthly *Tikkun* (30% percent of whose subscribers are apparently not Jewish) must be partly a result of a widespread hunger for intellectually serious criticism of politics and social problems.

But the problem, I fear, is one of demand as well as supply. There is a shortage of common culture. How often does one hear undergraduates discussing a novel they have read outside class? Reading for pleasure seems a quirky taste, the equivalent of building model railroads. College students seem ignorant of literary, philosophical, and artistic traditions; and maleducated students become maleducated teachers. The shortage of both accessible writers and interested readers is worsened by the thousands of childhood hours spent saturated with TV. But imagine, despite the hurdles, a well-read young academic, setting out to make a career as a public intellectual with an academic niche, possessed of a writing talent and possessed by a finite amount of energy (indeed, for feminist men, considerably less than in earlier decades, when domestic responsibilities were left to the wife). She or he makes choices. Why look to an unprofessional or cross-disciplinary journal when the reward is meager and there is even a certain risk? Young academics mapping careers are preoccupied by the advantages of publishing in refereed professional journals. Academic journals hospitable to post-New Left and interdisciplinary tendencies in the social sciences (*Theory and Society, Politics and Society*, and *Telos* among others) have been at pains to maintain their professional standing — at least in part for tenure-getting purposes — and have, to that end, maintained strictly, even baroquely scholastic styles. The readable feminist journal *Signs*, which cuts across academic boundaries, probably because of the transdepartmental esprit still remaining in feminist circles, gets short shrift from promotion committees despite being refereed — the assumption is that a feminist journal must be the property of a coterie. Meanwhile, for scholarly writers who cultivate accessible styles, there is something dispiriting about publishing an article in a public journal only to have it thunderously neglected. (Don Marquis said about an analogous literary exercise: "Publishing a book of verse is like dropping a petal down the Grand Canyon and waiting for the echo.")

I speak deliberately of the *cultivation* of accessible, let alone felicitous, style. Writers are encouraged to write in the styles they see published in the journals that serve as gatekeepers for their professions. Forced into disuse for long enough, accessible style withers.

CRITICISM IN SEARCH OF ITS OWN FOOTING

Many are the pressures and motives, in short, that drive sociology toward closed loops. The decline of a vigorous public confirms sociologists' turn toward a preoccupation with their own process — either in celebration (mistaking the discipline's scientific or theoretical "progress" for society's) or resignation (the dashing of revolutionary hopes for society having led toward hopes that, if nothing else, *theory* might be perfected — a hope often followed by a ritual genuflection toward the idea that "correct" theory will produce "correct" practice).

Social criticism, meanwhile, comes unmoored from a larger theory of society and a vision of social change — dilemmas that parallel those of the self-shriveling academy. In the 1960s, the most effective social critics operated outside the academy and, for the most part, reached ready-made constituencies: Michael Harrington, Betty Friedan, James Baldwin, Paul Goodman, Ralph Nader. In the 1970s and 1980s, by contrast, freelance critics with flair and scope have been scarce. Among academics, the reach of, say, my colleagues Bellah and Edwards (and I suppose myself to a lesser extent) beyond the academy is unusual. In practice, the dilemmas of public-minded criticism (leaving aside its considerable strengths) match those of cloistered sociology. When sweeping criticism of society (for example, Christopher Lasch 1979) finds a considerable readership, it fails to generate serious debate; it also fails to make itself practical — its accusations are too global, its eye for reform too jaundiced. Overarching critical frameworks like social ecology and cultural feminism remain ghettoized — they fail to collide with their contraries in a public domain. The narrower, ad hoc criticism of particular policies and practices — abstracted criticism, we might call it — is either squandered on the op-ed pages and talk shows or remains confined among specialists: circles of policy elites, lobbyists, and trainees. Ad hoc criticism fails to accumulate into a more general critique or a vision of society and transformation. The lure of influence can also be incapacitating. Critics who take social movements as their publics often find them unresponsive (at least in the short run) to intellectual demands — so eager are the movements to win ostensibly winnable short-run reforms, unwinnable as they prove to be, as in the case of the nuclear freeze; or empty as they prove to be, like the recently passed law that would restrict the advertising on children's television to 12 minutes per hour, or 10 1/2 on Saturdays, both more than the present industry average. Issues that arouse public controversy are usually trivial.

From the late 1970s through the 1980s, it was the right that proved artful and confident in framing political debate – in no small part because the Reagan administration and certain media elites were receptive. Think of the vulgarized New Class theories of Daniel Patrick Moynihan, Irving Kristol, and others as they made their way to a larger public via the *Wall Street Journal* and the widely quoted commentators of the Committee on the Present Danger, the American Enterprise Institute, and the Heritage Foundation. Think of Jeane Kirkpatrick's famous *Commentary* article (1979), which rationalized right-wing dictatorships in a manner tailor-made for the incoming president. While scholars of the left buried themselves beneath piles of statistics or scatter-gun disapprovals of authority – whether of texts or teachers – it was left to Allan Bloom (1987) and William Bennett to address public agencies with sweeping, if quarter-baked, ideas. But intellectual allegiance to the vertical virtues of Father, State, and Canon has more recently been contested in the public domain. The success of Paul Kennedy (1987) and other prophets of economic decline suggests the dawning of a different mood – a realism about America's place in the world coupled with a certain cultural gloom.

In the end, I agree with Norman Birnbaum's conclusion: We have fragmented theory aplenty – fragments that have not accumulated into overarching vision. Possibly, overarching vision is not in the cards – who knows? The parallel point can be made about sociologically based social criticism – there is actually plenty of it, modestly focused, and plenty more is possible, if for no other reason than that many social scientists are rampantly dissatisfied with precisely the conditions that Russell Jacoby has bashed away at. But healthy criticism requires more than improved prose. Criticism proceeds *from* interests that carry the viewpoints of constituencies; but to replenish the democratic ideal, it must proceed *to* a general public. Neither more specialist journals nor more talk shows will accomplish that. The restriction, fragmentation, and distraction of the general public, along with the shrinkage of the electorate, set a decisive limit on the larger resonance of *any* critical discourse now. Sociologically grounded social criticism has to stare at the damage, has to take it seriously.

Recently, I was told that an area designated for free speech at the University of Texas, Austin, was so inaccessible and overbuilt it was only infrequently used. I am asking: What shall it profit critics if their soapboxes occupy the periphery and they speak in tongues?

NOTES

1. A fuller discussion would also consider the very different models of Daniel Bell, Franklin Frazier, Nathan Glazer, Daniel Patrick Moynihan, Erving Goffman, and, more recently, Robert N. Bellah and his colleagues. The striking thing about Goffman, alone in this company, is that his influence was screened through a thick, relentless, deadpan academic prose – which over a long

sequence of books helped to certify that he had a system, more than a knack, for seeing through the structures of everyday life. The sense of a practical system made him, willy-nilly, an exemplar of anarchist suspicion, an austere poet of the counterculture.

2. In a less renowned but (for me, at least) also influential phase of his work, Riesman proceeded to address his colleagues, also approachably, on the most urgent political matters — the Bomb and the cold war. In the early 1960s, under his sponsorship and financing, the Committee (later Council) of Correspondence published a "newsletter" — really an informal journal — at first made up largely of his voluminous correspondence, later of more formal articles by academics (though still written with more tentativeness than more established journals invoked) on arms race matters. With varying but real impacts on the Kennedy Washington, on journalism, on the peace movement, and on the incipient New Left (including the about-to-be revisionist historians), the Council of Correspondence provided a valuable space for a thrashing out of critiques, positions, and policies — a noteworthy contribution for social science and social scientists.

3. Consider, by contrast to both Riesman and Mills, the work of one of academia's main composers of epistles to the public in the 1970s, Christopher Lasch. One of Lasch's running themes is the transformation of technologies of reason (social work, Deweyan school reform, psychotherapy) into instruments of class domination.

REFERENCES

Bell, Daniel. 1962. *The End of Ideology.* New York: Free Press.

Bellow, Saul. 1989. *A Theft.* New York: Viking Penguin.

Birnbaum, Norman. 1988. *The Radical Renewal.* New York: Pantheon.

Bloom, Allan. 1987. *The Closing of the American Mind.* New York: Simon & Schuster.

Blumenthal, Sidney. 1986. *The Rise of the Counter-Establishment.* New York: Times Books.

Engels, Friedrich. [1880] 1975. *Socialism: Utopian and Scientific.* New York: International Publishers.

Galbraith, John Kenneth. 1958. *The Affluent Society.* Boston: Little, Brown.

Gilder, George. 1981. *Wealth and Poverty.* New York: Basic Books.

Jacoby, Russell. 1987. *The Last Intellectuals.* New York: Basic Books.

Jencks, Christopher. 1988. "Deadly Neighborhoods." *The New Republic,* June 13, pp. 23-32.

Kennedy, Paul. 1987. *The Rise and Fall of the Great Powers.* New York: Random House.

Kirkpatrick, Jeane. 1979. "Dictatorships and Double Standards." *Commentary* 68:34-45.

Kuhn, Thomas S. 1962. *The Structure of Scientific Revolutions.* Chicago: University of Chicago Press.

Lasch, Christopher. 1979. *The Culture of Narcissism.* New York: Norton.

Mills, C. Wright. 1959. *The Sociological Imagination.* New York: Oxford University Press.

Murray, Charles. 1984. *Losing Ground.* New York: Basic Books.

Riesman, David. 1969. "Preface." In *The Lonely Crowd.* Abridged ed. New Haven, CT: Yale University Press.

Riesman, David, with Nathan Glazer and Reuel Denney. 1950. *The Lonely Crowd.* New Haven, CT: Yale University Press.

Whyte, William H. 1956. *The Organization Man.* New York: Simon & Schuster.

15

Social Criticism and Sociological Elitism

Joan Moore

No sociologist who has had a touch of activism is ever satisfied with what sociology is currently doing to improve the world. Some of us create new professional associations, like the SSSP, to rectify the situation; others bore from within, by creating sections within ASA to advance our cause. Some, like Messrs. Coser and Gitlin, also write papers.

Both of our inquisitors concentrate on topic of the evils of professionalism, giving it a special twist. But both make some odd assumptions that lead them to overlook a couple of fairly obvious features about sociologists as working professionals.

Both Coser and Gitlin indict sociology as a process and decry its end product. First, the question of process. Both men criticize an institutional infrastructure that produces boring sociologists rather than stimulating and transformative social critics. Coser (explicitly) and Gitlin (implicitly) blame our graduate schools for overemphasizing technical competence and stifling social concerns. In the end, therefore, our students do not get educated; they are merely trained. Both critics indict the tenure process. Gitlin goes further and charges the same tenure process for killing off the vitality of such New Left journals as *Telos* and *Theory and Society*.

Second, the products of modern sociology: Both agree that, while "abstracted empiricism" may be socially useful, it is not the equivalent of social criticism. Sociological theory also takes its lumps, but on different grounds. Coser regrets the dilution of concepts that should focus on social criticism. Gitlin sees even so-called critical theory becoming yet another cultist bit of esoterica. But, of course, he doesn't see it as really critical theory. Mastery of this theory simply admits sociologists to an elite group — but a group that is now irrelevant.

Coser and Gitlin also hold up the same kind of sociological role models — Marx, Weber, Riesman, and C. Wright Mills. Yet as a group these stars cannot really be generalized as "sociologists." Very few of us will be stars of this magnitude, let alone theorists with ideas that will endure over many generations. And, really, it's a little chauvinistic to claim most of these men as "sociologists." Even their occupation is irrelevant: Do we remember Marx as a journalist, Weber as a minor German bureaucrat?

In fact, Coser and Gitlin focus on what Jacoby called "public intellectuals" — writers and thinkers who address a national or international educated audience rather than sociologists per se. The public intellectual is their model of the social critic.

But this is a narrow view, very arbitrary. America's public intellectuals are all too often regionally parochial and still Eurocentric, overlooking major national concerns that fall outside of the restricted "intellectual" purview. Perhaps the concept of national speaker and national audience is as outmoded as the *Partisan Review* itself. Surely there are other target audiences for social criticism, and other kinds of social critics. What about those who address specialized audiences? What about those who address localized audiences on localized issues? What about those who address uneducated audiences with, perhaps, some intent to change a level of consciousness? Are they to be denied the label of "social critic"?

Let us take seriously, as a professional question, the goal that sociology should be more transformative. New questions appear immediately. What kind of critic do we want to produce? On what level, with what kind of product? What kind of professional process or infrastructure do we want? (The question of what curriculum would best produce social criticism is outside the scope of my discussion. But social criticism is taken seriously enough as a goal for some people to create graduate curricula that build in local social action. Perhaps our professional associations would find it useful to promote such efforts.)

What kind of critic do we want to produce, and at what level? And how well are we doing it? Gitlin parenthetically allows for some specialized publics. Implicitly a specialized public implies that there are specialized critics, and I hope that Gitlin develops this idea further.

Here we are reaching out for something much closer to the fabric of modern American society. Once we forsake fantasies about sociological superstars writing in national intellectual journals and moving the hearts and minds of an educated national audience, we are free to look for critics at a more realistic level. And I think we really do find amazingly committed critics within contemporary sociology. These are not superstars. They are run-of-the-mill, ordinary, working sociologists. They are specialized social critics, dealing with specialized audiences and specialized professional processes and institutional arrangements.

We have two sets of good examples in fields familiar to me — women and minorities. Black, Latino, and women sociologists are playing significant — but specialized — roles at both local and national levels. Rose Brewer, for example, lists several sociologists as among the leading black feminist intelligentsia and social critics.

During the past twenty years, women and minority sociologists have put serious pressures on the world of academia. In the tenure process, it has been possible to acknowledge the worth of publications in black, feminist, and Hispanic journals (such as *Phylon, Aztlan, Signs,* and *Gender & Society*). In many schools, they have been counted in tenure hearings along with so-called mainstream journals. Service in specialized minority and feminist associations is now counted. In some cases, forms of social action on local issues have been admitted and counted for tenure purposes. To be sure, such efforts may be doomed to failure at Harvard or Berkeley, but there are real successes at Austin, SMU, UWM, and other not stellar but nonetheless respectable universities. American public intellectuals may not be aware of these developments because they have no reason to follow events at such universities. But this is no reason for sociologists to overlook the fact that American universities offer support and encouragement to social critics on a scale that would have been unthinkable thirty years ago.

These are not trivial gains but an important legitimation of social criticism. These are not elite mass audiences but real constituencies. Any academic who is not white, male, and middle-aged knows that the moment he or she stands in front of a class, a portion of the class expects something that will illuminate their place in the social structure. This is a constituency. It is not a public. The woman or minority sociologist feels instant pressure to act as a social critic. And, of course, the pressure continues far beyond the classroom into struggles about framing research topics and about dissemination of research findings. It is this set of constituencies, in and out of the classroom, that helps generate and sustain minority and women sociologists in their roles as critics. I cannot say this strongly enough. It is not possible for a women or minority sociologist to walk into a classroom in modern America and not face instantly and squarely the twin issues of equality and poverty, which, I submit, cover many of the issues that public intellectuals purport to address.

I do agree with Coser and Gitlin that sociology should be transformative. But, as a practitioner, I prefer to identify variations in the sociological profession that *en*courage as well as those that *dis*courage sociologists as social critics. And I have to admit that I secretly prefer sociological criticism (at least some of it) to the punditry that often passes as social criticism by public intellectuals. Before we get too nostalgic about the good old days of *Partisan Review* and *Politics*, we should recognize that the general level of sociological sophistication, both national and local, is much higher than fifty years ago or even twenty years ago.

Reading those essays now, many of them were ill-informed, narrow, and often too short on solid information to support meaningful social criticism. We owe at least one small nod to the importance of empirical research.

Both Coser and Gitlin are curiously mute on the importance of some acute sociological critics who are also recognized by our profession. In particular, the election of Herbert Gans and William Julius Wilson to the presidency of the American Sociological Association indicates that the *profession* rewards social criticism. Perhaps these two men may be considered superstars, but they are also working sociologists whose writings touched off significant social policy debates. Neither one set out to "do" social criticism. They studied what they felt to be important and interesting as sociologists.

A final point: Both Coser and Gitlin are ambivalent, at best, about the role of right-wing social critics. This unnecessarily limits the range of social criticism. Sociology has its conservative social critics, and they have an effect. Furthermore, the recent appearance of conservative social commentary has challenged sociological empiricists. It is interesting that empiricism gains new stature in the responses to conservative pundits.

In short, I do not think it is useful to sociology as a profession to take a nostalgic and elitist view of what we can be as social critics. Change is often created in smaller and narrower arenas, where working sociologists can and do participate.

16

Born-Again Sociology

Peter H. Rossi

Reading the chapters by Professors Gitlin and Coser is very much akin to listening to revivalist preaching. A strong theme in both is a heartwarming nostalgia for the old days when giants like Saint-Simon and Karl Marx shook the world with their critical stances toward the modern societies of their times. Another theme also dwells on the evils in our discipline in the forms of abstracted empiricism, boring technical articles in *American Sociological Review* or *American Journal of Sociology*, group narcissism among critical theorists who write for each other, corruption in the meanings of such honorable concepts as social movements and deviance, not to mention bad writing styles. Both chapters end up with exhortations to the audience to return to the old-time social science, casting aside their structural equation models and their evil writing styles to walk in the paths of the righteous saints, mostly safely dead and gone.

I was about to go up to the altar and be born again, hopefully this time as Machiavelli, when a number of questions about what they were saying began to rise in my mind, which I will share with you.

First of all, the most shocking omission in both chapters is any answers to the question: What is social criticism in general or what is *sociological* social criticism? These issues are not addressed in either chapter except by implication. Of course, Gitlin characterizes sociology as "a way of knowing" and social criticism as "a way of acting," but those neither are good definitions nor are they paid attention to in the rest of his chapter. Indeed, I suspect he will drop these definitions from the final version of his chapter; they are just too superficial to justify setting into type.

Many of the heroes and heroines cited by both speakers were hardly activists. But perhaps this is a minor matter. After all, "everyone knows" who is a social critic and who is not. If you don't know, than you can't be either one.

There are many examples given in the two chapters of social critics. Perhaps we can learn from these examples? The heroic examples are instructive: We learn that, among the dead, Marx, Saint-Simon, C. Wright Mills, Machiavelli, and several others were social critics. We also learn that, among the living, the few heroes are persons such as Riesman, Harrington, Betty Friedan, and Christopher Jencks. The first question that arose in my mind is why it is that so many were not or are not sociologists. I suppose Machiavelli might be forgiven because, after all, sociology had not yet been crafted in his lifetime. But what is Harrington doing there? And Betty Friedan? I raise this question not out of disciplinary turf claiming but because, in these examples, the connection between sociology and social criticism is not revealed. If we are to learn from these heroes and heroines how to be sociological social critics, the connections are far from clear.

The second question that arose in the course of my reading of the two chapters concerns the omissions from the two rosters of heroes and heroines. We may note that, among the dead, Émile Durkheim, the Lynds, Lester Ward, Graham Sumner, Gunnar Myrdal, W.E.B. DuBois, and Pitirim Sorokin are missing. And, among the living, there is no mention of Robert Nisbet, James Coleman, Richard Cloward, Frances Fox Piven, and the like. Of course, no one would expect these two chapters to be encyclopedic, but every sample, when the processes of sampling are not explained, raises the technical issue of selection bias.

Trying to make sense out of this list, I came to the conclusion that the way to get into Gitlin's star class is to write well, sell well, and not be conservative. It is not necessary to be a good sociologist, as many of his examples are not sociologists and many of them are not very good scholars and even fewer are good researchers. I could not make much sense out of Coser's heroes except that they were either dead or European imports and, if alive, the criticism should come from the left and not the right.

A third question that came to mind when I read the two chapters was how little was said about how sociology and sociological work could be used as the basis of social criticism. Social criticism, especially from left of center, is what is being pushed in both chapters, not necessarily *sociologically relevant* social criticism. Perhaps this is why both authors are so ecumenical in their views of disciplinary origins. I believe that there is much that sociological work can contribute to social criticism and, by ignoring this subject, both chapters provide little guidance to the reader. Certainly, one of the heroes written about in both chapters is C. Wright Mills, a man who believed that he could learn from knowledge about our society what those features are that critics should highlight.

Indeed, neither chapter deals with the extremely important issue concerning what are and should be the connections between sociological work and social criticism. For example, I believe that the greatest achievement of postwar

American sociology has been the development of its research capacity. Sociological research can be and has been the provider of information about our society that has served the critical stances of some critics very well. Harrington would not have been able to write about the "other America" if the sociologists and other social scientists at the Bureau of the Census had not made the 1950 Census into among the best of modern censuses. Jencks's work also rests heavily on survey data collected by working social researchers, using designs devised by the technicians whose achievements are denigrated by Coser. Although not at the highest level of technical adequacy, there is also no doubt that Riesman's *The Lonely Crowd* rests on empirical research.

The point is that sociology has contributed mightily to the development of a knowledge base upon which social critics may draw. By that token, American sociological criticism ought to be the best in the world. That it may not be, I believe, is due to several perverse factors. On the one hand, in these two chapters, social critics are judged by what they support rather than by whether what they say is supported by grounded knowledge about our society. If that is the criterion, then sociology or any other social science discipline is not needed.

On the other hand, sociological researchers have largely relied on research paradigms that do not make easy the translation of findings into critical thinking. There is no doubt that a lopsided development of modern social research technology has not made matters easy. Ours is a research technology that is marvelously suited to the enumeration of individuals and households and to social psychological measurements. The main aggregations we deal with are geographic — such as census tracts, counties, cities, and states — and diffuse social groups — such as racial/ethnic, religious denominations — formed by aggregating individuals. Our research technology is primitive for studying organized social units such as kinship networks, political parties, economic firms, government agencies, and the like.

This technical inadequacy or failure is a shortcoming that has largely prevented sociologists from consistently being concerned with social structural issues. This shortcoming is especially handicapping for sociologists trying to serve also as social critics. For example, from Sorokin's early work on social mobility to the most recent structural equation mobility models is in one sense a long step backward. Social mobility is best conceived of as an institutional process, the institutional level being largely omitted in the more recent work with some notable exceptions. With our current conventional research design paradigms, it is far easier to study status attainment in terms of the capacities and experiences of individuals than in terms of the institutional structures that channelize mobility.

The implication for social criticism, with its emphasis on societal processes and large-scale organization, is that much of sociological work is irrelevant. Indeed, it is not that articles in *ASR* and *AJS* are written badly or in inaccessible technical jargon but that what is written about is found to be so irrelevant to social criticism — that is, if you have sufficient command of the technical vocabulary to be able to figure out what the articles are about.

It is instructive to contrast the situation in sociology with that in economics. The economists have traditionally been more concerned with macro-economics than with micro-economics. As a consequence, they have had over the past century considerably more to contribute to public policy than the sociologists. Both Marx and Keynes sparked "revolutions," albeit of quite different sorts. The current crop of monetarists and free market types may not like to think of themselves as revolutionaries but, by providing the intellectual rationale for the current worldwide epidemic of deregulation, they are as much revolutionary as Keynes.

I doubt that the conservative economists write any better than sociologists: Reading the major economics journals is just as much of a chore, if not more, than reading *ASR*. Economists may have wider and more attentive audiences, but then, if you have something to say, it may be easier to find people to listen to it. I am sure that John Kenneth Galbraith writes in a more accessible style than Talcott Parsons did, but that is not the main reason that Galbraith was listened to by a wider audience; he also had something to say that was relevant to the social policy issues of the time while Parsons had very little to say.

For their sake, I hope that the economists now concerned with micro-economic issues do not get sidetracked the way sociologists have into ignoring macro-level social processes. The study of individual differences and processes going on within individuals is seductive because it is easier to do and the appropriate but limited research methods are at hand. Sociologists have been suckered into becoming social psychologists, a legitimate and valid discipline, but one that is more conducive to fiddling with people to make them fit into our institutional structure than with redesigning the structure so that more people fit.

It is not the sloppy corruption of language that has turned *deviance* into a term that has no sharp edges, as Coser suggests, but that the study of individual differences in behavior provides no handles within itself to distinguish socially innovative deviance from self-centered evasion of institutional rules.

I get the sense from Gitlin's chapter that he would like to see a mass audience for social criticism. I think I would too. But the problem, as I see it, is a bit different than his analysis suggests. First of all, we have seen the growth of audiences for conservative social criticism. It is instructive to note the left to right shifts in *Commentary* and *The New Republic*, and the sad fact is that *Mother Jones* reads more like a more wide-ranging Ralph Nader, uncovering but not providing understanding. I cannot pretend to know why *Commentary* drifted to the right; all I know is that, when it did so, the magazine augmented its readership.

Gitlin suggests that the major competition to journals with leftish opinions are the mass media. It would be comforting to believe he is right because it is easier to bear losing out in a struggle with a massively robust giant opponent. Unfortunately, I fear the problem is that the major competitors to journals of liberal and radical opinion are not the mass media so much as the journals of conservative and centrist opinions. It may just be that the conservatives apparently have greater appeal to the literate elite audience that is not composed of couch potatoes. Journals of opinion never had mass audiences, at least in the last fifty years. To rail against the mass media is to pick on an enemy that is easy to rail against: To successfully compete against the conservative journals of opinion is much harder. The latter are winning because they may be better, in some sense.

Note that I am not endorsing the content of conservative thought as being better but that the conservatives appeal more to audiences of our time.

A final comment: In the two main chapters of this section, the implicit sense of a sociologist-social critic is one who is a social critic and happens to be a sociologist. The emphasis is on being critical rather than using sociological theory and sociological knowledge as the basis for being critical. I would like to turn that emphasis around and use the term *sociological critic* to designate someone critical of our society whose criticism is based on a thorough understanding of what is known empirically about our society tempered by an understanding of societal processes. I share Coser's and Gitlin's judgment that description is not enough — facts do not speak for themselves. But that statement should not be interpreted to mean that description is not necessary: Facts do not speak for themselves but they do provide the materials about which others can speak.

The Bureau of the Census did not write *The Other America,* and it probably should not have written it. But without the Census Bureau's descriptive tables, Harrington's book would have been much less effective. Without the Current Population Study's data, Christopher Jencks's work on inequality would have been much less effective.

These last remarks suggest that we should recognize that there can be a productive division of labor within our discipline. We need technicians to develop finer and more perceptive ways of knowing. We need persons concerned with developing meticulously collected descriptive data on our society so that we can use those data as the bases of our critical comments on this society. And we need sociological critics, persons who know what the technicians are doing and what the data tell about our society and who can interpret what the implications are for molding our society into a better one. We also need the social critics to tell the technicians and the describers what they should be measuring and counting. The reverse path is also worth traveling: The critics need to be told what it is that is being measured and whence the descriptions come. The current situation, as portrayed by Coser and Gitlin, in which all sneer at each other, can only be counterproductive.

I would be very proud if our discipline did produce a number of good sociological critics who managed to reach significant audiences and whose critical comments were based on a thorough knowledge of what grounded empirical research has told us about our society. For one, I would prefer it if the sociological critics were more concerned with equality and distributive justice than with efficiency and productivity, but sociological critics of the sort I have just described, either from the left or from the right, are all valid and very welcome.

Part VII
Foreign Sociologists Look at U.S. Sociology

17

American Sociology Viewed from Abroad

Alain Touraine

To talk about "American sociology" is a matter of limited importance. Our reactions toward sociology, when reading publications and using their results, are not grounded in nationality as such. When we refer to urban sociology, the study of juvenile delinquency, or analysis of hospital life, we feel we are using more useful categories and exploring fields of sociological research that have their own history. We all have clearer opinions about Park, Lynd, Parsons, Lazarsfeld, or Goffman, to mention but a few American sociologists who have passed away, than about so vast a domain as "American sociology," which cannot be more precisely defined than the "English novel," "French theater," or "German music."

What first attracts the attention of foreign observers is not so much American sociology's orientations and trends, which are diverse, but the way it is organized. In the United States, more than in other countries, sociology is a profession based in the universities, which, more powerful than elsewhere, provide a nearly unique model, much as the University of Berlin did in the nineteenth century, of how institutions of higher education should be organized.

Accordingly, we might say that American sociology exists more for Americans than for foreigners. It is the professional and intellectual world wherein the large majority of American sociologists live and work; and they do not have enough time to read all of the American books and journals of interest to them. For this reason, and despite these initial remarks, it is useful, even necessary, to analyze American sociology.

Among other things, sociology is an interpretation of specific social experiences. Although it seeks to formulate and prove general propositions, it is so embedded in the reality it has observed that it is, in fact, part of this reality. Before attempting to interpret American sociology, I would like to make one last qualification: This attempted interpretation can be, at best, but frail because it is guided by personal experiences and concerns.

THE TWO FACES OF SOCIOLOGY

I discovered America and its sociology as a Rockefeller fellow in 1952-53. I acknowledge the liberalism of this institution, which, at the height of McCarthyism, enabled a young French intellectual, strongly marked by the leftist climate of his own country, to spend time at Harvard — attending T. Parsons's seminar — and Columbia — with Paul Lazarsfeld, Robert Merton, and Martin Lipset — and also at Chicago, the Mecca of all sociologists at that time. The shock was sudden and the attraction so great that, since then, I have spent much time thinking about this experience. Sometimes, I felt that I belonged to a foreign intellectual and political culture, threatened by America's. But sometimes, on the contrary, and just as often, I took sides, as Tocqueville had done, with my host country and criticized my own society, in particular the way the social sciences were organized and evolving there. In both cases, I felt differences between American and European approaches were deeper than similarities.

These differences correspond on the whole to the opposition or, at least, separation between the two major problems that have, independently of each other, been repeatedly studied by sociologists. The first is this: How does society exist? How do *groups* — in the broadest reach of the word, whether national societies, institutions, or organizations — manage to maintain their cohesion through external change and internal strains? What goes into the making of social bonds or into the formation of collective conscience? This sort of inquiry, which has been pursued since Hobbes, Locke, and Rousseau, lies at the center of Durkheim's thought. The second question is this: How are culture and society historically created and transformed by work, by the specific way nature and its resources are put to use, and through systems of political, economic, and social organization? This second type of question has been central for the nineteenth century, from Marx to Weber, while the first question had received more attention in the eighteenth century. Now, my view is that, although questions about social groups and their cohesiveness or degree of integration have been asked everywhere, they have been central in the United States, whereas questions of the second sort have been predominant in Europe. Roots of American intellectual and political culture are in the eighteenth century; roots of European culture in the nineteenth. That does not mean that all of either American or European thinkers are on the same side. We must admit that Durkheim is nearer to American sociology and Bendix or Barrington Moore nearer to what I am calling the European tradition.

These differences in intellectual orientations stem from historical experiences. American thought has been shaped by the experience of creating a nation by the will of the people through legal processes. The foundation of this nation started with "We, the people," a phrase directly inspired by eighteenth-century European concepts of trust and social contract. Hence, American sociology has dwelt on a central concept, institution, and that demonstrates the impact of eighteenth-century thought upon American life. What a French person, for instance, has the hardest time understanding about your country — and what he admires most — is its legal system, specifically, its judiciary. This fundamental act of a people creating a nation through law was reinforced by the action of creating a nation through territorial conquest and the integration of successive waves of immigrants. Those who founded the modern American university system, in the last third of the nineteenth century, consciously sought to create a national elite from New England across to California (going through Chicago) that would be able to withstand both cultural chaos and the pressure exerted by immigrants and the lower classes.

This concern with integration has always been associated with modernization, defined in terms of openness and pragmatism. But, although American society may have been materially shaped by military actions and by the quest for profits under the leadership of industrial and financial entrepreneurs, it does not think of itself as such: its self-image is not basically economic. This society defines groups and individuals less in quantitative terms, in terms of up and down, than in terms of belonging or being excluded, terms of in and out; hence its constant fascination with themes such as delinquency, social control, socialization, and the institutional settlement of conflicts. American sociology is at its best when it deals with ethnic groups, segregation, or discrimination; it is less convincing when it refers to social classes or economic power. The importance given to the concepts of institution and socialization becomes all the more evident if we look toward Europe, whose self-image has come out of a quite different founding experience.

In Europe, modernity was not something decided and instituted. It was won out of a struggle against political, cultural, and social traditions. Just as *institution* is the key work in America, *revolution* has been, for a long time, the key work in Europe, as well as in Latin America and other regions of the world. *Revolution* refers to much more than violently seizing power and taking over the government in the name of the People. When it is used in phrases such as *industrial revolution* or *moral revolution,* it designates a constant struggle between, on one side, modernity and freedom and, on the other, tradition, parochialism, and authoritarianism. For Europeans, modernity works like a steam engine (to borrow an image from Claude Lévi-Strauss), running on the opposition between cold and hot poles — concentrating power and wealth on one pole and generating class struggle on the other. Whether conflict takes place between economic actors (social classes) or between political and ideological ones (state and church), life in European society has always been taken to be the unstable, changing result of a conflict-laden history.

In the United States, it is difficult to separate society and culture; in Europe, it is difficult to separate society and history, hence the crucial importance in Europe of labor and economic problems in contrast with the American preoccupation with institutions (the family, firm, hospital, or city). It would hardly be an exaggeration to say that the city has been as much at the center of American sociology as the factory has been in European sociology. This contrast accounts for the greater diversification of American sociology and R. Merton's emphasis on the necessity for middle-range theories. The theme of the social system and its cohesion or integration is so broad that it has no actual contents unless one specializes in order, for example, to study the congruence of statuses, the role set, or labeling processes, or to describe hospitals, prisons, or neighborhoods. European sociology, on the contrary, has been constantly dominated by the quest for the center, for the central social conflict; hence the importance of economic sociology but, also, of religion.

This contrast between two faces of sociological analysis, despite its generality, applies to several fields of research of which I would like to mention but two. The first one is of special interest to me. On each side of the Atlantic, we use the phrase *social movement,* but with meanings nearly always so different that we cannot be sure we are talking about the same facts. Now and then, misunderstandings arise; and research from the opposite shore is dismissed without much thought being given to it, without recognition being given to the different perspectives guiding it. In the United States, this phrase refers to social or cultural demands that, because they do not receive an adequate response from within the institutional system, give rise to "wild," "marginal," or violent action. Such crises have two main causes: the blocking of institutional channels and the resistance by social or cultural groups, in particular, ethnic, regional, occupational, or moral minorities, against the assimilation of dominant norms and values or integration into dominant forms of organization. Social movements are taken to be symptoms of a lack of integration. It is not surprising that they have come under increasing study since the 1960s, when American society, hitherto confident in its capacity for integration, was suddenly faced with the student movement, the civil rights movement, the violent resistance of racist groups, and demonstrations against the Vietnam War. Although conservatives, liberals, and radicals have interpreted these phenomena differently, they have generally defined the problem in the same way, namely: Why have institutions failed to respond adequately to certain social demands? And how can they be improved, or reformed, so as to take these demands into account?

This problem has guided research in Europe too and does so more and more often (a point to which I shall return); however, the European tradition has studied social movements from a very different standpoint: It does not consider them to be a symptom that institutions have not worked as they should. Nor does it take them to be a measure of the cultural distance between minorities and the majority. Instead, social movements are seen as coming out of a *central* struggle between opposite — dominant versus dependent — social categories for the control of major cultural resources and orientations of the economy but also in matters of ethics and knowledge. The European labor movement provides us with an example of this: It came into existence only when wage earners in industry began sharing the same cultural values as their managers — notedly, confidence in technology, productivity, labor, and progress — and, at the same time, fought against the power of capitalists who were accused of seeking profits rather than pursuing rationality (a choice that led to what American unions at the turn of the century called "industrial waste"). Today, when Europeans study the "new" social movements, they primarily seek to discover, within a society of communication and services rather than of industrial production, collective actions and conflicts that, despite having contents very different from the workers' movement, nonetheless, like the latter, are forms of protest against the social and political power that dominates this emerging type of society. The American approach insists on the number and diversity of social conflicts, whereas the European one attempts to see what unites the principal conflicts that break out in society. American sociologists are often irritated by this European obsession with the center and with grand theories, and Europeans, for their part, are often annoyed by what seems to them to be an effort to hide forms of power and cover up major social conflicts.

The second example of opposite interpretations of the same facts is not far from the preceding. In Europe, democracy is almost spontaneously defined as being representative. Parties represent social interests or even social classes. As a consequence, democracy has too often been analyzed not as a form of political organization but in terms of its social contents. For example, it was fashionable, even among sociologists (at least until the phrase *people's democracy* revealed the quite real dangers of this sort of analysis) to contrast "real" or "social" democracy with "formal" democracy. In the United States, on the contrary, law and due process of law have always been emphasized: Political analysis has also been closely related to the legal analysis of the conditions for upholding valid and collective rights and permitting interests, ideas, and programs to be freely voiced. In this example too, differing perspectives have often led to misunderstandings. Americans feel close to Tocqueville and agree with his criticisms of the Old World; and Europeans have often doubted the democratic nature of a society that they see as being both dominated by big business and unable to do away with racial discrimination. H. Arendt has given a classical analysis of the opposition between the American and the French revolutions.

Many other examples could be cited in addition to these two, and it would be interesting to ask why American sociology has a lead in precise fields, such as health and medicine or mass communications. However, I will not do this, because it would be false and dangerous to maintain that all of American and all of European sociology is integrated within a single intellectual orientation. I prefer diversifying this initial image of American sociology by situating other tendencies in relation to it.

COUNTERCURRENTS IN AMERICAN SOCIOLOGY

We can point to two major currents of thought in the United States that resist adopting an institutionalist, or functionalist, view of society. At the center of the first lies the notion of community, and at the center of the second, the notion of interaction. The first of these is easier to define.

Although America has been created out of the moral and legal determination to constitute a government through law, the country has long experienced waves of immigration, urban crises, juvenile delinquency, and the resistance of various groups to social and cultural integration and assimilation. This resistance has been enhanced by the importance of local life and the relative weakness of the central government. This contrasts with much more rapid integration in real melting pot countries such as Argentina and Uruguay (thanks to their centralized educational systems), in spite of the fact that immigrants made up a larger part of their populations. The importance of these social problems explains why American sociology has been so long identified with the Chicago School, human ecology, and a culturalist approach. All these have insisted on the autonomy, initiative, or resistance of primary groups, subcultures, minorities, neighborhoods, or regions. Nevertheless, it seems to me that the importance of this type of research proves, despite appearances, the centrality of the institutionalist approach and the idea of a social system. A European would have asked how minorities and subcultures become an integrated working class, whereas American sociology, in what has probably been its most brilliant specialty, namely, the study of juvenile delinquency, went, from Thrasher and Shaw to Cohen, from Cohen to Cloward and Ohlin, then to Matza and Cicourel, from an ecological and culturalist approach to a functionalist one, until, starting with Becker and others, it turned itself around to labeling, stigmatization, and exclusion, so as to show that *the principal subject of inquiry should be the social system, not a particular category of actors.*

The relationship between the concepts of interaction and social system is more complex. An American type of sociology — with its central idea that social organization implies a close, complementary relationship between institutions and socialization — is especially sensitive to crises of socialization when norms are no longer internalized by actors. The United States has never been seriously threatened by an authoritarian political power, a possibility that obsesses Europe. But, on the contrary, because it is so liberal, American society can become unable of integrating individuals and groups. That defines the second countercurrent in American sociology. Pragmatism and the pursuit of personal interests give rise to an individualism that strongly resists social integration. Hence, norms and values are no longer internalized. They constitute an environment, a set of constraints, of rules of the game; and individuals draw up *strategies* that combine their interests with an outward respect for these rules. This is the reason the sociology of interaction, notedly, in Goffman's work, has a cynical tone that brings to mind Balzac's and Stendhal's novels. Thus the vast domain of semisocial behavior has been opened up, which is explained both in sociological terms and by game theory. The farther we go in this direction, the more individuals seem to muddle through a world without any institutional rules, values, or convictions. How different a view from the interpretation of "marginal" groups and persons in developing countries, who are involved in political or religious movements (for instance, the communitarian revival movements). In the United States, interactionism has sprung up along the margins of functionalism, sometimes coming closer to it and sometimes going farther afield, especially in the case of Goffman.

Finally, American sociology has been constantly attracted by its direct contrary, which is not the sociology of historical conflicts (of crucial importance in Europe) but the rationalist sociology of interest (inherited from the liberal thinkers of nineteenth-century England). The study of rational choices, or decision making, in organizations rather than in the marketplace constituted the strongest criticism of the institutionalist model. What has been called the sociology of organizations, a name implying too narrow a definition, has followed an opposite course from the sociology of juvenile delinquency. Unlike the latter, organization theory has more and more taken its distance from functionalism. It criticizes the idea that the efficient firm functions according to the universal principles of Reason, an idea that management theorists have borrowed from the Enlightenment; and it lays ever more emphasis on limited rationality — according to Simon's formula — and strategies of actors defending their interests in a changing environment over which they have little control.

The importance of these two schools, interactionism and neorationalism, proves that American sociology has formulated its sharpest criticism of the functionalist model through an analysis not of the system but of the actors. This leads us straight back to the difference between our two continents. A crucial problem in any society is the absence of correspondence between actors and system. In America, the main preoccupation is with a lack of social integration and the development of selfish interests or of closed subcultures; in Europe, on the contrary, the most disturbing phenomenon has been totalitarianism, whether Stalinist or Hitlerian, and the suppression, restriction, or manipulation of actors and of social movements, who become victims or subjects. More recently, European thought has become acutely aware of another crisis, cultural rather than political: Doubt has been cast upon the notion of *modernity*, which, as I said at the start, was experienced as a barely won but continually threatened

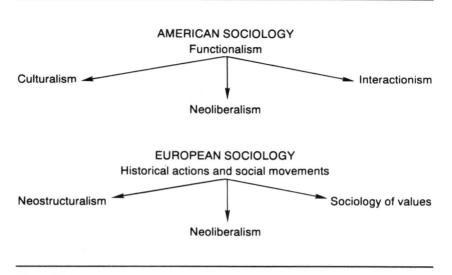

Figure 17.1

victory over all sorts of forces. This doubt runs through the themes of postmodernity or even posthistoricity, which have been rapidly diffused, among sociologists as well as among architects, artists, and art theorists. J. Habermas, because he has most actively resisted these themes, now stands at the center of European thought.

So I want to conclude this first and main part of my analysis by saying that the contrast between what I have called the American and European traditions of sociology is useful because it corresponds to the two faces of sociological analysis and makes it possible to define the relations between various trends or schools within each tradition (see Figure 17.1). There is a homology between these two traditions. American sociology's main orientation is institutionalist, analyzing processes and problems of integration. These orientations have succeeded absorbing large part of communist studies but are criticized and limited by interactionists. Neoliberals, in America as everywhere, proclaim the victory of Homo oeconomicus over Homo sociologicus and the end of sociology as an autonomous body of principles and problems.

In the European sociology, on the other side, the study of social movements and of historical action has come under attack, on one side, from cultural sociology (which undertakes a general inquiry into the values of a civilization and their crisis) and, on the other, from a purely critical sociology that sees in social organization only the logic of a central power and the mechanisms for maintaining or reproducing inequality. Farthest removed from the sociology of historical actions stands neoliberalism, associated with the theme of decision making and strategies, a theme common to both our continents. In neorationalism, the traditions of our two continents come closest together. The viewpoints of liberals and Marxists often converge in that, because they conceive of collective actors as being guided by the pursuit of their interests, and, because the problem of the ends is thus settled, what is to be studied is how resources are mobilized and used. This conception is opposed, on one hand, by those who remain faithful to an American type of institutional analysis and, on the other, by those who, interested (like myself) in a European type of approach to social movements, refuse to define their goals in purely utilitarian terms. On the contrary, Europeans like R. Michels and Americans like M. Olson are similar in that they are wary of collective action and organizations.

THE EUROPEANIZATION OF AMERICA AND VICE VERSA

Till now, the comparison between two sociological traditions has been static. But, obviously, these traditions have been changing. The European origins of a large part of American sociology have often been pointed out, and, during the Great Depression, American sociology sought to analyze the social and economic world crisis and it came close, especially in the case of R. Lynd, to adopting perspectives that I have characterized as European. During the same period, sociology in Europe was reduced to next to nothing as the social sciences were destroyed in Germany and the Durkheimian School was exhausted in France. Now, in the 1980s, even if during half a century the differences between American and European sociologies have been rather conspicuous, maybe the distance between our two continents is decreasing. Is it possible that even the orientations in sociology are being reversed?

What most strikes one is the Americanization of European thought. As major political ideologies have worn out, the Old World has begun turning toward a typically New World theme — integration. There is no better proof of this than the sudden emphasis on minority groups and racism, in particular racism against immigrant workers. At the same time, political sociology has been growing independent of the study of social classes and stratification, and it is devoting more attention to the protection of groups and individuals than to the social underpinnings of political power or collective efforts to defend class interests. Here too, European approaches are coming nearer to traditional American analyses.

Is American sociology, in turn, being Europeanized? The European visiting the United States is sometimes surprised to see Marxism being taught as widely as in Europe during the 1970s. He is interested in observing a renewed interest in the mechanisms of social domination and reactions to it, but he is somewhat surprised to see Marxist sociology considered as a special field more than as a general approach present in discussions of general problems. What interests him more is to observe that American thought had begun to be influenced by the image that others, in particular in the Third World, have of the United States. So that Americans are getting closer to the Europeans, who have, for a long time, been influenced by the way colonized people and other dominated categories view their society. Even more important, while Europe is getting out of the problems of industrial society with some difficulties, intellectually as much as economically, and maintains "gauchist" ideologies, that is, a mixture of new cultural and social demands with Marxist fundamentalism, American sociology has been more sensitive to new forms of domination and to social movements characteristic of societies wherein mass production and consumption of material goods are becoming less important and central than mass production and diffusion of symbolic goods, and characteristic of societies wherein domination is exercised not only over labor and material resources but also and primarily over information, images, language, personality, and culture. American social thought seems to be particularly interested in protest movements not of citizens or wage earners but of individuals or groups who feel threatened in their own personalities by the products and power of culture industries.

European thought, still often taken up with economic determinism and teleological conceptions of history, has a hard time understanding this return to problems having to do with ethics and personality. Maybe the moral traditions that are so strong in the United States have led Americans to broader interest in these new types of protest? The United States is the country where minority rights have been most actively defended. It is the country from which ecology as a protest movement has been launched, even though such themes have had a more autonomous political development in Germany. In the United States and especially within sociology, feminist thought has produced its major works of analysis and criticism. More generally, the basic unity of struggles having to do with class, race, and gender has been more actively proclaimed in the United States.

These new trends have often clashed with what I have called the central theme and inspiration of American sociology: They more easily relate either to interactionism or to the culturalist or human ecological tradition of the study of communities. The integration of these new fields and a more traditional orientation is difficult: Top-level universities have been divided and nearly paralyzed by the tense coexistence of professors of different tendencies. Nevertheless, there is a real danger that one kind of sociology, very professional but blind to the deepest movements in society, comes into conflict with another sociology, which, though sensitive to and involved in new social problems, acts more like an ideological pressure group than like a center of scientific research. Here, the European experience is more positive; it has more clearly demonstrated how critical reflection about the political and social situation can be combined with respect for professional rules of research. Such a combination is more difficult when sociology keeps giving a central importance to the concept of society instead of getting closer to the European tradition, namely, recognizing that historical transformations are carried out through central — but not necessarily centrally organized — social conflicts, whether these are handled through institutional channels or not. The classical functionalist or institutionalist perspective has already been reversed as far as developing countries are concerned. A generation ago, the prevailing idea was that these countries where disorder, poverty, and violence were visible would, thanks to modernization, become not only prosperous but stable and democratic. Very few American or European sociologists now defend this point of view, either because they emphasize the "dependency" of these countries upon developed countries or else because they have replaced the idea of stages of growth with that of paths of development, based on the diversity of social and political forms of historical change, forms that depend on economic modernization but also on external domination, the process of building of a nation-state, social class conflicts, and populist or antipopulist policies as well. Should we not apply this same approach to all societies and not only to the so-called underdeveloped ones?

THE LIMITS OF SOCIOLOGICAL ANALYSIS

But it would not be adequate to conclude that European sociology is becoming partly Americanized and vice versa. It is more important to observe that both are trying to get out, each one in its own way, of a general orientation they had in common. During a long period of time, they both believed that modernization meant the elimination of subjective factors, faith, conviction, values, and intentions, and the formation of social systems that are defined by their "organic solidarity," by their internal rationality, by a growing interdependence of their components. At that level, both traditions have been functionalist. The European tradition now rejects the idea of a rational society, coming from the Enlightenment and translated both by liberal economists and by Marxists. The American tradition, which culminated with T. Parsons's general theory, becomes weaker because more and more actors cannot be reduced to roles and roles to functions. A large part of present-day American sociology deals with the weakening of social controls and the growth of individual and collective behavior that neither respects nor attacks social norms but gives a priority to personal interests, values, and preferences over the needs or norms of the social system. American sociology is more influenced by its libertarian or individualistic mood than by conservative or radical orientations.

The American modern expression of the sacred *Society* and the European one, *History,* are rejected by a diversity of reactions from the most individualistic to the most sectarian, and by social movements that no longer refer to a rational society or to the end of history or prehistory. It is rather insufficient to oppose conservative and radical sociologies because both can share the same general view of social life, differing only about the capacity of institutions to adequately respond to new demands. We need a more complete reappraisal of the intellectual foundations of our discipline. Has sociology, as the heir to the social Philosophy of the Enlightenment, not replaced a religious with a social principle of order, in that it has turned society — in America — or history — in Europe — into principles that are as transcendental as "God" or national culture were before its development? In more general terms, might there not be a crisis of our common traditional conception of *modernity* as the creation of a rational society, which functions on mechanical or organic models borrowed from the natural sciences? Has sociology not arbitrarily laid too much emphasis on collective integration instead of on the diversity of actors? On instrumental rationality instead of on the ethics of conviction? On socialization instead of on personal autonomy? In short, has sociology not taken sides in a debate that has been raging for centuries between two conceptions of modernity: on the one side, the triumph of rationality and, therefore, of a rationalist conception of social organization as a system of communication, and, on the other, the emphasis on freedom of conscience and the defense of human rights against institutions and rules?

For a long time, we have felt assured that human rights coincided with the citizen's duties, as American and French declarations of rights had taught us, but nowadays, has not our conception of democracy led us, particularly in the United States, to protecting individuals and minorities from society and from the requirements of its integration and rational functioning? Our society seems to work less and less like a system but more and more like a situation wherein behavior, movements, and conflicts develop that are less and less oriented toward social integration and more toward self-development and ethical experiences. The traditional domain of sociology seems to be invaded, on one side, by international problems and, on the other, by the increasing importance of personality and interpersonal problems. It is high time to give up defining sociology as the study of society; it is more aptly the study of individuals and groups trying to act as subjects, behaving in a more and more tightly controlled social environment. This crisis affects the American tradition as much as the European one, but perhaps less deeply because Europeans have been more confident in the possibility of building a rational society, while Americans have generally been more sensitive to individual and group autonomy and have not considered it as sheer resistance of traditions and privileges to rationality and modernity.

So my conclusion is that, instead of going on putting the emphasis on the differences between two traditions, it becomes more urgent to consider how both of them are trying to get out of their common definition of sociology as the study of rationalization and of rational systems. I think that such a basic transformation of our field is likely to progressively eliminate the formerly central concept of society both in its American and its European forms and to give a central importance probably in different ways in different parts of the word to the concept of social actors. This evolution of the discipline will limit and already limits the differences between the two major sociological traditions.

SOCIOLOGY AS A PROFESSION

A European author has said that sociologists constitute a regular clergy in Europe but a secular one in the United States. I began by pointing out that American sociology is a profession whose strength is proved by the organization of the meeting on which this book is based. The American sociologist is, first of all, a teacher; and sociology is an important part of your country's intellectual culture. In Communist countries of central or eastern Europe, on the contrary, many more sociologists work with companies and planning agencies. However, in France, researchers are financed by public agencies outside the universities more frequently than in the United States. Thus it is not surprising that textbooks and publications of introductory sociology are more plentiful in the United States than in Europe and that American sociologists address, above all, other professionals and make a clear distinction between their writings and parasociological essays for a general public. They are sometimes consulted as experts, but they are seldom seen in public. On the contrary, European sociologists are more involved in public affairs, partly because the university environment to which they belong is narrower and weaker, so much so that they do not always identify themselves at first as sociologists. I recall a seminar in Paris that brought together the teachers, historians, economists, sociologists, anthropologists, and mathematicians of the Ecole des Hautes Etudes en Sciences Sociales, to which I belong. Journalists asked Roland Barthes and myself, as organizers of the seminar, to which occupational category we thought we belonged. Spontaneously, we both replied that the term that suited us best was not sociologists or even social scientists but intellectuals.

One of the consequences of these differences is that there is more communication in Europe than in America between social sciences and mass media. The fact that European sociology has many contacts with intellectual and political circles is in many ways positive. In turn, the solidity of their professional circles and universities helps American sociologists to analyze new social and cultural phenomena in a more professional language; but there is the risk of them maintaining a view of social life that corresponds more to their teaching traditions than to the actual social situation and to social actors' behavior.

Because I have much experience with the advantages and disadvantages of European professional life, I would like to end by voicing my admiration for American universities, whose campuses are fertile meeting grounds for those involved in cultural and intellectual innovations and in scientific work where communication is easily established between the heritage from the past, stored in impressive libraries, and the most imaginative experiments. More concretely and personally, I would like to express to your country and to its social scientists my gratitude: It is in your country that I discovered sociology, which was, at that time, little and poorly taught in my own. American sociology is one of the intellectual creations that has most deeply influenced our century. No other society has been more actively involved in understanding its own organizational change for the sake of the knowledge itself. For this reason, sociologists can never feel completely foreign in your country.

18

General Theory and American Sociology

Niklas Luhmann

I.

The sociology of sociologists is an empirical science not only in the United States but everywhere. It is not my intention to engender any doubts about this. Looking with European eyes on American sociology, it could be a temptation to notice the degree, verging on the exclusive, to which Americans are committed to short-term empirical projects, and to mention their sophistication and the average excellence of their oral and written contributions. Presenting themselves abroad, American sociologists underline their positivistic approach (see Smelser 1986), but, to repeat this essential point: This is not something that deserves reproach. Citing a comment Stendhal made about the love behavior of Americans at the beginning of the last century, I could almost repeat: "We admire them, we don't envy them" (Stendhal 1959, p. 176). However, this is not my point. Rather, I wish to draw your attention to certain problems that result from the American commitment to empirical research.

As a first problem, the empirical concept of sociology itself becomes unclear precisely when we conceive sociology as empirical research. About what are we going to talk: about people (sociologists), about organizations, about publications? This would lead us to neglect the fact that research is selection, that results are contingent, that sociologists process information that they themselves have previously constructed. Considering this, we would have to say that sociology is the total sum of possible explanations. But what is the referent of this realm of possibilities, which is — in medieval terminology — its "contraction"? Or in Kantian terminology: What are the conditions of admittable possibilities?

It seems that empirical methodology and even the prevailing epistemology (including the recently prospering sociology of science) do not prepare us to answer such questions. An answer would involve self-reference and circular reasoning. It would require eating the forbidden fruit. Without tackling such problems, the empirical sociology of empirical sociology would reduce its object (including itself) to a kind of natural drift (Humberto Maturana). It does what it does. It can be observed, but there is no control of standards or even of expectations against which it could be evaluated. And the so-called postmodern predicament will give its blessing to this approach: There are several possibilities of evaluating and criticizing sociology. Choose one of them!

A second problem can be presented by an inductive argument. So far, empirical sociology has not been able to propose a convincing theory of modern society. Conceptualizations as capitalistic society, industrial society, and postindustrial society lack empirical support in their conclusions. They point to some obvious facts, to some trends that can be demonstrated by selected data, but they change like fashions; and they do not describe the total system but only some of its characteristics. Most of the more theoretically inclined sociologists — and, again, in the United States as elsewhere — return to our classics, if no longer to Marx then to Weber or Durkheim or Simmel (see Alexander 1987; Parsons 1988). These people are told to have made binding decisions, if not about theories then about problems sociologies are supposed to pursue. Poor classics — they may remain hostages of academy sociology forever and may serve to replace theoretical research with exegetic erudition. And if we were to ask whether any new view of society has emerged since the time of our classics, we should have to answer in the negative. But we are living toward the end of the twentieth century. We are observing irritating realities — ecological problems, lack of integration of highly autonomous functional systems, deviation amplifications in the direction of structural developments with high inherent improbability, acceleration of structural changes, a radical turnover of classical and even so-called modern semantics, and an increasing degree of risk awareness and risk aversion without convincing alternatives.

This incapacity of present sociology to give an adequate account of modern society may result from epistemological obstacles. According to Gaston Bachelard (1947, pp. 13 ff.), epistemological obstacles prevent progress of knowledge committing us to formerly convincing conceptualizations. So, sociologies normally describe society by reference to a certain species of free-moving objects, called humans or subjects. In this perspective, society consists of humans and/or of relations between humans. This idea has its roots in the old European notion of "animal sociale." It is clearly incompatible with modern developments in physics, chemistry, biology, and psychology.

Another obstacle is the description of society as a regional unity. Then the United States is one society and the Soviet Union, or Mexico or even Canada, another one. The most important problem of sociology, that is, to define the boundaries of the encompassing system, is abandoned to geography; and, even worse, the theory of society has to use names to refer to its object, although names have no place whatever in theory.

Both the humanistic and the regional definitions of society make it impossible to provide for a clear definition of the societal system, to locate its boundaries, and to describe the type of operation that recursively reproduces the system as the unity of its own reproduction. It will be obvious that such deficiencies can be removed only by general theory. Such a theory has to be an empirical theory. It has to refer to reality (and not simply to self-validating conceptual constructions) but it cannot limit itself to a prediction of the outcome of empirical research in the form of correlations between empirical data. Its object is a self-referring system. Its empirical adequacy can be achieved only by taking self-reference into account.

II.

In recent decades, only one attempt has been made to formulate a general theory of sufficient complexity — the theory (or conceptual "framework") of general action, the lifelong preoccupation of Talcott Parsons. For some time it has been a joint venture of European and American thought. About twenty years ago, this enterprise fell into disrepute in America, but it gained increasing attention in Europe, particularly in Germany. Recent neofunctionalist or neo-Parsonian interests in the United States, therefore, draw to some extent on German sources; but, normally, Germans who accept systems theory as their research program meet astonished looks if they dare to enter the United States — as if they were not quite au courant with present sociology.

As far as I can see, there has never been an adequate — although there has been some semiadequate — discussion and refutation of this general theory of action, particularly in its systems — theoretical implications. It starts with an analysis of the concept of action, presupposing that action can come about only in conformity with its concept — as applied concept, so to speak. Parsons then proceeds to analyze the components of this concept and arrives at four components whose cross-tabulation produces the famous AGIL-Paradigm. In this sense, *action is system*, and it can evolve only by functional differentiation according to the directions indicated by the four components or functions.

There are many important insights derivable from this scheme. I mention only two. The most important corollary leads to a completely un-Weberian sociology. The person is not the subject of his action but a subsystem of the action system. This makes it anachronistic to discuss action theory and systems theory as different paradigms. The only relevant discussion should be whether or not the basic operation constituting the social system could be conceived as an action — or perhaps rather as an *inherently social* operation, that is, communication.

A second advance is the insistence on functional differentiation at the level of the general action system and at the level of the social system as well. This means that the society no longer can be characterized by pointing to one of its functional subsystems only and claiming priority for it. Functional primacy in Parsons means only that at the next higher level the subsystem is specialized to serve only one function whereas in itself it again has to fulfill all four functions. This eliminates the traditional reference to one of the functions as the top function of the total system — be it the political function or the economic function. All functions now have to be seen as having the same degree of importance, and the structure of a system has to be characterized by the degree to which it realizes the functional differentiation of subsystems and subsystems in subsystems.[1]

These are important theoretical innovations, and they show that Parsons himself was not quite at the level of his own theory when he claimed to continue and synthesize classical traditions. Be this as it may, I do not have the time to discuss with sufficient care the merits and problems of this approach. My point is rather that Parsons's approach will not help solve the problems that I outlined at the beginning of this chapter. It has no place for the fundamental problems of self-reference, curtailing all reflections of this kind by the assumption that action is the applied concept of action. Moreover, it does not offer a sufficient theory of modern society. Parsons retains the regional concept of society — insisting for one of his books on the title "The System of Modern Societies." And, even worse, he cannot systematically distinguish between the general concept of the social system and the concept of the encompassing system of the society. (I may mention in parenthesis that this problem had been solved by the Greek concept of *koinonía politiké* (societas civilis), which postulated the Koinón as the general concept and described the political koinonía as the most excellent whose goals include all others in itself.[2]) In Parsons, the diffuse and uncontrollable relations between the differentiation of the social system (or, for that matter, the action system) and the theory of society reduce this theory to a series of more or less convincing impressions, ad hoc statements, and feuilletonisms — as very often in Hegel too.

Looking from the outside at American sociology, I see increasing interest in Parsons as a historical author — like other classics. I don't see much continuity in research within the Parsonian grid. The impression is paradigm lost, but no paradigm regained.

It might be possible to do some repair work. One could consider describing the action system as a completely closed system, using the distinctions of the variables of the cross-tabulation as a technique for reflecting its own relations to time and environment. This would eliminate the reference to an external observer, and Parsons himself would have to reenter his system in one of the tiny boxes within boxes within boxes.[3] But then, the whole theory would become contingent on the decision of the action system to use these kinds of distinctions for purposes of self-identification. Considering all the problems of such repair work and the difficulties of even then arriving at a sociological theory of modern society, I rather prefer to make a fresh start. But how?

III.

A highly general but nevertheless instructive lesson can be drawn from these considerations. A theory of society has to be a theory of a self-referential system. Moreover, if we continue to define society as the encompassing social system, this system will include its own description. At least if we take observations and descriptions as social operations, that is, as communications, we have to admit that with reference to society there can be no external observer. Science itself is a social system and as such a subsystem of the societal system. This should not come as a surprise to sociologists. In particular, a sociology of sociology has always looked for social conditions of social research. This program could be executed by standard methods of empirical research or by speculations in the guise of empirical statements — see Gouldner's insights on "Parsons at Harvard." But we should not stop at this point. Such insights have consequences for the theory of society. Society has to be conceived as a self-observing and self-describing system; and its self-description has to include even this statement.

This amounts to saying that society on the level of its own operations (not in terms of causality, of course) is a completely closed system. There is neither input nor output of communication, or even information, connecting the society with its environment. Communications are by necessity internal operations. Pieces of information are constructions made by the system itself. The system reacts by communication to irritations and perturbations stemming from its environment. It cannot connect itself by communication with the environment. It cannot communicate with its environment. It extends or contracts the realm of its own operations by making communications possible or impossible, by the invention of language, of writing, of phonetic writing and its equivalents, by the printing press, and, to a not yet observable degree, by the invention of electronic media. These extensions — and not demographic growth, as Durkheim would have it (de la division du travail social, Paris, 1893) — require changes in the form of differentiation.

Writing an empirical research program along these lines would not present major problems. It could include a revised sociology of knowledge, correlating semantic changes with advances in communication technology and changes in terms of differentiation. I should mention at this point Walter Ong or Eric Havelock (for example, Ong 1967, 1971, 1977, 1982; Havelock 1963, 1978,

1982, 1986). Perhaps sociologists will join in considering their recent interest in "culture." They will meet considerable problems, due to the incompleteness and defectiveness of the semantic materials of ancient times and the overwhelming amount of publications immediately after the invention of the printing press. This, however, is not the main problem, even taking into account that it is unknown territory for most sociologists. The question is rather: What kind of theory fits this kind of research program, admitting that a research program as such is not yet sufficient as a theory.

A theory of society should be aware of, and responsible for, the assumptions and distinctions built into its concepts and research programs. Some of these premises are as follows:

(1) A theory of an operationally closed system has to make a distinction between operational closure and causal openness as different forms of observing the difference of system and environment.

(2) With respect to cognition, operational closure means that there can be no representation of the environment within the system but only construction; when considering its environment, the system is bound to use the forms in which the system itself reproduces its own operations.

(3) If there is no representation, there is no increasing adaptation of the system with respect to its environment. The rejection of any representationist theory of cognition requires the rejection of any adaptationist theory of evolution (see Varela 1984). And, in fact, don't we have the response of a forceful and even increasing maladaptation of the modern society in relation to its environment as the observable outcome of its evolution?

(4) The unity of the society would then be the result of its own interconnected operations; it would be the network of its operations, recursively producing and reproducing the network of its operations. This has close parallels to the biological notion of autopoiesis (see Maturana and Varela 1980). It could also be related to what Lyotard calls "le différend" — that is, the inevitable production of a difference by the enchainment of phrases, a concept that founds the much-discussed theory of postmodernity by denying the possibility of any meta-account that does not by itself produce a difference (see Lyotard 1983). But, taking this for granted, how could we include the operations of self-description in the system if observations and descriptions imply distinctions and indicate identity only as a component of a previously distinguished distinction? Does the theory of society depend on the paradoxical operation of a reentry of the distinction of system and environment into the system? How could we see and describe this paradox without assuming the position of an outside observer? Should we reanalyze the great logic of Hegel as the most elaborated theory of processing distinctions placing the observer at the end of history? Or should we use the logic of George Spencer Brown (1971) that claims to include the problem of the reentry of a distinction into the distinguished?

IV.

I mention these topics not for the sake of the argument. I am not trying to sell a specific brand of theory, such as a theory of self-referential social systems. I recalled the names of Lyotard and Spencer Brown to indicate that systems theory is not the only choice available, even if it is, at present, the option with the highest degree of elaboration and range of correspondences. My task is not to recommend certain approaches but to demonstrate the total incapacity of present-day sociology to tackle such questions.

In fact, whereas in the 1950s and early 1960s, sociology seemed to be a promised land full of fascinating conceptual advances and intellectual discoveries, nowadays the prospects seem to be quite different. Theoretically inclined sociologists are ill-advised if they peruse sociological literature in search of theoretical discoveries. They will find secondary literature about secondary literature about classics. The stimulating, intriguing, albeit highly inconclusive, suggestions will be found elsewhere. Sociologists will have to cross the boundaries of disciplines, and the most promising fields seem to be the new transdisciplinary enterprises such as cybernetics, general systems, or the new cognitive sciences.

Any further remarks will have a highly selective character. They are meant not as directives but as examples.

There is an increasing interest in self-referential relations in objects and in theories as well. This requires the inclusion of tautologies and paradoxes in objects (systems) and in theories seen as objects observing other objects (see Luhmann 1988b). This leads to the intriguing questions of whether there are certain types of systems that can operate only as self-observing and self-describing units, and whether this is true not only for conscious systems but also for social systems. But then, what exactly is the operation that constitutes itself by observing itself? And then, what exactly is meant by "observation"?

Systems theory itself is no longer the theory of a special type of *object,* called systems, but of a special type of distinction, namely, the *distinction* between system and environment. Virtually all innovations in systems theory during the last thirty years change the conceptualization of this distinction (see Luhmann 1988a), in recent years particularly by introducing the concept of operational closure and, correspondingly, the concept of *structural* coupling between systems and their environment, such as between social systems, based on communicative operations, and psychic systems, based on consciousness and fascinated by communication. Introduced into the sociological discourse, this would enforce a revision of current ideas about individual and society and about the individual as the quasi-"natural" subject of action, and it would have implications for the theory of language as the mechanism of structural coupling of conscious and communicative systems, which, on the level of their own operations, are completely closed systems (see Luhmann 1988d).

Within this theoretical context of operationally closed, self-referential sys-tems, the biologists Humberto Maturana and Francisco Varela have proposed to call the circular network of the reproduction of the components of a system by the network of the components of the same system *autopoiesis* (compare also Varela 1979). This concept transfers the logic of self-reference from the level of structures (or self-organization) to the level of the elements of the systems. In this sense, autopoietic systems have no substantial (or "atomic") base whatsoever, except the enclosure of their own operations. They are based not on matter or on molecules or on individual consciousness but on the difference between system and environment. There is by now an extensive discussion in Europe on whether or not this idea can be used in sociology and, if so, how the concept of autopoiesis must be changed or rendered more abstract (see Luhmann 1984; Haferkamp and Schmid 1987; Teubner 1988; or, for the Italian discussion, Sciortino 1987). As far as I can see, American sociologists, with rare exceptions, are not yet aware of the fact that this discussion implies a revision of virtually all concepts taken for granted in their normal discourse.

A last remark within this transdisciplinary section concerns the so-called constructivist (or even "radical" constructivist) approach to epistemological questions, based on empirical research in different disciplines, among others, the history and sociology of science. At first sight, and perhaps for most philosophers addicted to their textual tradition, this looks like a revised idealism. In fact, however, constructivism is based on empirical research on real cognitive systems in real environments, on brains, for instance. The most exciting state-ment seems to be that cognitive systems can produce cognition only because they have, on the level of their own operations, no contact with their environ-ment. Knowledge then presupposes not knowing what you are knowing, and this not as a transcendental but as an empirical condition, exemplified, for instance, by the indifferent coding of neurophysiological operations. The empir-ical condition of "no contact" or "closure" is, of course, a highly impossible evolutionary achievement that leaves no room whatsoever for arbitrary imagi-nations. The condition of closure has at the same time to provide for the sensibility and *Betreffbarkeit* (ability to be struck) of the system by outside events. The reduction of complexity by indifference is the condition for building up internal complexity that increases and differentiates the points at which the system can construct an irritation or perturbation if hit by outside events.

A remarkable side track of this constructivist movement is what has been called success-order cybernetics or the cybernetics of observing systems (see Foerster 1981). This shifts the interest of epistemology from the problem of access to a common reality for many or all observers ("intersubjectivity") to an interest in observing how and what other observers observe *and* — and this is the additional achievement — in observing what other observers can*not* observe. Medieval theologians already have had an interest in observing the devil, who, in observing God, tried to observe what he could not observe,[4] and made up his mind in view of the unthinkable by a decision that, *therefore,* was free. But the interest in observing what other observers can*not* observe became prominent with the eighteenth-century love novel, with the romantics, with Marx and Freud, and, finally, with the sociology of knowledge of this century. Academic epistemology on one side, but also the discourse on the postmodern society on the other, seem to neglect this perspective. But a sociology of modern society cannot be formulated without taking into account this curious neo-Enlightenment habit of trying to observe what others, for structural reasons based in their very apparatus of cognition, can*not* observe.

V.

This report on interdisciplinary developments and their possible impact on sociological theory will have been almost incomprehensible to an audience of American sociologists and, this, indeed, is part of the message. I can try to be as clear, as circumspect, as accurate as possible within the limits of my linguistic competence. This will make understanding not less, but more, difficult. The theory design required by the scientific developments that I mentioned must lead to an increased elaboration of conceptual issues and their consequences and probably to a higher sophistication with respect to distinctions (e.g., operation/observation, system/environment, medium/form), including Spencer Brown's distinction of distinction and indication. Observing the use of distinctions (e.g., Parsons's cross-tabulation or his pattern variables) will amount to observing the blind spot, that is, the latent premise, of a theory. This means that we are approaching what has been called the age of postmodernity without any true representation of the world within the world or any one true representation of society within society. The complexity of the society then has to be conceived as hypercomplexity, that is, as the multiplicity of incompatible self-descriptions (see, on a more general level, Rosen 1977). But this postmodernity will find its expression not in the style of the joyful science of a Nietzsche or of the pleasing madness of his French successors nor in the "new literary forms" of recent British adventures in reflexivity (see Woolgar 1988); it will require a new severity.

Is there any prospect of realization? I shall abstain from predictions. However, we could try to define the present situation of sociology by the distinction — again a distinction that creates a blind spot — of negative and positive feedback, that is, of stabilization versus deviation amplification. Most factors seem to work in the direction of negative feedback, for example, all the epistemological obstacles mentioned at the beginning of this chapter and, in addition, the habit, particularly strong in American universities, to define the limits of serious sociological work by the standards of empirical methods. This seems to indicate that sociology simply will jog on. You will find the widespread opinion, particularly in agencies financing research, that theoretical questions must be cleared in the process of preparing an application as if only empirical work could be in need of money; and even in Germany you need a large scientific reputation to overcome this barrier. The situation is somewhat different at the level of scientific conferences and in teaching. But scientific conferences are incredibly superficial.[5] Their function is to test the newest fashions. And, in teaching, you have to suggest to students a long-term commitment to learning how to move with a sufficient degree of freedom and with sufficient insights into the construction problems of theory designs in a field that is without professional rewards. The tight planning of postgraduate studies in the United States, which we are going to imitate in Germany, erects additional barriers. Some of my advanced students who continue in the United States complain about this lack of freedom and tight supervision in the guise of "helping behavior." And, in all European countries, the lack of career chances within the university (zero growth means that one university professor has to educate only one successor during his whole active life) discourages, of course, specialization in theory.

But there are also chances of positive feedback in the sense of an increasing deviation from the present state. The remarkable tediousness, even dullness, of normal science may act as a background against which the discipline becomes sensitive to the fads and fashions of the academic market. Moreover, I can see possible breakthroughs in relatively specialized fields — say, family therapy with its obvious need to understand what people meant when they began to talk of paradoxes, counterparadoxes, and systems therapy. Or the constructivist approach in the sociology of science, which may find support in contacting the epistemological constructivism of Heinz von Foerster, Humberto Maturana, or Ernst von Glasersfeld or even Piaget. But above all, sociology in its post-neo-Marxian or its Weber-editing phase will be aware, sooner or later, that it contributes nothing to the self-description of modern society within modern society.

If we trust once more the distinction of negative and positive feedback, we shall see a possible bifurcation. Bifurcation theory says that in such a situation small events may have large effects. But again and again: This is not the difference between empirical research and theoretical interests. The problem is to admit theoretical work on a highly abstract level within the boundaries of discipline that is and has to remain predominantly empirical.

VI.

Let me conclude with a few very personal impressions. It is an annoying fact that sociology at the end of this century has not much to contribute to what I call the self-description of modern society. The job is abandoned to the mass media (see Heintz 1982).[6] Even such an interest is rather the exception among sociologies and, as you can see from the references cited, pursuing such an interest requires transcending the boundaries of the discipline. This is a worldwide phenomenon and not a special trait of American sociology. However, looking back at the golden 1950s, you will see a different picture. At that time, the widely recognized leading role of American sociology was based on theoretical ambitions and on offering a description of modern society. It was not the methodological equipment alone that carried the day. It was the commitment to modernization as a joint venture of theoretical and practical efforts.

Today, it is impossible to continue this kind of engagement, and it may be impossible to continue this very American mix of theory and practice. With this shift in intellectual climate, American sociology has lost its capacity to impress European (and I even dare to say American) intellectuals. There are too many obvious facts that point to embarrassing negative consequences of modernization, and these are by no means limited to the consequences of industrialization. The alternative of elaborating on highly sophisticated and differentiated perplexities may not look very attractive to an American audience and it may look like a French or a German specialty; but there are also new chances for conceptual and theoretical rigor and it could be an attractive way out to further explore these possibilities.

NOTES

1. This requires a reinterpretation of hierarchy as a cybernetic hierarchy of control and conditioning from above resp. below (see Baum and Lechner 1987).

2. See Aristotle's Politica 1252 a ff. The Middle Ages, not prepared to give the city (politics) this excellent status, and conceptually more circumspect, normally used the term *universitas* as the concept which includes domestic and political societies.

3. I consider this possibility in Luhmann (1988c).

4. The conceptual language was, of course, "thinking." See Anselm of Canterbury (De casu diaboli IV: "Si deus non potest cogitari nisi ita solus, ut nihil ille simile cogitari possit: quomodo potuit diabolus velle quod non potuit cogitari?" ([1938] 1968, Vol. 1, p. 241).

5. Observing recent developments in literature and literature about literature, Miklós Szabolczi coined the phrase "la nouvelle sévérité" that may also serve to anticipate theoretical trends in sociology (see Szabolczi 1988).

6. This too is a self-referential statement.

REFERENCES

Alexander, Jeffrey C. 1987. "On the Centrality of the Classics." Pp. 11-57 in Social Theory Today, edited by Anthony Giddens and Jonathan Turner. Stanford, CA: Stanford University Press.

Anselm of Canterbury. [1938] 1968. Opera Omnia. Stuttgart-Bad Cannstatt: Fromann. (reprint)

Bachelard, Gaston. 1947. La Formation de l'Esprit Scientifique: Contribution à une Psychanalyse de la Connaissance Objective. Paris: Vrin.

Baum, Rainer C. and Frank J. Lechner. 1987. "Zum Begriff der Hierarchie: Von Luhmann zu Parsons." Pp. 298-332 in Theorie als Passion, edited by Dirk Baecker et al. Frankfurt: Suhrkamp.

Foerster, Heinz von. 1981. Observing Systems. Seaside, CA: Intersystems.

Haferkamp, Hans and Michael Schmid, eds. 1987. *Sinn, Kommunikation und Soziale Differenzierung.* Frankfurt: Suhrkamp.

Havelock, Eric A. 1963. *Preface to Plato.* Cambridge, MA: Belknap.

———. 1978. *The Greek Concept of Justice: From Its Shadows in Homer to Its Substance in Plato.* Cambridge, MA: Harvard University Press.

———. 1982. *The Literate Revolution in Greece and Its Cultural Consequences.* Princeton, NJ: Princeton University Press.

———. 1986. *The Muses Learn to Write: Reflections on Orality and Literacy from Antiquity to the Present.* New Haven, CT: Yale University Press.

Heintz, Peter. 1982. *Die Weltgesellschaft im Spiegel von Ereignissen.* Diessenhofen, Switzerland: Rüegger.

Luhmann, Niklas. 1984. *Soziale Systeme: Grundriß einer allgemeinen Theorie.* Frankfurt: Suhrkamp.

———. 1988a. "Neuere Entwicklungen in der Systemtheorie." *Merkur* 42:292-300.

———. 1988b. "Tautology and Paradox in the Self-Descriptions of Modern Society." *Sociological Theory* 6:26-37.

———. 1988c. "Warum AGIL?" *Kölner Zeitschrift für Soziologie und Sozialpsychologie* 40:127-39.

———. 1988d. "Wie ist Bewußtsein an Kommunikation beteiligt?" Pp. 884-905 in *Materialität der Kommunikation,* edited by Hans Ulrich Gumbrecht and Karl Ludwig Pfeiffer. Frankfurt: Suhrkamp.

Lyotard, Jean-François. 1983. *Le différend.* Paris: Les Éditions de Minuit.

Maturana, Humberto R. and Francisco J. Varela. 1980. *Autopoiesis and Cognition: The Realization of the Living.* Dordrecht: Reidel.

Ong, Walter J. 1967. *The Presence of the Word: Some Prolegomena for Cultural and Religious History.* New Haven, CT: Yale University Press.

———. 1971. *Rhetoric, Romance, and Technology: Studies in the Interaction of Expression and Culture.* Ithaca, NY: Cornell University Press.

———. 1977. *Interfaces of the Word: Studies in the Evolution of Consciousness and Culture.* Ithaca, NY: Cornell University Press.

———. 1982. *Orality and Literacy: The Technologizing of the Word.* London: Routledge and Kegan Paul.

Parsons, Talcott. 1988. "Structure." *American Sociology, Sociology Theory* 6:96-102.

Rosen, Robert. 1977. "Complexity as a System Property." *International Journal of General Systems* 3:227-32.

Sciortino, Giuseppe. 1987. "Teorie dell'Autopoiesis e Paradigmi Sistemici: Una Critica." *Stigma* 1(4):69-99.

Smelser, Neil. 1986. "Die Baharrlichkeit des Positivismus in der amerikanischen Soziologie." *Kölner Zeitschrift für Soziologie und Sozialpsychologie* 38:133-50.

Spencer Brown, George. 1971. *Laws of Form.* 2nd. ed. London: Allen & Unwin.

Stendhal [Marie-Henri Beyle]. [1822] 1959. *De l'Amour,* edited by Henri Martineau. Paris: Garnier.

Szabolczi, Miklós. 1988. "Neue Ernsthaftigkeit." Pp. 909-13 in *Materialität der Kommunikation,* edited by Hans Ulrich Gumbrecht and Karl Ludwig Pfeiffer. Frankfurt: Suhrkamp.

Teubner, Gunther, ed. 1988. *Autopoietic Law: A New Approach to Law and Society.* Berlin: de Gruyter.

Varela, Francisco J. 1979. *Principles of Biological Autonomy.* New York: North-Holland.

———. 1984. "Living Ways of Sense-Making: A Middle Path for Neuro-Science." Pp. 208-24 in *Disorder and Order: Proceedings of the Stanford International Symposium* (September 14-16, 1981), edited by Paisley Livingston. Stanford, CA: Anma Libri.

Woolgar, Steve, ed. 1988. *Knowledge and Reflexivity: New Frontiers in the Sociology of Knowledge.* London: Sage.

19

Notes on American Sociology and American Power

R. W. Connell

I.

We all agree there is something paradoxical in the idea of a national sociology. Sociology is known by its concepts, and no theorist worth her salt wants her concepts imprisoned in one country, however large or splendid. The "nation" is, as Luhmann points out, not an apt unit for most social analysis. Hence the unease foreign sociologists feel when confronted with American introductory textbooks that your publishers — who often own ours — regularly try to sell us. Most are written on the assumption that "sociology" means the current social problems of the United States; and one feels that some things are missing. Canada for one. Hence our unease also when American researchers let political geography define their conceptual world. I pick up a volume on social aspects of AIDS and encounter a blood-donor case study with a title about protecting "the nation's blood supply" — as if nothing that happened outside this particular nation were part of the authors' field of vision or moral concern.

So there is a problem about our problem. Yet no one is likely to say Tocqueville or Gans was mistaken in formulating such a problem. "Sociology in America" is about a real issue, the connection between intellectual work and its context. This is a peculiarly appropriate topic for us, because sociology as an intellectual approach is particularly concerned with contexts. Here I dissent from Luhmann's argument for "closed" communicative systems as a model for social analysis. The great accomplishments of European cultural analysis in this century — from Lukács on classical philosophy through Goldmann on Jansenism to Kristeva on poetic language — have characteristically involved a setting-in-context, a discovery of wider connections around and through communicative activity. This is not surprising, given that the condition of intelligibility of human social practice as practice (i.e., as distinct from "behavior" or from the instantiation of a structure or a discourse) is its historicity, its reference to a concrete, developing context recursively created by practice. There are, very properly, names in social theory. And "America" may be one of them.

Yet this has to be shown, not postulated. To analyze "sociology in America," we have to identify its "difference," define its place in a larger structure, give some account of how it got there. Touraine attempts this formidable task by a broad contrast between two continental traditions, American and European. He not only defines the dominant traditions, as such essays usually do, but also the structure of opposition and intellectual conflict within them.

The development of these themes is both lively and subtle. Yet when Touraine says that "the American and European traditions" correspond to "the two faces of sociological analysis," I become uneasy. Who is this speaking here? And who is this listening? It's me listening, and I come from a country whose antipodes are in the North Atlantic ocean. In my country, the wild animals hop rather than gallop. In my country, it is winter when it is summer in Europe and North America, when the sociologists gallop off to their conferences. If your two faces are looking at each other, the rest of us may have difficulty seeing anything but the backs of your heads.

Atlantic sociology, if you will forgive the coinage, is constituted by the network of intellectual and practical relationships both Touraine and Kon have described.[1] Kon's account illuminates a key process in its historical production, highlighting not just the "sociology of sociology" but also the "sociology of *reading* sociology," the way intellectual work is received. The theme has wide relevance beyond the case of the Soviet Union.

I come from outside the Atlantic world, though not from the Third World. Australia has been described by one of its economists as "a small rich industrial country"; for the past century and more, it has also been one of the most urbanized in the world. Its main exports are not crocodile skins but the products of high-tech mining and its main import in the last generation has been an industrial labor force. Our place in the world has given Australian intellectuals a lot of practice in analyzing relations with the metropole. We now have the distinction of having two metropoles. Australia was invaded from Europe 200 years ago, became a colony of British settlement, and in the mid-twentieth century became a political and economic satellite of the United States. A couple of years ago, the United States sent the old battleship *Missouri* to visit my home town of Sydney and allow a few of the locals to climb aboard. More than 200,000 people came. The event symbolizes the usual relationship between Australian and American sociology; we come to watch your big guns.

As a well-trained watcher, I am interested in what American and European sociology have in common. Atlantic sociology can be defined in terms of its themes, presuppositions, and intellectual exclusions; in terms of the way it is institutionalized and funded; in terms of its practical consequences, impact, and

1. Professor Connell refers here to the paper presented in Atlanta by Professor Igor Kon, of the Ethnographic Institute of the Soviet Academy of Sciences in Moscow. Unfortunately, Professor Kon could not contribute a chapter to this volume.

applications. I would be bolder than Touraine if I tried to characterize both halves in less space than he takes for one; so I will simply gesture. Atlantic sociology was mainly constructed by men, and its intellectual concerns mainly reflect the social world seen from men's point of view; in that sense, it is classically patriarchal. It makes little basic conceptual reference to the world outside Europe and North America; its intellectual structure relates to modernization in that context, and it relegates the "world system" to a subfield. Atlantic sociology is institutionalized in a way that brings it close to the state (whether liberal capitalist or liberal communist) as patron and consumer but it maintains a claim to professional independence. This claim is made good mainly by the general autonomy of universities; sociology in itself does not have the intellectual or political prestige of economics or physics. Atlantic sociology is funded at levels that make it, in world context, very rich. This invites a high degree of internal specialization and a striking preoccupation with questions of method, both at the level of empirical research and at the level of theory. Questions of practice are less central. Nevertheless, Atlantic sociology is connected to practice, mainly in the form of social policy administered through the state and the "caring professions." It has lost most of its historical links with the labor movement. In style, Atlantic sociology is talkative, even argumentative, but rarely impassioned. To an outsider, it is endlessly fascinating, and thoroughly dangerous. If this intellectual world is taken as the definition of sociology per se, a set of implicit power relations come into play with far-reaching consequences for intellectual work.

II.

The richness of Atlantic sociology is most visible in America as numbers and diversity. Having looked round the intellectual bazaar of the conference on which this book is based, no foreigner could fail to be impressed by the complexity and scale of what was going on. In Australia, there are perhaps a dozen and a half social scientists of all disciplines working on AIDS questions; here there are a dozen papers or meetings on AIDS in a single discipline's conference. The range of topics dealt with, from microcomputers to masochism, is stunning.

The richness is organized mainly as an elaboration of subfields. This is not only a question of the 26 (soon to be 27) specialties that have more or less official existence as ASA "sections." It goes to a specialization of topics and research styles within these sections, and a penumbra of specialties-in-formation around them. I am charmed to see that ASA was so eager to fill every void that it scheduled a session titled "Neglected Topics."

Such specialization could be thought a professional "division of labor," an arrangement to distribute effort where needed across the face of the discipline.

But the idea of a division of labor implies that something is being jointly produced, implies some budding rationality or joint purpose; and here the observer hesitates. Touraine, Luhmann, and Kon, in their different ways, all detect a kind of anomie. Sociology in America was founded on a moral program of social amelioration and an intellectual program of understanding the mechanisms of social progress. Though both ambitions can still be found among sociologists today, it is difficult to see either a moral or an intellectual program that gives shape to the discipline as a whole. Its shape and program, rather, are given by the practice of specialization itself, which seems to have become self-justifying. This process has left the specialties vulnerable to implicit ideologies, to a greater extent than one finds in eastern Atlantic sociology. It is notable that "applied" fields, such as the sociology of education or medical sociology, often use frameworks (such as role theory) that are obsolete in mainstream theory.

The formidable professional and financial organization of sociology in America makes a striking contrast to the entrepreneurial fragmentation of its content. This suggests a tension that is worth exploring. The structure of academic careers here seems to pressure people to lay claim to new fields, to become known as the pioneers of a new topic, the creators of a new scale, or the inventors of a new concept.

But it also fiercely reins in dissident thought, by demanding lots of publications in refereed journals, lots of papers at properly professional conferences, before you get your tenure. I was fascinated to see that even the roundtable discussions on Marxism at this conference were announced as "refereed," a striking indicator of the pressures for social control and occupational advancement within sociology.

This implies that the fragmentation of content, the impression of anomie, does not mean a political incoherence. When I last spent some time in America, as a postdoctoral innocent at the University of Chicago in 1970, the graduate students with whom I mostly mixed had a perfectly clear view of what mainstream sociology meant. To them it was the soft side of the American establishment; the part of the system that regulated the poor, cooled out the blacks, and bought off the working class while the tougher part of the system got on with napalming the Vietnamese and shooting down the Black Panthers.

The position is certainly more complex than that. Sociology embodies opposition as well as manipulation. It has not been taken over by the New Right and is open to certain forms of dissidence, the most important case at present being feminism. On the evidence of the 1988 conference, sociology in America has taken its distance from the more militaristic and managerial approaches of the 1960s. It is not easy to see another Project Camelot happening.

Yet it is still true that the researchers reporting to this conference are more often "studying down" than "studying up." I took three pages of the program at random and counted cases where the group being researched was recognizably more or less powerful than the researcher: In 14 cases, the research was about the relatively powerful; in 33 cases, it was about the relatively powerless. Sociology in America readily takes the political stance of *advising the powerful* about the conduct of affairs. ASA dramatizes this with a plenary about what sociology should say to the next president. It does not have a plenary about what sociology should say to the American working class.

The hegemonic moral/political stance in U.S. sociology might be characterized, by analogy with the phrase "corporate liberalism," as "professional liberalism." The curiosity about high school dropouts or Latin immigrants is benign; the advice to the rich and powerful is mostly in the direction of improving the welfare state. But there is little doubt about the boundaries. This might be sociology in favor of the powerless, but it is not sociology *for* the powerless. The socialist project is admitted, tellingly, as a specialization. No sociologist outside the "Marxist sociology" section is, so to speak, professionally obligated to think about class privilege and exploitation. And that "specialization" is disempowered, under a political regime as vehemently anticommunist as the United States, by its very name.

The main current alternative to professional liberalism as a moral and political stance is a kind of professional abstentionism. In this, the social contexts of both observed and observer are methodologized out of existence, and the social scientists in principle talk only to each other. I doubt this could ever be the hegemonic stance, as it is unsalable in the outside world. But it could be inflected in a technocratic direction and become more politically powerful.

III.

Atlantic sociology is the product of a history: not Atlantic history but world history. Europe and North America are the heartlands of modern imperialism and have in succession provided the dominant states. Sociology's autobiography connects its foundation with the "industrial revolution" and the accompanying social transformations. It is now clear from historical work that the advent of industrial capitalism was not a domestic accident in Manchester but had to do with the prior existence of a global structure of exploitation and accumulation. The connection between this history and sociology's concern with class is familiar; what "Introduction to Sociology" course fails to touch on Marx and Weber? But the connection is even broader. In the case of gender relations, for instance, sociology's long-standing interest in the family and its historical connection with the "woman question" cannot be divorced from the sexual politics of imperialism: the problems of masculinity imperfectly institutionalized in mass armed forces and bureaucratic states; the disruption and reconstitution of households in mass labor migration and new cities; the exclusion of women from citizenship in state structures organized for conquest and war.

The United States is a child of European imperialism, beginning as a settler colony. This year happens to be the bicentennial of the white settler colony in Australia, whose "celebrations" are being strongly protested by Australian aboriginal people. With that experience, it is difficult for me to accept Touraine's characterization of the United States as a nation created through law. It was created, more fundamentally, by invasion and genocide. The realm of law was created as an internal arrangement among a specific, privileged minority group — white male property owners who created a political and legal regime to which native people, blacks, women, and the propertyless were only gradually and reluctantly admitted.

The dynamic of expansion in the American case went much further than in any other settler colony, with the remote settlement eventually becoming the dominant world power. During the twentieth century, the American state in tandem with American corporations created new forms of imperialism, whose dividends can be seen in the enormous wealth that surrounds us here. We talk loosely about a bipolar world with two "superpowers," as if there were two systems of about the same size. As a matter of fact, the combined GDP of the OECD countries (the core, but by no means all, of the countries whose economies and politics are organized under American hegemony) is five times the combined GDP of the Warsaw Pact countries. The material conditions for the kind of intellectual hegemony described by Kon are obvious.

At the center of the process of expansion is the American state. It is clear in much of this conference that the state is the implicit audience, that some branch of the state is generally assumed to be the agency that will bring about change. Yet the state is not a major intellectual *problem* for sociology in America. While not entirely absent from the agenda, questions about the nature of the state and strategies of state action are certainly nowhere near the focus. They are significantly missing from most feminist sociology and most cultural sociology, to name two themes that were prominent in the conference.

Here, I would argue, American power shapes American sociology. It is only those who live under the aegis of a rich, flexible, and successful state who do not problematize that state. To the rest of the world, the American state is a conspicuous, even overwhelming, problem.

The situation is even less comfortable than that reflection suggests. Sociology is not only conditioned by American power. It is itself an aspect of American power. At this point — because I have my own career to consider — I will propose a new concept, a distinction between "inverted" and "everted" sociologies.

Inverted sociologies are self-constituting and self-referring; their members talk to each other, worry about each other, define standards for each other. *Everted* sociologies are constituted around a relationship with some other intellectual center and refer constantly to it; their inhabitants talk both to each other and to inhabitants of the center, worry most about what's going on in the center, and adopt the center's standards. Some years ago, I read a fascinating article by two Polish sociologists who had actually read other people's footnotes. They discovered that Polish sociologists cited Poles and Americans; British sociologists cited Britons and Americans; Italian sociologists cited Italians and Americans; while American sociologists cited other Americans. That neatly illustrates the distinction.

Atlantic sociology is the one inverted sociology in the world today, and its American wing is the only "national" sociology that is inverted. If the rest of the world vanished as an intellectual force tomorrow, sociology in America could go on much the way it does now; and this is not true in any other country. In every other part of the world outside the North Atlantic region, sociology is everted. It defines itself intellectually and organizationally with reference to what goes on here. In Australian universities, for instance, what one wants for promotion is not publication in refereed journals but publication in what are called "international" journals, meaning American and European.

That is as material a form of cultural domination as *Dallas* and *Dynasty*. We cannot escape you. We cannot fight you. We cannot be your comrades and exchange favors on even terms; we have no battleships to send to Savannah. Our problem is how to relate to you constructively without being colonized again. The damnable thing is that, if we fail, most of you would not ever know it.

Your problem, if I can put it bluntly, is to recognize your own conditions of existence. An inverted sociology can be self-sufficient, and American liberalism as an ideology invites you to elide the state and imperialism from your arguments. Yet there are countercurrents: highly sophisticated work on patterns of class and privilege, the growth of feminism and its intermittent but important concern with race and class, the invention of the world-systems perspective. American sociology is capable of self-critical leaps, as is shown by the inclusion of a session on foreign sociologists' views in a program of reflection on "sociology in America." I hope the discussion will be pushed forward. It isn't comfortable to do, and it probably isn't comfortable to listen to. But it is important for the people at both ends of this discussion.

Part VIII
Sociology and the
Other Social Sciences

20

Sociology and History: Producing Comparative History

Jack A. Goldstone

Sociologists in America, in conjunction with colleagues throughout the world, are breathing new life into an old discipline — comparative history. It is not exactly history or exactly sociology; it is a distinct endeavor that draws on talents and individuals from both disciplines as well as from economics, political science, and other fields. To understand what is going on in that endeavor today, it is necessary to be clear what comparative history can contribute to historical studies, and what is holding sociologists back from still greater contributions.

I want to claim first that social theory has often befuddled attempts by sociology to contribute to our understanding of history. It has done so by taking what should be *empirical* problems and raising them to the level of *theoretical* disputes. Unfortunately, as these problems are unresolvable at this level, theoretical discussions have tended to be endless and inconclusive and to divert attention from real historical issues. It is, therefore, necessary to show how these theoretical blinders can and should be cast aside.

I want to claim, second, that history and sociology should not merge, for they are different disciplines with different methods and foci of investigation. But I claim there is a sphere of inquiry — comparative history — that is not merely a border zone or a marriage of history and sociology; it is instead a distinct endeavor, with its own problematic and own techniques, that must be understood and defended for what it attempts and not as a variant of other fields.

THE BARRIERS IMPOSED BY SOCIAL THEORY

One does not apply theory to history; rather one uses history to develop theory."

— Arthur Stinchcombe (1978, p. 2)

There are many controversies in social theory today that, viewed from the perspective of historical analysis, make no sense. The questions as to whether one should rely primarily on conflict or consensus, idealist or materialist, and micro or macro models of behavior are presented as issues that can be settled *theoretically* for all societies and all times. Indeed, they are sometimes presented as issues that *must be* be settled before setting out on historical analysis, or the result will be muddled. Yet the truth of the matter seems to be the reverse — the theoretical debates have been muddled by not starting first with historical analysis.

Perhaps the prime culprit is formulating the task of social theory as solving "the problem of order": How can individuals create and maintain patterns of group behavior that transcend the lives and intentions of the individuals involved? (See Parsons 1937 for the classic formulation of this problem.) Yet it is absurd to reduce all the complexities of social behavior to a single "problem of order." Do natural scientists attempt to solve "the problem of nature"? No. Though a grand unified theory may be the holy grail of some physicists, most scientists — biologists, chemists, geologists, astronomers, zoologists — get on with the business of solving the *myriad* distinct problems presented by nature, using a *diversity* of models and theories to solve their particular problem. Perhaps, someday, models developed for different problems will be shown to have common elements, and a reduction in complexity can be achieved. But the *first* order of business is to solve specific problems in research — reduction is an elegant final course, not the initial step.

Yet sociology seems to have gotten it backward. The interminable arguments over whether "*the* social order" is based on conflict or consensus, on whether "social change" is founded primarily on material or ideal factors, on whether "micro" or "macro" behavior is the fundamental object of sociological concern, all reflect this notion that there is *a* problem of social order that, once solved, will allow all social behavior to be explained and understood. It should be evident by now that no such single solution is possible. History and current experience present *many, many* kinds of social order — that is, sustained patterns of multi-individual behavior. Some are based on conflict, others on consensus; some instances of social change may be primarily rooted in material changes, other instances may be primarily rooted in ideological factors; most show a mixture of both. *The only way to find out where a particular social order or social change of interest is on the scale of these factors is by close empirical examination.* In other words, the problem of order is not a single problem and hence is not amenable to solution by theoretical clarification and reduction. It is an empirical problem, or rather problems, for there are many actual social orders and hence many *different, valid* solutions to their description. The useful question, on which cumulative progress can be made, is to identify particular behaviors, or social orders, of interest, and seek to establish how *they* are developed and maintained, being aware that different answers are likely to hold at different times and places. To seek a universal answer first is to engage in fruitless and primitive monism.

To compound its difficulties, sociology often adds the error of Manicheanism to its monist view of the social order. That is, if there is *one* problem of order, and a single solution, then everything other than that solution is considered an evil deception. Modern social theory tends to divide its adjectives into opposed pairs, declaring one element of the pair to be essential or fundamental, the other to be secondary at best, mere superstructure or even illusion at worst. Too often, sociologists treat "micro" and "macro," "ideal" and "material," and "conflict" and "consensus" as mutually exclusive categories rather than as ideal types that denote extreme ends of an empirical scale. Because reality is dominated by various mixtures in the middle, arguing about the polar extremes merely diverts attention from real social processes.

To give an example, consider the terms *micro* and *macro*. As Alexander and Giesen (1987) have pointed out, this is a purely conceptual *distinction*. All *social* behavior involves both individual actions and socially generated resources — language, symbols, or institutional arrangements.

Yet debates about this distinction have steered sociology on the wrong course. Scholars use exchange theory to explain the micro foundations of macro structures (Homans 1961), or "structuration" (Giddens 1976, 1979) or "linkage" (Alexander and Giesen 1987) theories to emphasize that micro actions are constantly generating and maintaining macro structures, and vice versa. But they have *not* escaped from the dichotomous concept itself. And there lies the nub of the problem. For social behavior is not, not even in any alternation or continuous generation, merely a movement between "micro" and "macro" levels. The shape of complex societies is neither micro nor macro; it is *fractal*.

Geometry has recently embraced the term *fractal* to denote structures that show the same features, regardless of the scale on which they are observed. For example, a shoreline is indented with bays and inlets, but each bay has its own little bays and inlets, and so on. It is the same with society. At the national level, one finds political authority, business firms, political parties, status hierarchies, unions, voluntary organizations, and the like. But within the nation are provinces that act like little states; within the provinces are counties and municipalities that are similarly structured; within the municipalities are voluntary groups, clubs, business firms, and the like, that are in some ways similarly structured. Even families — as settings for authority, conflict, coalition formation, and intergenerational conservancy of property — have certain characteristics in common with the nation-state as a whole. *A focus on micro versus macro excludes an awareness of this whole phenomenon.*

Once this "fractal" character of society is recognized, a host of empirical problems present themselves. To what extent are the structures of subnational (or transnational) organizations and groups congruent? That is, to say a formation is fractal does not imply all scales are identical — it is a key problem to establish how similar or different they are. For example, a nation-state with elected officials usually has state and local governments with elected officials, and voluntary associations and labor unions with elected officials. Conversely, nation-states dominated by a party apparatus and party-appointed officials usually have party-appointed officials in charge of local governments, unions, and the like. Yet there are exceptions. How is it that precisely at the time political structures of greater democracy were becoming established in nineteenth-century England, economic structures of greater authoritarianism — the factories — were simultaneously developing? Even today, although publicly held firms elect their officers, voting is weighted by share ownership rather than the equal vote of all participants that is preferred in the political system. How do these variations manage to subsist? Are they holdovers on the way to a more congruent future? Or are they stable? To what extent does socialization in family units — which are undemocratic — impede later appreciation of individual rights and responsibilities? Is the movement for "children's rights" an inevitable extension of national norms into the lower levels of the fractal hierarchy?

These issues are of crucial importance, for example, in judging the prospects for successful restructuring in the Soviet Union and China — to what extent can they avoid fractal congruence and maintain party-dominated political organizations in the same society with "free" business firms and elective unions? This crucial problem of modern politics immediately springs forth when one considers the fractal structure of societies. Yet it is completely obscured (and hence has been ignored) by the traditional micro versus macro categories.

Indeed, the key dynamics of social reproduction and social change generally operate at the level of coherent groups — families, peasant villages, urban working classes, regional elites, business firms, local governments — that mediate between individuals and the society as a whole. Are these dynamics micro or macro? Of course, they are neither, and explanation is lost, rather than gained, by trying to fit them into one category or the other. Jettison the theoretical blinders that confine us to one or the other end of the scale, and the rich reality in the middle is revealed for empirical examination.

Similarly, asking whether social order and social change are based on material or ideal factors — or a wishy-washy blend of both — is often posed as a theoretical question that could be answered and then used to guide empirical inquiry. Adopted in this fashion, it can only lead to rejection of empirical variation out of hand. It may be that, in some cases, or certain aspects of a complex social process, material factors *do* dominate; in other cases, ideological factors may do so. To assume that it is *always* one, or always the other, or always both, is to theorize historical variation out of existence.

In short, theory can never solve "the problem of order," and indeed committed perhaps its biggest error in framing its task in this fashion. We have erred wherever we have taken Marx and Weber's categories, which were for them the end product of long empirical investigation, as *our* beginning point. Instead, we too need to begin with empirical inquiry and *then* amend the theoretical categories as needed.

It is some sociologists' tendency to begin with theoretical categories and then apply them to history, which confounds and distresses historians. Their tendency to treat sociologists as people describing the world by viewing it through the wrong end of a telescope, therefore, has some foundation.

Comparative history is *not* the application of social theory to history. What then is it?

COMPARATIVE HISTORY: A MANIFESTO

Mais ce n'est pas l'histoire!

> — Pieter Geyl, commenting on
> Arnold Toynbee's A *Study of
> History* (cited in MacDougall
> 1986, p. 26)

Variation in History

Paul Mantoux (1903, p. 122) wrote, 85 years ago, that "the particular, whatever occurs only once, is the domain of history." This view, often expressed earlier and echoed since, has remained dear to historians' view of what they do. Yet we must be clear what this means. The "particularity," the "uniqueness," is the property of a sequence or collection of events. The task of all historical inquiry is to explain those particular sequences of events that have occurred. However, this task would be quite impossible if all of the components, in every aspect, of such sequences were totally unique.

Consider the history of a nation, such as England. If every moment in English history were *utterly unique, in all aspects,* what value would there be in talking of England? Presumably, *some* aspects were common to the society that existed in the southern two-thirds of the island of Britannia over several centuries. Language, form of government, and ethnic heritage all changed somewhat, but not so much that they were totally different at every moment from what they were at the next.

Once it is grasped that, even though *in toto* historical sequences are unique, it is still possible to recognize *some aspects* of those sequences that are similar to those of other times and places, the historians' claim of the uniqueness of particular sequences generates a useful problematic. For we then face not an a priori theoretical assertion of absolute incomparability but an empirical task — investigating the *degree* of difference between nonidentical, but possibly some-what similar, selections or sequences of events. History, in short, shows both continuity *and* change. It is thus possible to ask such questions as this: In *what* respects did England's eighteenth-century monarchy differ from that of the seventeenth century? *What* changes occurred in England's economy from 1750 to 1850, and was change greater than in the preceding century? If such questions are unanswerable in principle (and no practicing historian would claim this, except in the heat of debate with recalcitrant social scientists) then the "history of England" can have no meaning.

If there is both change and continuity in history over time, the same variation is found over *space*. An eighteenth-century traveler from England to France would recognize certain features of the landscape — monarchy, nobility, agricultural techniques — as differing in detail; but they would not be completely unrecognizable. One can, therefore, ask *what* were the differences between English and French government (or agriculture, or incomes, or religion) in the eighteenth century? Again, the historical claim of uniqueness is a matter of degree, to be established by empirical inquiry.

Here too, our conceptualization has been a slave to a simple, mutually exclusive categorization generated by a priori theorizing. Historians and social scientists tend to argue over methods as if there were only two ways to look at history — either every historical sequence is unique, or there are general principles or "laws." Neither is quite true. The reality (and, again, this is something every good historian knows and practices) is that of historical *variation* — that is, elements that have greater or lesser continuity over time that vary and combine in distinctive ways across time and space. Doing history — that is, reconstructing, describing, and explaining particular sequences of events — is almost always a matter of identifying *which particular aspects* of a complex situation are changing, which are remaining more or less the same, and why.

Yet if historical variation is the very stuff of history, large-scale historical variation poses certain problems. These are problems that neither history nor sociology, as generally practiced in the core of those disciplines, can solve.

A Tale of Two Disciplines

Philip Abrams (1982) has recently argued that sociology and history should merge. This advice is not likely to be taken, and for good reason. These disciplines rightly have distinct methods, training, and goals.

Historians' main business is the reconstruction of past sequences of events from the traces left by those events. This is an enormously difficult, challenging, and sensitive task that requires specialized training. No sociologist who is unfamiliar with the demands of this task, who is not aware of the evidence and methods by which historical accounts are produced, should presume to "know" history.

Sociology uses quite different methods to collect its data. The observing tools of sociology (and much political science) are survey research and participant observation. Some techniques may be useful for both sociology and history, such as a knowledge of sampling and statistical methods of data analysis. But the collection of the basic data and their skillful assemblage into useful form — the analysis of survey or poll data or of participant observation notes — proceeds quite differently.

Validation is different as well. The historian, if his or her conclusions are challenged, will point to the value of the historical witnesses he or she cites — the judgment and access of a diary-writer to the events he or she describes, the comprehensiveness of the set of police records, the representativeness of a sample of slave prices. A sociologist, if similarly challenged, will point to the quality of the survey data — the appropriateness of the sampling method, its internal reliability, the skill of the poll takers — or the validity of the statistical techniques used to establish key relationships.

These different techniques reflect different problematics. The sociologist who studies crime is generally concerned with the general process of crime in his or her own and in other contemporary societies — how widespread is crime, and is it found more in some social groups than others? How does a person become a criminal? And what kinds of policy interventions might affect the answers to these questions? Surveys, participant observation, and planned experiments are appropriate means to answer these questions. Yet the historian who studies crime is denied these methods. He or she may ask similar questions but must use different sources and methods. The nature of historical sources, and the difficulty of identifying, collecting, and mastering primary materials, mean the historian will usually specialize in studying crime in a particular time and place.

Of course, there may be useful cross-fertilization of techniques. Once historians (or historically trained sociologists) have collected their data, they may borrow statistical tools of data reduction developed by sociologists. And sociologists are wise to be aware of the historical context of the society they live in and study. Yet these borrowings cross the border zone between two recognizably distinct disciplines.

Let us now ask a question of a type that often arises: How was the government of eighteenth-century England different from those of eighteenth-century continental European states?

The core skills of the historian — the reconstruction of particular sequences from their traces — are poorly suited to answer this question. This is because it can take a lifetime to master the primary source of materials required to reconstruct events even in one country over a period of a few decades. Thus historians quite sensibly specialize; only then can their primary skills be used most effectively. To become familiar with the primary sources of a dozen nations over a period as broad as a century is an imposing, almost impossible task (although diplomatic historians do so, in covering international relations; yet they then must almost entirely exclude direct engagement with the materials of social history. Thus they too specialize in a "slice" of history).

On the other hand, the primary skills of the sociologist — describing the behavior and experience of individuals or groups of individuals in a complex society by interviews, observations, and surveys — are also ill-suited, for the past has passed and is no longer accessible by these means.

Who then can answer such questions? I would argue that explaining large-scale historical variation, whether across many different societies, or across long stretches of time, calls for a distinct specialty: comparative history. The skills and problematic of this specialty are not those of history, or of sociology, as practiced in the core of either of those disciplines, or, for that matter, of economics, political science, or anthropology. Certainly detailed knowledge of a particular society is useful, but so is knowledge of how various social processes — government, crime, social mobility, revolution — have developed in different societies. Neither skill is sufficient in itself, though both are excellent starting points. Thus comparative history has drawn its practitioners from a variety of disciplines, though chiefly from history and sociology. Indeed, this is a field known best not through a particular set of methods or recognized departments but by its practitioners. Modern comparative historians comprise distinguished scholars whose initial training occurred in a wide variety of fields — as a few examples, consider Paul Kennedy (1987), William McNeill (1982), and Robert Brenner (1978) in history; Theda Skocpol (1979) and Charles Tilly (1986) in sociology; Mancur Olson (1982) and Eric Jones (1988) in economics; Eric Wolf (1970) in anthropology, and Ned Lebow (1981) and Robert Jervis et al. (1985) in political science. What these scholars have in common is, first, a curiosity that led them to delve deeply into a broad range of secondary literature to complement their initial research specialty and, second, the ability to produce insights into particular cases of large-scale historical continuity and variation.

Cases and Critical Differences

How then to approach historical variation? We must backtrack a moment, for I have misled us by suggesting that large-scale historical variation is the defining characteristic of comparative history. This is not quite true. What distinguishes comparative history is its use of the *case-based* method to study historical variation.

Thus a historian might present a long-term history of disease or of income distribution. A historian might write a history of Europe that spans several countries or several centuries. Such general histories, long-term histories, or world histories are *not* comparative history. They have in common with it an interest in large-scale historical variation and a necessary recourse to secondary sources. But they differ in approach. The long-term or general history attempts to recount what happened in a given, possibly very large, time frame.

Comparative history is more focused, and much more thematic, than such general long-term or large-scale histories. Comparative history begins with a question: Why did Japan respond more successfully than China to Western incursions in the nineteenth century? Why did serfdom fade after 1500 in Western Europe, while something very much like it expanded in Eastern Europe? Did ideology play different roles in Communist and non-Communist revolutions? Such questions arise from noticing a critical difference in the record of historical variation — two sequences of events that seem to share some characteristics but are strikingly different in others. It may be that the apparent similarities are, on close inspection, illusory. Or it may be that only a small, but crucial, factor separated quite similar situations and led to striking differences. What makes comparative history interesting is that the answer is not known in advance — it is an empirical inquiry to discover what happened and why.

The goal of comparative history is thus not merely to find analogies or generalities in historical experience. Its goal is finding *causal explanations of historical events*. It proceeds by asking, given that historical *variation* reveals both continuity and change, *which* elements of the historical record were crucial? Thus to merely study the history of two cities, or two countries, is parallel, but not comparative, history. The latter depends on identifying some key difference between the cases and asking which of the many differing elements in these cases was responsible for the *particular* difference in question.

It is common to take different countries as cases. But this is certainly not necessary. Mark Traugott (1985) has recently analyzed the forces on either side of the barricades in Paris in 1848 — his cases are the insurgents, on the one hand, and the members of the Mobile Guard, on the other. His comparison of these two groups is the basis for his argument that the Mobile Guard remained loyal to the government not because of its class makeup but chiefly because of its socialization under military-style training and discipline between February and June of that year. Similarly, Craig Calhoun's (1982) study of the English working class takes as his cases the artisanal workers of the early nineteenth century and the factory workers of the later nineteenth century; by identifying the differences between these groups, he is able to challenge E. P. Thompson's earlier claims of continuity in a single English working class. William Brustein (1985, 1986) has used regions as cases to shed light on patterns of French political protest in the seventeenth and eighteenth centuries.

Both historians and sociologists often ask "sociological" questions of the historical record: What was the pattern of social mobility in nineteenth-century Marseilles (Sewell 1985)? Or they may turn to history to explain features of the present-day sociological terrain: How did physicians become such a powerful profession in America (Starr 1982)? Answers to such questions draw on *both* the historians' skills of analyzing primary sources and the sociologists' knowledge of social processes. Such inquiries, therefore, do produce a blend of the sort Abrams envisaged, which goes under the name of "social history" or "historical sociology." Though enormously valuable, this is distinct from comparative history, which rests on the case-based approach. In this sense, comparative history is only a part, although perhaps the most controversial part, of a broader historical sociology. (More wide-ranging analyses of historical sociology are provided by Skocpol 1984, and Hamilton and Walton 1988.)

Robust Processes in History

Comparative history often starts with apparently similar situations, among which there is nevertheless a striking difference that calls for explanation. Yet the reverse pattern of historical variation also sometimes arises — that is, in historical situations that seem markedly different, *similar* sequences of events unfold. There are striking similarities between the French Revolution of 1789 and the Russian Revolution of 1917, despite their vast separation in time and enormously different historical settings. Thus the comparative historian may also approach historical variation from the angle of *significant similarities*: Why, in contexts that seem to widely differ, are similar patterns of events observed?

Examination of similar sequences of events in different historical settings has provoked enormous controversy and even scorn. Comparative history has been given a bad name by attempts to overextend limited generalities and pretensions to lawlike findings. Such pretensions marred the otherwise valuable work of Marx and the Hegelians, including, in his own way, Arnold Toynbee. Suspicions have also arisen that, in seeking generalities, comparative history is disdainful of facts. To lower the barriers between comparative historians and history, it is necessary to dispel the notion that good comparative history shares these attributes.

First, it should be recognized that comparative history cannot simply "use" historical narratives as data. This is because historians do not tell us what happened in a particular time and place; they *argue* about what happened. At any given time, certain patterns of events may be generally agreed on and others hotly disputed. Given the nature of historical evidence and the problems of reconstruction, it could hardly be otherwise. That is why it is essential for comparative historians to fully engage the secondary literature of the cases they study, to be aware of the historical arguments, the uncertainties, and issues at stake. A comparative historian does not approach historical scholarship as a miner approaches a mine. Instead, he or she approaches the literature as a historian would, to engage in a conversation about what happened.

Second, identifying similar sequences of events in different historical contexts is not the same as identifying general laws independent of historical context. Rather than discovering laws, this is more like the geologist mapping different regions and discovering similar fossils in similar rock strata at widely divergent places. The geologist will then hypothesize that a common process occurred in both places and will attempt to carefully reconstruct what that process was. But this process is not a "law" in the same sense as the law of gravity.

A "law" is a relationship that holds regardless of varying initial conditions. It is true that, to make predictions, one must know the initial conditions of a system. Thus, to predict the motions of two gravitationally bound bodies, one must know their mass and the distance between them. But the existence of gravity, and the inverse square law of its operation, does not depend on those masses or positions. The initial conditions are merely parameters that can vary without affecting the operation of the law. The law is *independent* from the initial conditions. The geologist's claim that similar processes occurred in different sites, however, is precisely a statement about initial conditions. It is a claim that, at some particular times in history, physical laws, such as gravity, leading to the sedimentary deposition of rocks, and chemical reactions, leading to fossilization of animal remains, must have acted on similar enough initial conditions in distinct sites to create a similar rock/fossil bed.

What the geologist has found is evidence of a "robust process." Such a process is not a law but a combination of *characteristic initial conditions* with particular laws that produce a characteristic outcome. It cannot be used to make precise predictions, for it has no parameters to be plugged into a "law" that then predicts precise outcomes. Thus the geologist would not hope to predict the precise number and location of fossils in a particular sort of rock. Geological processes act in historical context with initial conditions that are never exactly alike. Yet the geologist would predict the *type* of fossils, and their rough proportions, if he or she knew that the rock was formed at a time when certain species lived. That is, if the initial conditions were similar (even though not identical), then regular laws would produce similar (though not identical or exactly predictable) results.

Similar "robust processes" also occur in history. This is because most men and women do act in something like a consistent or rational fashion. Indeed, we rely on this every day — we count on generals not to betray their countries, and on bankers and bureaucrats not to give away or destroy their organizations. Of course, there are traitors and saints; yet we label these individuals with special words to indicate their exceptional nature. If most generals were traitors and most bankers were saints, these words would lose their meaning; and, needless to say, history would be very different.

Thus the key to historical explanation is knowing that, in a given situation, most people will react in some consistent fashion. This does not mean that *all* people have the same goals. In some groups of individuals, honor may be so important that an honorable defeat is valued more than a base victory. In others, spiritual status is more valuable than material rewards. Yet we do not consider all human action to be random or inexplicable. This is because we believe we can discover, for a given person or groups of persons, what they value. We then expect, in most cases, a certain consistency of their behavior. Because this is the case, if one can identify certain sets of salient initial conditions that confront a particular actor or group, one can expect that people will react in a particular (though not identical) fashion, to produce a characteristic (though not completely predictable) outcome.

This does not imply that everything that happens happens because someone intended it. On numerous occasions — as when many people seek the same quiet stretch of country trail and thereby so crowd it that it ceases to be a quiet country trail — people make choices that, because of the simultaneous or reactive choices of other people, or because of a lack or misunderstanding of information, lead to something like the opposite of what any one individual intended. Rational-choice theory makes this explicit and seeks to examine the consequences (Schelling 1960; Olson 1965). This can be extremely useful, for it is quite valuable to be aware of the kinds of circumstances in which the intended acts of individuals, in their interaction, produce collective outcomes that no one intended or foresaw.

A splendid example is the work of Theda Skocpol (1979) on revolutions. Skocpol identifies a historical process that led to social revolutions in France, Russia, and China. The process involves the collapse of state power due to failure to cope with external pressures from competing states, and peasant rebellions mobilized at the village level. Though monarchs and peasants sought changes in their current condition, the combination of their actions produced social revolutions of a kind that neither monarchs or peasant villagers intended.

Yet to merely describe this process is only beginning. The key parts of Skocpol's work consist of tracing how the processes unfolded in her several cases. She notes that the process could differ in specific details: States could fail to cope with external pressures either because of inadequate economic development (as in Russia in 1917) or because powerful elites blocked changes necessary to improve state efficiency (as in Imperial China and Old Regime France). What makes these accounts convincing is that they show how state leaders, faced with the situations of limited resources and external pressures, were trapped into taking actions that angered elites and led to state paralysis. This created openings for peasant rebellions from below. Then, Skocpol demonstrates how villages with local autonomy and village organization could plausibly react spontaneously, while villages in China — which lacked autonomy from local elites — could not react similarly until Japanese invasion and mobilization by the Chinese Communist Party had created a village-level organization in China that was autonomous of local landlords. There is no single cause, or single combination of causes, that created social revolutions. Skocpol presents no "law" of revolutions that would apply in all contexts, regardless of initial conditions. Instead, she delineates a *specific historical set of conditions* that occurred in similar fashion in several places. Under those conditions — a situation of state paralysis and peasant organization, which could be produced by slightly differing combinations of causes — the reasonable actions of state leaders, elites, and peasants would likely result in social revolution. The identification of the critical elements of their situation that led actors to take similar actions — even though the situations were not in all respects identical (nor were the consequences) — is the essence of good comparative history.

A robust process in history is a sequence of events that has unfolded in similar (but not identical or fully predictable) fashion in a variety of different historical contexts. Yet it is not a mere "limited historical generalization" or an analogy between different events. The statement "European monarchs in the seventeenth century were crowned" is a limited historical generalization. But we have no idea what produced it — was it a mere coincidence? Or did the choice of coronation as a symbol of monarchy have roots in a process of symbol manipulation and inheritance of a common symbolic heritage? If so, then there was a robust process *behind* the limited generalization and responsible for it. Similarly, one may note an analogy in the contestations of power between the French Assembly and French monarchy in 1789, and between the Petrograd Soviet and the Provisional Government in 1917, and label this situation "dual sovereignty." But is the resemblance coincidental or superficial? What makes such an analogy historically meaningful? It is meaningful if we can identify a process of initial conditions leading to similar choices by actors in the two situations — that is, a causal process connecting the similar elements in each situation. As Stinchombe (1978, p. 117) has pointed out, "The causal forces that make systematic social change go are people figuring out what to do." Thus a "robust process" is less than a law but more than a limited historical generalization or analogy. It is a causal statement, asserting that a particular kind of historical sequence unfolded because individuals responded to particular specified salient characteristics in their historical situation. If the salience of those characteristics is great, one can reasonably expect that, in a wide variety of historical contexts, actors will respond somewhat similarly to them, and their likely actions can thereby be predicted or explained.

Robust processes are not universal or determinate, because if the initial conditions are too different, or an additional element of a situation with these characteristics proves sufficient to destroy their salience, actors may then act quite differently and the process not occur. Because a law is independent of initial conditions, one can test and reject a law if one varies the initial conditions and fails to obtain consistent results. Thus one "tests" the law of refraction by examining the path of light under a variety of angles of incidence, and with substances with varied indices of refraction, to confirm that the law holds in these varied cases. But one does not "test" a process in this manner.

Enormous confusion has arisen because of a belief on the part of many historians and social scientists that pointing to robust similarities in history is akin to alleging the existence of predictive, determinate laws. Historians argue that, because historical sequences are unique and subject to accident, the search for causally meaningful regularities is a hopeless, misguided quest. Social scientists, on the other hand, argue that the search for causal regularities should be sought through large numbers of cases, testing for valid predictions as well as exceptions that might invalidate them. But *both* these views err, for they fail to grasp the difference between robust processes and laws.

To give an example from natural science, Darwin's theory of evolution by natural selection presents a process: It argues that when certain initial conditions exist — species with variation among individuals who are in reproductive competition — the law that progeny inherit the traits of parents creates a process whereby traits of more reproductively successful individuals are diffused throughout the population, giving rise to new species. But one can adduce exceptions: Laboratory mice (or other domesticated species) do not experience natural selection. Their reproductive success is controlled by owners, and individual variation is purposefully minimized (among laboratory mice) or moved in specific directions (such as in particularly attractive or valuable features for animals or crops). Yet this does not invalidate the theory of evolution. Nor does the confirmation of Darwin's theory depend on finding "negative" cases — whether populations that do not experience natural selection do not show speciation is not at issue. Darwin's theory does not depend on finding large numbers of identical cases for reinforcement, for no two cases of speciation *are* identical. Nor does it have to explain *all* speciation to be valuable — genetic drift and catastrophic extinctions are now believed to play roles equal to, or greater than, natural selection in the evolution of species. Precise, determinate prediction is not at issue either — the theory of natural selection makes no prediction of any particular new species or of the precise time of its emergence. As Cohen (1984, p. 96) notes, "Darwin showed that the way of progress in all of the sciences was not necessarily mathematical in style. . . . [His was the] first major scientific theory of modern times that was causal, but not predictive."

The power of Darwin's theory is that, by pointing to a simple process that has unfolded, in similar fashion, in a number of different circumstances, a large number of details of the historical record can be related to each other in a fashion that had previously been unrecognized or misunderstood. The validity of the theory of natural selection depends on whether it can be shown that, for a number of species, the variety of present species *did* develop through the diffusion of new traits from prior species. This means a close examination of the fossil record to see if the evidence conforms to the alleged process. One "tests" an alleged process by examining if, in the actual historical sequence that it is intended to explain, the details of what occurred are consistent with that process.

Similarly, the allegation that a particular process in human history occurred in specific historical settings requires a detailed examination of the historical record for those cases. A process can be considered robust if the workings of this process can be traced in different contexts — that is, if in different historical circumstances actors nonetheless were faced with situations that, in certain respects, were similar, and hence acted, in certain respects, in similar ways. The "certain respects" are presented in terms of a model that abstracts and simplifies certain details out of the complex and varied reality. But the validity of the demonstration depends on whether those actual historical details are consistent with the alleged process. Thus validating a *process* does not depend on exact prediction, or on matching positive and negative cases, or on finding large numbers of identical cases. The demonstration of validity depends on what Alexander George (1979) has described as *process-tracing* — showing that observed outcomes could reasonably be expected to result from actions likely to be taken in the specified situation.

Once a robust process has been identified for particular cases, prediction to cases other than those initially examined, and the treatment of exceptions, is quite different than in the case of a law. To use a law to predict, one simply applies the law to the initial conditions. To use a robust relationship, one must ask: In this situation, are the conditions considered to be salient still likely to be salient to the key actors? Or are new factors likely to outweigh them? Do the actors have differences in resources, or in goals, that may lead the process to unfold differently or not occur? Where similar situations do arise, without evident countervailing factors, knowledge of robust relationships can form a useful starting point for predictions about sequences of social behavior. Yet, where conditions are different, one would not expect the same process to occur. Thus a relationship between external pressure and revolution may be robust for large agrarian monarchies, but it may not hold equally for twentieth-century Iran.

Yet this does not "invalidate" the robust relationship for the cases for which it was developed — that validation rests on the process-tracing of the history of those cases. Instead, a knowledge of robust processes that occurred in several cases, when confronted with an exception, raises an *empirical* problem: *Precisely what factors or conditions* prevented the process in question from occurring? Perhaps the actors had different motivations, or perhaps the actors were similar but the initial conditions were different. Or perhaps the initial conditions were somewhat similar, but one crucial difference interfered with the process. In other words, one does not simply "reject" a process that has been found to be robust in different contexts by producing an exception. Instead, knowledge of the process then becomes a useful step in identifying a critical difference.

The key point is that the goal of comparative history is not simply to discover robust processes. The reality of history is *variation*; the goal of comparative history is to better *understand* that variation. In some cases, explanation may be facilitated by pointing to a robust process at work; in other cases, explanation may require elucidating crucial differences that led to particular variations in outcome. The value of a work of comparative history depends not on how well it abstracts regularities from historical details but on how well it handles the *details of what has occurred*, on whether it points out relationships among those details that were hitherto unrecognized or misunderstood.

This emphasis on process-tracing of causal processes sharply differentiates comparative history from mere correlational studies using many cases, which are often conducted in political science or sociology when doing cross-national research. Any limited generalizations found in this latter fashion, though useful, are only hypotheses whose basis in causal processes remains to be demonstrated. In this sense, comparative history and large data set correlational analyses are complementary but are not competitive or substitutes for one another.

Good comparative history must, therefore, "sink a huge anchor in details" (Gould 1986, p. 47). It is in confronting the historical details, in demonstrating certain connections between them, that comparative history makes its mark. Of course, as with geology or evolution, it is not possible to explain *all* the details of a historical sequence; it is enough to elucidate a process that connects *many* details of what happened to produce a work of great value.

A Summation

Comparative history does not mine history to develop laws. Let us instead list what comparative history *does* do. (1) Comparative history uses case-based comparisons to investigate historical variation. (2) Its seeks to engage in historical debates by offering *causal* explanations of particular observed sequences of events. (3) It may develop such causal explanations either by identifying critical differences between somewhat similar situations or by identifying robust processes that occurred in somewhat different settings. (Outstanding comparative histories often do both.) (4) Comparative history uses simplifying models, but this does not mean it is precisely predictive. (5) It validates its findings by process-tracing rather than simply by correlation. (6) It sinks an anchor in historical details, for its validity rests on how well the relationships it describes correspond to, and make sense of, those details. While its findings may have some predictive value, and may be generalizable, that is not the critical test. Instead (7) the test of the worth of a work of comparative history is whether it identifies and illuminates relationships heretofore unrecognized or misunderstood in particular sequences of historical events that have occurred.

As Geyl said of Toynbee's efforts, in words that apply to all comparative history — "but it's not history." True enough; it is not the reconstruction of what happened in a particular place at a particular time from the remaining evidence. Nor is it a broad chronological narrative of the sort recognized as general national or world history. It is a different endeavor, with different goals and methods. Yet it shares history's concern for getting the sequence right and for human action. It seeks to engage in the same conversation with historians, as they argue about those sequences. No less than history, comparative history seeks to explain why certain things happened, and how the world we live in today got to be that way.

REFERENCES

Abrams, Philip. 1982. *Historical Sociology*. Ithaca, NY: Cornell University Press.
Alexander, Jeffrey C. and Bernhard Giesen. 1987. "From Reduction to Linkage: The Long View of the Micro-Macro Link." Pp. 1-42 in *The Micro-Macro Link*, edited by Jeffrey C. Alexander, Bernhard Giesen, Richard Münch, and Neil J. Smelser. Berkeley: University of California Press.
Brenner, Robert. 1978. "Agrarian Class Structure and Economic Development in Pre-Industrial Europe." *Past and Present* 96:16-113.
Brustein, William. 1985. "Class Conflict and Class Collaboration in Regional Rebellions of 1500-1700." *Theory and Society* 14:445-68.
———. 1986. "Regional Social Orders in France and the French Revolution." *Comparative Social Research* 9:145-61.
Calhoun, Craig. 1982. *The Question of Class Struggle*. Chicago: University of Chicago Press.
Cohen, I. Bernard. 1984. *Revolution in Science*. Cambridge, MA: Belknap.
George, Alexander L. 1979. "The Causal Nexus Between Cognitive Beliefs and Decision-Making Behavior: The 'Operational Code' Belief System." Pp. 95-124 in *Psychological Models in International Politics*, edited by Lawrence S. Flakowski. Boulder, CO: Westview.
Giddens, Anthony. 1976. *New Rules of Sociological Method*. London: Hutchinson.
———. 1979. *Central Problems in Social Theory*. London: Macmillan.
Gould, Stephen J. 1986. "Cardboard Darwinism." *New York Review of Books* 33:47-54.
Hamilton, Gary and John Walton. 1988. "The Future for History in Sociology." Pp. 181-199 in *The Future of Sociology*, edited by Edgar Borgatta and Karen Cook. Newbury Park, CA: Sage.
Homans, George Caspar. 1961. *Social Behavior: Its Elementary Forms*. New York: Harcourt, Brace & World.
Jervis, Robert, Ned Lebow, and Janice Gross Stein, eds. 1985. *Psychology and Deterrence*. Baltimore: Johns Hopkins University Press.
Jones, Eric. 1988. *Growth Recurring: Economic Change in World History*. Oxford: Clarendon.
Kennedy, Paul M. 1987. *The Rise and Fall of the Great Powers: Economic Change and Military Conflict from 1500 to 2000*. New York: Random House.
Lebow, Richard Ned. 1981. *Between Peace and War: The Nature of International Crises*. Baltimore: Johns Hopkins University Press.
Mantoux, Paul. 1903. "Histoire et sociologie." *Revue de synthèse historique* 1:121-40.
MacDougall, Walter A. 1986. " 'Mais ce n'est pas l'histoire': Some Thoughts on McNeill, Toynbee, and the Rest of Us." *Journal of Modern History* 58:19-42.
McNeill, William. 1982. *The Pursuit of Power*. Chicago: University of Chicago Press.
Olson, Mancur. 1965. *The Logic of Collective Action*. Cambridge, MA: Harvard University Press.
———. 1982. *The Rise and Decline of Nations*. New Haven, CT: Yale University Press.
Parsons, Talcott. 1937. *The Structure of Social Action*. New York: Free Press.
Schelling, Thomas C. 1960. *The Strategy of Conflict*. Cambridge, MA: Harvard University Press.
Sewell, William H., Jr. 1985. *Structure and Mobility: The Men and Women of Marseilles*. Cambridge: Cambridge University Press.

Skocpol, Theda. 1979. *States and Social Revolutions*. Cambridge: Cambridge University Press.
————., ed. 1984. *Vision and Method in Historical Sociology*. Cambridge: Cambridge University Press.
Starr, Paul. 1982. *The Social Transformation of American Medicine*. New York: Basic Books.
Stinchcombe, Arthur. 1978. *Theoretical Methods in Social History*. New York: Academic Press.
Tilly, Charles. 1986. *The Contentious French*. Cambridge, MA: Belknap.
Traugott, Mark. 1985. *Armies of the Poor*. Princeton, NJ: Princeton University Press.
Wolf, Eric. 1970. *Peasant Wars of the Twentieth Century*. New York: Harper & Row.

21

Sociology, Economics, and the Economy

Harvey Molotch

What utility has sociology for understanding the economy? What sort of sociology would usefully clarify the nature of economic relations? My response begins with a critique of traditional understandings of economic activity, whether organized through the market or within bureaucracies, whether in the capitalist realm or the socialist countries. My complaint is that the dominant views embody a notion of rationality that is inconsistent with the way people actually operate. These views come too close to portraying humans as automatons whose plans and schemes are subservient to market or bureaucratic machina. But real rationality, practical rationality, operates in a way that makes markets and bureaucracies as contingent on human action as the other way around.[1] At the micro level, this means that economic relations are produced through the same sort of interactional methods that are part of behavior generally; at the macro level, it means that markets and bureaucracies are always structured by exogenous social forces that give rise to them in the first place and sustain them over time.

The received wisdoms are increasingly being questioned, especially in those places — like the United States and the Soviet Union — where models of the putative rational human have been dominant. The self-examination in the Soviet Union is dramatic: A brittle form of organizing production is being blamed for a stagnant economy. In the United States, the issue is less prominent, but gaining momentum. After decades of blaming unions and shiftless workers for U.S. economic problems, even conservative analysts have turned to issues like the "culture" of the corporation, the time horizons of corporate managers, and the dubious contribution to productivity of corporate takeovers and other forms of

AUTHOR'S NOTE: *Paul DiMaggio, Bill Domhoff, and Herbert Gans provided helpful critiques of this chapter.*

financial engineering. There is also serious talk of worker participation, as in the "quality of work life" movement. Although calls for reform in the social organization of the economy have come before in U.S. history, they have tended to come from the left, primarily to foster social justice; the current mood grows from a growing concern, quite consensual, that innovation and productivity are at risk.

Both the U.S. and socialist economic systems have always rested on particular sociological views, however tacit, of how economies best work. While Soviet lip service pays Marxian homage to the perfectibility of humans, the society is massively Weberian (a Weberian caricature) in its reliance on bureaucracy to hold itself together. Production and distribution of goods occur through formally organized agencies with offices of delimited function, chains of command and written rules that supposedly guide actors toward their proper jobs and duties. Aptly termed the *command economy,* the system rests on the assumption that bureaucracy (at least when controlled by the state) efficiently organizes production. This is the macro-sociology. The micro assumption is that humans really can operate bureaucratically and still get the job done: They respect authority and jurisdictional lines and act according to rules.

American sociologists have a long and distinguished tradition of pointing to the ways the Weberian assumptions fail to explain actual bureaucratic life (there are informal norms, for example). But even this research fails, for reasons I will later explain, to go far enough in showing how actual bureaucratic life differs from the ideal type. This has left a void; sociologists have not established a clear alternative to the rational person model. Thus the dominant sociological assumption in America (not necessarily shared by professional sociologists) invokes the invisible hand—the economist's term for a macro social structure of competitive markets that optimally organizes human behavior. At the micro level, the market functions because people have an inherent tendency to truck, barter, and exchange, to materially self-maximize through rational means-ends action. The market sets individuals free to do their thing (maximize utilities), and the result is a division of labor that directly optimizes productive efficiency and, at least indirectly, the moral good.

Both the command bureaucracy and the free market theories rest on similarly deterministic, "oversocialized" conceptions of humans (Granovetter 1988). Bureaucratic legitimacy leads to conformity, which will aggregate to production and justice; markets lead individuals to self-maximize and this aggregates to production and justice. This lynchpin in both versions tying individual action to organizational outcome is their view of human rationality. Bureaucrats will respond to plans, directives, and rules in the way they were formulated; market actors will atomistically pursue material interests, restrained only by the rules or norms of the market itself. In both versions, individual rationalities aggregate to societal rationality.

EMPIRICAL PRODUCTION

Studies of Eastern bloc countries make it easy to critique underlying assumptions of their bureaucratic economies.[2] We learn that workers, managers, and members of the top elite must rely on extrabureaucratic tools to get work done. Plant managers horde supplies because otherwise a crucial ingredient will be unavailable when needed. Informal arrangements within and across industries provide for exchanging tools, technologies, and raw materials. Rivalries within and across agencies and production units account for many decisions, often at the expense of formal goals. Members of the "new class" may have one eye on the rules contained in recent party directives but seem equally guided by personal desires and the social solidarities provided by their special status. Workers routinely disobey rules precisely so they can get their jobs done; at other times they shirk because of their own demoralization and antagonism toward the system. Workers also invent small industries of their own and manufacture in their homes or in their factories during off-duty hours, even when forbidden to do so.

The U.S. market system is less dissimilar than it may appear. As in the East, there is a vast "informal economy" of people who work out solutions to livelihood irrespective of laws and apparent informal norms (e.g., the drug trade, prostitution, sweatshop labor). More crucially, the formal economy is itself informal in its actual operations, relying on ad hoc solutions of actors to make production occur. Some of this is technically criminal, like price-rigging or zoning violations, while much is not only legal but indispensable to production.

Workers often know best how to do their jobs; they operate out of an "action-centered" orientation (Zuboff 1988) that does not depend on formal rules or incentives.[3] They see what needs to be done and, under the press of circumstance, intuit how to combine physical movement with thought to solve a problem. Such behaviors, whether at work or in other settings, are as natural as play or rest and need no special reward structures to explain (see McGregor 1960). Sometimes workers' resistance to management springs not from a desire to defeat authority but, ironically, from a desire to sustain production (Roy 1954; Zuboff 1988). Rather than self-maximizing at every turn, they want to make things go well out of some sense of craftsmanship (Burawoy 1979). Even when supervision is direct and tyrannical, discretion is still at work; in the extreme case of the concentration camps, many of the victims acquiesced to the micro routines necessary to maintain "production" and some creatively concerned themselves with such goals. Building the bridge over the River Kwai was not fiction.

As with workers, managers' actions do not rely on the type of means-ends calculations or atomistic, asocial procedures implied by either the market or the bureaucratic models. In one authoritative study, corporate managers are described as people who "act first and think later" (Isenberg 1884, p. 89); a manager-informant describes the process as a series of "preoccupations": "You have a preoccupation with working capital, a preoccupation with capital expenditure, a preoccupation with people . . . and all this goes so fast that you don't even know whether it's completely rational, or it's part rational, part intuitive" (Isenberg 1984, p. 85). As part of this same intuitive mechanism, managers (even in competitive firms) "work together" through all manner of informal arrangements that seem inconsistent with either rules or the profit motive (see Donaldson and Lorsch 1983).

Managers repeatedly turn to the same suppliers and subcontractors even if it means paying more because prior encounters (some business, some in other social forms) lead them to expect reliability, fair treatment, and perhaps friendship. In the building trades, for example, circles of subcontractors tend to work repeatedly together on the same projects because they rely on one another's knowledge of routines and techniques as well as on their mutual experience of fairness and reliability (Eccles 1981).[4] Speaking of "communities of trust" among business actors, Storper and Scott remark that "trust and personal experience are . . . important pre-conditions of much . . . behavior in modern business complexes." Thus, even when disputes arise in business transactions, they are "frequently settled without reference to the contract or potential or actual legal sanctions" (Macaulay 1963, p. 61, as quoted in Granovetter 1985, p. 497).

Because of the social nature of production, firms choose their locations in part to gain proximity to those who can be trusted. Even when it comes to locating branch operations, social factors intervene: Executives make the decision, in part, based on their contacts with others who have made similar moves, even in unlike industries (see Pred 1976), rather than through any clear-cut optimizing strategy. Other management behaviors are similarly social in nature: Discrimination against women, minorities, and the physically unattractive has been a mainstay of corporate behavior, despite its nonoptimizing waste of human capital. Firms grow with little positive consequence for efficiency or profitability.

The examples have been piling up in both the business press and the scholarly literature attesting to the failure of neoclassical economics or the Weberian bureaucratic ideal type to explain what really goes on. Economists, sometimes noticing these empirical failures, try to "patch up" the rational-choice model (Frank 1988; see also Hahn 1981), sometimes by bringing nonmaterial rewards into the utility-maximizing matrix. Workers who seem to be unselfishly helping the firm reach its goals are gaining the admiration of peers or some other psychic kick. The fact that parents risk their lives for their children's, that majorities of people are shown in well-designed experiments to return wallets to strangers (cash intact),[5] all must be explained as either exceptional (and hence deviant in some way) or evidence of a hidden goal. Old people, for example, who say they refrain from spending so they can leave more for their children are interpreted as selfishly motivated because they enjoy contemplating the consumption of future generations (Laitner 1979, p. 403, as discussed in Etzioni 1988). Through such tautological reasoning, the rational utility-maximizing assumption is unfalsifiable.

Somewhat more plausible patching involves use of the economist's concept of opportunity costs: Executives who imitate business friends' plant location decisions are "satisficing" as a way to avoid the costs of a full search. Similarly, entrepreneurs reply on one another's reputation for reliability because this saves them money in the long run. On the issue of irrational discrimination, minorities or women are kept out of business positions because their presence would distress other workers with resultant productivity declines (for a critique, see Blau and Jusenius 1976). Regardless of the analytic creativity involved in dealing with the apparent exceptions, at some point the paradigm has to be changed to facilitate observation instead of treating observations as problems. Otherwise, the efforts to patch, always as an afterthought to a surprise conse-quence, enervate economic theory that comes to resemble a Rube Goldbergian contraption of fixes.

PRACTICAL RATIONALITY:
A SOCIOLOGICAL IMPERIALISM

While there are indeed an increasing number of sociologists (as well as restive economists) who are creatively addressing these issues, our discipline has not been very audacious in pressing an alternative view (see Zelizer 1988, pp. 2, 3). Contrary to the grand vision of Comte, sociology has allowed its queenly self to be defined by the economic perspective and not the other way round (Swedberg 1987, p. 20). To gain admission to the academy, sociology had to take, as Albion Small commented, the "leftovers" (Swedberg 1987, p. 20). And given the political need to stay off the economists' turf (as well as those of political science and anthropology), the main leftover was the irrational. Econ-omists study behavior oriented toward production and distribution of material goods and the rational processes that presumably characterize such efforts. Consistent with Samuelson's dictum that economics' subject is rational behavior and sociology's, the irrational, sociology's early spin was to focus itself upon such phenomena as suicide, deviance, authoritarianism, and status anxiety. Sociologists study the institutions, events, and loci where the putative irrational aspects of life hold sway, like the family, mass media, popular culture, revolu-tion, and the street corner. Even when they move beyond such topics to areas like class analysis and social mobility, sociologists look for the ways that what people say or think is not what they do, or what they take to be true information about the world is, in fact, false and thus irrational (e.g., stereotypes, false consciousness, or simple naïveté).

The search for such ironies, their causes and consequences, has been a mainstay of sociological research (see Garfinkel 1967; Cicourel 1964), albeit often useful in a populist way. A number of these studies have had important implications for how the economy works (e.g., father's occupation versus IQ effects on income), but sociologists have seldom used their findings to redefine the nature of economic relations. They could: All this "irrationality" might be seen as evidence that rationality, in the economist's sense, does not exist at all. But sociologists, perhaps in part because their intellectual roots share too much with the economists, use their piles of findings more modestly. They (along with economist fellow travelers — see, for example, Leibenstein 1981; Hirschman 1986) stress that these other matters also "count" and should be taken into consideration in understanding society. The scenario implies partial variance explained by the sociological "factors." Sociologists have not gone very far in arguing that the economy is itself social and that no economic relation occurs outside the sociological frame because every economic act is inherently a social act.

Indeed, our most famous modern link with economics was provided by the exchange theorists like Homans and Blau, who, rather than using sociology to explain the economy, used neoclassical economic concepts to explain realms of social life otherwise treated as sociological (e.g., friendship, helping behavior, family). Now economists like Gary Becker have invaded the sociological turf with a vengeance, leaving nothing outside the domain of their "economic imperialism," as they unabashedly term it (see Radnitzky and Bernholz 1986; Becker 1976).

A number of sociologists have begun to overcome the fear and/or loathing that has kept economic matters beyond the sociological pale. Granovetter (1985, p. 495), adapting Polanyi's term, argues that economic relations are "embedded" in social relations. "Transactions of all kinds are rife with . . . social connections," Granovetter says. I want to advance this line of thought by showing what "embedded" or "rife with" might mean. At the outset, it does not mean that economic relations are merely modified (or defiled) by the social; instead, it means that economic relations are made possible by the inherently social nature of human rationality.

To the extent that human beings are rational at all (and some of them are completely nuts), their rationality works in a different way than either the Weberians or the neoclassical economists would suppose. The usual concept of rationality so misunderstands actual human behavior that it presumes humans to be, in Garfinkel's[6] (1967, p. 68) term, "judgmental dopes," or in the somewhat related phrase of the renegade economist Sen (1977), "rational fools." The supposed cunning of the economist's trucking, bartering, and exchanging human or of Weber's dutiful bureaucrat who has mastered the list of complex rules and procedures is really a very restricted cunning. Humans are much brighter, and their brightness is, broadly speaking, a constructive and productive force that must be appreciated to understand economic behavior or build economic institutions.

A few examples from bureaucratic and economic life can help. Zimmerman (1970) studied a U.S. welfare office to determine the nature of rules in that setting. A cardinal rule for the receptionist to follow was "first come, first served" when assigning clients to their interviews with case workers. Zimmerman noticed, however, instances when this did not occur. Sometimes clients were sufficiently disruptive that they were moved ahead of the queue. The receptionist knew that such a client could upset all the other interviews (carried out in adjoining cubicles) and risk an escalation of emotional displays that might prove contagious. The result might be that no one could be interviewed. The appropriate action, one contained in no rule book, was to take care of the disturbing client first. How did the receptionist know to do this? In the rule-following schema, there is no way to account for such discretion. In the modification proposed by Blau, receptionists follow informal rules that exist side by side with the formal ones, but Blau does not tell us what happens when there is no such rule or where such rules come from or how the actor might know which one (out of a multitude) to apply under what circumstance. In any event, the receptionist's bureaucracy had no such "informal rule" evident in any clear way; she was a solo practitioner, trained by being put on the job, without recourse to any scheme of operation except her own common sense.

In Zimmerman's ethnomethodological explanation, that common sense consisted of the receptionist's complex understanding of the whole scene, including her own biography and future prospects—a scene she grasps as a kind of evolving *gestalt* and to which she can quickly adapt as circumstances change. The receptionist is context-sensitive and understands what makes organizations work; she has *practical rationality*. She does what "must" be done to keep the organization, including her role in it, operational. Indeed (more on this later), the receptionist's—and others'—active empathy for what a welfare agency is provides the only way that the agency, qua agency, gets its reality.

Often, Zimmerman saw the receptionist serve people on a first-come basis, but she did this because it ordinarily works out well organizationally, not because of a master rule book. Instead, the master rule, if we can speak of such a thing at all, is to make the system work. When bureaucrats' social and physical situation puts them in a position to follow that rule, there can be recognizable efficiency.

People with practical projects (doing a job, getting welfare benefits, building a fortune for posterity) interpret the swirl of rules, norms, values, dictums, notions in light of their circumstance. "Thou shalt not kill," perhaps the most universal and fundamental of all behavior guides, has been readily transformed, on a case-by-case basis, to permit murder in the streets, in the concentration camps, under the gallows, on the battlefield, in the womb, at the hospital ward, in the old age home, and under the insect fumigation tent. If people aren't going around killing one another, willy-nilly, it's certainly not because there is a rule against it.

A well-known example from the marketplace can be used to make the same point about how institutions come to exist and how people operate in their midst. Individuals who travel the New Jersey Turnpike for the first and last time presumably leave tips for those who serve them food. Why? A neoclassical patch-up is that people are so used to tipping under conditions where they must maintain their restaurant reputations that they continue to do so when the conditions do not apply, rather than go to the trouble (opportunity costs) of rationally recalculating. This seems farfetched; some people are consistent travelers who have had ample opportunity to figure out that there is "no reason" to tip. The conventional sociological perspective is to invoke norms — informal rules "out there" that somehow guide behavior as conscience, superego, or some other disembodied force.

The explanation I prefer is the same as in the receptionist's case: Eaters are organizationally (in the largest sense) empathic. People understand that U.S. restaurants exist, rightly or wrongly, through tipping; it is restaurants' nature. Folks understand there is a standard (about 15%) that helps prompt a cooperative response of doing one's share: As in game research simulations, most people[7] choose the cooperative outcome — especially when it is a solution perceived as generally known and available.

It isn't just that the restaurant is helped along by nice behavior like tipping; the relation between behavior and institution is, as in the welfare agency, more intimate and mutually determinative. The restaurant is "done" through the tipping behavior just as the behavior is invoked by the institution. The setting gets its "restaurantness" via activities like tipping (as well as being given a menu, selecting from a delimited choice of food, paying a bill, and so forth). To recognize an institution as a certain sort and to act accordingly so as to sustain its integrity as that sort of institution embeds social action in an institution and in this way constitutes the institution (Wilson forthcoming). This requires interpretive skill (usually found in cultural natives) as well as benign intentions — that is, a stance not oriented toward "making trouble" (like insisting on Chinese food at a pizza restaurant or not tipping because it isn't legally required or economically rational). This "practical ethics," in Garfinkel's wise phrase, is evident in mundane behavior generally. Social order requires (and ordinarily gets) behavior that is "intrinsically 'biased' towards solidary actions" (Heritage 1984, p. 286) and a cunning that is organizationally alert.

This is the necessary social psychological underpinning for what Giddens calls "structuration" — the mutually reflexive determination of structure and action. It helps solve the conundrum of the relation between action and institution, still vague in Granovetter's "embedded" usage. The social is embedded in the economic in the same way it is embedded in structure of any sort: It is only through humans interpreting, acting, and attending to organizations as particular and peculiar in certain ways that those organizations have their special and enduring forms, much less operate smoothly as instances of those forms. An institution, including economic ones like restaurants and markets, come alive only through people's alert conceptualizing of their plausible organizational natures; these institutions' resultant health and efficiency depend on just how this is done.[8] People get into the swing of things, as workers, executives, or bureaucrats, by lending their sense-making apparatus to the cause. A job task is done by a worker who senses and sustains a specific organization through mobilizing knowledge of a wide range of relevant particulars.

Now we are in a position to see what is really wrong with patch-ups like opportunity costs. To explain tipping as an avoidance of opportunity costs trivializes the matter. The costs would not just be high; they would be overwhelming. Nontipping would require the transformation of the restaurant as an institution and a suspension of the human proclivity to attend to an institution in a way that let lets it be, helps it go on, and makes one appear as competent to exist in a world that has restaurants. To not tip "for no reason" is to border on insanity. People tip not because they are nice, not because they are selfish, but because they are rational.

The overarching source of order is not a zeal for self-maximizing or the fact of a rule book but the need to appear accountably rational — that is, to perform as a competent social being. This is how structure emerges through action and action through structure. At the individual, social psychological level, there is a structuration urge. If there is a basic human nature, this, I would argue, is it. It links individual with social organization through the effort to perform as an accountably sane and competent person.

Cunning of the sort I describe proceeds quickly (in the gestalt instant — hence, "action-centered," "intuitive," and so on) and is time- and place-contingent. Tipping is less universal than I have implied. Its usually not done at MacDonald's and is more ambiguous still at places where you stand to order food but then someone brings it to you, like Sizzler's. It's not done at all if the service is bad enough, except when the problem seems to have been caused by the chef or the host or mechanical problems not under the server's control. If the restaurant server is one's lover or spouse, a tip would be so inappropriate as to threaten the relationship. Similarly, first-come, first-served varies in all sorts of ways: What if Jackie Kennedy comes into the beauty shop? A bank robber into the bank? Or a starving child to the supermarket? But then suppose its the tenth exception in a row: Will the old rule again be invoked or will still another guideline be brought into play? What needs to be done is contextually and sequentially determined in an ad hoc way that neither greed nor norm/rule following can explain.

This lack of material or normative drive does not mean people are *laid back* or *shiftless* — although these are the terms often flung at Californians and members of the underclass in response to their respective efforts to struggle through a day. It's almost the opposite: Oh, if only we had a clear goal with efficient means to reach it and norms/rules to instruct us along the way. That would put us all on automatic pilot, a bit boring but stress-free. In contrast, real rationality as opposed to textbook rationality is tense. That life is hard is evidence that the essence of rationality is not the ability to follow rules or atomistic greed but the capacity to appear appropriate under diverse settings and ever-changing circumstances.

Humans' theorizing and action do not, of course, spring out of nowhere; the dead hand of the past exists as a structuration history, as sticks and carrots recalled, as visible cues and memories of what works, as physical forms and spatial configurations that can be seen and experienced. Self-preservation, sacred canons, and material aggrandizement are also among the powerful details; but rather than being determining, their meaning can be situationally transformed by the nature of the other particulars — as when the bottom line transforms them into suicide, genocide, and potlatch, respectively.

Rendering our actions rational and hence mutually intelligible is the basis for accomplishing anything real together, including the production (or destruction) of goods and services. In doing that work, we often must invoke bureaucratic rules, informal norms, and material interests. In a society dominated by the rationalist ethic, among behaviors to be appropriately displayed is conformity to a putative market-driven social order, defending one's actions — especially in business affairs — as calculating, unemotional, and hard-nosed. The surge of interest among corporations in the post-1950s period in "strategic planning" (see Swanstrom 1987, p. 141) explicitly injects a radical model of the rational actor and rational organization into the corporate setting. Firms should create "mission statements," then conduct "environmental scans," leading to "resource audits," followed by implementation, which is "viewed as a relatively automatic and unproblematic process" (Swanstrom 1987, p. 145). About a decade behind, government agencies and nonprofit organizations are now infatuated with the same lockstep models; the education establishment teaches teachers to approach the classroom a similar way (the infamous lesson plans) and now even the children in some schools are under the gun to sign "learning contracts." Given the hegemony of this discourse, actions and agreements need to be discussed and justified in terms of means-ends rationales.[9] Fealty to economist decision making or bureaucratic obeisance must be displayed — hence falsely making it appear as though markets and rational rules run the world.

But the stipulations of bureaucratic rules and market contracts are secondary to the social bonds, human empathies, and informal understandings that permeate transactions. These go beyond Durkheim's "noncontractual elements of the contract"; they reside in the essential imprecision of all dictums and agreements, due to the fact that every clause is inherently ambiguous because every word of any language is construable in a virtually infinite variety of ways. All contingencies cannot be specified in advance (not even most of them); there is always more, infinitely more, to say (what Garfinkel calls, in a more general context, the "et cetera clause"). Instead, the ongoing systems of trust and reasonableness are used to solve the problem of what, precisely, the agreement really meant all along. To be clear: The trust is not, as others have more conventionally argued, in the other party's reputation for adhering to a certain contractual provision or for adhering to contracts generally. Rather, the trust is in the other party's willingness and capacity to be reasonable — that is to say, in the other person's willingness to use the full array of contextual details to work out together what the contract means in light of all the evolving circumstances. Rationality consists in the capacity to display and recognize this attitude of practical ethics.

I reiterate: The capacity to know what to do when and where, and how to provide intelligible accounts, is not at all the version of rationality as it plays itself out under the ideology of Homo oeconomicus or command bureaucracies. Indeed, these two thought systems have great potential for screwing up real human accomplishment by depriving people access to their own social talents. Executives and planners who insist on sharp divisions of labor, who require rule reliance, who insist that hierarchical divisions be obeyed eviscerate the resource that problem-solving humans bring into settings. British unionists long ago learned that an excellent way to disrupt an organization is by "working to rule" — which means instructing workers to follow formal procedures. By deliberately approximating such conditions through their directives, management may enhance titular power and generate data demonstrating conformity (what Gordon 1976, in another context, calls "capitalist efficiency"), but organizations degenerate. They cannot function effectively without continuous and routine discretionary human action, even if such action is a threat to management authority. Techniques of domination not only breed resentment and counterconspiracies, they disallow workers' own human skills from being mobilized on behalf of production — an indispensable ingredient of economic activity. The deviant dope goes macro, aggregating into a dopey organization.

OPPORTUNISM AND STRUCTURE

This failure to recognize the omnipresence of human scheming and cooperation carries into law and politics as a presumption that markets and bureaucracies tend toward self-regulation. This invites the very opportunism that both the market and the bureaucratic orientations hold as exceptional. Adam Smith was himself aware that markets are not naturally self-policing and that norms may not work so well either. He warned against "the mean rapacity, the monopolizing spirit of merchants and manufacturers" (see Swedberg 1987, p. 14).[10] Abolafia reminds us that, based on the history of the U.S. stock and commodity markets, "increasingly rigorous constraints were found necessary to keep these markets from being cornered." If any tendency in markets exists, Abolafia says (1985, p. 13), "it is anti-competitive as a result of the desire of successful competitors to reduce their uncertainty through monopoly. It is *constraint* which is 'natural' in the midst of competition." As Commons (1959, p. 713) remarks: "Competition is . . . an artificial arrangement supported by the moral, economic and physical sanctions of collective action." If it is to be attained at all, it is "to be attained by restraints upon the natural struggle for existence." And key to this "constraint" and "natural struggle" is the practical urge of humans to make structures through micro social tools.

Under the neoclassical scenario, not only do markets serve efficiency but they arose in the first place because they were functional for this goal. But regardless of their putative macro effects, markets have to be invented through proximate stages and proximate acts. Maureen Jung (1988) has recently completed a study of just how these acts proceeded in the formation of the nineteenth-century mining companies of California and Nevada and the markets through which their stocks were exchanged. These firms were among the pioneering modern corporations of the world in that their stock was easily traded, they were heavily capitalized by distant investors, and they helped transform the technology and social organization of their industry. Jung learned that these first corporations, and the western stock markets newly developed to trade their shares, were both opportunistic in their very creation. The dual social invention of the stock market and the corporation, as they together took form in these early ventures, was designed to attract capital from naive investors who could be bilked. For example, insiders ran up the value of market shares by putting out media stories of bonanza mineral strikes (whether true or false) and then selling out at the propitious moment. They set up privately held firms to milk the publicly held ones. There were a range of such schemes, which is why, according to Jung's data, the publicly held firms' aggregate economic performance was dismal. For the majority of firms, stockholders were forced to pay more money as special assessments into the firm than was ever dispersed as dividends (Jung 1988, p. 197). Further, it appears that the firms that did pay significant dividends issued them only when insiders held predominate shares of stock. After the great gold and silver rush was transformed from lone panhandlers working small claims to modern corporations using heavy technologies, the bulk of a nonrenewable resource was exploited from the American West at a great net loss to the investing public. By this criterion, the corporation was an inefficient form.

The historic record suggests that far from an aberration, such shenanigans as insider trading and nonproductive asset manipulation were intrinsic to the creation of the modern economy. The great fortunes, and many small ones as well, were built by God-fearing men who seized the opportunities that came their way, relying on collusion to structure and exploit the firms and markets that were their practical projects.

However reified it has come to be, the nature of a corporation, like the nature of a restaurant, is continuously up for grabs and those with the most power to make reality are the most crucial players or, to awkwardly adapt Giddens's term, the crucial "structurators." Restaurant making is a rather democratic enterprise, but establishing the meaning of stock markets and corporations is not. Rules, norms, and values are reinterpreted ad hoc as they inevitably must be by all social creatures to determine what to do next; the powerful are more brazen and have special access to making their interpretations stick on matters of importance to them. The market is itself structured, as is the bureaucracy, through the substantive ends it might serve, including the distribution of money, power, fame, and honor. The current legal and moral controversies surrounding raider groups' use of junk bonds (a new invention) to control corporations and make stock killings is only a recent manifestation. Whether the outcome is socially beneficial or not, economic projects occur through empathy and proximate cooperation that modifies structures (to varying degrees) as they are exploited. When it comes to any but the simplest project, there is honor (and rationality) among thieves or there would be no thieves.

By sustaining the myth that the natural equilibrium point of economic relations is a nonopportunistic state, we miss the truth of our history and present — and with it the capacity to set up contexts that will facilitate one sort of collusion and not another, one sort of market and not another, one sort of bureaucracy and not another. The Soviet case teaches clearly that efficiency and rational action at the individual level should not be equated with efficiency and rational action for a bureaucracy; the U.S. corporate economy teaches that efficiency and rational action for an individual manager or owner should not be equated with efficiency and rational action for the firm or the society. Disaggregation of interests and nested and cross-cutting rationalities among those making up a firm or bureaucracy are a necessary prologue for intelligent institution building.

If people's primary urge is affiliatory, they will get together to make common cause, whether in matters having to do with production or any other. This sociability can be labeled, depending on one's attraction to the outcome, as "conspiracy," "cooperation," or "community." "The social animal" is as plausible a starting point for understanding human nature as is the utility maximizer. The desire to be with and make league with other people is as basic as the drive to truck. When fused with the production and distribution of material goods, it determines the way such activities occur and who will gain or lose as a result. A society that encourages exchange in a market cannot banish sociability as part of the arrangement.

Given the contingent nature of rules and contracts (their "indexicality") and the socialness of humans (including their hypersensitivity to one another's presence, intentions, and commonalities), collusive opportunism is an obvious solution to concrete problems. It is the grass that will grow in every crack. Again, by ignoring this proclivity and its permeation of the economic realm, there is a disarming of the potential for creative problem solving at the macro level — for creating a framework through which social solidarities will result in productive and fair material outcomes.

Thus, in the United States, we need to end the tiresome debate, one that goes back to Durkheim's quarrel with the economists of his day, between intervention into the economy versus a free market strategy. Extending the thinking of Polanyi a generation ago, it is now clear that collective intervention is intrinsic to economic relations (and not just modern ones), even more radically than Granovetter indicates. This makes the only question not whether to have intervention but the nature of the institution that does the structuring — guilds, church, clubs, worker councils, neighborhood groups, corporations, cliques, cartels, unions, or government — and the purposes for which the structuring will be put — world domination, ecological preservation, wealth redistribution, or helping a Texas family corner the silver market.[11]

Obviously involved in these decisions are matters of power and politics. The social organization of markets, prices, and wages means that scholars will, in participating in these debates, be taking positions that are moral in their nature and distributive in their implications. Once rationality is no longer the mark of goodness, ethics surfaces as a topic rather than remaining submerged in the pursuit of amoral optima.

At the factory and office level of putting together productive environments, as well as at the macro policy level of framing national directions, reforms must take into account the nature of people to ad hoc invent, collude, and connive, regardless of their station in life or the collective benefits that result. Sociologists have only begun to delineate these processes, to study "in detail," as one economist urges, "what the standard (economic) theory simply assumes" (Leibenstein 1981, p. 109). To play their larger role, sociologists will need to become less shy about intruding on the sensibilities of economists and embrace a conception of humans as creative, methodic beings whose rationality (for good or ill) can be profitably studied.

NOTES

1. I am not the first to try to "bring the human back in" but, as I will later argue, most previous efforts have not gone far enough in breaking with the "economic [or bureaucratic] man" models.

2. See, for example, Granick (1960), Burawoy (1979, 1985), Stark (1986).

3. Zuboff implies this action-centered mode is contingent on specific ways of organizing production. I'm making a more universal claim for its relevance.

4. Such relations characterize vast portions of the Japanese economy, which is organized as a series of hierarchical layers with conglomerates at the top that subcontract to medium-sized firms that then subcontract to still smaller units, sometimes made up of as few as three working individuals. The number of layers varies across sector, but the personalistic (and paternalistic) tenor of relations is characteristic (Hill forthcoming).

5. Studies demonstrating such altruism are reviewed in Etzioni (1988, pp. 51-63), a highly useful source for this chapter.

6. While, in his excellent review of economic sociology, Swedberg (1987, p. 128) correctly observes that sociologists have generally "neglected" the topic of rationality, he misses the detailed empirical attention of ethnomethodologists to the subject.

7. "Most people" may not include most economists; economics graduate students were found by Marwell and Ames (1981) to be less likely than other subjects to choose cooperative options in game experiments.

8. The ethnomethodological scheme seems compatible with the "Austrian school" of economists, which criticizes the "mechanical quality" of the Keynesians who "somehow blithely believed [it] possible to analyze the interaction of various 'macro' variables without any examination of the micro-underpinnings of these aggregate entities. . . . Economic theory needs to be reconstructed so as to recognize at each stage the manner in which changes in external phenomena modify economic activity strictly through the filter of the human mind" (Kirzner 1981, pp. 120-122).

9. This is the source of the tendency for social scientists to see the market as "boundless" (Zelizer 1988), overstating the invasion of capitalist modes into all realms, including consciousness and micro interactions. They take people's accounts too literally.

10. Smith's precise comment on *truck*, barter, and exchange was that this was a "certain propensity in human nature"; this "certain propensity" has become reified as a compulsion through which all economic behavior (and a good deal of noneconomic behavior) can supposedly be understood.

11. If socially progressive goals are selected, there is no need to presume that productivity declines; research suggests that regulation on behalf of enhancing the social wage is associated with strong, rather than weak, economic performance among the market societies (Friedland and Sanders 1985; Korpi 1985). Capitalizing on workers' creative instincts is similarly a likely productivity plus.

REFERENCES

Abolafia, Mitchel Y. 1985. "Market Crisis and Organizational Intervention." Paper presented at the annual meeting of the American Sociological Association, Washington, DC, August.

Becker, Gary S. 1976. *The Economic Approach to Human Behavior*. Chicago: University of Chicago Press.

Blau, Francine D. and Carol L. Jusenius. 1976. "Economists' Approaches to Sex Segregation in the Labor Market." Pp. 181-200 in *Women and the Workplace: The Implications of Occupational Segregation*, edited by M. Blaxall and B. Reagan. Chicago: University of Chicago Press.

Burawoy, Michael. 1979. *Manufacturing Consent: Changes in the Labor Process Under Monopoly Capitalism*. Chicago: University of Chicago Press.

———. 1985. *The Politics of Production: Factory Regimes Under Capitalism and Socialism*. London: Verso.

Cicourel, Aaron. 1964. *Method and Measurement in Sociology*. New York: Free Press.

Commons, John R. 1959. *Institutional Economics*. Madison: University of Wisconsin Press.

Donaldson, Gordon and Jay W. Lorsch. 1983. *Decision Making at the Top*. New York: Basic Books.

Eccles, Robert. 1981. "The Quasifirm in the Construction Industry." *Journal of Economic Behavior and Organization* 2(December):335-57.

Etzioni, Amitai. 1988. *The Moral Dimension: Toward a New Economics*. New York: Free Press.

Frank, Robert H. 1988. "Patching up the Rational Choice Model." Paper delivered at the Conference on Economy and Society, University of California, Santa Barbara, May 20-21.

Friedland, Roger and Jimmy Sanders. 1985. "The Public Economy and Economic Growth in Western Market Economies." *American Sociological Review* 50(August):421-37.

Garfinkel, Harold. 1967. *Studies in Ethnomethodology*. Englewood Cliffs, NJ: Prentice-Hall.

Gordon, David. 1976. "Capitalist Efficiency and Socialist Efficiency." *Monthly Review* 28(3):19-39.

Granick, David. 1960. *The Red Executive*. New York: Doubleday.

Granovetter, Mark. 1985. "Economic Action and Social Structure: The Problem of Embeddedness." *American Journal of Sociology* 91(3):481-510.

————. 1988. "The Old and the New Economic Sociology: A History and an Agenda." Paper read at the Conference on Economy and Society, University of California, Santa Barbara, May 20-21.

Hahn, Frank. 1981. "General Equilibrium Theory." Pp. 123-38 in *The Crisis in Economic Theory*, edited by Daniel Bell and Irving Kristol. New York: Harper Torchbooks/Basic Books.

Heritage, John. 1984. *Garfinkel and Ethnomethodology*. Cambridge: Polity.

Hill, Richard Child. Forthcoming. "Comparing Transnational Production Systems: The Automobile Industry in the United States and Japan." *International Journal of Urban and Regional Research*.

Hirschman, Albert O. 1986. *Rival Views of Market Society*. New York: Viking.

Isenberg, Daniel. 1984. "How Senior Managers Think." *Harvard Business Review*, November-December, pp. 81-90.

Jung, Maureen. 1988. *Corporations and the Structure in Markets: The Comstocks and the Mining Economy in the Far West, 1848-1900*. Ph.D. dissertation, Department of Sociology, University of California, Santa Barbara.

Kirzner, Israel. 1981. "The 'Austrian' Perspective." Pp. 111-22 in *The Crisis in Economic Theory*, edited by Daniel Bell and Irving Kristol. New York: Harper Torchbooks/Basic Books.

Korpi, Walter. 1985. "Economic Growth and the Welfare State: Leaky Bucket or Irrigation System?" *European Sociological Review* 1:97-118.

Laitner, John P. 1979. "Bequests, Golden-Age Capital Accumulation and Government Debt." *Economica* 46:403-14.

Leibenstein, Harvey. 1981. "Microeconomics and X-Efficiency Theory." Pp. 97-110 in *The Crisis in Economic Theory*, edited by Daniel Bell and Irving Kristol. New York: Harper Torchbooks/Basic Books.

Macaulay, Stewart. 1963. "Non-Contractual Relations in Business: A Preliminary Study." *American Sociological Review* 28(1):55-67.

Marwell, Gerald and Ruth Ames. 1981. "Economists Ride Free, Does Anyone Else?" *Journal of Public Economists* 15:295-310.

McGregor, Douglas. 1960. *The Human Side of Enterprise*. New York: McGraw-Hill.

Ogburn, William F. and Meyer F. Nimkoff. 1956. *A Handbook of Sociology*. London: Routledge & Kegan Paul.

Pred, Allan Richard. 1976. "The Interurban Transmission of Growth in Advanced Economies: Empirical Findings Versus Regional Planning Assumptions." *Regional Studies* 10(2):151-71.

Radnitzky, Gerard and Peter Bernholz, eds. 1986. *Economic Imperialism: The Economic Approach Applied Outside the Traditional Areas of Economics*. New York: Paragon.

Roy, Donald. 1954. "Efficiency and 'the Fix.' " *American Journal of Sociology* 60:155-66.

Samuelson, Paul. 1983. *Foundations of Economic Analysis*. Cambridge, MA: Harvard University Press.

Schrank, Robert, ed. 1983. *Industrial Democracy at Sea*. Cambridge: MIT Press.

Sen, Amartya. 1977. "Rational Fools: A Critique of the Behavioral Foundations of Economic Theory." *Philosophy and Public Affairs*, pp. 317-44.

Stark, David. 1986. "Rethinking Internal Labor Markets: New Insights from a Comparative Perspective." *American Sociological Review 51(4):492-504.*

Storper, Allan and Michael Scott. 1987. "High Technology, Industry, and Regional Development: A Theoretical Critique and Reconstruction." *International Social Science Journal 39(2)*: 215-32.

Swanstrom, Todd. 1986. "The Limits of Strategic Planning for Cities." *Journal of Urban Affairs* 9(2):139-57.

Swedberg, Richard. 1987. "Economic Sociology: Past and Present." *Current Sociology* 35(1, Spring).

Wilson, Thomas P. Forthcoming. "Social Structure and Sequential Organization." In *Talk and Social Structure*, edited by D. Boden and D. Zimmerman. Cambridge: Polity.

Zelizer, Viviana A. 1988. "Beyond the Polemics on the Market: Establishing a Theoretical and Empirical Agenda." Paper read at the Center for Economy and Society, University of California, Santa Barbara, May 19-21.

Zimmerman, Don. 1970. "The Practicalities of Rule Use." Pp. 221-38 in *Understanding Everyday Life*, edited by J. Douglas. Chicago: Aldine.

Zuboff, Shoshana. 1988. *In the Age of the Smart Machine: The Future of Work and Power*. New York: Basic Books.

Appendix A:
The Atlanta Thematic Sessions[1]

1. AMERICA'S IMPACT ON SOCIOLOGY

Organizers: *Herbert J. Gans*, Columbia University; *Robin M. Williams, Jr.*, Cornell University

Presider: *Robin M. Williams, Jr.*, Cornell University

Cultural, Scientific, Academic, and Government Influences on Sociology: *Neil Smelser*, University of California, Berkeley

The Curious Centrality of the Small Group in American Society: *Allan Silver*, Columbia University

Discussion: *Marvin Bressler*, Princeton University; *Ernest Q. Campbell*, Vanderbilt University

2. THE IMPACT OF SOCIOLOGICAL METHODOLOGY ON AMERICAN LIFE

Organizer and Presider: *John W. Riley, Jr.*, Consulting Sociologist

Opinion Surveys: *Eleanor Singer*, Columbia University

Demographic Research: *Mathew Greenwald*, Matthew Greenwald Associates

Market Research: *Arthur J. Kover*, N. W. Ayer, Inc.

Health and Medical Surveys: *David Mechanic*, Rutgers University

Discussion: Have Our Research Methods Made a Real Difference? *John W. Riley, Jr.*, Consulting Sociologist

3. SOCIOLOGY'S IMPACTS ON AMERICA

Organizer: *Kai Erikson*, Yale University

Presider: *Arlene S. Skolnick*, University of California, Berkeley

Sociological Ideas and American Culture: *Dennis Wrong*, New York University

The Creation and Destruction of Meaning: *Joseph Gusfield*, University of California, San Diego

Discussion: *Wendy Griswold*, University of Chicago

4. SOCIOLOGY AND ITS CONSTITUENTS

Organizer: *Paul M. Hirsch*, University of Chicago

Presider: *R. Stephen Warner*, University of Illinois, Chicago

Sociological Theories and Their Constituencies: *Alan Sica*, University of Kansas

The Organizational Politics of Sociology: *Marshall Meyer*, University of Pennsylvania

The Cultural Contradictions of Teaching Sociology: *Paul J. Baker* and *William Rau*, Illinois State University

Discussion: *Ann Swidler*, University of California, Berkeley

5. DISSEMINATING SOCIOLOGY TO THE GENERAL PUBLIC: WORKING WITH JOURNALISTS AND NONACADEMIC PUBLISHERS

Organizers: *Ronald Milavsky*, National Broadcasting Company; *Herbert J. Gans*, Columbia University

Presider: *Ronald Milavsky*, National Broadcasting Company

Panel: *Patricia Horne*; *John Leo*, *Time* magazine; *Malcolm Ritter*, Associated Press; *David Streitfeld*, *Washington Post*; *Martin Kessler*, Basic Books

Discussion: *Eleanor Singer*, Columbia University

6. SOCIOLOGY AND SOCIAL CRITICISM

Organizer: *Herbert J. Gans*, Columbia University

Presider: *Bennett Berger*, University of California, San Diego

The Virtues of Dissent in Sociology. *Lewis A. Coser*, Boston College

Sociology for Whom? Criticism for Whom? *Todd Gitlin*, University of California, Berkeley

Discussion: *Joan Moore*, University of Wisconsin, Milwaukee; *Peter H. Rossi*, University of Massachusetts, Amherst

7. SOCIOLOGY AND U.S. SOCIAL POLICY

Organizer and Presider: *Victor Nee*, Cornell University

Sociologists as Engineers and Story Tellers: *Peter Marris*, University of California, Los Angeles

Small Findings, Large Problems: Synthesis in Policy Research: *Steven Caldwell*, Cornell University

Discussion: *Ronnie Steinberg*, Temple University

8. SOCIOLOGY, THE CIVIL RIGHTS MOVEMENTS, AND RACE RELATIONS

Organizer and Presider: *Hylan G. Lewis*

Sociological Foundations of the Civil Rights Movement: *Lewis Killian*, University of West Florida; *Charles U. Smith*, Florida A&M University

A Sociology of the Civil Rights Movement: A Participant-Observer's Perspective: *Joyce Ladner*, Howard University

Discussion: *Kenneth B. Clark*, Kenneth B. Clark & Associates; *Robert Moses*

9. THE UNDERCLASS:
SOCIOLOGICAL PERSPECTIVES AND CRITIQUES

Organizer and Presider: *S. M. Miller*, Boston University

A Structural (Nonracial) Explanation of Slavery in the United States: Implications for the Contemporary Study of "Race": *Richard Williams*, State University of New York, Stony Brook

Debunking the Underclass: The New Culture of Poverty: *Walter Stafford*, Community Service Society; *Joyce Ladner*, Howard University

The Underclass: Disaggregating Race, Class, and Culture: *Stephen Steinberg*, City University of New York, Queens College and the Graduate Center

Conceptualizing the Underclass: An Alternative Perspective: *Robert Aponte*, University of Chicago

10. SOCIOLOGY AND THE WEALTHY AND POWERFUL

Organizer and Presider: *Michael Useem*, Boston University

Inside the Dominant Class: *Maurice Zeitlin*, University of California, Los Angeles

Gender, Class, and Career in the Lives of Privileged Women: *Arlene Kaplan Daniels*, Northwestern University

Power, Control, and Networks of Corporate Influence: *Walter W. Powell*, University of Arizona

Discussion: *Paul DiMaggio*, Yale University

11. SOCIOLOGY OF GENDER AND INEQUALITY

Organizer: *Elizabeth Long*, Rice University

Presider: *Judith Lorber*, City University of New York, Graduate Center and Brooklyn College

The Response of Feminists to Social Inequality: *Carole Joffe* and *David Karen*, Bryn Mawr College

Gender and Race: *Bonnie Thornton Dill*, Memphis State University; *Maxine Baca-Zinn*, University of Michigan-Flint

Gender as a Structure of Power: *Robert Connell*, Macquarie University, Sydney

Discussion: *Joan Huber*, Ohio State University

12. SOCIOLOGY AND THE WORLD

Organizer: *Victor Nee*, Cornell University

Presider: *James M. Skelly*, University of California, San Diego

Sociology and Nuclear War: *William A. Gamson*, Boston College

War, Warmakers, and Sociologists: *Charles Tilly*, New School for Social Research

Discussion: *Susan Eckstein*, Boston University; *Louis W. Goodman*, American University

13. FOREIGN SOCIOLOGISTS LOOK AT U.S. SOCIOLOGY

Organizer and Presider: *Ivan Szelenyi*, University of California, Los Angeles

Social Actors Versus Social Systems: The Transatlantic Debate: *Alain Touraine*, Ecole des Hautes Etudes en Science Sociales, Paris

General Theory in Sociology: A Talk to an American Audience: *Niklas Luhmann*, Bielefeld University, West Germany

American Sociology in the Context of the Development of Soviet Sociology: A Personal View: *Igor Kon*, USSR Academy of Sciences

Discussion: *Robert Connell*, Macquarie University, Sydney

NOTE

1. The sessions are presented in the order that the Program Committee had in mind for them.

Appendix B:
Sociology in America:
The Discipline and the Public.
American Sociological Association,
1988 Presidential Address

Herbert J. Gans

When I first began to think about the presidential address, I planned to choose one of the research areas in which I've worked all of my professional life. I considered a paper on Sociology and the City, urban sociology currently being in an exciting intellectual transition, and also one on Poverty and Inequality, a topic about which sociologists have far more to contribute than they now do. I would also have liked to discuss Sociology and the Mass Media, an ever more significant field which still has not received the attention and respect from the discipline that it deserves.

Instead of writing a paper that might have been relevant to only some colleagues, however, I chose a topic in which all of us are or should be interested, the discipline.[1] More particularly, I want to discuss our relations with America's nonsociologists, the *lay public:* both the very large general public and the smaller well-educated one which does much of the country's professional-level analytic and creative work. Since the lay public includes the country's entire population, less the approximately 20,000 sociologists, my topic is also an intrinsic part of Sociology in America.

Although I shall concentrate on what we still need to do to serve the lay public and the institutions in which it is involved, in many respects we are doing better than we have in the past. Sociology has established a presence in many kinds of policy analysis and is moving into large numbers of other so-called practice areas, even if our ideas continue to be largely absent from the country's political thinking. As best I can tell from energetic but unsystematic observation, the news media pay more attention to us then before, and some journalists now want sociological angles on feature stories they are covering. Slowly but surely they are also becoming interested in sociological research. We even show up as sympathetic characters in occasional popular novels and films, although we continue to play villains and fools in high culture. I have the impression that the majority of the literary community still believes that only it can analyze society.

When one talks with publishers of general, nonacademic books as well as with editors and writers for so-called serious magazines and with foundation heads, the picture also

AUTHOR'S NOTE: *I am grateful to many colleagues who made helpful comments on the version of this essay presented in Atlanta, and to those at the Graduate Center of the City University of New York, the State University of New York at Albany, and Fordham University for allowing me to try out early versions of it on them. My thanks also to Anna Karpathakis for library research assistance and to Allan Silver for convincing me to use an allusion to Alexis de Tocqueville's classic work for the title of this paper and the theme of the 1988 Annual meeting.*

remains discouraging. Too many people still dislike sociology or, worse still, are not interested in it. To be sure, often they react to caricatures of sociology, but the very fact that they are not motivated to go beyond caricatures is itself depressing. In effect, we play a smaller part in the country's intellectual life than we should.

Many sociologists find nothing wrong with this state of affairs. For them, sociology is a social science with emphasis on the science, and reaching out to, or obtaining the attention of, the lay public is irrelevant. Others hold a stronger version of this point of view; being in touch with the laity, except when necessary for earning a living, impedes the progress of scientific research. Colleagues who feel most strongly speak of vulgarizing sociology or pandering to the uninformed.

I believe that these feelings are mistaken. Maintaining some relationship with the American public is part of our responsibility as members of society and as recipients of its funds, public or private, whether as tuition payments, salaries, grants or contracts. Moreover, when members of the lay public feel that our work is useful or enlightening or both, they have an incentive to give us their cultural and political support if we need it — when issues like student interest in sociology, the allocation of research funds, and freedom of research are at stake. The rest of the essay will show that paying more attention to lay America can be done without pandering.

This essay has three major parts. The first describes some of the research needed to analyze sociology's roles in America, for without it we cannot fully understand how we can best reach out to the lay public. The second part discusses some ways in which we can now improve our relations with the public. In the last part of the paper I focus on sociology itself, offering some ideas on what we can do better for ourselves even as we do better by the public.[2]

Before I start I must define the term "we." I use it broadly, referring to "we the discipline" and "we the collectivity," knowing all the while that the discipline is highly diverse while the collectivity is far from a functioning sociopolitical entity. "We" is therefore mainly a shorthand about how numbers of us act or how we should all act, but I must apologize to the practitioners that my "we" is mostly the academic discipline and collectivity, they being what I know best.

STUDYING SOCIOLOGY IN AMERICA

My initial topic is researching Sociology in America. At one level, I see the topic as a set of studies in the sociology of knowledge that tries to understand where we are coming from and going and how we are tied to the main structures and hierarchies of American society. In the process, we should identify our employers, sponsors, funders, supporters, and allies, as well as our clients or constituents — and our possible victims. In short, we must understand whose sides we have been on, purposely or accidentally (Becker, 1967).

At another level, Sociology in America is evaluative, the application of our analytic tools and our values to understand and assess what we are doing for and to the country, as well as to all the sectors on which we might impinge, from underdogs to top dogs, for instance. We need to know whom we help and whom we injure and damage, intentionally and unintentionally, so that we can figure out what we should be doing and not doing in behalf of a better society, however "better" may be defined.

"Sociology in America" is a good title for an ASA annual meeting theme, but the topic could also be called sociology and society, in part to emphasize that it must be cross-national and cross-cultural as well (Kohn, 1987). A first priority is conceptualizing the basic subject, and many alternatives are possible. One can begin by looking for and at sociology's *contributions*, identifying activities and institutions in which sociologists have participated directly or in which their work has been used indirectly. A major problem with looking at contributions is that we tend to forget the negative ones and the ones we fail to make, but this problem can be corrected.

A slightly different approach would be to ask what *roles* sociology has played and is playing, adding the evaluative element by also asking how well these roles were played, and which should be played in the future. Some roles are self-evident, but the concept allows us to wonder whether, for example, we somehow also represent particular interest groups, or falling, not to mention rising, classes. Or are we mainly one of a set of academics whose role it is to add a touch of cultural polish and a smidgen of social conscience to the socialization of young Americans able and willing to go to college? Yet how do we fit into the scheme of things when we play what I think of as the Martian role, distancing ourselves and going to Erving Goffman's backstage — or back of *it* — to report on how society or some of its constituent parts operate.

My own thinking takes me in the direction of *effects* concepts, because what matters most is not what we have done but how our work has affected others. Somewhat the same outcome as a study of effects can be achieved by the use of functional analysis, for functions are operationalized as consequences — as long as we always inquire into functions and dysfunctions of what for whom, and assume the possibility that some of our activities are functional mainly for ourselves. Alternatively, one can look at sociology's benefits and costs — if these are not treated solely as quantitative concepts. We must also remember that researchers will not always agree on what is beneficial and costly, and that the determination of benefits and costs must reflect the views of all those who actually win and lose. Moreover, we must never exclude the possibility that our work has neither significant benefits nor costs — nor major independent effects. We are, after all, only 20,000 in a country of 230 million.

I am aware of all the methodological difficulties of studying effects, functions, and benefits and costs, but we *must* discover what impact we have had. Furthermore, any properly sociological effects study has to examine the agents and processes that have shaped sociology to achieve whatever impacts it is having. Thus, a study of sociology's impact on America must be preceded by research on America's impacts on sociology (Gouldner, 1970; Vidich and Lyman, 1985). However, if we analyze the roles we have played, we must likewise ask what helped us play these roles and how we were invited or shoehorned into them.

Needless to say, there are other conceptual schemes for looking at sociology in America, but whatever the schemes, the questions I have raised also have to be answered historically. In fact, it may be strategic to begin with historical analyses because the historical view can give us a better fix on the primary theoretical or empirical issues on which we must concentrate in order to understand the present.

Although the teaching of sociology has still not obtained enough respect from the discipline, the fact remains that virtually all academic sociologists, including those at the most elite research universities, earn their living by teaching. Consequently, one of the first and most important questions to be researched concerns the effects, and thus also the effectiveness, of our teaching.

ASA estimates that 75 percent of America's sociologists — or 15,000 — are still academics. If each teaches four courses a year, and many unfortunately teach many more, that comes to 60,000 courses a year, and of these the most frequently taught continue to be introductory, marriage and the family, and social problems. Although studies have been made of the major texts used in these courses, we ought to start finding out what is actually being *taught* in them: not only what kinds of sociology, but what descriptions of and prescriptions for American society. For example, a multicampus sample of marriage and the family courses could be analyzed to identify what models of marriage and the family sociologists teach, and what postures they encourage students to take toward them, explicitly or implicitly. To what extent do we teach conformity to the culturally dominant models, and if we suggest the desirability of sociopolitical change, what new or old models do we have in mind?

After that, we ought to begin on the more urgent but also more complex task of looking at what students *learn* from these basic courses, for their own lives and their citizen roles, to see if we can establish findings about the effects of their exposure to sociology. Since sociology has begun to drift down to the high schools, similar research can be done there. Schools not being the only teaching institutions in America, however, someone should also take a look to see whether sociology has yet had any visible impact on the country's news and entertainment media.

Parallel kinds of research can be undertaken among sociological practitioners. Indeed, now is an ideal time to begin, for before-and-after studies should immediately be conducted at some of the many public agencies and private companies that are first hiring sociologists, so that we can learn what early effects they are having. Now that sociologists are being employed in market research, for example, it would be useful to look at a sample of firms to discover what, if anything, the sociologists do differently — and with what effects — from the previous market researchers who have generally been MBA's and psychologists. Do sociological market researchers have more empathy for the subjects of market research than had their predecessors, and what effects does this have to their work, the resulting firm policies, and the profits? Or are sociologists in big organizations more likely to practice what their organizations prescribe rather that what their discipline has trained them to practice? Incidentally, an interesting study of *academic* practitioners, the increasing number of sociologists who become deans and provosts of their universities, could be done to see what, if anything, they do differently because they are sociologists.

The effects studies of the greatest urgency are those with potential public policy significance. I will limit myself to two examples. One is the roles and functions sociology has played in past culture-of-poverty research and is now playing in the study of what is currently called the underclass. We could begin, for example, with the effects the most widely-read new sociological book of the last few years, William J. Wilson's *The Truly Disadvantaged* (1987), has had for the public understanding of the underclass, and for the policies needed to bring it into the country's mainstream. As sociological underclass research proliferates, however, we must also look at what we may be doing against the people now assigned to that class.

The term *underclass* was first used in recent times by Gunnar Myrdal (1962) as an economic concept for describing a set of people being driven to the edges or out of the economy. While most current underclass research seems to be in the hands of economists, they have generally adopted a different definition, perhaps of journalistic origin, in which the members of that class are also associated with a variety of criminal, pathological, or stigmatized activities and are generally black or Hispanic.

No laws prevent us from studying the impact of economists alongside of, or in comparison to, our own, and many questions deserve answering. Do studies using the underclass concept call attention to people who need economic and other kinds of aid? Or are researchers primarily giving scientific legitimization to the latest buzzword for the undeserving poor and concurrently helping to disseminate a new code word for the covert expression of racial hostility? More generally, what role do researchers play in the emergence of a new public stereotype, and how can they prevent a social science generalization or an ideal type from being interpreted as a stereotype?

To the extent that underclass studies are seen and used by social workers and other street-level bureaucrats as well as policy-makers, we have to ask whether these studies mainly help the people of the underclass or help government to control them? Once again, what sides are we on, intentionally and unintentionally, as we study this newest "hot" topic? Perhaps the biggest problem stems from unintentional "putdowns" of poor people, because of either lack of researcher reflexivity or the use of data from agencies that exist in part to be punitive toward the poor.

I have the impression that sociologists doing research among underclass people are more likely to be on their side while the economists tend to treat them as a dangerous class. Even so, sociologists and economists play only a small causal part in the tragic relationship between the underclass and the rest of America. Indeed, the current research is itself an effect of public appetites for information, scapegoats, and, of course, solutions. These appetites have themselves emerged for such reasons as the increasing fear of crime — and of dark-skinned Americans — the rise of homelessness, the economic insecurity created by the Reagan economy, and the relentless pressures by the Reagan administration on people who cannot afford the values of mainstream cultures.

My second example might serve as a model not only of what we have done well as sociological researchers but also of the ways in which sociology can be useful, and relatively easily. I think here of the large set of findings which indicate on the one hand that informal groups and related social supports have both illness-preventing and healing functions, and on the other hand that isolation and loneliness as well as alienation produced by hostile or distant formal institutions can breed and worsen physical and mental illness. The basic idea goes back to 19th-century sociology, but since World War II many researchers have shown how the presence or absence of kin, friends, neighbors, and other informal groups and networks affect health (Litwak and Messeri, 1989).

For the study of sociology in America, and for the making of health policy, we must examine whether and how such findings are, or could be, providing competition for purely medical models of health and illness. In addition, we need to know whether and how these findings are leading to changes in medical activity, from physician practice to national health policy. Conversely, we must also study why changes did not take place, so that we can try to understand how they could take place. Since informal groups should cost less than doctors and hospitals, social supports would help reduce medical costs and might be welcomed for that reason alone — unless hospitals and doctors decide to turn them into a medical specialty, and charge accordingly.

Whether the study of Sociology in America involves basic, applied, or policy-oriented research, we will, in effect, be studying ourselves. I need not list the dangers of a disciplinary-wide self-study, and in a utopian world, another social science would study us while we study yet a third. However, in this world, *we* have to do the needed studies and *we* have to learn how to deal with the likely conflicts of interest.

An essential ingredient for self-study is the right mixture of deliberate and systematic reflexivity and an equally deliberate and systematic distancing. Appeals for more reflexivity without structural underpinnings and instrumental incentives being the material of sermons, I am reluctant to go further except to hope with Alvin Gouldner that what I have in mind here does not become "just another topic for panels at professional conventions and not just another little stream of technical reports" (Gouldner, 1970, p. 489).

Consequently, as relevant studies are undertaken, we have to begin to think about what we will do with the results. Even before we know more about our contributions, roles, and effects, we must debate how to increase sociology's positive effects and cut back the negative ones. We ought also to confront once more an old, recently forgotten question: What is a good society and how can sociology help bring it about?

I have no illusions about how much we can agree on the nature of the good society or how much we can do to bring one about, but the discussion of these questions will have beneficial results for the discipline itself. The very innocence of the notion of the good society may be a useful antidote for our too frequent tendency toward excessive abstraction. Moreover, asking fundamental general questions, even the kind that cannot be answered easily or completely, forces us to address issues of widespread interest in America and is, in addition, a way of reaching out to the general public.

SOCIOLOGY AND THE LAY PUBLIC

The second part of my paper is about improving relations with the public and its institutions. I begin again on an empirical note, because at least two further topics badly need study if we are going to act intelligently to improve our relations with both the large general and the smaller well-educated public.

One study seeks to identify *lay sociology*, the generalizations about society and its parts that all people — we included — start learning as children, long before knowing of the existence of professional sociology. True, lay people do not label their knowledge about society *sociology*, but nonetheless it consists of ideas and data in all of the fields we study. Much lay sociology is learned during the process of socialization, yet more is discovered through the applied participant observation we all do constantly in everyday social life, and some comes from nonprofessional, or so-called pop, sociology: research done by nonprofessional sociologists who use some of our methods but few of our concepts and theories.

For my purpose, the significant questions center on what happens when people's lay sociology comes into contact with our professional sociology. We have to discover what impacts we have on lay sociology, and whether and how we add to and change it. Perhaps even more to the point, we have to find out if and why we are ignored or rejected. When the generalizations of lay and professional sociology diverge, we generally seek to replace the lay kind, and our students may fail to learn because they are not persuaded that our sociology is more valid than theirs. I wonder, for example, what happens when working-class and poor students, whose lay sociologies are particularly rich in the fields of class and inequality, take a course in social stratification which sees society solely from a middle-class perspective. Although we assume that professional sociology is always better than the lay version, that assumption also deserves some inquiry.

The other study strikes at the heart of our relations with the educated public because we need to know in detail how our sociology is judged by that public. If, when, and where our standing is not as good as it should be, we have to identify the reasons and causes. In addition, we have to find out what the members of this public want from sociology, ours and theirs. There is clearly a great demand for applied organizational research, for the management literature is full of pop sociology on this topic, much of it so poor that every six months yet another new analysis becomes a brief best-seller.

In their nonoccupational reading, however, many members of the educated public seem to specialize in literary and historical works, which is one reason why just about all of the important magazines and publishing houses catering to this public continue to be run by people from literary and historical backgrounds. Why the reading public is so fond of history and why it ignores — and perhaps dislikes — some or much sociology is a research topic of fundamental importance, for until we have a comprehensive answer our work will not get much attention from the journals of cultural and political opinion, the large circulation "class" magazines such as *Time, The New Yorker,* or *The Atlantic,* and "trade book" publishers who publish nontechnical books in the social sciences.

Despite the need for these researches, many suggestions can be made *now* for how to improve our relations with the lay public, but I will limit myself to five I consider particularly significant.

First, I assume the lay public — general and educated — will pay more attention to professional sociology if and when our research addresses salient subjects and issues. Many of these center on the family, the economy, and health — subjects about which we have something to say that can help people's understanding, if we can present our ideas and findings in plain English. Other lay concerns touch on or are set off by current events, and we should figure on how we can do more studies on significant topics of the moment. Many years ago Gladys and Kurt Lang proposed "firehouse research" for such studies, and their proposal is as timely as ever. We can also supply useful comments on topical issues, especially as debunkers and correctors when the early journalistic reports and nonprofessional sociology are wrong. In addition, we can report on trends underlying topical subjects and can often provide more systematic explanations of events and trends than do journalists and pop sociologists.

An already existing lay interest in our sociology has to do with the diversity of American life. Because of that diversity, some members of the lay public want to know how other Americans cope with common problems such as familial and community ones, as well as how they interpret, or substitute for, the conventional rules and norms of American life. It is no coincidence that the best-known sociological works of the last 75 years — *Middletown, The Lonely Crowd,* and *Habits of the Heart* — respond to one or another of these lay inquiries.

These studies also exhibit what I consider one of sociology's distinctive qualities: They are based on research among ordinary Americans. While other sciences concentrate on elite decision-makers, exotic subcultures, or laboratory subjects, sociology has always done much of its work with and among typical Americans. This is one reason why professional sociology, when properly presented, appeals to the lay public. That appeal is widened when we use the research methods that seem most attractive to this public: the depth-interview, in which people have a chance to talk and to explain themselves fully; and fieldwork, in which sociologists are on the scene to hear them on a continuing basis, and inside the social structures in which they act and interact.

The ideal study format may be the community study, not because I have done a few but because it is broad; it allows researchers the opportunity to report on a variety of people across a wide range of institutions and situations. If the communities and people studied are reasonably representative or thoughtfully chosen deviant cases, the sampling is done properly, and the research is focused on significant theoretical and substantive questions, this is the best way to look at America, for both the discipline and the lay public (Keller, 1988).

Community studies are hard work; they can take a long time and, like many qualitative studies, do not fit the currently dominant definition of science. As a result, funding agencies have not been supportive — a serious mistake that helps to explain why sociology is not as much in the public eye as it should be.

The *second* of my five suggestions is a corollary of the first: that undergraduate sociology courses should concentrate, whenever possible, on sociological analyses of American institutions and society rather than on sociological principles illustrated with samples from America. There is nothing like an overly concept-filled introductory course to turn many students against sociology forever. Courses that teach sociology through an analysis of American society also require research on topical issues and current events.[3] Unfortunately, even reading a first-class newspaper or weekly news magazine with a sociological eye is not normally part of the graduate school training program. If we carried out more analyses of topical issues and current events, sociology could make more original contributions to understanding both. If any sociologists now prepare such analyses for their classes, we should find a place where the best of them can be published for the rest of us.

My *third* proposal is that we must recruit and encourage talented sociologists who are able and eager to report their work so that it is salient to both their colleagues and the educated lay public. Borrowing Russell Jacoby's concept of public intellectuals (Jacoby, 1987), they might be called *public sociologists*, and the public sociologist par excellence that comes at once to mind is David Riesman. Public sociologists are *not* popularizers; they are empirical researchers, analysts, or theorists like the rest of us, although often their work is particularly thoughtful, imaginative or original in some respect.[4]

Public sociologists have three further distinctive traits. One is their ability to discuss even sociological concepts and theories in the English of the college-educated reader, probably because they enjoy writing as well as doing research and may even think of themselves as writers. Their second trait is the breadth of their sociological interests, which covers much of society even if their research is restricted to a few fields. That breadth also extends to their conception of sociology, which extends beyond research reporting to commentary and in many cases also to social criticism. To put it another way, their work is intellectual as well as specific.[5] A third, not unrelated, trait is the ability to avoid the pitfalls of undue professionalism described by earlier ASA presidents (for example, Hughes, 1963, p. 890; Lee, 1976, pp. 927-29).

I do not know how one recruits fledgling or mature public sociologists, but I fear that too many young people with an interest in society get Ph.D.'s in English, literature, or history — and then do public sociology instead of us. Consequently, sociology must encourage those it does attract, beginning in graduate school. It also has to assure them that they can be both sociologists and writers and will not be discriminated against for this combination of skills. For example, they must be rewarded for being writers, and their major sociological writing in nonscholarly publications must be treated as equivalent to scholarly writing in promotion and tenure decisions. We should also find outlets for their writing inside sociology so we do not lose all their work to other publications.

I have been around long enough to remember when David Riesman was not considered a sociologist in many parts of the discipline, although even today some colleagues who hold fervently to a natural science conception of sociology reject public sociologists. Worse yet, they may dismiss them as "journalists," a term that we should never use as a pejorative for yet other reasons I will come to shortly. I am told that John Kenneth Galbraith, dean of public economists, has never been accepted as an economist by many of his colleagues, but then economics is a backward social science in other respects.

The *fourth* suggestion for adding to our impact on the lay public requires revitalizing an old mode of public sociology: social criticism. I oversimplify only slightly to point out that American sociology began in part as social criticism, and while a handful of sociologists have continued this tradition, today's American social criticism is almost entirely in the hands of journalists, essayists, literary critics, and philosophers. Europe is quite different in this respect, because many European sociologists and researchers double as newspaper or magazine columnists, writing regularly the kind of social commentary found here in journals of opinion and cultural criticism.

We are not Europeans and we should not even imitate America's current social critics. Our task is *sociological* social criticism. Journalistic and humanistic critics too often view social ills by what makes them personally unhappy, and they may also misunderstand the causes of these ills or offer solutions that reflect the values of a single group — be it intellectual elite or working class. Partly as a result, conventional criticism is frequently nostalgic or apocalyptic, with good old days being mourned right and left and many institutions thought to be in permanent rapid decline — headed almost always by the family.

The sociological social critic can do much better! The identification of social ills ought to be based both on empirical data about what the public or several parts of it feel to be wrong, *and* on the critic's own concerns. Proposed solutions can likewise transcend the perspective of the critic's own immediate circle, and they should draw on systematic causal analyses of the problems to be solved.

Social criticism is not for every sociologist, but it should become part of the discipline just as social policy research became a part of it in the last 20 years, once we were able to move beyond the primitive conceptions of value-free sociology on which the early disapproval of social policy research was based. Sociological social criticism will never grow as large as social policy research, however, because it cannot, and should not, become a government function.

My *fifth* and last proposal is particularly focused on the general public. Since its major contact with professional sociology comes from the mass media, we should try to get more of the sociological perspective and our own studies into these media. Reaching the general public requires *popularizers*, sociologists and others who can turn the ideas and findings reported in our journals and books that should be of general interest into everyday English.[6]

Concurrently, we should encourage the journalists who also popularize our work: the small number of free-lancers who do it from time to time, as well as the handful who have regular social or behavioral science beats. We should assist journalistic popularizers as much as we can, for good popularization will increase public interest in sociology. At the same time, we may be able to head off some inaccurate or sensationalized popularization.

In addition, we should help nonprofessional researchers who undertake pop sociology, which I described earlier as research based on the concepts and ideas of lay sociology. We can be particularly helpful with advice on methods. After all, the rules of sampling, question construction, field work, and statistical analysis apply equally to professional and pop sociology. True, nonprofessional sociologists often cannot apply these rules as rigorously as we do, for the lay public is not interested in professional subtleties and qualifications, whether in sociology or in physics. Still, our common interests in good methodology can make us useful as long as we understand and are tolerant about the differences between their sociology and ours.

Good nonprofessional sociology is useful to us for the same reasons as good popularization. We have a special interest in reducing bad pop sociology, however, because its low quality can reflect on us directly and quickly since the general public may not distinguish between professional and nonprofessional sociology.

Professional sociologists should keep an eye on pop sociology, if only because it has a much larger audience than we do. They should also distinguish between good and bad pop sociology, but unfortunately too many of our colleagues look down on all of it, as they do on popularizers of our work. This stance can only hurt the discipline, for when some of us appear distant and superior, we may turn off members of the lay public otherwise ready to pay attention to our work. Worse yet, wholesale rejection of sociologies other than ours may end up by biting the public hand that feeds us.

An ideal solution, allowing us to have our cake while eating it, is an ASA-run or supervised magazine of high-quality popularized and pop sociology, but that solution is unrealistic since the current lay constituency for sociology is too small to support such a magazine. Sociology may be inherently less newsworthy than, for example, psychology or economics, since both give advice about everyday life of a kind that we cannot supply — or anthropology and psychiatry, which can tell more dramatic stories than we. Thus, a *Sociology Today* modeled on the monthly *Psychology Today* is not in the cards.[7]

Today's most significant disseminators of our sociology to the general public are magazine and newspaper journalists who incorporate our work in their stories, occasionally because they judge a sociological study to be newsworthy but increasingly often because they want sociological commentary on and in their stories. In these cases they may look for appropriate sociological findings, a sociological perspective to increase the quality of their story, or a quote to provide the story with some sociological legitimation.

These journalists are a crucial resource for us, a veritable disciplinary treasure, and they should be given our full and immediate cooperation (Gans, 1988). That we are being called more and more often by reporters, feature writers, and their equivalents in television can only be viewed as a compliment. I hope it is all a sign that the old days, when sociology was good only for a cranky feature exaggerating our shortcomings, are coming to an end.[8] Besides, the more we help journalists with their stories, the more interested they may become in reporting our studies.

We can be helpful further by eliminating the mindless attacks on journalism that are still heard in the discipline. At one level they reflect a disciplinary stereotype that all journalism is superficial, but at another level they may express unhappiness with the competition journalists provide us in the study of society. While journalism *is* often superficial, sociology would be superficial equally often if it had to report to a diverse and often poorly educated lay audience; if it had a two- to six-hour deadline for data collection, analysis, and writing; and if the research report had to be condensed into a few hundred words. Journalism has other faults too, but we must learn to distinguish between good and bad journalism. Indeed, we should not refrain from criticizing bad news stories about our work and ideas, as long as we make clear to the journalists involved how and why their work was inadequate. Conversely, we have every right to expect that journalists will learn to distinguish between good and bad sociology, to give up their stereotypes of us, and to stop thinking of the term *sociological* as a pejorative.

I end this section of the paper with a modest proposal: that the abstracts of our journal articles and the summaries of our academic books be written in nontechnical English.[9] Journalists may then become interested in our work instead of becoming discouraged at the very outset, and while they will probably still have troubles with the technical writing in the body of the text, they may be motivated to get in touch with the author for help in clarifying his or her work. They may also wean us away from writing so many of our article and book texts in "Sociologese."

SOCIOLOGY FOR *AMERICA*

The third of my three topics is the discipline itself and what we can do to help as well as improve ourselves. I again limit myself to the academic side, mainly at the research university level I know best. I will not systematically evaluate that side of the discipline, however, and I cannot even go into some specific problems that badly need discussing: for example, the ways we still often mistreat graduate students and part-time instructors, which is in part a reflection of long-standing inequalities within the discipline. These inequalities are currently worsened by the ever-expanding star system and the treatment of some colleagues as celebrities.

Here I want principally to outline what we need to do for and in the discipline in order to obtain a better reception from the public, particularly the educated one. This goal requires attention to the intellectual level of our work and the imperfections that intellectual observers and other members of the educated public see in that work. I will limit myself to two such imperfections. Both can also be found in the other social sciences, which means that their causes transcend our own discipline. However, the imperfections of the other social sciences do not excuse ours — and besides, we should be the first to overcome them, thus leading the way for the others.

The initial imperfection is *mindlessness*, research that is poorly thought through. Mindlessness cuts across fields and methods. It is the use of proxies or indicators because tangentially appropriate quantitative data are accessible, even though these proxies have only the most tenuous logical or empirical connection to the phenomena under study. Mindlessness is grounding the analysis of a complicated phenomenon on survey questions without any idea of how respondents understood the questions. Mindless fieldwork supplies thick descriptions of what is already common knowledge but fails to provide the thick analyses that are sorely needed. And whatever the research method, there are still occasional sociological analyses that, once translated into ordinary English, turn out to be examples of what we have often been accused of: restating the obvious.

Another kind of mindlessness sacrifices substantive validity to a favored analytic technique of the moment. That kind of mindlessness is part and parcel of our passion for methodology, which is actually long-standing. Jules Poincaré, who was writing at the turn of the century, even then described sociology as "the science with the most methods and the fewest discoveries."[10] Otis Dudley Duncan, whose theme I am here repeating, has put is more pointedly:

> Writing on "methodology" cultivated for its own sake produces a bifurcation of scientific effort that is stultifying. You have on the one hand inept researchers who think they have no responsibility for the methods they use because they can cite the authority of some "methodologist" and on the other hand "methodologists" whose advice is no good because they do not actually know how to do research (otherwise, we must suppose, they would have done some). (Duncan, 1974, p. 2).

The second imperfection, also of long standing, is what I think of as *overquantification*. I have no quarrel with statistical or mathematical analyses per se; they have advantages and disadvantages just as the various qualitative methods do. However, overquantification takes place when the research problem calls for qualitative analyses but quantitative ones are used instead, or when the use of such analyses changes the research problem. Overquantification occurs when elegant statistical analyses are performed on sloppily collected data, or on data forever made unclean by the covert or overt agendas of the collectors. And it takes place when quantitative analysis is not preceded — or driven — by concept and theory formulation, when researchers are literally merely crunching numbers. Needless to say, equivalent sins happen on the qualitative side. There may be no phrase for qualitative data crunching, but it occurs, and fieldwork alone is inappropriate when the research problem calls mainly for frequency distributions.

Some unfortunate effects of overquantification result from its ideological character. One is the inability of overquantifiers to tolerate disagreement, and their resulting stigmatization of and discrimination against qualitative research. Perhaps as a result, some advocates of qualitative method have also become ideologists. Consequently, a *scientific* discipline, in which research problems ought to determine the methods, and in which many problems are best solved by the use of both types of methods, is locked into an ideological dispute over a dubious typology — which is, moreover, actually about the nature of sociology.

A related effect of overquantification is the time and energy academic departments, individuals, and the discipline as a whole waste in endless battling over the two types of methods. Robin Williams was recently quoted as calling this a sham battle, adding rightly that "energy should be better utilized in applying whatever techniques seem to produce reliable knowledge" (Hirschman, 1987, p. 5). However, by now the crucial battle is less over ideas than over "scarce resources . . . jobs, research funds, editorial policies of our journals, professional recognition and prestige," as Mirra Komarovsky has pointed out (Komarovsky, 1987, p. 562). *Such* battles are not sham, and were they to end now, the superior resource position of quantitative sociology would become permanent. Those of us who believe in the virtues of qualitative empirical and other sociological work have to continue the struggle for equality of resources. I consider it scandalous, for example, when funding agencies with public mandates or tax exemptions nonetheless base their grant policies on the power balance inside disciplines.

A final effect of overquantification that needs mentioning is its tropism toward secondary analysis, which makes it possible for sociologists to study society for their entire lives without ever leaving their offices to talk or listen to the people they study.[11] The reliance on secondary analysis also makes us increasingly dependent on officially produced data. Worse yet, the resulting impersonalization of research is thought to make sociology more scientific, whereas in fact intensive interviewing and fieldwork are generally more scientific because the researchers get to know closely the people and social structures they are studying.

The problems I have described are familiar and have been discussed in previous presidential addresses (e.g., Coser, 1975). Thus, nothing is gained by further elaboration. What can be useful, however, is more sociological research into why sociology and the other social sciences have been developing what I see as imperfections. If I were doing the study, I would want to look particularly at three sets of current academic arrangements.

The first of these arrangements might be called scholarly insulation and a correlative lack of reality checks, which can disconnect our work from what is generally referred to as the real world. Unlike practitioners, our research does not need to be accountable to nonsociological kinds of validity, so that, for example, we are not open to and thus do not receive corrections from the people we have studied. We are accountable to funders to some extent, but many tend to base their judgments on peer reviews and, whatever their other virtues, peer reviewers can be as insulated from the nonsociological world as other researchers.

The absence of reality checks, which is also one cause of intellectual mindlessness, could actually be remedied somewhat by instituting such checks as part of our empirical procedure at the start and just before the end of our research. Basically such checks would involve informal reconnaissances, through the use of informants, informal interviewing, and fieldwork, among the people or institutions under study, as well as the application of independent statistical data, already available or newly collected from a small sample. Even theoretical papers and quantitative secondary analyses can be improved by reality checking.

Another kind of reality checking would identify thoughtful nonsociologists to critique our work and identify errors of omission and commission. Where possible, these must also include the people we study. Reality checks seem to me to be at least as important as literature reviews, and we will be well served if we can make them intrinsic parts of our research procedures.

The other two causes of imperfection are less easy to remedy. One is *scientism*, the modeling of sociological (and social science) research methods on a highly idealized version of the methods of the natural sciences. Although this modeling began even before sociology first became systematically empirical, it continues today when we know full well, in part from research in the sociology of science, that natural scientists do not operate according to the idealized conception of their method. Indeed, the ideal is humanly unworkable; nevertheless we cannot let go of it. We also know that social structures are not molecules and cannot be studied like them, but we cannot seem to let go of that analogy either. Nor have we yet learned to appreciate Donald McCloskey's lesson that "scientific work is rhetorical" and that it is so "even in its stylistic appeal to a rhetoric of not having a rhetoric" (McCloskey, 1985, p. 98).

Idealized natural science is a kind of civil religion in modern America, and there may be a quasi-religious element both in the ideal and the consensus behind it. The ideal also continues to justify the search for sociological "laws" — the nomothetic approach to sociology — but that search may express the latent hope for power — in an ideal society in which these laws — and their formulators — would play a central decision-making role. Such a society is as millenarian as those of the major religions: when salvation has been achieved, the Messiah has come, Mohammed has returned, or the State has withered away.

The search for sociological laws is, furthermore, sufficiently abstract to be "above" cultural or political conflicts of the moment. It is perhaps no accident that nomothetic sociology — like overquantified work — is usually noncontroversial, and unlikely to produce criticism of economic, political, and cultural power holders who are behaving in undemocratic or unjust ways.

The third and last cause of imperfection in sociology I will discuss concerns that strange institution in which academics work and in which all academic scholarship is therefore embedded. Although we are paid for the number of courses we teach, we are promoted by how much we publish, and only sometimes by the quality of our publications as well. In effect, our strange institution operates like a machine shop in which publications are treated like piecework. And like employees in any other kind of machine shop basically concerned with amount of productivity, we may overspecialize to study one part of the "social machine."

Moreover, again like workers in other machine shops, we are periodically greeted by new technology oriented to improving productivity, most recently of course the computer. The virtues of the computer for both quantitative and qualitative sociology far outnumber the vices, but there are some downsides too. Despite its potentials for high-quality research, the computer facilitates the speedier and thus greater production of piecework. It further encourages secondary analysis and the use of official, rather than self-generated, data. Although creative researchers can make creative use of the computer, the new technology even reduces the need to think and analyze once the right computer program has been found. Like many other industries, we too are becoming less labor-intensive.

These patterns are also symptoms of the continuing bureaucratization of research and, as often happens, the new technology is merely handmaiden to the socioeconomic process. In fact the computer nicely fits the academic shop routine, for it enables academics to do their research during the interstices of a full teaching load, and to publish more work at a faster clip.[12] The computer adds further to the impersonalization of research, and thus fits in with the worship of the idealized natural science method. What comes out of the computer is therefore automatically judged to be scientific, and insufficient attention is frequently paid to what human beings put into it.

The imperfections I have described not only stand in the way of a better sociology but also damage our discipline and its reputation. The public, general and educated, cannot understand, or even see the jurisdiction for, much of what we produce, since in too many cases our work appears to have no benefit, direct or indirect, for people's understanding of society or for their lives. The reactions of the lay public *must not* determine social science policy or shape our research, but they cannot be ignored either. Meanwhile, the leaders as well as the foot soldiers of today's dominant sociologies ought to remember that a good deal of the intellectual standing and good will our discipline has developed comes from the work of public sociologists. They — and books like *The Lonely Crowd* and *Habits of the Heart* — essentially persuade much of the lay public and its politicians that sociology ought to be cared about and funded![13]

OUR SOCIOLOGICAL IDENTITY

To conclude my highly selective analysis of the discipline and to end this essay, I want to raise the issue of our identity as sociologists in an era of ever-greater specialization of fields and subfields within the discipline.[14] That identity should concern all of us, to further our own well-being *and* to help us make our case for the desirability of sociological knowledge to the lay public.

Sociology is once again no different from the other social sciences, although the degree of specialization may be greater than it is among our peers because we are the residual social science. We are more diverse to begin with than economics (even though it is now branching out beyond the economy) and political science, which is basically still concerned with politics only in government.

In any case, it is worth looking into the benefits and costs of further sociological specialization. Among the major benefits are the intellectual vitality usually found in new fields and subfields, as well as the intensive personal contact among researchers as long as these fields remain small. Indeed, because of the vitality that accompanies work in the new fields or at the frontiers of research, we ought also to be moving deliberately across the accepted or imagined boundaries of sociology, and in two ways.[15]

For one thing, we should look more closely at other social science disciplines to see what we can learn from them as well as to discover how we can improve on their work, jointly or by ourselves. To mention just a few: social history, the study of symbols and symbol systems which we share with anthropology, and empirical research in and of economic institutions can all gain from such a look.[16] Disciplinary boundaries in the social sciences are arbitrary anyway, and they should be crossed freely, preferably for substantive, not imperialistic, reasons. We should act similarly toward boundaries beyond the social sciences and take a greater interest in the humanities. Among other things, the study of the interrelations between culture and social structure can benefit from the concepts and ideas of literary scholars. These can put some of our concepts and ideas to use as well in their work on literature and society — for instance, what we have learned about the roles of audiences in the production of culture.

Increasing specialization inside sociology also carries costs, however. For one thing, the more sociologists specialize in particular fields, the more are some likely to limit themselves to really tiny specialties within the discipline as a whole. Moreover, when new fields and subfields develop, they quickly breed their own technical languages.

The end result is that [the discipline] looks like a wheel. People sit on their own spokes and talk less and less to those on the other side. Eventually the wheel may become a doughnut, with a huge intellectual hole in the middle. (Winkler, 1986, p. 7)

The person I quote is geographer Sam Hilliard talking about his own discipline, but his comment is starting to apply to sociology as well, and the challenge is to prevent both the wheel and the intellectual hole. The hole cannot, however, be filled by pining for one approach or theory that will reintegrate sociology, as some of our colleagues do, for such reintegration is neither likely nor desirable in a pluralistic discipline.

Instead we should ask ourselves what can or should bring us together as sociologists. One approach may be to identify intellectual cores that are common to many of us. These can be concepts, frames, theories, methods, or other intellectual forms and qualities that we continue to share. A related approach is to look empirically at some major old and new fields and subfields and determine what ideas, concepts, and theories are operationally similar in the significant research and theorizing in them, even if the terminology is different.[17] Such a project might even increase the sharing of terms and reduce the excessive number of terms in the discipline. The more we emphasize elements of sociology that we share in annual meeting sessions, other conferences, and various kinds of publications, the more we will discover to what extent we can remain a single discipline. Even my previously mentioned question, "What is a good society?" can perform this function. Imagine a medical sociologist, an ethnomethodologist, a specialist in gender and sex roles, a market researcher, and a mathematical sociologist, all with roughly the same values, being asked to come up with a single answer to this question!

Identity is social as well as intellectual; consequently, we should also look at social mechanisms that can contribute to being and feeling a part of a single discipline. ASA does what it can along these lines, but only a bare majority of all sociologists belong, and much too small a number of them are involved in ASA as other than receivers of its services. Also, the organization still relies excessively for its agenda and leadership on academics from the major research universities to be fully representative. The Annual Meetings bring about 3,000 of us together for a hectic few days, although the sessions themselves increasingly are vehicles for specialization. In 1988, for example, 43 percent of the *regular* sessions were run by sections, and many other regular sessions were on subjects for which there are sections.

Publications could bring us together as well, but I wonder if they do since our journals tend to appeal largely to specialists, whatever the editor's hopes. For example, *ASR*, being the flagship journal, is supposed to represent the best in sociology. However, for this reader and I imagine many others, it is also a journal of lengthy research reports on specialized topics, only some of which are of general interest. In addition, *ASR* is dominated by often elegant quantitative research. In fact, some have suggested that *ASR* is actually a methodological journal for quantitative sociologists not able or willing to work through the yet more technical articles in *Sociological Methodology*. There are exceptions in *ASR*'s emphasis, to be sure, and recent editors have published more exceptions than past ones. On the whole, however, most major articles continue to be research reports of roughly the same format and from basically one kind of sociology. Sometimes one gets the impression that *ASR* is "run" by its contributors, the editors functioning primarily as quality controllers and traffic cops even if they might personally prefer to publish a different journal. Like the organizations we study, *ASR* has become institutionalized.

CS may be the most general of the journals, for it reviews a large proportion of all the books sociologists publish. While the reviews are classified by sets of specialties, *CS* readers can get a kind of overview of sociology by reading all of the reviews. Conversely, anecdotal evidence suggests that many of *ASR*'s readers scan the abstracts, read an article or two, and leave it at that. Over the years many have reported in the discipline's grapevine that they have difficulty understanding or getting involved in many of the articles, and there are regular complaints, some published (Wilner, 1985), that *ASR* almost never deals with any of the severe problems or controversial issues abundant in American society.[18]

None of these observations are intended as criticisms of present or past editors of *ASR*, for they work harder and longer at less celebrated tasks than any other active ASA members. Furthermore, I do not think *ASR* should be anything else than what it is now: a journal of research papers, although it should publish more reports of qualitative research and theoretical as well as historical papers.[19]

Instead of making basic changes in *ASR*, we need another sociological journal that publishes what *ASR* cannot: articles of general interest to sociologists. Although such a journal should be published for sociologists and not the lay public and should be of high intellectual quality, it must not be a technical journal. This should also add to its appeal and help make it profitable for an academic publisher. We would not even be pioneers in establishing such a journal, for in 1987 the American Economic Association began to publish *The Journal of Economic Perspectives*, which described itself in its first issue as "a scholarly economics journal for the general audience of economists" (Stiglitz, Shapiro and Taylor, 1987, p. 3).

The editors of this new journal would have to use their intuition, experience, and values to decide what their sociologist-readers want and need, but I will describe some kinds of articles this reader would like to see:

1. Analyses of general intellectual issues in sociology, including, for example, studies of the roles and effects of sociology in America, the relevance of sociology in postindustrial societies, and the relation between American sociology and the American economy.

2. Extended debates about, and critiques of, current theories or trends in theorizing, as well as fundamental or controversial issues in empirical research, teaching, and practice.

3. Review articles of sociologically relevant work in other disciplines, such as institutional economics, literary criticism, and theories of knowledge.

4. Nontechnical research reports and *Annual Review of Sociology*-style articles about currently significant or controversial trends in American society: for example, downward mobility in the middle class, causes of drug use and abuse, convergences of and relations between high culture and popular culture. This category could also include analyses (and corrections) of pop sociology, for example, of the decline of the nuclear family, the rise

of greed and materialism in the 1980s, and the cultural and economic power of "yuppies" and "baby boomers" in American society.

5. Sociological analyses of current events that have been or should have been in the headlines, domestic and foreign, economic, political, and cultural.

6. Long reviews, of *New York Review of Books* quality, of important sociological books, well known *and* unfairly neglected, as well as of books of significance to sociology but written by nonsociologists.

7. Articles of professional relevance not likely to appear in *Footnotes, The American Sociologist*, or the practice journals: for example, analyses of sources of conflicts in academic departments, reviews of graduate sociology programs from the student perspective, and problems of sociological practice in profit-making organizations. These articles would frequently need to be anonymous.

8. Sociological biographies of influential figures in sociology, not necessarily from the past.

9. Provocative pieces that suggest unusual if untested (and even untestable) hypotheses, or offer thoughtful analyses of the discipline by relevant outsiders.

10. Shorter or lighter articles: for example, sociological reviews of art, literature, and films — highbrow, middlebrow, and lowbrow; studies of the depiction of sociologists in American novels, films, and television, and even cartoons of sociological significance or relevance.

A lively journal that speaks to interests we share may help a little to bring us together as specialization moves us ever further apart. Nevertheless, perhaps the best way to add some unity to the diversity takes me back to the major theme of this essay: our being more useful to the public and to its various sectors. Being useful, as teachers, researchers, writers, practitioners, *and* as experts, advisers, and critics, will make us *feel* more useful — and this will strengthen the commonality of purpose among us. Being useful should also add to our pride in the discipline, and pride is itself a potent social cement. But if we have further reasons to be proud of sociology, we will surely grow intellectually and in other ways in the years to come.

NOTES

1. I had, however, made presentations about where I thought sociology was going to seminars at Columbia University in 1980 and 1985, each time before large enough audiences to suggest that there was considerable interest in the topic.

2. Some of what follows was also said by presenters at the Atlanta thematic and special sessions, but I wrote this essay before reading their presentations.

3. Some time ago I received a blurb for an annual review of sociology text for undergraduates and discovered that the vast majority of contributions were not written by sociologists.

4. I distinguish public sociologists from visible scientists (Goodell, 1977) because the visible scientists she describes earned their visibility not only as scientists but also as popularizers and as commentators on social issues far outside their scientific fields.

5. Jacoby's hopes notwithstanding, public sociologists also have to be academics or practitioners, there currently being no free-lance writing market to provide a living for even one sociologist.

6. Actually, a number of sociologists are already working with ASA's Public Information Committee and ASA staff to write popular articles from papers in various sociological journals. Now

we need to find ways to get their work into the media, which also requires learning what kinds and subjects of sociology will appeal to the general public, and the editors who supply their newspapers and magazines.

7. *Psychology Today*, which was founded as, and is once again, a commercially owned magazine, was for some years published by the American Psychological Association, which lost several million dollars in the process and proved that even a giant social science organization is not necessarily commercially adept.

8. Such features, which criticize us for the use of jargon, too many numbers, irrelevance, academic restatements of the obvious, as well as for triviality *and* excessive seriousness, still appear from time to time, and we should make sure that we do not act according to this now-aging caricature.

9. Moreover, article abstracts should not be repetitions of the first and sometimes the last paragraphs of the article but should supply readers with a summary of the article's findings.

10. I am indebted to Otis Dudley Duncan for this quotation. Robert K. Merton has planned to include it, with its source, in a collection of social science quotation which he and David Sills are editing.

11. David Riesman has pointed out that some survey researchers draft their interview questions, have others obtain the answers and then analyze the data and never leave their offices either (personal communication).

12. Perhaps the current crisis in university library finances, brought about in part by the ever-increasing number of journals which charge ever-increasing subscription rates, will eventually put a damper on the publish-or-perish syndrome.

13. Their reasons for supporting sociology could shrink if cultural anthropologists who can no longer do fieldwork overseas and who learn to cut back on their appetite for exotic U.S. subcultures replace us even further in doing American community studies.

14. Again, I must omit the practice side of sociology, but the discipline's most serious long-term identity problem is our continuing to conceive of identity in academic research terms, as I do here. Thus, we neglect the fact that many practitioners may have little reason to identify with an academic discipline, especially if and when they are pushed or pulled by industry/agency- and job-specific demands for their loyalty.

15. Both of these boundary-crossing themes were considered by the 1988 Program Committee and translated into a number of Special Sessions at the Atlanta meeting.

16. The intellectual vacuum created by the economists' emphasis on econometrics and model-building could and should be filled in part by more ethnographic and other institutional studies by sociologists of the giant, and the small but innovative, firms that currently play a significant role in the American economy.

17. Harriet Zuckerman has suggested, in a personal communication, that some sociologists' practice of changing fields and the migration of problems and approaches from one field to another may act as countertendencies to fragmentation.

18. Despite the high reliability and validity of the sociological grapevine, my evidence is anecdotal, and we badly need sophisticated readership studies of the discipline's major journals.

19. In fact, the number of historical papers in *ASR* is now rising and one way to begin to assure the publication of qualitative research reports and theoretical papers is to submit them in large enough numbers and at such high levels of quality that *ASR* cannot want to do other than to publish them.

REFERENCES

Becker, Howard S. 1967. "Whose Side Are We On?" *Social Problems* 14:239-47.
Coser, Lewis A. 1975. "Presidential Address: Two Methods in Search of a Substance." *American Sociological Review* 40:691-700.

Duncan, Otis D. 1974. "Duncan Requests Reconsideration of Award!" *Footnotes* 2, 9:2.

Gans, Herbert J. 1988. "Improving Sociology's Relations with Journalists." *Footnotes* 16, 4:8.

Goodell, Rae. 1977. *The Visible Scientists.* Boston: Little, Brown.

Gouldner, Alvin. 1970. *The Coming Crisis of Western Sociology.* New York: Basic.

Hirschman, Charles. 1987. "Eastern Sociologists." *Eastern Sociological Society News* 2, 8:3-5.

Hughes, Everett D. 1963. "Race Relations and the Sociological Imagination." *American Sociological Review* 28:879-90.

Jacoby, Russell. 1987. *The Last Intellectuals: American Culture in the Age of Academe.* New York: Basic.

Keller, Suzanne. 1988. "The American Dream of Community: An Unfinished Agenda." *Sociological Forum* 3:167-83.

Kohn, Melvin L. 1987. "Cross-National Research as an Analytic Strategy." *American Sociological Review* 52:713-31.

Komarovsky, Mirra. 1987. "Some Persistent Issues of Sociological Polemics." *Sociological Forum* 2:556-64.

Lee, Alfred McClung. 1976. "Presidential Address: Sociology for Whom?" *American Sociological Review* 41:925-36.

Litwak, Eugene and Peter Messeri. 1989. "Organizational Theory, Social Supports and Mortality Rates: A Theoretical Convergence." *American Sociological Review* 54:49-66.

McCloskey, Donald N. 1985. *The Rhetoric of Economics.* Madison: University of Wisconsin Press.

Myrdal, Gunnar. 1963. *The Challenge to Affluence.* New York: Pantheon.

Stiglitz, Joseph, Carl Shapiro, and Timothy Taylor. 1987. "Foreword." *Journal of Economic Perspectives* 1:3-5.

Vidich, Arthur J. and Stanford M. Lyman. 1985. *American-Sociology: Worldly Rejections of Religion and Their Directions.* New Haven: Yale University Press.

Wilner, Patricia. 1985. "The Main Drift of Sociology Between 1936 and 1984." *History of Sociology* 5:1-21.

Wilson, William J. 1987. *The Truly Disadvantaged: The Inner City, the Underclass and Public Policy.* Chicago: University of Chicago Press.

Winkler, Karen J. 1986. "New Breed of Scholar Works the Territory That Lies Between History and Geography." *Chronicle of Higher Education* 33, 4:6-7.